Food and Women in Italian Literature, Culture and Society

Also Available from Bloomsbury:

Feminist Theology and Contemporary Dieting Culture, Hannah Bacon
Food, Masculinities, and Home: Interdisciplinary Perspectives, Edited by Michelle Szabo and Shelley L. Koch
Representing Italy Through Food, Edited by Peter Naccarato, Zachary Nowak and Elgin K. Eckert

Food and Women in Italian Literature, Culture and Society

Eve's Sinful Bite

Edited by
Claudia Bernardi, Francesca Calamita
and Daniele De Feo

BLOOMSBURY ACADEMIC
LONDON • NEW YORK • OXFORD • NEW DELHI • SYDNEY

BLOOMSBURY ACADEMIC
Bloomsbury Publishing Plc
50 Bedford Square, London, WC1B 3DP, UK
1385 Broadway, New York, NY 10018, USA
29 Earlsfort Terrace, Dublin 2, Ireland

BLOOMSBURY, BLOOMSBURY ACADEMIC and the Diana logo are trademarks of Bloomsbury Publishing Plc

First published in Great Britain 2020
This paperback edition published in 2022

Cover design: Terry Woodley
Cover image © SolStock/Getty

A catalogue record for this book is available from the British Library.

A catalog record for this book is available from the Library of Congress.

ISBN: HB: 978-1-3501-3778-3
PB: 978-1-3501-8930-0
ePDF: 978-1-3501-3779-0
eBook: 978-1-3501-3780-6

Typeset by Deanta Global Publishing Services, Chennai, India

Contents

Contributors

Claudia Bernardi is a Senior Lecturer in Italian at Victoria University of Wellington, New Zealand. She holds a PhD in Italian from the University of Bath, UK. Her research focuses on contemporary Italian fiction, in particular twentieth-century women writers. She has published widely on the works of Silvia Ballestra. Her more recent research has focused on the representation of gender, sexuality and national identity in popular fiction and cinema, with articles on women's crime fiction and Italian film noir.

Pia L. Bertucci holds a PhD in Romance Languages from the University of North Carolina at Chapel Hill and is, since 2010, Director of the Italian Program at the University of South Carolina. Her current research interests and publications focus on Italian food culture and Italian women writers. Currently, she is completing a textbook on Italian language and culture, *Illumina: Nuovo Corso di Lingua e Cultura Italiana*, that will be published in 2020.

Francesca Calamita is Assistant Professor and College Fellow at the University of Virginia where she teaches Italian Studies and collaborates with the Department of Women, Gender and Sexuality. Author of a monograph (*Linguaggi dell'esperienza femminile*, 2015), a co-edited volume (*Starvation, Food Obsession and Identity*, 2017) and a number of articles in the areas of transnational gender issues, she holds a PhD from Victoria University of Wellington and carried out her postdoctoral project at the Centre for the Study of Contemporary Women's Writing, University of London.

Danielle Callegari (PhD, New York University) is Assistant Professor in the Department of French and Italian at Dartmouth College and Councillor for the Dante Society of America. Her research focuses on Italian literature and food and wine studies. She has published on a variety of subjects including Dante, medieval food and wine culture, early modern women's writing and religion, and modern Italian food and politics. Her first monograph, *Dante's Gluttons: Food and Society in Medieval Italian Literature*, is forthcoming.

Luca Cottini is Associate Professor of Italian Studies at Villanova University. He holds a PhD in Romance Languages and Literatures from Harvard University. His research focuses on Italian literature, culture and social history of the nineteenth and twentieth centuries. He has published several scholarly articles (among others, on silent cinema, D'Annunzio, Palazzeschi, De Amicis, Fenoglio) and two books, on Italo Calvino (2017) and the birth of industrial design in Italy (2018).

Daniele De Feo is Lecturer in the Department of French and Italian at Princeton University where he teaches Italian Studies and the course 'Literature of Gastronomy'. He holds a PhD from Rutgers University, and his publications focus on the nineteenth-century European discourse of taste, both in its sensorial and its metaphorical significance, and consider the contribution of literary, philosophical and culinary writings in their ability to challenge aesthetic and social boundaries.

Rossella Di Rosa holds a PhD in Italian from Rutgers University. She currently teaches Italian at the University of Georgia. Her academic interests focus on Italian modern and contemporary literature, material ecocriticism, posthumanism and gender studies. She has published several articles on Giacomo Leopardi's proto-ecological conception of nature, on the influence of María Zambrano's philosophical thought in the works of Anna Maria Ortese and Elsa Morante, and on the relationship between human and non-human animals in Italian women's writing.

Teresa Di Somma is an Italian researcher based in João Pessoa, Paraíba, Brazil, with academic interests in postcolonial literatures and cultural studies. She recently got her MRes at the Graduate School of Literatures, Languages and Identities (PPGLI) of the Universidade Federal do Acre, in Brazilian Amazonia, with a dissertation on the Sanremo Music Festival. On that occasion, she pursued a study on the representations of race, gender and disability within the famous song contest. She collaborates with the Brazilian journals *Muiraquitã* and *Tropos*.

Niki Kiviat is a PhD candidate in Italian Studies at Columbia University. Her dissertation focuses on the continuities and ruptures in Italy's filmic foodscape from 1954 to 1973. Her research interests include star studies, the continuities of fascism and neorealism in post-war media and representations of disordered eating. She is the co-editor of *(In)digestion in Literature and Film: A Transcultural Approach* (forthcoming).

Laura-Marzia Lenci is Assistant Academic Director and Internship Coordinator at Boston University, Italy programs. She holds a PhD in Italian Literature from the University of Verona with a dissertation on Luigi Malerba. She teaches Italian Migrant Literature, and her researches currently focus on Luigi Malerba and Gianni Rodari poetics, and the representation of the identity in migrant Italian writers. She has published several articles in these fields. She recently worked on a research project financed by Boston University on the assessment of the learning outcomes of American university programs abroad.

Marcello Messina is a Sicilian composer and academic based in João Pessoa, Paraíba, Brazil. He holds a PhD in composition from the University of Leeds (UK), and is currently *Professor Visitante Estrangeiro* at the Universidade Federal da Paraíba. He has been recipient of the Endeavour Research Fellowship at Macquarie University, Sydney, Australia, and of the PNPD/Capes postdoctoral bursary at the Universidade Federal do Acre, Brazil.

Maria Morelli is Marie Sklodowska-Curie Fellow at the University of Milan, Italy, and acts as Expert Evaluator for the European Commission. She holds a PhD from the University of Leicester, UK, and has taught Italian literature and language at the University of Leicester and at Wheaton College, USA. She has published several articles and book chapters on gender, sexuality and embodiment in Italian women's literature and theatre, co-edited the volume *Women and the Public Sphere in Modern and Contemporary Italy* (2017) and published the edited collection *Il teatro cambia genere* (2019). Her monograph, *Queer(ing) Gender in Italian Women's Writing*, is forthcoming.

Maria Grazia Scrimieri is an Italian language assistant and she holds a PhD in Langue, littérature et civilisation italiennes from the Université Côte d'Azur (Nice), France. She focuses on contemporary Italian fiction, in particular twentieth-century women writers, on representations of food in Italian family novels and in the novels of the Resistance. Her latest publications have examined the works of Dacia Maraini, Clara Sereni and Rossana Campo.

Giovanna Summerfield is a Professor of Italian and French and Associate Dean in the College of Liberal Arts at Auburn University. She holds a PhD in Romance

Languages and Literatures with a minor in European and Mediterranean History from the University of Florida. Her research focuses on the long eighteenth-century French and Italian (with emphasis on Sicily) literature, women's studies, Mediterranean studies and religious movements. She is also a published poet and short-story writer.

Georgia Wall is a translator and language tutor. Her PhD thesis (University of Warwick, 2018) was part of the 'Transnationalizing Modern Languages' project, and it explored the experience and expression of Italian migration to London through various food-related sites. Her contribution to this volume was developed as part of a postdoctoral fellowship at the Institute of Modern Languages Research (London). Her current research focuses on incorporating everyday material culture and ethnographically informed approaches into modern languages.

Introduction

Claudia Bernardi, Francesca Calamita and Daniele De Feo

The multifaceted relationship between women and food in Western culture is captured by the Christian myth of the Fall narrated in Genesis with the well-known episode of Eve and the apple. Eve's sinful bite represents a key symbolic meeting between women and food in a long list of metaphorical meanings associated with the act of eating and ideas of femininity in society and culture. This myth is all the more resonant for Italy, a country where religious and food traditions have historically played a crucial role in shaping its culture. Food and eating-related activities, such as cooking and serving meals to the family, have often been seen as signifiers of something else in women's lives: lust, affection and desire for emotional shelter and expression of frustration, to mention only a few of the nuances associated with food consumption.

As Maria Giuseppina Muzzarelli and Fiorenza Tarozzi remark in *Donne e cibo*: *una relazione nella storia* (Food and Women: A Relationship Through History),[1] and as Muzzarelli and Lucia Re confirm in their introduction to *Il cibo e le donne nella cultura e nella storia. Prospettive interdisciplinari* (Food and Women in Culture and History. Interdisciplinary Perspectives),[2] food and women are two inseparable protagonists of historical discourse: talking about women in history and culture means talking about food, and all discussion about food includes women. For example, if we look back at the time of the unification of Italy in the second half of the nineteenth century, neurology, psychiatry and gynaecology, supported by patriarchal ideology, explicitly identified women as naturally unbalanced beings, underdeveloped from a biological and physiological standpoint. They were considered to be physically and psychologically akin to children more than to their male adult counterparts. As a result, a rigorous diet was recommended to control their voracious feminine behaviour.[3] From the Risorgimento (the term normally used to refer to the process of Italian unification) onwards, the accepted female diet was to be 'delicate', comprised of foods that would leave women lethargic and unprepared to participate in civil and political life, as desired and preached by the patriarchy. Women's domestic role, anchored in the maternal act of breastfeeding, was defined by their duty to prepare meals for the family, which was synonymous with traditional expectations that women should take care of others. However, eating some dishes or abstaining from them was also seen as contributing to regulate female disorderly conduct. Similarly, current Western societies continue to try and control what is the appropriate relationship between women and food, especially in relation to its preparation and consumption, using the media, rather than religious, medical and psychological discourses, as a powerful platform to showcase how women should look and act. For a long time, television and magazines have been the most prominent perpetrators of women's conflicted eating habits, by producing and distributing ads that glorify thin women and promoting the importance of eating 'light' or 'fat-free' foods to maintain a slim figure, often disguising the underlying misogynist discourse as concern for women's health. Adjectives that describe food pathologies, such as 'anorexic' and 'bulimic', have entered everyday language; along the same lines, food-related illnesses are regularly discussed on both popular and specialized platforms. A look at how Italian women have been historically expected to behave – cooking for and serving others, while often denying themselves the pleasures of the table – can therefore help us to understand the complex and nuanced interplay between food and women's lives. In this volume, we aim to precisely do so from a cultural perspective, by presenting essays that discuss how the relationship between women and food has been portrayed in a wide range of media and genres, from narrative fiction to memoirs, from cookbooks to women's magazines, from film to television.

The popular post-unification Italian writer Marchesa Colombi ends her 1885 novel *Un matrimonio in provincia* (A Small-Town Marriage) with a significant comment by Denza, the young and unfortunate protagonist: 'The thing is, I am gaining weight'.[4] Earlier in the novel, she had been forced by the cultural constrictions imposed on *fin de siècle* Italian women to marry a forty-year-old notary with whom she goes on to have three children. Denza is neither in love with nor attracted to him; however, her stepmother reminds her that as she was thirty years old, she should accept his proposal in order to fulfil her female destiny. As Giuliana Morandini notes, at the end of Marchesa Colombi's novel, the protagonist's emotional and physical spheres come together to express her frustration with her life.[5] Indeed, by gaining weight, Denza's body tries to communicate a non-verbal message, a protest against an unjust female fate that has trapped her into an undesired life since childhood. Following what distinguished feminist psychoanalyst Susie Orbach says about bulimic women, '[t]he resulting fat has the function of making the space for which women crave'.[6]

Like a present-day compulsive eater, Denza tries to satisfy her needs by eating, thus masking and compensating for her desires and frustrations. According to feminist scholars,[7] eating disorders and troubled relationships with food are indeed employed by women in order to say what they cannot express with words; they are a self-destructive language that, however, gives them the opportunity to replace conventional verbal communication. And as recent research shows,[8] Italian culture in general and literature in particular have often been at the vanguard of capturing this complex strategy used by women to negotiate their anxieties, whether personal or political, using food and eating habits as a non-verbal language.

Our volume explores how, since Marchesa Colombi's ground-breaking intuition of Denza's bulimia as a strategy to express her dissatisfaction with her marriage, maternal role and prescribed femininity, women's relationship with food has been represented in Italian literature, cinema, scientific writings and other forms of cultural expression since the nineteenth century, when, following the country's unification, Italian identity along with women's role in it were being defined. Contributions to our collection offer a close reading of the symbolic meanings associated with food and of the way these intersect with Italian women's socio-cultural history and the feminist movement, addressing issues of gender, identity and politics of the body. The discussion is articulated in four parts, each focused on a key theme.

The three chapters in Part I analyse the interplay between numerous types of food texts (etiquette and hygiene manuals, cookbooks, culinary memoirs) and the role of gender promulgated within them. In Chapter 1, Daniele De Feo examines how women during the Risorgimento and the post-unification period were told to host, eat, dissimulate and remain socially and politically subdued due to their 'physiological' makeup. De Feo traces women's expected behaviour and food practices through authors who worked to unify the nation culturally through matters of taste and food, all the while promoting the notion of a specific role for women as good Italian citizens around the table. In Chapter 2 Danielle Callegari analyses how Marcella Hazan used the cookbook and the domestic space it inhabits to achieve fame and dictate the reception of Italian food culture in America. Her chapter engages with recent research on the social and political intentions of premodern and modern Italian cookbooks to demonstrate how the most famous Italian-American food writer of the twentieth century exploited this unique genre and its perceived 'effeminacy', tapping into the unexpected power it could wield to control the conversation between Italian culture and American culture. Chapter 3 by Georgia Wall looks at the act of making bread from sourdough leaven, 'lievito madre', as a point of departure for a critical analysis of femininity in the texts of Anglo-Italian author Simonetta Agnello Hornby. Wall draws on a feminist reading of happiness as possibility and offers a close reading of the sensory recreation of the past enacted in *Il pranzo di Mosè* (Lunch at Mosè) and *Un filo d'olio* (A Drizzle of Olive Oil). Focusing on the themes of kin work, haptic pleasure and memory, these narratives are discussed for how they work simultaneously to uphold nostalgic visions of rural Italy and to query the role women are assigned within this frame.

Part II of the volume looks at the depiction of Southern Italian women in post-unification and contemporary literature, as well as contemporary cinema and television, through their relationship with food, whether real or culturally constructed. In Chapter 4, Luca Cottini observes how Matilde Serao's *La virtù di Checchina* (Checchina's Virtue, 1884) offers a precious insight into the condition of women in post-unification Naples and Italy, as well as a powerful metaphor of the nation's ambiguous quest for modernity in the late nineteenth century in the protagonist's hoped-for, yet never realized, love affair with the Marchese d'Aragona. Food plays a significant role in the plot, as the lunch planned, cooked and served by Checchina to her husband and the Marchese ignites her passion for the latter, and acquires a multifaceted range of meanings that challenge women's societal status quo. Pia L. Bertucci continues the discussion on the important legacy of Serao's work, drawing comparisons with Elena Ferrante's recent writings. In Chapter 5 Bertucci argues that there is an organic and intimate relationship between food and language, one that can reveal the culture and history of a people. For Matilde Serao and Elena Ferrante, the cuisine and dialect of Naples serve as sensory conduits for a female Neapolitan identity. This connection is forged between mothers and daughters, enabling them to persevere against the harsh realities and challenges of the city in enclaves of female relationships that are simultaneously supportive and stifling. Although separated by a century, both Serao and Ferrante depict similar familial dynamics, with semi-symbiotic relationship between mothers and daughters bound by sense memories of food. Food traditions and the Neapolitan vernacular reinforce this sensory threshold creating a liminal sphere forever caught between the past and the future, the real and the imaginary. International literary phenomenon Elena Ferrante is also included in Giovanna Summerfield's wider analysis of the Italian Southern kitchen in her chapter. Summerfield contends that, contrary to the traditional notion that sees women solely as food preparers and servers, a woman's presence in the kitchen represents action, reaction and often subversion rather than submission, demonstrating how alterations to recipes may mean to harm or to entice control of others. This is particularly notable in some of the Neapolitan works of Ferrante and Marosia Castaldi, as well as in the writings of Sicilian author Giuseppina Torregrossa, in which pain and pleasure follow each other while the female protagonists become self-aware and self-confident, and ultimately reinvent themselves through food preparation and serving, and through the responsibilities taken in performing those acts. In Chapter 7 Marcello Messina and Teresa Di Somma interrogate the artistic trajectories of such actresses as Marisa Laurito and Tosca D'Aquino, as well as others, noticing how their respective personas are often constructed on the basis of a combination of clichéd Southern Italian identity, exuberant appetite and extravagant personalities. Messina and Di Somma highlight how, in most cases, their characters are relegated to secondary/gregarious roles, and, most importantly, are excluded from the main love plots that normally characterize comedies. The 'greedy southern woman', they contend, is a fairly recurrent cliché in Italian popular culture, deeply anchored to a national imagery that, in different ways, perceives both women and southerners as potential anomalies to be constantly domesticated.

Part III of the volume examines how food becomes the symbol of womanhood and Italianness from the hey-day of Italian cinema in post-Second World War Italy to contemporary and migrant literature. In Chapter 8 Niki Kiviat looks at Sophia Loren, one of Italy's foremost cultural exports, arguing that the actress and her characters helped to bridge the gap between 1940s and 1950s cinematic neorealism and the Hollywood-influenced aesthetics of the economic boom. Kiviat argues that despite Loren's films being mostly written and directed by men, Loren's stardom highlighted everyday Italian women's stakes, both inside and outside of the kitchen, in a transitional period of Italian history; moreover, by authoring her own cookbooks, Loren also embodied a historical change when women started speaking for themselves in the wake of international feminist movements. In the same vein, but from a literary perspective, in Chapter 9, Rossella Di Rosa analyses food's pivotal role in Fabrizia Ramondino's debut novel *Althénopis* (1981). Di Rosa argues that the ways in which the grandmother (one of the main characters in the book) prepares and serves meals to the family represent a revolutionary act on many levels: the fact that she cooks, together with the fantastic realm of the kitchen, the utensils she uses and the recipes she modifies according to her mood and the availability of the ingredients, reveal an unconventional and 'nomadic' attitude and world view. Following on the theme of food preparation as a challenge to societal norms, Laura-Marzia Lenci concludes this section with an analysis of food in Italian migrant literature, particularly focusing on author Igiaba Scego. In Chapter 10 Lenci contends that in Scego's novels and stories, female characters are usually self-confident, eccentric and strongly willing to affirm their uniqueness. As a woman herself, Scego is interested in investigating the female roles inside the family, the meaning of being a woman and, particularly, as a Somali-Italian woman in Italy, the process of building a female identity that is not defined in exclusively linguistic or national terms. Purchasing, cooking and consuming food represent for Scego's characters acts of cultural transfiguration: linguistic registers are mixed together with personal, culinary and religious traditions, and the experience of migration. Ultimately, this chapter investigates Scego's poetics and the centrality of women and food in the process of identity creation.

Part IV of the collection delves into contemporary literature and film to examine social, political and global facets of Italian women's relationship with food and their traditional domestic roles. In Chapter 11 Maria Morelli examines the recourse to the food imagery, both literal and figurative, in a number of Maraini's works. Morelli demonstrates that, in these novels, the act of preparing, presenting or consuming meals, while reaffirming food as central in the shaping of the female experience, also bespeaks the author's preoccupations with an essentializing model of female identity that casts women in the role of nurturers and providers. In the novels Morelli analyses, food plays a crucial role not only in shaping the subjectivity of their female characters and their relationship with, and position within, family and society but also in understanding Maraini's social and political attitudes to her own times. Similarly, Maria Grazia Scrimieri, in Chapter 12, uses Rosi Braidotti's redefinition of female subjectivity to investigate literary works *sub specie culinaria*, that is to say by analysing food not only as social activity but also as a metonymy of cultural and social belongings, especially in autobiographical novels or in memoirs. In contemporary Italian women's literature, Clara Sereni's narrative work is certainly one of the richest in terms of food references and food-related activities, and Scrimieri's analysis considers Sereni's take on women's relationship with food from the perspective of a Jewish woman who fully experienced the labour movement, feminism, the battle for divorce and terrorism, choosing to face these complex, contradictory and personal forms of conflict through the table and through writings saturated with food images. Francesca Calamita's chapter then goes on to discuss the current debate on the portrayal of eating disorders in contemporary Italian women's writing, and the multifaceted meaning of the body/weight perception in the development of these disorders. Drawing from current feminist readings of anorexia and bulimia that understand these pathological behaviours as controversial yet powerful answers to patriarchal dictates in women's lives,

Calamita relates the paradoxical behaviour of Schelotto's female protagonist towards food and body to women's socio-cultural position in contemporary Italian culture and society, providing a reflection on how this leads disorderly eaters to split their mental desires from their corporeal bounds. Finally, in Chapter 14 Claudia Bernardi focuses on Silvia Ballestra's novel *Amiche mie* (My Friends, 2014) where food features as a cultural signifier for anxieties of white, middle-class, heterosexual women in contemporary Italy, but also offers them an opportunity for social engagement and political activism. Through a polyphonic structure that gives voice(s) to different women's experiences of family life and marital disillusion, the novel portrays a generation of women who cannot or will not cook like their mothers and grandmothers, but who, supported by their reciprocal friendship, find intellectual clarity and personal agency in their commitment (or resistance) to feeding themselves and their families.

The chapters collected in this volume confirm that a nuanced and intricate relationship between women and food is at the very core of how Italianness has been constructed from nineteenth-century nation building to the multicultural, diverse, increasingly globalized and contradictory country it is today. Across a number of cultural expressions and a variety of genres – from literary to filmic, from scientific to artistic – we see how women in the Italian context have been portrayed, subjugated and emancipated symbolically through food. In these portrayals, women have been shown starving to emaciation and overindulging to obesity to conform or to react to systematic oppression and cultural conventions, practices of conformity and resistance that have often been called 'sinful'. From the very first bite of that biblical apple, to a forced continence at the table, female food consumption had been considered socially immoral; yet women's preparation and service for others have been seen as socially good and indeed eminently female responsibilities. As many of the essays collected here remind us, due to their maternal duties and traditional domestic roles women have been historically designated as nurturers, confined to the kitchen but also empowered in it with a vital female space, one they have often turned into an opportunity for female bonding and legacy-building across generations. While the studies presented here confirm that that women in Italy have been controlled by food roles created by a patriarchal society, they also suggest how cultural representations of the kitchen and cooking (whether embraced, reclaimed, revolutionized or explicitly rejected) have also been transformed by women themselves into tools of domestic, social and political liberation.

Part I

Gender and social norms in food writings

1

She is not selfish enough to analyse and favour these sensual pleasures

The role of women in nineteenth-century Italian taste

Daniele De Feo

> Taste is evidently the first in rank *[of the senses]* . . . you can exist though deprived of the active use of each of the four senses, but you cannot live . . . without the active exercise of the sense of taste . . . . Gormandism . . . will be the magnetic needle of health and of wisdom . . . it will only lead man to work to satisfy the senses of others, at the same time he is satisfying his own, and securing health to all. It will constitute the science called Gastrosophy, which will place good cheer in strict alliance with honor and the love of glory.
>
> (Fourier Vol. 1, 29, 33)

The aforementioned quote from the famed French utopian Charles Fourier (1772–1837) allows us to enter into the novel nineteenth-century philosophy of taste: one that was both science and art, both realism and utopia – a philosophy for the modern century. However, as the quote itself underscores (*man; he*), *gastrosophy* is a masculine arena, a philosophy of contemplating food as art that could only be enjoyed by men, practised by men and ultimately appraised by men. One need not look further in the Italian context than Pellegrino Artusi (1820–1911), dubbed the father of Italian gastronomy, who, with his *Scienza in cucina e l'arte di mangiar bene* (Science in the Kitchen and the Art of Eating Well, 1891), purportedly unified Italian culture through the promulgation of the nation's regional cuisine.[1] Artusi, similarly, espoused the same philosophy of food in which taste reigns over the other senses, where food is indeed art and its consumption a cognitive process, where reason and the senses work in unison. All of this is articulated in his recipe book through the figure of Olindo Guerrini

(1845–1916): friend, collaborator, famed poet, and the first Italian to look at cuisine as a historical and aesthetic subject matter for the new Italy.[2]

Yet another of Artusi's friends and collaborators, Paolo Mantegazza (1831–1910) – pathologist, anthropologist and novelist, to name a few – also advocated for this newfound rhetoric of an aestheticized food for the bourgeoning Italy. In doing so, Mantegazza promulgated an analogue of music and food by dividing the pleasures of taste into two components – 'harmony' and 'melody' – therefore allowing the author to argue the 'sublimity' of gastronomy. It is this sublimity which finds its utmost expression in a meal that the author defines as 'a concert of harmony and melody of taste . . . that is brought to maximum perfection by the genius of the artist'.[3]

The sublimity preached by Mantegazza has a very important precedent: one found in the pages of the most important etiquette manuals of the nineteenth century, *L'arte di convitare spiegata al popolo* (The Art of Banqueting Explained to the People, 1850, 1851). Giovanni Rajberti (1805–1861), the *Medico-poeta*, translator of Horace and author of humorous yet scathing satires, also rendered the table an arena for *beauty*: 'of all the arts that are called beautiful, because they are understood to satisfy the intellect and emotions, this one should be called truly beautiful, because it aims to satiate the mind, the heart and even the belly'.[4]

With this new art, Italians could find a common denominator. If culturally, the regional, socio-economic and political differences were too difficult to overcome, Italy was to become Italy through the one art all could enjoy: its food. Italians were to become Italians by learning about each other's culinary practices, versing themselves in the language of their cuisine; simultaneously, they were to educate themselves about the nutritional aspects of what they ate, which would provide, as Mantegazza states, 'that much more strength in the veins of the entire Italian people'.[5]

It is of great import to understand how the Italian woman was to play a part within these burgeoning taste ideals. In what capacity were the new nation's women to partake? Probing these author's texts, in particular those by Rajberti and Mantegazza, two medics who delved into matters of the kitchen and who went to great lengths to define the Italian woman's role in both preparation and consumption, we can better comprehend (a) the propagated role of women within the praxis of bourgeois *gustus* and (b) how this role was limited due to the preached physiological 'inferiority' of her organs of taste. The dialogue between these Milanese men from different generations, brought together by their respective relationships with an extraordinary woman (Laura Solera

Mantegazza),[6] ironically unearths the Risorgimento and the post-unificatory period's chauvinism in culinary customs, etiquette and the science of eating.

From chef to 'the woman of the house'

Guerrini and Artusi shared a vivid correspondence in which they discussed a plethora of gastronomic and philosophical topics, and from which Artusi drew inspiration. Guerrini's influence is evident by the numerous references and citations found in *La scienza in cucina*: one that is of note was from a conference held at the Exposition of Turin on 21 June 1884 in which Guerrini lamented society's prejudice against cuisine as a vulgarity. The poet alternatively contended that *la cucina* is elegant and intelligent, and exhorted its rehabilitation.[7] With this in mind, Artusi advanced the premise for the future of *la gastronomia*, with which he intended to 'train young female cooks, who are naturally more economical than men and less wasteful, they would easily be employed and would possess an art, which when brought to the middle-class households, would be a medicine to the many frustrations that often occur in families because of poor dining'.[8] Within this context, we see woman's role as key to the gastronomic cause. Unlike the experience in France, where a bourgeois taste was forwarded through the figure of the chef and the proliferation of the restaurant, in Italy, the caretaker of the household (i.e., *la donna di casa*) was to be the disseminator of taste. Her culinary education was fundamental to the construction of a new Italian society, as it was considered the most effective way of influencing the middle-class household. It is, however, clear that the ideal conveyed by Artusi and Guerrini is of a woman who is preparer, not gastronome.

On the one hand, with this declaration, we see the culmination of a shift that occurred historically. The most celebrated cookbooks written by the likes of Bartolomeo Scacchi (1421–1481), better known as Platina; Bartolomeo Scappi (1500–1577), the legendary 'secret chef of the popes';[9] and Domenico Romoli, known as Panunto, were geared, for the most part, towards male aristocratic chefs. Texts addressed to the bourgeoisie did not begin to appear until the eighteenth century, and many were mere assemblages and translations of French counterparts.[10] Others laid the foundations for what would become known as regional cuisines.[11] However, it was not until the nineteenth century that the male chef was superseded by the female cook as the primary intended audience. This shift coincided with the growth of the middle classes as well as with the prominence of the household cook and the figure of the bourgeois mother.

Therefore, it is clear that there was a keener focus on how the Italian woman was to manage the household's gastronomic matters. Ultimately, she was to be the eminent purveyor of this new Italian art.

On the other hand, this role of prominence was equivocal. Despite this newly founded stature, a further examination into the way she was to behave is revelatory of a trend that ostracizes, or at the very least demonstrates, her as ancillary to the gastrosophic cause. For all the progressive and democratic elements that authors such as Rajberti and Mantegazza represent (e.g. education, political and cultural unification), they were reflective of a conservatism that could be found in contemporaries such as Antonio Rosmini (1797–1855).[12] In his *Filosofia del diritto* (Philosophy of Law) from 1845, a seminal text in the construction of the roles of men and women during the Risorgimento, the philosopher defined the natural qualities of the Italian woman: she is 'timid sweetness, gracious weakness, attentive docility: [she] is delicate, tranquil, homely, patient'.[13] Man, conversely, has qualities that 'render him fit to command, courage, strength, authority, a firm mind or certainly a more developed one'.[14]

If women were viewed as intellectually and physically inferior to men, as is evident with Rosmini, then for the aforementioned taste authors, she was also inferior in matters of *gustus*. Her role is clearly delineated: she was to endure the difficulties of preparation in addition to the duties of hostess, all the while carving out a space for herself in the background. She was expected to artfully divest herself from her function as housewife to become, for all intents and purposes, a *Signora*: that is, a figure of perfect decorum. It is precisely with this oscillation between preparer and hostess that she was condemned to convivial, and, of course, taste subordination.

Rajberti's hostess: Dissimulation as poetry and the indecency of eating

As Gabriella Turnaturi has indicated, the table was the arena for the greatest dangers dreaded by the nineteenth-century bourgeoisie, or, in other words, naturalness, spontaneity and sensuality.[15] Therefore, as consequence, the manuals on etiquette preach moderation, restraint and equilibrium for the convivial setting, with a particular focus on the continence needed by women in the context of a meal. With this in mind, Ida Baccini, who wrote over fifty years after Rajberti's *L'arte di convitare*, declared that the first duty of a hostess is to hide 'the behind the scenes of the domestic theater' (108).[16] If the table was envisioned to be the venue of performance, then, as with all actors, the hostess was to hide the rules and tricks of her trade: 'it is necessary to make it seem as one is not adhering to rules or faking'.[17] Therefore, the difficulty of the mise en scéne of the convivial performance, no matter how arduous, need not transpire.

Rajberti's text was indeed the first etiquette manual for the table written exclusively for *la classe di mezzana fortuna* (the class of average fortunes),[18] and as such the *Medico-poeta* was the first to promulgate this ideal of a theatricalized meal to the middle classes. The medic wrote that 'in a woman there is not only the poetry and beauty of her quirks and of her spirit, but there is the hostess who we guests want to imagine seated in the room busy with gentle work, and not working on the burners'.[19] The woman of the household portrayed here needed to maintain a level of propriety that concealed all workings underlying the preparation, arrangement and organization of a meal. The author goes so far as to state: 'Let her be in the kitchen the whole day if need be: let her prepare lunch with her own hands; but do not tell us, because these are things that we should not know.'[20] Details of any sort should not be revealed, particularly when it comes to dishes: 'Praise of dishes easily leads to the description on how to cook them; and it is not rare that the hostess disillusions enumerating the ingredients of a sauce or pasta.'[21]

What is thus evident within Rajberti's work is the need for the hostess to become a creature of dissimulation, or, rather, an expert in secreting all phases of her art. The author made it clear that 'dissimulation is poetry, and truth a horrible prose'.[22] However, Rajberti's diffused etiquette did not stop with this form of *sprezzatura*,[23] as the gastronomic space he constructed was predominantly a masculine one. The woman's role was considered fundamental, as its primary responsibility was to ensure the happiness of the others at the table, in particular, her male counterparts. For example, the medic recommended: 'Advise your women that if they need to absent themselves, that these absences be brief and rare: and that in the end they do not demonstrate engaged in anything but us.'[24]

The hostess needs to render herself available and willing to serve, as well as display another, more complex, behaviour: the necessity of publicly demonstrating a disinterest in food. The notion of restraining oneself from eating during a meal connoted that one was at the complete disposal of others. If good propriety, therefore, entailed limited consumption (at least publicly), then the notion was easily brought to extremes: Rajberti speaks of a woman who stated that 'it always seemed a strange and inconceivable thing, how in this world one needs to open their mouth for that mundane vulgarity of eating and drinking'.[25] This notion of an 'indecency of food', as Meldini called it (451), and of a healthy appetite being a vulgar quality for women, became widespread in the nineteenth century. Studies such as those conducted by Anna K. Silver assert that the idea of self-starvation developed and was central to Victorian England's notions of femininity.[26] She made the case that Victorian gender ideology can be read through an 'anorexic lens' (3). It was precisely in this time period that the first diagnosed anorexic cases were confirmed in England by Sir William Gull (who coined the term *anorexia nervosa*) and Ernest Lasègue (who published a report on the condition he called *anorexie hysterica*).[27] This phenomena is widely present in the Italian Ottocento as well, according to Ludovica Costantino. In *La ricerca di un'immagine. L'anoressia mentale* (The Search for an Image. Mental Anorexia), the author isolates in the figure of Elizabeth of Austria (more commonly known as Sissi; 1838–1898) an emblem of the 'new woman' (63). Due to a fixation with exercise and sport, the empress demonstrated that one could be thin without the use of a corset. Her obsession with her body dominated her life, leading Costantino to claim that 'she searched for a personal identity her whole life, hoping to find it with her body'; therefore, 'she became the progenitor of modern anorexia' (63). With the empress, we see the birth of a fashion of thinness that transforms the new woman of the nineteenth century into a pale and emaciated figure, replacing the robust *mater familias* as the new ideal of femininity (64).

Along with this new female ideal, the notion of food consumption and the satiation of one's appetite was conflated with that of the satisfaction of one's carnal appetite. In her ground-breaking work on the origins of *Anorexia nervosa*, Joan Brumberg confirms through Sigmund Freud and Pierre Janet that there is, in fact, a link between consumption of food and female sexuality, which contributed to cases of anorexia in the late nineteenth century.[28] Brumberg demonstrated, mainly by citing Freud, that eating or not eating became a proxy for sexual appetite.[29] The dinner table was the site for the expression of the bourgeoisie's worst fears,[30] namely, the expression of an uninhibited spontaneity, including sexuality, that contrasted proper middle-class conduct. It is then apparent that the suppression of one's appetite suggested the repression of one's carnal urges, thus becoming further impetus for feminine convivial fasting.

Mantegazza's 'delicate' woman

Addressing the new fashion of thinness that prevailed in the second half of the nineteenth century, Susan Bordo claimed that it was necessary to follow a specific praxis of 'straitlacing, minimal eating, reduced mobility', which rendered the female body incapable of participating in activities outside the roles designated to her by society (181). It is precisely this routine that was advanced by the scientific literature of the day, in particular by the most diffused of Italian authors, Paolo Mantegazza. The self-proclaimed *polygamist of the sciences* (*La bibbia della speranza* [The Bible of Hope, 1909] 1), who published countless volumes of hygiene manuals and treatises, forwarded a biological analysis of the sexes that physiologically privileged men for their gustatory abilities, leaving women disadvantaged by nature itself:

> man was privileged by nature . . . . Woman, although more sensitive than man, is too little selfish to analyse and to favour these sensual pleasures. After all, the delicateness of her organs and the many peculiarities of her bizarre tastes, more often than not, preclude more intense pleasures.[31]

Here Mantegazza ratified the prominent image of a woman who was incapable of partaking in the gastronomic endeavours of her male counterparts due to what he implied was an innate deficiency. The fact that the author referred to woman's nature as 'too little selfish' to be able to evaluate and privilege the sense of taste corroborated the need to suppress her individuality for the benefit of others. The focus was on her role as caretaker – as someone always at the disposal of others before herself.

Even when not focusing on taste, Mantegazza divulged a concept of womanhood that condemned her to be a creature of vanity who found recourse in dissimulation:

> Woman, vain par excellence, studies herself in all her movements and in all the external features of her person, attempting to draw the most interest possible to the assets granted to her by nature, and to hide her defects with all the artifices possible.[32]

In many ways, Mantegazza's depiction was perfectly in line with that of Rajberti: a woman was a figure of continence and grace, keen to mask any indiscretions, particularly in the convivial setting. Mantegazza, however, went further than his precedent, as he preached female physiological inferiority due to what he contended to be her biological underdevelopment. In what became a sort of leitmotif, the author associated women physically and psychologically to boys (and even brutes), that is, man in a partially developed state: 'She in her general form resembles a young male . . . [and is] even psychologically close to him . . . [with] an infantile and, above all, atavistic personality.'[33] They were likened even in terms of physiognomy: 'A woman's forehead almost always has (at least in the superior races) extremely weak or missing eyebrow arches; they are narrow and have marked frontal humps; all characteristics of the infantile cranium.'[34]

This tendency derives from Darwin, who indicated in *The Descent of Man* (1871) that woman was evolutionarily inferior.[35] She was 'in essence, a stunted man', associated with the young of both sexes.[36] We can trace this thought to other Italian writers as well. For example, Cesare Lombroso, the famed positivist criminologist, claimed: 'Women, like children, are notoriously misoneistic.'[37] And, in describing youth, he declared, 'The impulsiveness that is noted in women is also found in children.'[38] Furthermore, in his text *La donna delinquente: La prostituta e la donna normale* (The Delinquent Woman: Prostitutes and Normal Women, 1893), Lombroso went on to outline differentiating biological characteristics of the sexes, concluding that 'in their entirety, [normal] women are more infantile then men', and later condemning her as someone possessing a smaller brain and lacking originality (48, 161).[39]

Another Italian text that demonstrates this Darwinist trend was published in 1886 by Francesco Tanini: *La donna secondo il giudizio dei dotti e dei proverbi di tutti i popoli* (Women According to Scholars and Proverbs of all the People). This is a work that defines an epoch's depiction of women by anthologizing proverbs and phrases that characterize their physical, psychological and physiological natures. Within this collection of sayings from throughout the centuries, Mantegazza alone is quoted forty-two times. For example, while discussing the pleasures of the table, Tanini references the *polygamist of the sciences* to demonstrate how 'the pleasures of taste and of gluttony are felt more by males than by females'.[40] Additionally, the collection demonstrates how this link between woman and child was indeed widespread.[41] In twenty-nine cases, the statements anthologized by Tanini demonstrate this correlation, leading the author to surmise the following:

> There are great connections between the female sex and masculine youth: they have sensitivities and passions in common. The makeup of their organs is equally soft and full of moisture; their limbs are delicate and round; their hearts are sensitive and mutable; their observational spirit is little profound . . . woman is an adult child and needs the moral and material help of man.[42]

With this description, the nineteenth-century woman was clearly depicted by the male writers of the period as lacking the maturity and the refinement necessary to partake in the endeavours of her male counterparts. Because of her 'biological inferiority', which was understood as a lack of evolution, woman's societal roles were to be limited (at least in the eyes of the patriarchal and clearly sexist society in which these writers worked). It was, therefore, no different for matters of taste, and the leading disseminator in the Italian context of the proper feminine diet was Mantegazza himself.

Throughout his texts, Mantegazza creates an image of a woman whose nourishment is based on the limited societal responsibilities prescribed to her, completely opposing that of man. Since, according to the author, man's brain and muscles are more active, he must consume more meat and nervine foods *(alimenti nervosi)* (*Igiene della cucina* [Hygiene in the kitchen] 6, 80).[43] A woman's diet, for the medic, was to be more vegetarian and frugivorous, specifying that vegetables were 'innocent'; in other words, they did no harm nor good, to the system (colourfully stating that Dante would have put them in reign of Limbo) (24). Nervine foods, such as alcohol, were out of the question for women due to their 'weak wills' and penchant for addiction.[44] Because of this food regimen, woman, not surprisingly, was, 'close to a young boy and is anthropomorphic'; in other words, she embodied human characteristics, yet was not fully (hu)man (*Fisiologia della donna,* Vol. 1, 103). On a very basic level, the author communicated that the diet of the Italian woman was to be a diet of a non-developed man. Furthermore, it was through not only what she consumed but also how she consumed it that her infantile or stunted nature was conjured: 'She eats less than us, but she prefers to eat more often . . . this too is a characteristic of an infantile diet.'[45] Ultimately, women were biologically structured for passivity: 'in the female we have the tendency of composing molecules, in other words, a corresponding inactivity or passivity. The male expends energy, the female accumulates it.'[46] What Mantegazza argued was innate inactivity that was fostered by a specific manner and mode of consumption and that suppressed her possibilities for active societal roles. Her passivity was both cause and product of how she nourished herself. Furthermore, the medic's postulated female diet, by nature, promoted an image of woman that was delicate, consumed little and would seldom participate in society – an image that certainly promotes thinness, an inhibited individuality and, ultimately, an overall lack of impetus.

Mantegazza's dissemination of a truly patriarchal science of the sexes can be encapsulated in a single phrase written as part of a book analysing women: 'Is a woman an angel or a demon? – neither: she is man's.'[47] He claimed that women would be free to develop on various levels in a society that were not male-controlled. He even emphasized that it was due to 'male despotism' that women could not indulge in their desires, in particular, their sense of taste. As the leading Italian anthropologist,[48] he adduced Paraguay as exemplar: women there enjoyed an advanced use of their gustatory sense and enjoyed nervine foods such as coffee, tea and tobacco since their male society did not condemn it (Vol. 1, 103). He went even further by stating that women could even equal men in physical labour, citing his studies on the peasants of Liguria and Lago Maggiore as salient examples (Vol. 1, 105). The author claimed that it was the 'tyranny of man' that stagnated woman's societal progression (Vol. 1, 105); however, it is clear that he did very little to rectify this matter. On the contrary, his conception of woman was reflected in a nutritional inferiority that only worked to further widen the taste gap between the sexes.

Conclusions

Whereas the French model of food aestheticization (the European model par excellence) found propagation through the public sphere – through aristocratic and intellectual classes, journalists and the explosion of newly developing restaurants in the 1800s – the Italian model advanced via domesticity. It was geared towards mothers, sisters and servants, who, as caretakers of the home, became prominent purveyors of an attempted Italianness. As Lucia Re stated, 'the economy of the home, and women's role in it were increasingly envisioned as a source of healing for the society at large'.[49] Women, as nurturers of the domestic space, cultivated the larger social body and, in turn, spurred a sense of national community.[50] The authors showed that food became a national tool that was divulged through women, and, since food preparation and consumption 'involves the production of meaning and identities',[51] women's role in nineteenth-century Italian societal culture was of paramount importance.

Simultaneously, this food-centric and scientific literature dictated that women eat and act in a certain fashion at the table, thus delimiting their role. Authors such as Rajberti and Mantegazza made great strides to portray new gastronomic and gastrosophic ideals while acting as national unifiers. Yet their work did very little to include women in the convivial sphere. They reflected and further diffused the patriarchal hegemony of their day, yet their success was, in every sense, constructed on woman. Artusi, for example, could not cook. His book was a compilation of recipes that were tested by his personal cook, Marietta Sabatini, and that were, in many instances, taken from the hundreds and hundreds of letters that he received, the vast majority of which were written by women. Guerrini was a neophyte in the kitchen, and his recipe collection *L'arte di utilizzare gli avanzi* (The Art of Making Use of Leftovers, 1918) was nothing more than a collage of dishes taken from historically significant cookbooks for an audience he hoped would comprise home cooks and the 'woman' of each house. Despite women being essential to the call of Italianness around the table, the aesthete and the gastro-philosopher were to be males, making the realm of taste exclusively masculine. Women were to prepare and organize, assimilate, dissimilate and serve, yet they were not to partake. Female identity at the table was constructed around the social parameters that precluded them from self-expression and indulgence; therefore, 'woman' was caretaker, cook, *gastrophilanthropic* (the nineteenth-century term meaning 'The Benevolent Purveyor for the Belly of Others')[52] and hostess, but never *gastronoma.*

Notwithstanding this attempt to condemn women to the kitchen, to the dining room and to a delicate diet, women did indeed find a voice within this food-centric literature. The first published female-penned Italian cookbook came out in 1897: *Come posso mangiar bene?* (How Can I Eat Well?) by Giulia Ferraris Tamburini. It was the inauguration of an Italian woman writing to Italian women and a *padrona di casa* writing to others, paving the way for writers such as Ada Boni, who would find immense success with her *Il talismano della felicità* (The Talisman of Happiness, 1927). Boni became a household name that was on par with, if it did not surpass, the likes of Artusi. When it comes to etiquette manuals, we can see that women authors begin to rise precisely in the period of our taste authors: from Marchesa Colombi's *Gente per bene* (Proper People, 1874) to Emilia Nevers's *Il galateo della borghesia* (The Etiquette Manual for the Bourgeoisie, 1883), Caterina Pigorio Beri's *Le buone maniere* (Good Manners, 1893) and Ida Baccini's *Lo spirito del galateo – il galateo dello spirito* (The Spirit of Good Manners – Good Manners of the Spirit, 1904), there is a significant promulgation of a female-led decorum, guides for women to be *Italian* women as written by *italiane.* Ultimately, the patriarchal society still highly influenced their works, and women were still to be the embodiment of bourgeois propriety as the orchestrator of the household (i.e. the private sphere), as agreed upon by male intellectuals and politicians as a means for the new Italian society.[53] However, female gastronomic writers broke into the 'public' sphere, in many ways defying the very roles intended for them.

2

Marcella cucina

Marcella Hazan and the gendered authority of the Italian cookbook

Danielle Callegari

In a review of her by then canonical Italian cookbooks, the American food writer Craig Seligman complained that while Marcella Hazan's recipes were invaluable, her tone was 'impatient and judgmental', making Hazan herself much harder to love than her food:

> For more than 25 years now Marcella Hazan has been goading, browbeating, hectoring, shaming and, not incidentally, inspiring her readers into preparing Italian cuisine the proper way, which is to say, according to the traditional methods of the Italian kitchen . . . . Marcella Hazan's impatient and judgmental tone often makes her seem like a pain. (She is one hero I've never wanted to meet.) But her recipes are so beautiful and so reliable and, most of the time, so brilliantly simple that what can you do but venerate her and love her in spite of herself?[1]

Hazan, who is generally credited as the individual who brought 'real' or 'authentic' Italian cuisine to the American audience through her English-language cookbooks, is almost universally described as difficult and critical, even by those who only met her through her writing.[2] Sitting in on one of her classes, and making careful note of how expensive the privilege was, Scott Simon similarly called her 'sturdy and uncompromising' and her instructions 'blunt and specific'.[3] Though David Sipress was decidedly more loving in his depiction, he too described her as 'a short, compact lady, a tough biscotti [*sic*] with a raspy voice who didn't suffer fools gladly and had a surprising preference for Jack Daniels over a glass of wine'.[4] Unlike Seligman, however, Sipress was pleased that she provided him with precise rules to follow and took advantage of an opportunity to meet her, becoming overwhelmed when she anointed him with her approval after he revealed he had conquered a challenging recipe. Mark Bittman instead found her to be a generous teacher, and he eventually afforded her the highest praise of all by deeming her even more important than the *other* mononymous cook in his canon, Julia. Yet in granting her this, he also suggested she was unaware of, or at least unwitting in her participation in, the Italian culinary–cultural project that resulted from her efforts: 'the woman who was largely responsible – however unintentionally – for bringing real Italian food to the United States'.[5]

This oscillation between portraying Hazan as a tough and headstrong master, who is decidedly authorial but hard to take, and a hospitable instructor, whose books against all odds were effective, points to the peculiar space occupied by the writer of cookbooks and the genre as a whole. Hazan's profilers all conclude the same thing: as a woman who takes an authoritative, and thus male, stance, Marcella is herself 'off the map', and her books, bossily unfeminine in their succinct prescriptive style, are practical but discordantly assertive.[6] Deviations from this interpretation often move to lift agency from her writing: a passionate cook and teacher in person, it was only a coincidence that her writing managed to communicate a universal expertise to a wider audience. In this way, Hazan can exist outside of and separately from her texts – so that the cookbook might be revered while the cook is loved.

The discomfort with the unstable space a cook and their cookbook can inhabit inadvertently picks up on an overlooked aspect of the genre and authors who have experimented with it. Recipe collections have only recently begun to be appreciated by historians as primary source artefacts, at least in part because they have long been perceived as domestic and effeminate in the modern Western household. More broadly, though cookbooks have been acknowledged as resources for social history, they have rarely in any tradition been perceived as consciously developed tools in a grander plan of cultural or political construction, despite the explosion of interest in food studies and particularly the politics of food economies in recent decades.[7] In fact, the cookbook has successfully acted as inscriber of social anatomies and power systems, taking advantage of its ability to speak to or through both professional chefs and home cooks, both heads of household and primary nourishers, and thus both men and women. The Italian cookbook in particular has historically been used to consciously construct authority and impose cultural programmes – from Renaissance recipe collections that were designed as social ladders for their court chef authors to the nation-building aspirations of Pellegrino Artusi's

1891 *La scienza in cucina e l'arte di mangiar bene* (Science in the Kitchen and the Art of Eating Well) – sometimes through the commanding, dismissive voice of a master in the kitchen, and sometimes through the familiar, coaxing voice of an adept amateur.

Born in the small seaside town of Cesenatico in the Italian region of Emilia Romagna and holding degrees in biology and natural sciences, Marcella Hazan was neither classically trained as a chef nor even much of a cook in her premarital life. Yet after moving to New York in 1955 with her husband Victor, she embarked on a career in which she established herself as the authority on authentic Italian food in America.[8] Her first two cookbooks, *The Classic Italian Cook Book: The Art of Italian Cooking and the Italian Art of Eating* (1973) and *More Classic Italian Cooking* (1978), later collected and revised under the title *Essentials of Classic Italian Cooking* (1992), defined Italian cuisine for the Anglophone audience and have remained fundamental points of reference even for professional chefs, despite the vastly expanded availability of sources for the contemporary cook.[9] This chapter will use recent research on the social and political intentions of premodern and modern Italian cookbooks and their authors to demonstrate how through her bestselling English-language Italian cookbooks, Marcella Hazan utilized the genre and its fluidly gendered authority, tapping into the power it could wield to control the conversation between Italian culture and American culture through food.

There is a growing interest in the interpretation of the cultural–historical dialogue that takes place in the cookbook, and significant archival and philological reconstructions have provided the foundation that might facilitate further research. Most recently, in his comprehensive study of European cookbooks from the medieval to the modern period, Henry Notaker has observed that everything from the material form of the texts themselves to the para-texts incorporated to the organizing principles employed can reveal values and ideas governing a cookbook. He emphasizes that culinary texts reflect and respond to social, economic, cultural and political realities of their historical moment.[10] Importantly, Notaker points out that cookbooks and recipe collecting seem to have always been for both men and women, and only in the eighteenth century, if not later, did the audience begin to become primarily female.[11] While contemporary European culture regards the kitchen and its associated culinary texts as the domain of the woman, especially the housewife, cookbooks were objects where oral and written literacy merged, and public and private life blurred together; even at their inception they occupied a grey area between male-coded and female-coded spaces. Because the cook is flexibly gendered –

traditionally the home cook is female, the professional cook is male – so too the cookbook enjoys a certain flexibility.

The studies that have focused specifically on Italian cookery texts have suggested compelling evidence for the implicit agendas of the recipe collection, and its potential as a model for use beyond Italian borders.[12] In their comprehensive study of Italian gastronomic history, Alberto Capatti and Massimo Montanari have pointed to the more profound nature of this uniquely durable didactic genre: 'Created by men who were professional experts in specific areas of service at the courts of nobility, [early Italian] cookbooks are far from miscellaneous collections, and in the course of their publishing history they became more diversified.'[13] As Allen Grieco has emphasized, while tracking the real application and intended audience of cookbooks can be very difficult, careful attention to the dialogue between culinary texts and their historic contexts can measure how accurately recipe collections reflect tastes and habits of their time.[14] Grieco has used the rich Italian archival sources available to trace recorded recipes back to buying practices and into literature, to sketch an outline of what was eaten and why in the late Italian Middle Ages, pointing to dietary restrictions that align with civic responsibility and social class.[15]

Expanding on this, the extensive archival mapping by Anna Martellotti has demonstrated that the first Italian recipe collection, the anonymous *Liber de coquina* (Book of Cookery), was produced at the imperial court of the Emperor Frederick II of Hohenstaufen (r. 1220–1250), at the behest of the emperor and in dialogue with a culture that valued food preparation as a political art.[16] Perhaps the first European text to collect ingredients and instructions in the format that is today recognizable as a cookbook, the *Liber de coquina* became an urtext for later culinary works, with the rich and cosmopolitan courtly milieux of Frederick II as its backdrop. This imperial inception of the genre provided the Italian cookbook with a firmly patrilineal genealogy, and suggests that even in its earliest iteration, it was conceived expressly as a text that would use culinary expertise to engender cultural hegemony and reinforce existing power structures. The many highly successful pre- and early modern recipe collections that appeared in the *Liber's* wake certainly capitalized upon this, often being presented by their authors or publishers as an essential component to an élite or courtly education for the complete man. However, these same texts were also forced to acknowledge – if backhandedly – that even if the ideal held that the power of the kitchen was masculine, the person actually cooking might well be a woman.

Following the anonymous *Liber*, compilers of recipe collections became more persistently visible and the relationship between author and text was more thoroughly elaborated. Figures like Maestro Martino – whose biography is only scarcely known but whose cookbook, the *Libro de arte coquinaria* (The Art of Cooking, ca. 1465), was circulated widely in manuscript form and earned him the title 'prince of chefs' – began to pave the way for a long line of esteemed, authoritative chefs. His friend, and perhaps direct collaborator, Bartolomeo Sacchi, better known as Il Platina, cemented the place of the recipe collection in the canon and affirmed its *auctoritas* by publishing Martino's recipes in the context of a larger Latin humanist treatise, *De honesta voluptate et valetudine* (On Honorable Pleasure and Health, 1474). By the high Renaissance, many court *scalchi* (heads of household) turned to the published recipe collection as a stepping stone towards greatness, among them the famous Este court *scalco* Cristoforo Messisbugo, who published the well-received *Banchetti, composizioni di vivande et apparecchio generale* (Banquets, Compositions of Meals and General Table Setting, 1549) and earned the title of Count Palatine. The method was also employed by the Venetian chef Domenico Romoli, with his encyclopaedic *La singolar dottrina* (The Singular Doctrine, 1560), and the celebrated Bartolomeo Scappi, who achieved fame with his *Opera dell'arte del cucinare* (Complete Work on the Art of Cooking, 1573).

In her thorough investigation of Scappi's *Opera* and of the early modern cookbook more generally, Deborah Krohn has demonstrated that many of the recipes that appear in these early modern cookbooks acknowledge a larger, more diverse audience than their dedications would suggest. To be sure, while Cristoforo Messisbugo distinguishes himself from a 'common little woman' in the preface to his *Banchetti*, he nonetheless includes several recipes that are clearly meant more for a humble home cook than his courtly peers.[17] As Krohn points out, Messisbugo's claim that he will not waste time on the things 'any simple woman knows how to make perfectly' in fact reveals his awareness of an audience that is not composed solely of princes, and that the cookbook's ability to be both literature and practical manual – both for an educated male élite and a working, mixed gender household staff – was precisely what could best guarantee the success of his volume.[18] Scappi (or at least his publishers) similarly seems intensely focused on the elevation of the occupation of the cook, excluding any women from the extensive illustrations that accompany his text. Yet other contemporary visual companions to gastronomy from artists like Vincenzo Campi betray him, depicting a less professionalized, and thus less strictly male world.[19] The anxiety that Messisbugo and Scappi display points to the tension inherent to the genre – one that they feared but also used to their advantage. By grafting their texts onto the deep roots born at the late medieval imperial court, but simultaneously exploiting the familiarity and universality of the genre, these authors helped the cookbook medium become a versatile tool for social mobility.

In the modern period, increased literacy and the growing ease with which printed books could be obtained allowed a much wider audience to have access to cookbooks, and now the home cook, usually a woman, was just as likely to benefit from and be willing to invest in a text that guided daily work in the kitchen. As cookbooks became a more common presence in the homes of the burgeoning bourgeoisie, the potential arose for such a text to act as a Trojan horse for a political agenda. At the end of the nineteenth century, as the newly formed Italian state endeavoured to find its footing, Pellegrino Artusi took this opportunity to use the cookbook, combining its fluid nature and its increasingly ubiquitous presence, for a Risorgimento project. His *La scienza in cucina e l'arte di mangiar bene* has long been recognized as a coherent effort to depict a unified Italy by collecting regional recipes under the umbrella of one national cuisine during the delicate post-unification years.[20] Artusi, as Martino, Messisbugo and the many others before him, used the socially constructed and collectively shared values of food and its preparation to communicate a political message – in this case reaching beyond the interest of individual fame and fortune. However, Artusi began to deviate from the overtly male posturing of the genre in his more modestly composed cookbook, which explicitly positioned itself as a guide for the non-professional.[21] Less concerned with elevating the chef than the cuisine, Artusi takes on a warm, genial tone, and includes poems and proverbs to counterbalance his more prudent overtures to hygiene and cleanliness. The dedication to his two cats, Biancani and Sibillone, and his concern for the frequent indigestions of the latter, presents a patently different approach, couching his efforts in an explicitly female voice:[22]

> Whenever my dear friend Sibillone used to suffer from indigestion, he would go a day or two without eating and work it off on the rooftops. We should therefore deplore those pitiful mothers who, in an excess of maternal sentiment, keep a forever watchful eye over the health of their little ones, and the instant they see them a bit listless or not evacuating with regularity – obsessed as they are with the silly notion of worms, which most often are only in their imagination – immediately resort to medications to enemas, instead of letting nature take her course.

With this tangent on the health of his cats and proper mothering, Artusi is not undermining the seriousness of his text; he is exploiting its adaptability to his own ends. He disparages bad mothers in the voice of a mother himself, fretting over Biancani and Sibillone who wait patiently at his feet to taste his recipes. Striking this maternal pose, Artusi carves out a comfortable seat that the genre permits him to find in the space between masculine potency and feminine intimacy. While he reminded his readers that his cats were always his first concern and his first critics, Artusi also created a standardized lexicon for food items that were known under a range of regional names and proposed a set of rules for maintaining a clean and safe kitchen.[23] Speaking to this careful balance in tone, Luigi Ballerini has observed 'Artusi's voice may be that of the well-meaning schoolteacher with a sense of humour as preposterous as the nonchalance with which it is proffered, yet his style is never obscure and ridiculous (or ridiculously obscure), as was often the case in the history of culinary writing'.[24] Artusi's impositions had consequences beyond the culinary for the Italian audience, in large part because they were delivered with this structured combination of ambiguity and calculation.

Artusi's manipulation of the flexibly gendered authority of the cookbook does not seem to have been an exception, but rather one star in a constellation of modern Italian recipe collections that used these techniques – a constellation to which the prodigious work of Marcella Hazan belongs. Hazan's position here stands out because, among other things, she is the first female author to be named in this culinary genealogy. As Notaker has underlined, there is a striking distance between the cook and the cookbook writer.[25] If cookbooks are literature, then their writers have authority that allows them (or is, counter-intuitively, derived from their ability) to act as authors, which is traditionally a male territory. While the audience for cookbooks might have always been less strictly delineated than other genres, female-*authored* cookbooks are almost non-existent in the pre- and early modern periods, and still somewhat rare later, though more common in the Anglophone world.[26] However, the unique opening presented by Artusi's acceptance of, and delight in, the inherent femininity in a text that discussed methods of nourishing did not go unnoticed. In the twentieth century, Marcella Hazan would have at least one significant example of a woman writing in the genre before her and on whom she could rely: Ada Boni.

Continuing to stretch the elasticity of the cookbook, in a notable contrast to the gentle, tolerant tone of Artusi, came the voice of Ada Boni, who composed what would soon be one of the most important cookbooks of the twentieth century for the Italian audience, *Il talismano della felicità* (The Talisman of Happiness). As a woman, Boni seems to focus on appropriating the masculine weight or seriousness of the cookbook, and spends little time indulging her reader. In fact, the 'impatient and judgmental' tone Seligman laments in Hazan is literally a page out of Boni's book:

> Many of you, ladies, may know how to play the piano well or to sing with exquisite grace. Many of you may have prestigious degrees, may speak foreign languages or be pleasant writers or fine painters. Others of you may be masters of tennis or golf players, or know how to drive a luxurious automobile with a firm hand. But, alas, if you examine your conscience, I am certain that not all of you can honestly say that you know how to make a perfectly coddled egg![27]

Il talismano della felicità stood in stark contrast to *La scienza in cucina* in many ways. Designed to speak to a serious cook with pretensions to mastery, Boni writes deliberately and forcefully, expecting her readers to already be in charge of their kitchen and to understand the trickle-down effect of a confident cook. Boni separates her antipasti into 'simple' and 'complex', denoting levels of progress to be achieved, and adds a section on 'intermezzi' for formal meals. As Montanari observes, editions of her text contain double portraits of her and her husband, visibly cementing her position as author of the text and as equal partner in the maintenance of her healthy, stable household through her prowess in the kitchen. This is perhaps, as historians have suggested, what makes Boni less appealing than Artusi. While Boni became the face and voice of a class-bound haute cuisine in Italy, Piero Meldini has joked that 'grandma's cooking' in Italy is actually 'grandpa's cooking' – a transgendered translation of the appeal and comfort of Artusi's cooking, which is de facto associated with the female despite the male voice that proposed it originally.[28]

But if Artusi was the victor in the great gastronomic battle for the hearts and minds of Italians in Italy, Hazan reveals that it was the *Talismano* she turned to when she decided to learn to cook Italian cuisine in America: '[My husband Victor] bought a copy of Ada Boni's *Il Talismano della Felicità*, the cookbook that became my first reference when, shortly after we were married we moved to New York and I began to cook.'[29] Her choice is especially significant because, as she underlines repeatedly, she saw no particular connection between cooking and housewifery, and she was explicitly not interested in the latter: 'Aside from cooking, which I enjoyed, the role of housewife did not fit me well.'[30] While she originally begins to experiment with cooking out of the essential need to feed her family, she takes it on pragmatically, and does not seem to even momentarily consider allowing her environment to influence her. On the contrary, Hazan is unapologetic in her discrimination against American taste and 1950s kitchen expedience. She remains horrified by supermarket frozen sections – memorably describing them in *Essentials of Italian Cooking* and again in her memoir, *Amarcord*, as 'cemeteries of food, whose contents are sealed up in waxed boxes marked, like some tombstones, with photographs of the departed'.[31] Like her decision to learn English better to tell off the rude Italian-American shopkeepers she encounters in her early days in New York, Hazan first begins to cook because it is a practical need, but she then works to master it because the uncouth American audience seems to require her intervention.[32]

The resolve she expresses repeatedly has nonetheless been left unrecognized. Though Hazan is formally credited with introducing America to 'real' Italian cuisine, she is also depicted as having allowed this privilege to happen to her, as in the case of Bittman's appraisal of her legacy. Yet Hazan provides significant insight into this element of her personal history in *Amarcord*. Craig Seligman rightly notes in his review of the autobiography – not missing the chance to emphasize once again how 'witheringly stern' Hazan can be in her cookbooks – that she spends surprisingly little time on moments that would seem to be of great importance in her life.[33] At the same time, she dedicates a considerable part of her memoir to making explicit her mission to change the American diet (or at least the American view of the Italian diet), clearly stating that she set out to write a text that would be the principal point of reference for an Anglophone audience wishing to approach Italian cuisine. Hazan's decision to use a language and format that would be clear for her audience indicates explicit intention to avoid the dangers of cultural mistranslation. She relies heavily on her 'inseparable collaborator' and husband, Victor, to be sure that her limited English and tendency to elide details do not obscure the functionality of the recipes. She notes that she looked at several examples of Italian cookbooks and quickly dismissed them as models, knowing that an American audience would not have the necessary context or comfort in the kitchen to make recipes expressed in that style useful:[34]

> I had brought my favorite cookbooks from Italy and I studied them now, not, as I had been wont to do, in search of cooking ideas, but to see how they were organized and how the recipes were set down. They were of no help. In Italy, cookbooks are written for a public already familiar with the procedures of the cuisine. The instructions are in a cooking shorthand that I would have loved to use, but if I had, my recipes would have been inaccessible to most American readers.

Her culinary texts confirm this through their design and format. Hazan's first cookbook, *The Classic Italian Cookbook*, an unmitigated success despite her lack of experience, begins with a brief history of Italian cooking, followed by a list of standard Italian ingredients in Italian with English translations below, and finally a list and explanation of necessary kitchen equipment. Perhaps most notably, Hazan employed the artist George Koizumi to prepare extensive technical drawings for the text, providing a hand-illustrated visual apparatus not unlike the one included in Bartolomeo Scappi's 1573 *Opera*. The recipes that follow are all similarly presented, with their Italian title first and an English title below, creating a didactic template. Last of all, there is an explanation of how to use a traditional Italian coffee pot to make coffee in the Italian way – connecting the technology and the consumable product. The text concludes with this revelatory paragraph:[35]

> What people do with food is an act that reveals how they construe the world. It is no coincidence that the country that produced the Confucian system of ethical conduct imposes on the ingredients of its cooking a rigid discipline of cut and shape. The work of art that is a Japanese meal is a natural legacy of the only society where aesthetics, at one time, entirely governed life. And the achievement of classic French cuisine, its logic, the marvellous subtlety of its discoveries, could have occurred only in the country of Descartes and Proust.
>
> The world of the Italians is not a phenomenon that needs to be subdued, reshaped, arranged in logical patterns. It is not a challenge to be won. It is there simply to be enjoyed, mostly on its own terms. What we find in the cooking of Italy is a serene relationship between man and the sources of his existence, a long-established intimacy between the human and natural orders, a harmonious fusion of man's skills and nature's gifts. The Italian comes to his table with the same open heart with which a child falls into his mother's arms, with the same easy feeling of being in the right place.

If her designs were not clear before, Hazan announces here her structural conception of cuisine as a reflection and reinforcement of a cultural framework. She reminds her readers that learning how to cook and eat as an Italian is the means by which to inhabit this culture on intimate, if qualified, terms. She does not suggest that this is a simple undertaking. Hazan dares her audience to challenge themselves in the kitchen and on their palate, affirming that like her they can stand on the shoulders of the cooks that came before: 'Now, as these recipes are turned over to you, it must be your tastes that take charge. The dish will become yours, as much as it became mine, as much as it was that of the cook who preceded me.'[36] She further models this process, recounting her own search for this impossible-to-recreate experience in the preparation for her second cookbook, *More Classic Italian Cooking*: 'I went wherever I was told there was a gifted cook. I took down recipes the way one takes down unwritten folk songs and stories, traveling with a tape recorder slung besides my shoulder bag, a magic listening box so small and unobtrusive few people I talked to were aware it was there.'[37] Her concerted efforts are thus shown to go beyond the kitchen and into the world, acknowledging the need for an intrepid spirit as well as a sensitivity to the nuances of the development of cuisine. *More Classic Italian Cooking* also includes in its para-textual apparatus 'A Pasta Glossary', akin to the lexicon of terms in Artusi's *La scienza in cucina*, along with a list of producers from whom authentic, quality Italian ingredients can be sourced.[38] These parts taken together make Hazan's cookbooks the keys to unlocking another culture, and to consciously accessing good taste that goes beyond the palate.

In articulating her understanding that culture and cuisine go hand in hand, Hazan not only reveals a sophisticated appreciation of the terms on which food has meaning and value in society but also affirms the potential value of her work. In the vein of her predecessors in the genre, Hazan profits from the confidence that masculine mastery inspires, but as a female author writing in a genre of nourishment, she also shares an inherent intimacy and confidence with her audience, who come to her table 'with the same open heart with which a child falls into his mother's arms, with the same easy feeling of being in the right place'. As Hazan concludes in *The Classic Italian Cookbook*, 'I cannot expect from anyone a total conversion to Italian cooking, but if even a few of these dishes together with their proper placement within an Italian meal become a natural part of your life at table, I shall feel handsomely rewarded for my efforts.'[39] Her use of the word 'conversion' – the turn away from ignorance towards knowledge – suggests a desire to effect a more profound and lasting kind of change.

Indeed, her insistence on the larger scale implications even allows Hazan to be seen to dialogue with gastronomic and social historians. The broader dilemma of explaining the existence of certain eating habits has led scholars to suggest that cultural culinary particularities might be understood through economic determinism or geographic and climatic limitations. Yet case studies that reveal human eating patterns are just as frequently the product of ideological or cultural constructions, often even in the face of significant logistical challenges.[40] Hazan taps into a deep genealogy of cookbooks, one in which the author uses the text to judge and appraise, and to condemn if necessary. Her culinary works are not meant to provide the dilettante with an afternoon of gastronomic frivolity; her purpose is to impart culture along with skills that are indeed pleasurable, but also venerable, and essential to the complete cultural formation – the *art* of Italian cooking and the Italian *art* of eating. As fellow chef Jacques Pépin observed, '[p]eople didn't think of Italian as great food. She challenged that. She did what she did with very strong conviction, and that's the way it was regardless of whether other people liked it or not.'[41]

At the medieval imperial court, Frederick II marked cookery as one among many equally important pieces in a larger puzzle of court culture, as deserving of a treatise as falconry or music because it required attention and skill, and because it could be wielded as a subtle weapon. In this tradition that trickled down to Hazan through Renaissance court *scalchi* and Risorgimento projects, Hazan composed culinary texts that provided practical and technical details, anchoring her authority through both masculine and feminine channels. Her cookbooks are not for housewives; they are for cooks, whoever they might be. If it is perhaps possible to think of the cookbook as quintessentially multi-gendered, in its hedging between instinct and performance, Hazan finds that inscribing a cultural standard through food must have the seasonality of the market and the deliberateness of intellect. As she reflects in a later cookbook, *Marcella Cucina*, over the selection of greens at the market, '[i]f it seems like a lot of trouble to take over a salad, it is food that she is going to put on the table isn't it, and what could be more important? There are no decisions she will make, either that morning or in her life, to which she is likely to give more deliberate thought.'[42] With this in mind, it might be useful to revise Pépin's observation and say instead: Marcella cooked, whether other people liked her or not.

3

Domestic labour, everyday pleasure and perspective in Simonetta Agnello Hornby's culinary memoirs *Un filo d'olio* and *Il pranzo di Mosè*

Georgia Wall

Born in 1945 in Palermo, lawyer, novelist, and food writer Simonetta Agnello Hornby is a naturalized British citizen and has spent most of her adult life living in London. Her writings, which range in genre from autobiography to historical fiction, can be read as products born out of mobility across and between nations and eras – quite literally, as the author explains with an acknowledgement to British Airways in her first novel, *La Mennulara* (The Almond Picker).[1] Perhaps due to her professional experience of domestic violence cases, Agnello Hornby's narratives are also characterized by a special attention to domestic power relations alongside highly sensory depictions of food preparation and consumption. This chapter explores the themes of labour and pleasure in Agnello Hornby's recent culinary memoirs *Il pranzo di Mosè* (Lunch at Mosè, 2014) and *Un filo d'olio* (A Drizzle of Olive Oil, 2011), taking into account her perspective as an Anglo-Italian woman writer remembering the Sicily of her childhood. Informed by Jean Duruz's reflections on the gendered implications of nostalgia for the social relations of former domestic landscapes, the aim of this discussion is to invite further consideration of the various and potentially conflicting connotations of the broader appeal of nostalgic images of Italy, particularly in terms of domestic pleasure.

In Western culture, Italy is often characterized by nostalgic idealizations of its rural past and traditional family kitchens – a view of Italian culture that, Gisela Ecker points out, 'powerfully corresponds to Italian auto-stereotypes distributed in great quantity and best visual quality by local tourism boards'.[2] Beyond and within Italy, Italian food and the family table are exalted as symbolic of community and the security of the family home – in the rhetoric of media campaigns such as that of *Il Mulino Bianco*, which feature images of wholesome families enjoying life in sun-drenched rural cottages,[3] and, quite practically, in the *sagre* or village *fêtes* that celebrate specific local products and recipes, often with participants in costume. Of course, the apparent vogue for nostalgic re-creations and re-enactments of the past is not confined to Italy. Memory scholar Andreas Huyssen points to a broader pattern of social anxiety in the post-industrialized West, and argues that such a 'yearning for remembering' is related to the need for a more secure positioning when confronted with an indefinite future; it is the response to an 'informational and perceptual overload combined with a cultural acceleration that neither our psyche nor our senses are adequately equipped to handle'.[4] Italy's past has been shown to lend itself to commodification more so than other geographies.[5] At the same time, to attribute these romanticized imaginings exclusively to rapid technological development means overlooking the specifically gendered dimension of these ideals. With these two points in mind, the culinary memoirs of Agnello Hornby offer an interesting point of departure for reflections on the relationship between the wider 'nostalgia boom', as Huyssen puts it,[6] and conceptions of the home as a quotidian site of feminine labour and gratification.

In the long history of discourse on the home, the perspective of the beneficiaries of domestic nurturance has been the dominant one – a male prerogative, as Sharon Harr and Christopher Reed comment.[7] Reflecting on the current desirability of vintage commodities in relation to the absence of 'old-time kitchens', Jean Duruz makes the same point, highlighting the silence of the female figures in these images, and asking who stands to gain from 'nostalgic returns to traditional, gendered divisions of labor embedded in daily shopping, cooking and eating in the industrialized/postindustrialized West'.[8] Especially pertinent to this inquiry is Duruz's identification of the gaze that is privileged in nostalgic re-creations of the domesticity of yesteryear: it is, she highlights, one that effects

> a return to the world of childhood and to the pleasures of exploring its minute textures – to its tasting, touching, smelling, hearing. However, it is also a return to the primary position of the one who eats, who is nurtured, who is fed.[9]

Explicitly looking back to the rural Sicilian home of her childhood summer holidays, both *Il pranzo di Mosè* and *Un filo d'olio* seem to offer intensely nostalgic commemorations of Southern Italian rural life. 'Browsing supermarket aisles, I realise that the seasons have disappeared',[10] Agnello Hornby reflects in *Il pranzo di Mosè*, going on to mourn the loss of seasonal markets:

> Everywhere in Europe now you find everything, all year round; I mourn the disappearance of the markets' seasons and their lost influence on how we eat. For weeks at Mosè you eat the same fruit and vegetables which all mature at the same time; you preserve them in salt, oil, vinegar, and you work with them, you cook them, freeze them. All of a sudden, the plants don't bear fruit any more. Other things take their place. There is an ancient beauty in waiting for the start of the fennel season; it is comforting to make huge pots of apricot jam with the thought they will last an entire year, and there is a mysterious sensuality in a bellyful of figs or gorging on oranges, knowing that there will be no more for over eight months.[11]

In this passage, informal vocabulary and an emphasis on bodily pleasure – 'gorging', 'a bellyful' – mark the contrast between the clinical impersonality of the supermarket aisles of today and the deeply physical gratification the author associates with the seasonal diet of her childhood. Agnello Hornby's lexical choices in this extract bespeak loss, even grief: 'I mourn', 'the disappearance', 'the loss'. These choices can be considered in line with an established trope of narratives dealing with relationships between migration and home that privilege a language of mourning and reverence.[12] It is important to note, however, that the author has never been a permanent resident of Mosè. Rather, it appears that the country house has always been associated with a playful coming-and-going, and a related sense of a homely elsewhere that is reflected in the food consumed there. 'I could never understand why our diet at Mosè was so different from what we ate in Agrigento', she muses early in *Un filo d'olio*:

> Papa went to Agrigento or the towns nearby every day: he could have easily bought everything we needed – he would have liked to do the shopping, too. Instead, he would come back empty-handed. The first days I always wanted fish, which we were served every evening in the city, and the processed cheeses which were always on the table. Whenever I asked Papa to buy them, I always got the same blunt reply: 'In the country we live off the land, like the farmers'.[13]

Even in childhood, then, we can see that Agnello Hornby's experience of Mosè is both recreation and re-creation; these quotations suggest that the selective re-enactment of food preparation and dining rituals is, to the young daughter of an urbanite aristocratic family, a game. This is why Duruz's invitation to consider the implications of the narrative vantage point of the observing/helping child is especially pertinent. To see Mosè through the eyes of 'the one who eats, who is nurtured, who is fed' is also to see a world of everyday wonders; to explore with sight, smell, touch and taste; to pause and to listen, marvelling at the individual components that make up the quotidian; in short, to make the unremarkable, remarkable.

Consider the memory with which *Il pranzo di Mosè* opens:

> 'Simonetta, there it is, Mosè's gatehouse!' But I'd already spotted it, and my heart was thumping. I knew that after the gatehouse, the land folded into hills covered in olive trees and further beyond, hidden from the eyes of passing motorists, was our house. I couldn't wait to reach it. That was Mosè. 'Our' place.[14]

Five-year-old Simonetta is encouraged to spot the old country house, to notice the yellow stones of the Greek ruins, to observe the elements comprising the Sicilian countryside as she coasts through it in her father's car. 'Papa repeated the same words every time we drove past, I knew them by heart',[15] she tells the reader, accentuating the framing of Mosè in terms of the childhood delights of sensory discovery. And against the idyllic countryside setting, one female figure in particular is revered: Rosalia.

> In the farmyard hens and chicks clucked and chirruped; the horns of a local herd of goats peeped over the picket fence. Mamma told us that Rosalia – Luigi the groundsman's wife – whom she and auntie Teresa adored, had invited them for the special *caffè du parrinu* (priest's coffee) and fresh bread, still warm from the wood-fire oven.[16]

In both *Il pranzo di Mosè* and *Un filo d'olio*, Rosalia is presented as a largely silent figure; a mute and almost other-worldly guardian of the country house and its traditions. 'If I imagined an enchantress watching over Mosè, it would be her, Rosalia',[17] writes Agnello Hornby, introducing the reader to this figure with an account of young Rosalia's marriage to her paternal uncle (at the time, legal, and not an unusual practice in Sicily) and her duties as wife of the groundsman of Mosè. As in previous passages, the joyful memories of the rural kitchens is the prerogative of the recipient of this care, young Simonetta; 'Rosalia took care of everyone with extraordinary energy and generosity',[18] while the viewpoint of the cook, the countrywoman, the provider – Rosalia herself – remains obscured.

Given the construction of the kitchen table as a space of shared delight and happy recollections in both *Il pranzo di Mosè* and *Un filo d'olio*, feminist scholar Sara Ahmed's analysis of the very idea of happiness seems a useful perspective for the analysis of these texts. Opposing happiness 'as an exclusion not just of unhappiness but of possibility" on the grounds that unhappiness is always possible,[19] Ahmed explains that

> [h]appiness involves both reciprocal forms of aspiration (I am happy for you, I want you to be happy, I am happy if you are happy) and forms of coercion that are exercised and concealed by the very language of reciprocity, such that one person's happiness is not only made conditional on another person's happiness but on the willingness to be made happy by the same things.[20]

When we consider Agnello Hornby's memoirs in light of Duruz's discussion of the commodification of the notion of home and Ahmed's critique of happiness, it is easy to identify several instances where the sense of security promoted by the texts is one that is dependent on the public effacement of the specific subjecthood of the host in favour of her symbolic homeliness. Her responsibility is to silence and self-silence, to efface the contradictions that may threaten an imagined communal happiness. In other words, the host is a happy figure, because she *makes* her happiness dependent on the happiness of those she serves:

> The role of the women of the family was to look after their husband and children, to be good housekeepers and, when guests came, to take responsibility for their happiness, from the moment of their arrival up until they left.[21]

Rosalia, who is 'always ready to smile',[22] seems at first glance to be quite literally 'the iconic figure of the country woman';[23] she is a representative symbol or sign, meaningful only as the signifier of the happiness of others. The legacy of this role and its associated trauma is one that has been explored sensitively and with great insight across a range of genres, from memoir to critical scholarship, in relation to Italian–American heritage.[24] But to read Rosalia *solely* as the purveyor of domestic happiness would be to disregard Agnello Hornby's shifting understanding of this figure in her writings, as well as the specific positioning of the author herself. In contrast with the narratives of subsequent generations of Italian–Americans (and indeed, with the British–Italian experience, which, as Margherita Sprio identifies, 'has remained largely invisible'),[25] Agnello Hornby's texts address primarily an Italian audience and must be read in a different frame – a point we will return to presently.

First, though, let us note the attention the texts pay to her labour, to the pleasure associated with the performance of specific domestic tasks and to Rosalia's specific subjectivity within transgenerational female kin networks. Rosalia, we are told, 'listened to us all, grown-up women and little girls',[26] a comment that marks the domestic spaces of Mosè as a feminine world. Before we consider more closely the layers of the portrayal of Rosalia, it is important to recognize the complexity of this world; while the division between domestic and public sees the women of Mosè serving its menfolk, the women who inhabit this space are portrayed as experiencing its specific power dynamics, networks, meaning and gratification quite independently. As we will see subsequently, pleasure is derived from small quotidian acts in their own right, and not exclusively from the thought of pleasing the end recipient. Young Simonetta's understanding of 'playing host' highlights this well. In *Il pranzo di Mosè* Agnello Hornby recounts observing, as a young child, a lively table discussion in which she proudly remained a silent witness:

> They could have avoided the whole argument if they'd asked at the beginning what actually was in the kitchen; and Raimondo was right; you need small aubergines to make *melanzane a quaglia* (fried 'aubergine quails', a recipe in which aubergines are cut and fanned out to seem like bird feathers). I didn't say anything because it would have ruined the fun and, perhaps, the hint of reconciliation between husband and wife: it was an open secret that Raimondo had another family hidden who knows where.[27]

'I didn't say anything': the young protagonist is a good host because she knows not to reveal a truth that would threaten the apparent happiness of the home. But the position of the narrator here is clearly far from the voiceless figure Duruz describes. Simonetta interprets her own discretion as an indication of her understanding of some of the unspoken knowledge and of the hidden female world of Mosè's domestic politics; her self-effacement may be more accurately read here as a satisfied assertion of a specific female agency.

Rosalia is, of course, a central figure in this world of women, which spans age and class: 'Rosalia was the first to greet us with kisses, always. That reunion, warm and informal because there was real affection between us, was a female ritual in its own right.'[28] Rosalia's 'special coffee' is also emphasized in ritualistic terms, as a tradition that has 'bound together the women of Mamma's family and those of Rosalia's, who had lived at Mosè for seven generations.'[29] Again, this is presented as an explicitly female tradition, through which care and provision for kin is simultaneously skilled labour and a source of sensory pleasure.

> Each enchantress has her ritual, and Rosalia's was *caffè d'u parrinu*, which she offered only when Mamma and auntie Teresa arrived. The Neapolitan pot used for 'special coffee' – as Giuliana called it – grumbled away on the stove, its lid firmly sealed, but from the spout a warmly spiced scent escaped, a hint of the

> aroma to come, and it crept towards us, sneaked into our nostrils and then flooded the room: a mix of cocoa, vanilla, cloves, coffee and cinnamon.[30]

Described with pervasive sensuality, the recollection of this ritual, which we are told is performed only for Simonetta's mother and her aunt Teresa, is one that again places the narrator in the position of the watching child. Rosalia is clearly venerated by the child protagonist – and we can presume all the children of Mosè – as Agnello Hornby recalls that, 'desperate to be like Rosalia', the children's favourite game was playing at making bread and bread-ovens out of wood chips, clay and bricks lying around the farm.[31]

Crucially, though, it is not only through the eyes of *young* Simonetta that we see Rosalia. Later in *Un filo d'olio*, the author returns to the ritual of *caffè d'u parrinu*, and recounts how she dared, as a grown woman, to ask Rosalia for the recipe:

> Her lips, by that time thinned, were pursed by the same clear smile and, still beautiful, Rosalia said neither yes nor no. She listed the seven ingredients and explained that *caffè d'u parrinu*, made properly, required a lengthy preparation process, boiling, and then had to 'settle a wee while'. She did not give me the recipe, but for the rest of my stay at Mosè she brought me a full coffee-pot mid-morning, every day. No recipe. Her daughter Antonia told me years later that her mother, though an avid reader of books and magazines on religion, rarely wrote: she knew all her recipes by heart and was afraid of not being able to write them accurately. Antonia and now, Chiara, prepare *caffè d'u parrinu* in exactly the same way she did. But theirs, though excellent, is not quite the same thing – it lacks Rosalia's magic touch.[32]

The now-adult Agnello Hornby regards Rosalia with the same admiring wonder she did as a young child. In revealing Rosalia's reluctance to write down her recipes for fear of reproducing them imprecisely, Agnello Hornby emphasizes the essentially embodied nature of this intelligence; the sensitivity to touch, smell and taste, that Rosalia has refined over a lifetime of domestic labour, is not something that can be simply transcribed.

The author's revisiting of Rosalia and her memories of this woman also indicate the development in her own perspective from that of the observing/nurtured child to that of the nurturer and domestic matriarch; a shift that is reflected in the structure of both books. *Il pranzo di Mosè* is divided into four main sections, the first three of which combine Agnello Hornby's childhood memories of Mosè with practical advice on contemporary cooking, hosting and well-being; *Un filo d'olio* gives greater prominence to childhood memories and storytelling in the first two-thirds of the book, but the final section, 'Le ricette di Chiara Agnello',[33] as in the case of the fourth and final section of *Il pranzo di Mosè*, is firmly forward-looking: the reader finds a collection of the recipes featured in the memoir to try themselves. Significantly, these instructions are presented as 'a good starting point, because their development into different recipes seems to me the best result I could wish for'.[34] The para-text, too, is indicative of a fluidity of movement between past and present. *Un filo d'olio*, in accordance with the author's professed objective to 'bring back to life culture of the table of our home through recipes, old photographs and some "narrative" pages', features photographs of different family members during the childhood and adolescence of Simonetta, but is prefaced and concluded by notes dated 2011.[35] *Il pranzo di Mosè* features an older photograph, a full-cover close-up of the slightly sullen black-and-white formal portrait of an elegant young woman; 'Elena Giudice: mother of Simonetta and Chiara Agnello' – not quite the happy, anonymous symbol of blissful domesticity that we might expect – and turning the first page, we find the hand-written recipe notes from the notebook of Agnello Hornby's maternal grandmother, Nonna Maria. Portraits of family members from various periods up to the present day appear throughout, including reproductions from scenes of the book's corresponding television series.[36] In these memoirs, therefore, past and present, public and private are wholly interlinked; just as the childhood memories of the rituals of Mosè are interwoven with practical advice and accounts of the author's present life in London, so the jottings of her grandmother's recipe book are available in bookshops internationally.

In relation to the memories of the Italian–American experience, Edvige Giunta has discussed the importance of memoir *writing* (as distinct from oral history) in terms of catharsis, retrieval and remembrance, echoing Janet Zandy's identification of the role played by writers who can access a public audience as witnesses or mediators for those without opportunity for self-expression.[37] As we have noted, Agnello Hornby's happy scenes necessitate a different frame, but the connotations of the act of writing itself must not be overlooked, particularly given the author's authority as an Anglo-Italian 'writing back' in Italian, to the Italy she has left.[38] It seems that in publishing Rosalia's instructions along with the recipes of her own family members, Agnello Hornby wants to inscribe the value of this type of intimate, sensory and largely female knowledge in a public, global and 'masculine' sphere.[39]

The concept of 'kin work' that Micaela di Leonardo uses in her ethnography of Italian–American families is useful here. Mapping the significance of kin ties in terms of social capital,[40] di Leonardo rejects readings of the 'conception, maintenance, and ritual celebration' of kinship as a superficial activity, suggesting that

> [m]aintaining these contacts, this sense of family, takes time, intention, and skill. We tend to think of human social and kin networks as the epiphenomena of production and reproduction: the social traces created by our material lives. Or, in the neoclassical tradition, we see them as part of leisure activities, outside an economic purview except insofar as they involve consumption behaviour. But the creation and maintenance of kin and quasi-kin networks in advanced industrial societies is *work*; and moreover, it is largely women's work.[41]

A failure to recognize kin work as both labour *and* a potential source of pleasure merely reinforces the position of women as signifiers and agents of the happiness and opportunities of others, rather than as subjects capable of producing (and entitled to) gratification in their own right. Consider, for example, Agnello Hornby's description of the pleasure she takes, together with her sister Chiara, in continuing their mother's habit of preparing small home-made gifts for guests at Mosè:

> I enjoy snipping some bay leaves and sprigs of rosemary, arranging biscuits on paper trays, wrapping them in cellophane and tying them up with old silk ribbons – or ones I've bought especially – filling little bags with pistachios and almonds, making sure they are all good ones, and sealing them carefully, thinking of the person who'll receive them.[42]

Building on di Leonardo's findings, Terry Lovell has also argued for recognition of the domestic domain as 'not only an area in which unpaid labour must be undertaken, but also a realm in which one may attempt to gain human satisfactions – and power – not available in the labour market'.[43] And the fifth chapter of *Il pranzo di Mosè*, pointedly titled 'Mentre lavoro in cucina' (As I work in the kitchen), is persuasive evidence for a reading of Agnello Hornby's texts as narratives that seek to highlight the labour of domestic toil, but also to celebrate this kin work as a form of female agency and creativity. Here, Agnello Hornby compares the time-consuming preparation of *melanzane alla parmigiana* (aubergine parmigiana) to the work of modern artists: 'I arrange the fried slices of aubergine in geometric patterns, as a zigzag, or in a herringbone shape, I add the tomato sauce in brushstrokes, as if it were tempera.'[44] 'The humble task' of cleaning vegetables may be a social moment when shared with friends,[45] or an opportunity for reflection: 'I feel sorry for people who don't cook and don't know how to cook. They miss out on real pleasure and beautiful moments of contemplation.'[46] In this sense, Agnello Hornby's portrayal of household work is comparable to Anne Allison's phenomenologically informed approach to *obentō*, the elaborate lunch boxes traditionally prepared by Japanese mothers. Allison argues that it is impossible to separate the pleasure that mothers derive from this practice from the heavily gendered and ideological meanings of *obentō*; 'significantly, women find play and creativity not outside their social roles but within them'.[47]

It is important to distinguish between Agnello Hornby's description of her own role, however, and the more laborious work carried out by Rosalia. As *Un filo d'olio* makes clear, the task of breadmaking at Mosè is an arduous one, carried out largely in silence: 'exhausting group work, and a women's "thing"'.[48] Bread is the most important food of Mosè and as the chief – and most highly skilled – breadmaker, Rosalia commands a stern respect among all the women involved in the task. Indeed, 'her approval was greeted by sighs of relief from the other women',[49] Agnello Hornby tells us, revealing the petite, reserved figure we were first introduced to as a charismatic leader of considerable physical strength. After all, this is dirty, sweaty work: With the back of her hand Rosalia wiped the sweat from her brow and then, legs apart, leaning slightly back, gave the order to go and checked as the women pulled the loaves out of the oven.[50]

The association of Rosalia with the provision of daily bread highlights the significance of her labour, and we are offered no explicit insights into what she thinks of her lot. All we can infer, from the dramatic measures she takes to protect the sourdough leaven used to make the bread of Mosè when the house is attacked in the war, is the solemnity of her sense of responsibility:

> When they fled from the farm with the children, Rosalia took the *livatina* with her, the small ball of leaven that is preserved each time the dough is renewed and re-kneaded, kept aside to grow sour and to act as yeast for future baking. Mosè's livatina came from a sourdough leaven that the women of her family had kept alive since 1870. As they escaped, Rosalia put it under her clothes, against her body to keep it safe and warm.[51]

This passage inscribes the value of Rosalia's labour, and that of previous generations of her family, in the fabric of Mosè. Again, it alludes to the bodily nature of her engagement and echoes the description of her figure as an enchantress, a 'ninfa', that we observed previously. The question of how Rosalia conceives of herself – whether or not she finds pleasure and meaning in her social role – is not one to which the texts provide an answer. What her figure does do, I would argue, is open up new ways of conceiving femininity. Because the physical work with which Rosalia is associated has been traditionally considered as the constitutive limit of the feminine,[52] her portrayal merits further consideration as part of a broader assessment of the relationship between class and gender.

Returning to Ahmed's critical assessment of the history of happiness, I want to conclude with her reflections on the pertinence of the etymology of the word 'happiness' and attention to the 'hap', or the 'chance' of happiness. Ahmed offers the notion of happiness as 'a sense of possibility',[53] illustrating her argument with a quotation from the character Clarissa in Stephen Daldry's film adaptation of *The Hours* (2002) as heiress to the sadness (and namesake) of Virginia Woolf's *Mrs. Dalloway* (1925):

> I remember one morning. Getting up at dawn. There was such a sense of possibility. You know that feeling. So this is the beginning of happiness. This is where it starts, and of course there will always be more. It never occurred to me that it wasn't the beginning. It was happiness.[54]

Considered in light of Ahmed's understanding of happiness as a sense of possibility, the changing perspective of the narrator of *Il pranzo di Mosè* and *Un filo d'olio* becomes particularly meaningful: such a sense of possibility in these texts is, as we have seen, not confined to childhood, but represents a life-long engagement with the sensory work of cuisine and reflective response to one's surroundings.

The trope of traumatic memory in relation to Italian–American culinary heritage is one that has received a range of stimulating creative and critical interventions. Less attention has been paid, however, to the significance of non-traumatic memory, and to how these romantic images of the family table may relate to and be read in different contexts. Through consideration of the Anglo-Italian writer Simonetta Agnello Hornby's culinary memoirs *Il pranzo di Mosè* and *Un filo d'olio*, this chapter seeks to open up inquiry into the wider meaning of contemporary haptic re-creations of Italy.

Il pranzo di Mosè and *Un filo d'olio* have been analysed in light of Jean Duruz's caution, of a need to 'question whose remembering is at stake when one is mourning the woman at the wood stove or purchasing her symbolic products',[55] with the aim of focusing on the gendered connotations of these sensory memoirs. To be sure, the figure of the woman at the wood stove in these texts, Rosalia, is one that remains voiceless. At the same time, the narrator's shifting understanding of the labour Rosalia performs has been revealed as crucial: while it is true that the reader is greeted by a Simonetta positioned in a childhood world of carefree comforts, we have noted that the interweaving of past and present throughout the texts ultimately reconfigures Agnello Hornby as the provider of care rather than its recipient, and reveals the home both as a site of labour and a space through which quotidian meaning and pleasure are derived. This fluid mobility of the protagonist between the position of nurtured child and nurturing mother/host, underlined by the progressive mingling of childhood memories with recent anecdotes (including the filming of the 'Il pranzo di Mosè' television series) and recipes suggests meaningfully the continual re-construction of the perspective of possibility. In this way, *Il pranzo di Mosè* and *Un filo d'olio* may be most productively read in the context of a renewed understanding of femininity, as texts that invite critical reflection on the *possibilities* of domestic labour in terms of sensory gratification and meditative pleasure.

The aim of eliciting the reader's engagement with these traditions, of indicating the everyday and the home as spaces of both labour and personal gratification, can be seen as the author's antidote to the social anxieties of the post-industrialized West. At the same time, as published volumes, Agnello Hornby's narratives confer value on the practical tasks of homemaking, and bear witness to the silent toil and embodied knowledge of the women who populated her childhood. The texts thus can be interpreted as a personal and prescriptive response to the contemporary cultural environment, compelling the reader to recognize the meaningful nature of 'the humble work' of homemaking.

Part II

Food, womanhood and the Italian south

4

Food, adultery and the pursuit of the modern in Matilde Serao's *La virtù di Checchina*

Luca Cottini

Matilde Serao's novel *La virtù di Checchina* (Checchina's Virtue)[1] offers a precious insight into the condition of women in post-unification Italy, and a powerful metaphor of the nation's ambiguous quest for modernity in the late nineteenth century.

First published in four instalments in *La domenica letteraria* (The Literary Sunday) (between 25 November and 16 December 1883) and then turned into a book in 1884,[2] the novel dates back to the Roman years of Matilde Serao[3] – an intensely creative period in which she also published *Fantasia* (Fantasy, 1883),[4] the reportage *Il ventre di Napoli* (The Belly of Naples, 1884)[5] and the autobiographical novel *La conquista di Roma* (The Conquest of Rome, 1885).[6] *La virtù di Checchina* certainly retrieves some key elements of Serao's past narratives (e.g. the love of worldly life, the bourgeois admiration for nobility and the representation of impossible or even catastrophic loves),[7] but it also stands out among her works, for its masterful construction of the protagonist's 'psychological hesitation',[8] as well as for its belated critical fortune, against the backdrop of the Italian feminism of the 1960s and the 1970s.

After the publication of Anna Banti's literary autobiography of Serao in 1965 (leading to an overall re-appreciation of her work),[9] and Natalia Ginzburg's rediscovery of *La virtù di Checchina* (leading to its republication in 1974),[10] the novel gained new critical ground as both a historical testimony of a transitional moment in Italian society and a fundamental work in the underestimated repertoire of the late-nineteenth-century women's literature. The domestic narrative of *La virtù di Checchina* can thus be read as a mirror of the trends, customs and fashionable objects of Italy's early industrial society, and as a cultural manual, instructing female readers on their social codes and fashioning their awareness and imagination.

Serao's domestic narrative is part of a larger framework of women's literature of the age, which Antonia Arslan and Gabriella Romani delineate in their anthology of Italian female fiction writers from the late nineteenth century (*Writing to Delight*, 2006). They argue that the representation of the private space enforced a man-made vision of the woman, guaranteeing the moral stability of society by virtue of her capacity to properly run a household and passively accept her role as wife or mother.[11] Yet they also contend that these novels' domestic setting also led women writers to elaborate a new feminine space of self-education and creative freedom. Against the reality of social exclusion (manifested in high illiteracy rate, poor working conditions and limited access to education), and in opposition to the pre-made male constructs (of the femme fatale or of the woman as *regina della casa*),[12] domestic stories then represented for their female readership not just a leisurely vehicle to promote secular education for women of the newly formed Italian state but ultimately 'a means of self-improvement',[13] as seen in Marchesa Colombi's *Matrimonio in provincia* (A Small-Town Marriage, 1885) or Neera's *Teresa* (Teresa, 1886).[14]

Along these general interpretative lines, *La virtù di Checchina* similarly depicts in its protagonist an 'articulate system of behavioural norms and rituals that incorporated abstract mores into the everyday life of women',[15] and a fictional space of free imagination, granting them the possibility to interact with the world outside their daily domestic life, receive information about current events and gain 'knowledge concerning taboos surrounding female sexuality'.[16]

Far from merely mirroring women's condition in the Italian society of the late nineteenth century, *La virtù di Checchina* also offers a broader reflection on Italy's cultural environment vis-à-vis the growing phenomenon of its early industrialization that took off after the success of the National Exposition of Milan in 1881, capturing through the feminine gaze of Checchina the new wave of products brought forth by industrial modernity, and Italy's ambiguous relationship to it.

With extraordinary attention to detail, Serao reproduces the new plethora of items invading the social space in the early industrial age. Recent technologies enter her narration, such as the street lamppost (following the clamour of electricity's first appearance in Milan at the National Exposition of 1881); the umbrella (right before the presentation of the mechanical umbrella at the National Exposition of Turin of 1884); and the wristwatch (worn by Checchina's friend Isolina), reflecting the new feminine trend of wearing timepieces as bracelets and filtering the contemporary debate on universal timekeeping (which took place at the 1883 Geodetic Conference of Rome).[17] Moreover, commercial items and specific brands like perfumes, cleaning products or digestive remedies of any sort make their way into the literary space, mirroring the ad-filled pages of contemporary publications and foreseeing the practice of including commodities in literary texts, which would be evidenced in Aldo Palazzeschi's 1913 poem 'La passeggiata' (The Walk).[18]

By way of the novel's plot, featuring the hoped-for yet never realized adultery of a middle-class lady, Serao also outlines a powerful metaphor of the nation's quest for and fear of modernization. Suspended between her passions for the marquis and her frustration with her marriage to the Roman doctor Toto Primicerio, Checchina certainly embodies the interior drama of a contemporary woman. She is suspended between the thrill of a new experience of freedom and her anxiety, ultimately leading her to the final resolution to maintain her 'virtue' and refrain from breaking her codified gender role. At a deeper level, however, Checchina also reflects the ambivalent reaction of enthusiasm and disquiet pervading Italian society as a whole in the wake of industrialism, equally manifested as a hectic pursuit of an idealized modernity (in the frenzy to participate in and organize expositions) and a latent apprehension for its perceived 'radical break' from past traditions or a consolidated social order.

In parallel with this symbolic framework, I argue that the recurring appearance of food and the centrality of the meal scene in the plot function as defining elements of the novel's ideology, and not as a mere reflection of Serao's well-known culinary appetite.[19] Unlike other contemporary representations, such as Collodi's *Le avventure di Pinocchio* (The Adventures of Pinocchio, 1883) or Neera's *L'indomani* (The Following Day, 1889), where food is portrayed in connection to hunger and poverty,[20] the acts of preparing, serving and eating food are clearly expressed in relation to femininity in *La virtù di Checchina*. Subsequently, in accord with the previous observations, the food theme is then paired with an instructional moment (in the presentation of a correct set of practices and behavioural codes for women), and with the representation of Checchina's mixed feelings towards the illicit (as a mirror of her frustration with an unhappy marriage and ephemeral lust for the marquis).

The symbolism of food accompanies and enforces the exploration of Checchina's interior drama. In reference to her social status, it purposely replicates the 'middle-class doctrine of separate spheres based on gender and class in the new Italy',[21] defining the private and safe space of the home as the assigned area of her action. On the contrary, in reference to her aspired adultery, it defines a fictional space of physical and psychological investigation, mirroring the power of the passion that consumes her (both in positive and negative terms), and prompting her initiation into pleasure (moving from taste and smell to the unknown space of sexuality).

By focusing on the symbolism of food in the novel, this chapter contends that Serao's depiction of cooking, serving and dining scenes does not represent a secondary element in *La virtù di Checchina*, but rather a key factor in the narration of her failed adultery, overtly implementing its dialectic of pleasure and vanity.[22] In exploring the relevance of the food theme, I will consider first the different meanings and connotations of its textual occurrences and then the relationship between food (both represented and actual) and the other objects in the novel.

Food and adultery in *La virtù di Checchina*

Food defines the personality of Checchina and triggers her love affair with the marquis. From the novel's opening, the culinary realm is evoked by the figure of Susanna, who takes a break from cooking in order to open the door to Checchina's visiting friend Isolina. The contrast between the two women (the servant and the lover) is introduced by a singular olfactory notation, contrasting the disgusting smell of Susanna's 'stinking dust-cloth' over 'her rough cloth apron [. . .] covered in with greasy stains' with Isolina's scented 'handkerchief, heavily perfumed with *jockeyclub*',[23] with which she covers her nose. A similar dichotomy of repulsiveness (identified with grease or stains) and pleasure (identified with cleanliness and perfumes) will reappear in a later scene in reference to tact, when, in Chapter V, Susanna delivers Checchina a letter from her lover mixed in with and stained by the groceries. Although the setting is reversed (unlike the opening scene, now the servant arrives from outside, and the woman in love is at home), the food allusion is again paired with a dialectics of greasiness and cleanliness, in the contrast between the whiteness of the letter and the stain of red sauce tarnishing it ('then Susanna pulled out something white, a paper, a letter wet and stained with red sauce').[24] This alternation of bad odour (or greasy stains) and good scent (or tactile pleasure), in reference to smell and touch, will be a recurring theme in the central episode of the meal, as well as throughout the novel.

The preparation of the meal (Chapter II) and its consumption (Chapter III) constitute the narrative beginning of Checchina's adventure with the marquis, offering her the occasion to reconnect after a brief visit to his mansion in Frascati, and him the pretext to invite her to his Roman house on Via dei Santi Apostoli.

Chapter II opens with Toto Primicerio notifying Checchina that he has invited the marquis to dinner at their place as a way to return a courtesy and build a strategic connection with high society (as stressed by his 'he'll be useful to me').[25] In hearing about the meal while brushing Toto's coat, Checchina is immediately caught off guard. In contrast with her husband's irony about the scheduled hour of the lunch/dinner, she immediately recalls her first meeting with the nobleman in Frascati, and a later encounter with him at the farmer's market. In recalling that encounter, when, not by chance, she was negotiating with a peasant the purchase of some baskets of tomatoes, she realizes her need to figure out the logistics and menu for the meal. Checchina's fantasy is thus instantly paired with a mental catalogue of dishes and recipes (each accompanied by the necessary tools and ingredients), and followed by a rapid estimate of costs, and the mental review of the required manners and appearance.

The planning of her menu is intrinsically related to the design of the table, as attested in Checchina's elaborate considerations regarding silverware, dishes and cooking tools. The need for a salad sparks her concern over the lack of a bowl. Likewise, the idea of cooking a plate of fried fish elicits in her the awareness that 'she needed a new pan'[26] and her perceived need to cook the meat is coupled with the urgency to find an adequate oven – a relatively new item that had been on the market for only a few years. Checchina's mental list of items, both available and needed, also offers Serao a pretext to include a catalogue of current brands or products in her narration, as in the case of the set of dishes, bought 'at a Stella sale',[27] or of the wished-for Bianchelli coffee machine, seen at an exposition ('just a week ago Bianchelli had exhibited his coffee machines – all shiny and sparkling, they seemed like silver and gold').[28]

In terms of attitude, Checchina approaches the preparation of the meal in two different ways, depending on her mental dialogue with either the husband or the marquis. On the one hand, with her husband in mind, she estimates the costs for the meal (including silverware, cooking tools, and actual ingredients), and replicates Toto's stinginess and attachment to money, as seen in her repeated self-assertions about the price of ingredients. On the other hand, with the marquis in mind, Checchina carefully reviews her recipes ('a cake with cherry preserves? How many eggs, then, should she put with a kilo of flour, half a kilo of fine sugar, and half pound of butter?'),[29] and imaginatively plans her look, as in her final question to the servant who is preparing the broth: 'Susanna, would you know how to do curls?'[30]

Checchina's preparation of food offers her a way to disguise and nurture her interior planning of a lovers' meeting, which is reflected in her red cheeks, allegedly caused by the oven's heat ('her face was red, two patches of fire on her cheeks; the stove's blaze had really sent the blood to the head'),[31] or in her obsessive need to remove the smell of fish from her hands, as she tried to pair her look with a good fragrance ('four times she had washed her hands for fear that they smelled of fish, and she kept sniffing them mechanically like a sleepwalker').[32]

After the meticulous description of Checchina's preparations for the meal, the following chapter focuses instead on the consumption of the food and on the actual dinner, defined by the husband Toto as 'just a simple dinner in a modest home'.[33] During the meal, Checchina acts as a chef, a maître d' and a table guest, as she presents her handmade gnocchi (and later her cake). The taste of her recipes is followed by praise for her graceful hands, from Toto, in reference to her cooking skills, and from the Marchese, in reference to smell and touch, as the subtle fragrance of his arm reaches her 'soft and sweet [. . .] like a taste of sugarplum'.[34]

As Checchina carefully runs the meal, paying constant attention to the room's setting, lighting and temperature, she observes the manners of both men, swinging between her awe for the 'disinterested self-possession'[35] of the marquis and her unease towards her husband's 'coarse levity of a doctor on holiday',[36] emphasized even more by the out-of-place medical report of his daily surgical procedures. When Checchina finally joins the meal, she also gains participation in society. As a way to praise her cooking skills, or her 'virtue', Toto decides to open 'a bottle of vieux cognac that he had been given by a patient of his from France',[37] including her in the toast. Serao notes that Checchina 'in response, drank a glass of cognac – a liquor she'd never had before – in one draught',[38] thus establishing a clear comparison between the pleasure of drinking the liquor and the previously unconsidered adulterous passion growing in her.

In the aftermath of the meal, Checchina's discomfort towards her husband (leading the way for her to give in to this pleasure) is transferred from his unpolished manners at the table to his unsophisticated behaviour in the parlour, as Toto falls asleep on the couch. In parallel, Checchina's reawakened senses are transferred from the pleasing aromas of the food at the table to the violet fragrance surrounding the marquis, seated on the armchair, and inviting her to visit him.

In the following chapters, Checchina's wished-for adultery will be paired with a similar alternation of anxiety, disgust or fear, as she observes everything as a possible obstacle, and with secret inebriation, as she fictionally plans her visit to the house of the marquis in the secluded space of a dream.[39] The interior contrast between her 'exaltation of fantasy at night and the absolute lack of will during the day'[40] will once again find an external manifestation in a food-related metaphor, as attested in the reference to Checchina's indigestion, making visible her inner love torments, which now appear as a problem to hide and solve. In a way, her bitter mouth reiterates her repulsion and disgust for her husband. As she tries to hide the amorous dreams of the night, Toto Primicerio remains nonetheless incapable of catching any signs of them, as he observes only her exterior symptoms (in parallel with Charles Bovary, Emma's husband, who thinks he can cure his wife's disturbances with the sole remedies of medicine):

> it must be the pork chop that has you feeling poorly, Checca my dear. If you don't feel well, why don't you take effervescent magnesium citrate? It's a pleasant beverage and it sweeps out your stomach like a broom. Checca my dear, the more I look at you the more I think that you must have coprostasis. Really, why don't you opt for a bit of almond oil? Freshly squeezed, at Garneri's, it's a delight.[41]

In another way, Checchina's constant dusting, washing and cleaning (which previously related to her obsession for hygiene, good fragrances and the pursuit of sensual pleasure) is now linked to the self-imposed need to treat her stomach with bicarbonate, as a metaphor for the necessity to purify herself of her illicit thoughts. Cleaning then acquires the meaning of dismantling her fictional adulterous desires, as seen in the coupling of Checchina's list of mending or washing activities with her endeavour to forget about her secret life and regain a domestic routine. Now perceived with disgust, Checchina's act of cleaning is ultimately paired with her self-induced bigotry (as she mechanically prays with Susanna while pouring the lentils for the soup onto a plate) or with her self-inflicted neutralization of love desires (fully manifested in the end of the novel) as she cleans up the taste of the boiling lentils through bicarbonate.

Food, femininity and the vision of modern society

The appearance of food in *La virtù di Checchina* is part of a larger visual symbolism, which opens up, through the female perspective, a space of critique of contemporary society and cultural imagination with regard to industrial modernity. While offering Serao a pedagogical opportunity for showing her female readers how 'to deal with their limitations and predicaments as wives and mothers',[42] the food theme also works as a powerful instrument to communicate emotions and a synecdoche of class differences, gender distinctions or economic disparities in Italian late-nineteenth-century society.

With regard to male figures, food represents the gap between nobility and bourgeoisie. It marks the behavioural distinction of Toto and the marquis, separating the former's unpolished manners and repulsive odour from the latter's etiquette and pleasing scent. It highlights their class difference, in their different eating schedules (a dinner for Toto is a 'lunch' for the marquis) and menus (cooked, for Toto, by his wife and, for the marquis, by a personal chef). It also identifies their economic disparity, by imposing budgetary constraints on Checchina, and making accessible to wealthy noblemen the new, sought-after items (silverware, bowls), products (cooking pans, ovens and the coffee machine) and recipes, made available by industrialization.[43]

With regard to female figures, food is a signifier of gender distinction.[44] In the relationship between Toto and Checchina, food marks the division of roles between man, in charge of social life and professional duties, and woman, in charge of the responsibilities related to the home (also including dusting furniture and maintaining hygiene). As Toto allows Checchina to drink cognac, rewarding her for her good work in preparing and serving an important business meal, he implicitly reiterates this division and her condition of submission. By disguising his marital authority under the appearance of a generous recompense, however, he paradoxically introduces her to the seduction of a new idea of womanhood, one found in her awakened sensual desire for the marquis.

With regard to broader society, Checchina's emphasis on cooking tools, the room's lighting and heating, and digestive remedies (which reflects the new plethora of products in expositions or ads in contemporary magazines) mirrors a phase of transition in access to food, characterized by the formation of new culinary habits and eating practices. The new availability of products (made possible by faster means of transportation), new ways of cooking and conserving food (introduced by ovens, and later by refrigeration) and new social occasions for meals (guaranteed by the growth of the middle class) contributed to the expansion of menus and the configuration of a new national market. Within this context, Checchina's planning – portrayed in her attention to culinary products, her mental review of recipes and her care for hygiene in the preparation of meals – goes along with the post-unification push to create a national cuisine (as part of the formation of a new 'Italian' culture). It indeed foreshadows two key aspects of Pellegrino Artusi's seminal 1891 cookbook *L'arte di mangiar bene e la scienza in cucina* (Science in the Kitchen and the Art of Eating Well), similarly offering readers a collection of recipes, as well as valuable information on the proper conservation and treatment of ingredients.

While reflecting the trends, customs and contradictions of its time, the novel's treatment of food also enacts a symbolic space of cultural imagination towards industrial modernity, which interacts with other, similar contemporary representations. In parallel with the other objects of the house (reproducing on the page contemporary tastes, the psychology of the protagonist and the economic condition of the household), new culinary tools (like ovens and coffee machines), new grocery practices (reflected in Checchina's mental list of ingredients, costs and recipes) and new customs in cooking and serving meals are charged in the novel with an aura of thrill and concern. In a similar way, actual food is represented in association with the two semantic areas of consumption: in its connection with the theme of uncleanliness (e.g. the presence of dirt) and pleasure, in relation to the pursuit of an aesthetic experience involving different sensorial realms.

Food enforces Checchina's sense of self-consumption and suffocation in her house, as also confirmed by her obsession for dusting. Dust is ever-present in the house. It covers 'a small plate of artificial fruit' on the table ('these too of marble, vivaciously painted: a fig, an apple, a peach, a pear, and a small bunch of cherries'),[45] which needs to be dusted before the arrival of guests. It also covers actual food, as we see in the detail of Susanna blowing dirt off of the lentils ('she blew on them, shaking them, to get rid of the dust').[46] The deliberate presence of dirt responds to the narrative need to stage an act of cleaning, in reflection of the new association of modernity with cleanliness, and of Checchina's self-imposed purification from adulterous thoughts. At the same time, however, the symbol of dust in relation to food also refers to a recurring cultural iconography in the literature and painting of the 1880s, linking it with ephemerality, immobility and consumption.

Contemporary writers adopted the image of motionless objects, stored as dusty ruins in the old family house, as a metaphor of the intrinsic vanity and consumption of the modern world. A detailed list of objects and furniture items in the house, mirroring the protagonist's life (as in Checchina's parlour), would appear in *Un matrimonio in provincia* (A Small-Town Marriage, 1885) by Marchesa Colombi or in *Il piacere* (Pleasure, 1889) by Gabriele D'Annunzio, as a way to bring old memories to life or to suggest the need to contain the ephemerality of commercial artefacts. In connection with the topical scene of the house's sale or decay – in novels like Giovanni Verga's *Malavoglia* (The House by the Medlar-Tree, 1881) Marchesa Colombi's *Un matrimonio in provincia* (A Small-Town Marriage, 1885), Italo Svevo's *Una vita* (A Life, 1892), Emilio De Marchi's *Demetrio Pianelli* (1893) or Luigi Pirandello's *Il fu Mattia Pascal*

(The Late Mattia Pascal, 1905) – the image of dusty, immobile objects, turned into junk, defines a key metaphor of the *rovina* (ruin) brought about by modern life, revealing the inevitable consumption of everything.[47]

Contemporary painters also symbolized objects and food as consumable goods, pairing them with the concepts of ephemerality and perishability. In parallel with the immobile vision of food (often coupled with dust) in the recently rediscovered genre of still life painting (in French Impressionism and photography), the 1884 canvas 'Asfissia' ('Asphyxia') by Angelo Morbelli offers a striking representation of such relation of food to consumption and suffocation, which is parallel to Serao's narrative in *La virtù di Checchina*. The painting, later split into two halves due to its crude representation, stages the last banquet of two adulterers before their suicide in a hotel room. The elements left on the table – fruit in a bowl, bottles of champagne and flower petals – suggest the consummation of sensual pleasure, conveyed through taste and smell, and an ominous prefiguration of the couple's tragic end. A stopped clock displays the ephemeral nature of this instant of enjoyment, before their death, and the perception of the asphyxiating immobility of everything. In parallel with Checchina's (failed) adultery and sense of breathlessness, the canvas presents the image of food in relation to both pleasure and asphyxiation, making manifest its connection to the thrill and tragic breaking of an established order (in a clear echo of Madame Bovary's suicide, and in contrast with Serao's depiction of the sole omen of consummation).

In parallel with the rhetoric of consummation/consumption, food also defines for Checchina an experimental creative space, of aesthetic planning and inventive combination of senses. Checchina's attitude in planning the meal (including the disposition of objects within the surrounding space) and in constructing a multi-sensorial experience of food reflects her broader taste in the decoration of the house interior and her capacity to carefully arrange objects in her parlour, which emerges as her distinctive feature from the novel's opening. The emphasis on her creative attitude in furnishing a room or planning an event is a recurring element in Serao, as also documented in *La conquista di Roma* (The Conquest of Rome, 1885), where the protagonist Sangiorgio is portrayed in the act of meticulously preparing his Roman apartment for the arrival of his lover Angelica. Similarly, in *La virtù di Checchina*, objects are arranged in relation to a studied interplay of light and shade, to the combination/variation of colours and to the creation of a multi-sensorial experience. The singular presence of porcelain fruit in the opening description of the *salotto* (living room) certainly locates food within a larger composition of elements (including, as in a still life painting, flowers, drapery, furniture, cloths, folds, glasses, ceramics, dust and food), yet also connotes it as part of a larger process of creative combination of elements, prefiguring the act of cooking itself. In parallel with the objects, which act as symbolic reflections of Checchina's personality in the house, food ingredients, mental recipes and actual dishes then represent the tools of her creativity in the imaginative design of a multi-sensorial experience.

The appearance of food is thus not limited to providing the reader with a narrative pretext for Checchina's secret fantasy relationship with the marquis, but is also functional to manifesting a hidden side of Checchina's femininity, in her experimental capacity for the invention and elaboration of new forms. In its association with the senses, food indeed identifies an illicit space of freedom from social restraints, which is of course related to her desired adultery, but most importantly to her transgression of her pre-codified role: she elaborates an original taste, designs an aesthetic space and enacts the pursuit of pleasure. In an attempt to construct such an experience, involving all of the senses, food is paired, not by chance, with *smell*, in the deliberate contrast between the un-breathable air surrounding the husband and the violet fragrance of the marquis; with *taste*, in the descriptions of the different reactions to the meal by the guests and Checchina herself; with *sight*, in the explicit focus on the marquis's 'serious and thoughtful gaze'[48] at the table; with *touch*, in the husband's praise of Checchina's 'blessed hands' in preparing the gnocchi and the cake;[49] and with *hearing*, in detail of the marquis's soft voice ('he spoke quietly, with a very light *r* and an infantile *s* that were very sweet).[50] The connection of sensual pleasure to the senses of taste, smell and touch prefigures the overall experience of inebriation involved in her act of drinking cognac, as well as Checchina's later desire to write a thank-you note for the marquis on a 'fine paper that looks like satin [touch] and smells good', and not on 'broad sheets that reeked of carbolic acid like everything Toto touched'.[51] A visual equivalent of Serao's multi-sensorial rendering of Checchina's pleasure in drinking cognac (as a metaphor for her adulterous passion) will be later represented in a famous poster ad designed by Marcello Dudovich for *Liquore Strega* in 1903. Perhaps inspired by the scene of Checchina's first sip of cognac, the image displays the idea of liquor as an alluring fascination of senses, and of modernity itself as a state of luxurious decadence. As in Serao's narration, the ad experiments with a new visual language, by expanding the minimalistic depiction of the product (a small shot glass) onto the surrounding space in the construction of a deliberate synesthetic experience. The designer deliberately matches the orange of the drink to the woman's hair, associating her seductive allure (signified in her tempting gesture of lifting her skirt) to the liquor's suggested pleasure of the senses. By re-enacting the drink's actual consumption, through the juxtaposition of her clothes' contrasting colours (blue and red) with the drink's taste (a mix of cold freshness and burning warmth), of her whiff to its smell and of her semi-nudity to touch, Dudovich willingly breaks the bi-dimensionality of the poster and defines the essence of the present as an ultimate aesthetic experience, merging the arts and the senses in a personalized pursuit of beauty.

In light of these observations, it is possible to conclude that the theme of food in *La virtù di Checchina* not just provides an accessory element in the narration of Checchina's failed adultery but rather becomes a silent or hidden protagonist of this illicit love, offering a sensorial *trait-d'union* between the woman's private and public life, as well as embedding an intimate space of escape and freedom from social restraints. The scene of the meal (preparation, serving and eating) thus acquires a central role in the economy of the novel, prefiguring the adultery as a free space of pleasure, creativity and new self-identification, yet also anticipating its ruin, in the breaking of established codes, and its devouring power, ultimately leading Checchina back to 'virtue'[52] in her decision to renounce visiting the marquis at his house.

In light of it coinciding with the theme of adultery, food subsequently contributes to the depiction of modernity as a similar space of thrill and excitement. While further documenting Serao's exceptional capacity for observation, which makes the novel 'perhaps the best ever written by her',[53] the meticulous rendering of food (as an object and an experience) ultimately relates to the double-edged construction of a rhetoric of consummation/consumption, meant, in a way, as a figure of pleasure (in the context of Italy's growing industrialism) and, in another, as an omen of the instability, loss and decay intrinsic to its ephemerality.

5

Spiritual sustenance

Naples' soul food in the narrative language of Matilde Serao and Elena Ferrante

Pia L. Bertucci

Introduction: Food and women's writing

The relationship between food and women's writing can be traced back centuries, to a time when the kitchen served as a domestic space for women of various cultures and classes. Foodways and women's writing reveal so much more than mere accounts of submissive domestic duties. Sor Juana de la Cruz, the seventeenth-century Mexican nun and writer, extolled the virtues of cooking and inventing recipes as a platform for understanding science as well as for philosophizing, stating that 'if Aristotle had cooked, he would have written much more'.[1]

The motif of food transcends narrative strategies and serves as a vehicle for conveying sociological and historical accounts of women's lives, particularly the lives of the poor and the disenfranchised. It is fitting that the term *cucina povera* (peasant food) has come into mainstream usage by contemporary food critics to capture the essence of Italian cuisine. Referring to a peasant style of cuisine that makes the most of meagre resources, dishes such as *ribollita* (a soup made from old bread and vegetables) or *panzanella* (a salad made from stale bread), *cucina povera* is uncomplicated, but artfully prepared, resulting in a sort of elegant simplicity. Perhaps this concept is most evident in Naples, both historically and contemporarily, a city that has been defined in part by its hard times and by its ability to adapt beautifully and creatively to such hardship. Naples has always been a city of contrasts. Although its patriarchal structure ostensibly defines the city, within the Neapolitan societal structure, a substratum of that urban culture exists, a dominant community of women defined in part by the unique food and dialect of Naples. Patrizia Sambuco describes Naples as 'a context of blatant chauvinism, which is inherent in the city's culture and society and almost an element of urban description'.[2] This context, according to Sambuco, is reflected in Elena Ferrante's (b. 1944) novella, *L'amore molesto* (Troubling Love). Ferrante's Neapolitan narratives poignantly deconstruct the complexities of this urban space, primarily through the lens of the mother–daughter relationship.

Although they are chronologically separated by more than a century, the Neapolitan writer Matilde Serao (1857–1927) was the first woman writer to portray this community of women; her focus was also the mother–daughter dyad in much of her prose as well as her reportage. While not all women are mothers in Serao's and Ferrante's narratives, they are all daughters, and in this respect, the concept of mothering figures prominently. The mother–daughter relationship, whether told from the perspective of the daughter, or from the mother, reveals a liminal dimension of marginalization that perseveres, despite, as well as in reaction to, the outside world. In both Serao's and Ferrante's narratives, the cuisine and dialect of Naples serve as powerful sensory markers for a female Neapolitan identity. However, the way in which each writer approaches this identity is markedly different. This thematic is most graphically represented in Serao's novels and short stories, *Il ventre di Napoli* (*The Belly of Naples*, 1883), *Piccole anime* (Little Souls, 1884) and 'Terno secco'[3] (1885), and in Ferrante's shorter novels *L'amore molesto* (Troubling Love, 1999), *La figlia oscura* (*The Lost Daughter*, 2002) and *I giorni dell'abbandono* (Days of Abandonment, 2006).

To better understand Matilde Serao's representation of women in Neapolitan society, it is important to recognize her dual vocation as a journalist and fiction writer. Upon her death in 1927, *Il Giorno* heralded Serao as 'la più grande scrittrice del secolo' (the greatest woman writer of the century).[4] Serao's accomplishments – a collected oeuvre of more than 165 short stories, seventeen novels, and innumerable essays and collections of reportage as well as the founding of four newspapers[5] – would be considered admirable in the twenty-first century if only for her prolific output. However, when considered within her milieu, Matilde Serao's ability to transcend oppressive gender barriers is an exceptionally remarkable achievement. Serao's social narratives reveal that her accomplishments did not come easily. At the heart of her writing is the plight of the oppressed, particularly women and girls, and Serao vividly portrays the challenges and hardships of this marginalized subsection of Italian society. Food figures prominently in Serao's tales: it is an expression of motherly love, of solidarity between Neapolitan women and it is an essential element in establishing collective or social memory. Victoria A. Goddard, in her study

Gender, Family, and Work in Naples, connects food with Naples's collective memory emphasizing the vital role of the family:

> Food could be seen as the sensory point of entry into a web of sentiments, memories and fantasies which largely constituted a sense of identity, as a person and as a member of Neapolitan society. This has implications for family life and how it is perceived and remembered and for women, whose role as nurturers provides a thread of continuity within these identities.[6]

Neapolitan women, mothers in particular, are primarily nurturers in Serao's stories. Although the mother and the Neapolitan identity are central to Ferrante's narratives as well, her female characters eschew the very idea of nurturing, even when they are mothers. In Ferrante's texts, food and mothering serve as a foil to the heroine's growth and interpersonal relationships. However, Ferrante's negative, and at times toxic, portrayals of mothers, food and the Neapolitan identity are as revealing as Serao's affirming tales.

Both Serao's and Ferrante's female protagonists share similar motivations as well as challenges. They are primarily Neapolitan women who, for various reasons, are constrained to navigate their daily struggles alone, without a husband or father figure. In fact, this isolation of women naturally enables a sort of marginalization, as Tiziana De Rogatis maintains in her analysis of Elena Ferrante' s work. The Neapolitan women depicted in Serao's and Ferrante's narratives struggle to reconcile familial obligations with their personal desires and vocational aspirations. At the heart of these tales is food and food imagery, represented at times in vivid, historical detail, or as powerful metaphors for social problems as well as interpersonal dynamics. I have therefore chosen to organize my study by specific themes that dominate both bodies of writing by Serao and Ferrante. The first theme is the Neapolitan identity and the mother–daughter relationship as expressed through language and food. The second theme is the body as sustenance: food and sex.

The Neapolitan identity: Mothers, daughters, language and food

In an 1882 letter to the biographer Ida Baccini, Matilde Serao provided a brief autobiographical sketch highlighting some details of her life. In addition to detailing her vital statistics, education and employment history, Serao mentions her late mother, who she describes as *coltissima, intelligente angelica*, *divina* (refined, intelligent, angelic, divine).[7] She then punctuates her mother's immeasurable impact on her life with the statement, 'Da lei, tutto' (From her, everything).[8] Serao considered mothering to be a natural instinct for all women, as did many women writers of her generation, such as Neera (1846–1918,) Annie Vivanti (1866–1942,) and Grazia Deledda, (1871–1926), who ultimately embraced the self-sacrificing motif of motherhood as an irrefutable, inescapable fate for women.[9] Throughout Serao's short stories, novels and newspaper pieces, mothering is a recurring theme. For the most part, the paternal figure is either a negative presence or wholly absent in Serao's fiction. In narratives in which the mother figure is present, the relationship between mother and child (typically mother and daughter) is one of mutual support. This powerful bond between mother and daughter is beautifully illustrated in the following exchange from the novella 'Terno secco': 'Oh mamma, you carry me . . .', 'But you sustain me, little one.'[10].

The mother figure in Serao provides emotional support as well as sustenance: as long as the mother is physically present, despite financial adversity, there is always food. In 'Terno secco', the dire economic status of the household is revealed in the austere description of the apartment, infested with roaches and virtually devoid of furnishings. However, despite their financial hardships, Caterina, the fourteen-year-old daughter, is described as a thriving, *fanciullona* (big girl) with a *corpo robusto* (robust body).[11] She is well nourished physically and spiritually by her mother. Caterina is woken up tenderly to her mother's caressing words, 'up, little one, up',[12] and feasts happily on little sandwiches, apricots and her special Sunday treat of an *uovo sbattuto nel caffè* (coffee with a beaten egg in it).[13]

However, in many of Serao's narratives, such as the novella in *Piccole anime*, the significance of the maternal figure is paradoxically underscored by her absence. The novella 'Canituccia', features an orphaned girl as the protagonist, a girl who once enjoyed the nurturing and nourishment provided by her mother, but in the aftermath of her death, knows only cruelty and hunger. The heroine of 'Canituccia' is a seven-year-old child who has been abandoned by her prostitute mother, and taken in by a peasant woman, Pasqualina. Canituccia's primary chore is caring for a pig, Ciccotto. Canituccia's life is harsh – she sleeps on a single grain sack in the apple pantry – and is marked by privations, obvious in Serao's physical description of her: 'She had a head too small on a very skinny body.'[14] In the opening scene, Pasqualina mercilessly beats Canituccia when the young girl temporarily loses the pig. It is to the animal alone that Canituccia speaks with a maternal affection: 'Beautiful Ciccotto? My Ciccotto [. . .] where are you? [. . .] If I don't bring you home, mamma Pasqualina won't feed me.'[15] When the girl finally locates the pig and brings him to his stable to be fed, she becomes aware of her own hunger: 'She was also hungry like Ciccotto [. . . .] She no longer thought: she was simply and singularly hungry.'[16]

As the seasons eventually move towards winter, the pig grows bigger, as does Canituccia's maternal love and care for him. Eventually, Ciccotto is fattened to the point of virtual immobility, while Canituccia's rations dwindle, and her hunger increases. As the narrative draws to a close, the melancholy atmosphere of the farm is suffused with hope and elation, as the peasants busy themselves with preparations for their yearly feast. Canituccia is oblivious to the preparations until a servant informs her that because it is Christmas, they are going to slaughter Ciccotto. What is the source of joy and nourishment for the rest of the household is a death knell for Canituccia. In the final scene, Canituccia, who is described as being near starvation, refuses to have any part of the feast provided by the sacrifice of Ciccotto. In the end, the child, deprived of her own nutritional and emotional sustenance, pours her hunger into the nurturing of what is emblematically a surrogate child.

It is through her poignant depictions of maternal love as well as deprivation that Serao emphasizes the connection between mothering and food. Food is a signifier for maternal love: Canituccia sacrificially puts her own needs second to that of Ciccotto. The loss of this symbolic child effectively returns Canituccia to the role of orphan: she is motherless, but also no longer in a maternal role. Her extreme hunger and refusal to eat seals this fate.

Although the theme is represented in an entirely different light from Serao's work, the connection between food and mothering can be traced in Elena Ferrante's narratives, particularly the shorter novels *L'amore molesto*, *La figlia oscura* and *I giorni dell'abbandono*. The mother–daughter dynamic in Ferrante's short novels, whether written from the perspective of the daughter, or the mother, is always presented in the first person. The term *una madre snaturata* (a heartless mother), uttered by the protagonist Leda in *La figlia oscura* in an unapologetic self-confession,[17] aptly summarizes Ferrante's mother figure, a dominant presence in all of her narratives. However, unlike Serao's organic mother–daughter dyad that conveys maternal love and affection, the mother–daughter relationship in Ferrante can be described as complex, troubling and dysfunctional.

Ferrante's first novel, *L'amore molesto*, portrays an imperious mother figure, Amalia, who continues to dominate her daughter Delia even after her death. From the very first pages, the main theme of identity confusion is apparent.

The Neapolitan dialect and culture are bound up in the figure of the mother, who encapsulates the pain and trauma from Delia's childhood. It is both Delia's identification with her mother and her identity as a Neapolitan that she will try, unsuccessfully, to shed throughout the novel. This identity crisis is narrated through Delia's voice when she returns to Naples from her new home in Bologna for her mother's funeral:

> It was the language of my mother [. . . .] Not a joyous or nostalgic dialect: [rather] a dialect without naturalness, used with imperiousness, pronounced stiffly like an unknown foreign language [. . . .] Now that she was dead and I could have erased it forever together with the memory that it carried, hearing it in my ears caused me anxiety. I used it to buy a fried pizza filled with ricotta. I ate it with gusto after days of near fasting.[18]

The mélange of sense memories – smells and sounds associated with an urban setting, the Neapolitan dialect – all lead to Delia's musings on her connection to her mother and to Naples itself, ultimately leading to Neapolitan street food, a significant sensory marker. In particular, the power of olfactory memory has been recognized as the most powerful and expedient of sense memories, as Emily Brady explains in *The Philosophy of Food*: 'Many physiological theories have been put forward to show that memory is better through the nose than through the eyes. It has been claimed [. . .] that odour-related memory is more immediate, called up more directly than memories connected to sight or sound.'[19] However, the aforementioned pizza *fritta* (fried pizza) serves as the only positive food reference in the text. All other such references, even if they appear appetizing, are tainted sense memories that trigger a stream of painful recollections from Delia's childhood, mostly concerning the complex relationship with her mother. I will revisit these and other food-centric memories from *L'amore molesto* in the next section on the body as sustenance.

I giorni dell'abbandono, Ferrante's follow up novel to *L'amore molesto*, continues the idea of food as a negative sensory trigger, particularly in the mother–child relationship. The story traces the days leading up to, but mostly following, Olga's abandonment by her husband for a much younger woman, and Olga's subsequent descent into virtual madness. As Olga's mental and physical health begin to decline from the stress of her new situation, her tenuous relationship with her own two children becomes precarious:

> I was basically in a labile state, to which I reacted with a tense, exhausted self-control. My entire head was occupied with Mario, with fantasies about him and that woman, from a reexamination of our past, from the craving to understand

> what I had been; insufficient and, on the other hand, I desperately kept track of the mandatory tasks: pay attention to salt the pasta, and attention not to salt it twice, pay attention to the expiration dates of food, attention to not leave the gas on.[20]

Although Olga has a clear understanding of the nourishment and love that children need from their mother, she is at best only able to connect with her children in an almost mechanical manner. There are several instances in the text of Olga's perfunctory attitude towards cooking, such as the act of grating cheese: 'the gesture became so mechanical, so distant and independent, that the metal cut my nails, the skin of my fingertips.'[21] Perhaps the most illustrative example is when Olga recognizes the need for a semblance of normalcy after recovering from a temporarily debilitating virus: 'I started to cook again, endeavouring to entice them with new recipes. I began slicing, browning, salting. I even attempted to make desserts, but for desserts I had no vocation, I had no ability.'[22]

The acts of slicing, browning and salting are markers of domestic tranquillity, as well as of an idealized motherhood. However, Olga's heart is not in the task. This is further reinforced in her refusal to even consider making desserts or pastries; that is to say, traditional comfort foods. As the text progresses, it becomes clear that Olga's attitude towards cooking is not only a lack of interest but also one that is bound up in all things related to mothering, and which is ultimately revolting: 'I experienced a nausea that had always been foreign to me for the green streaks of parsley mixed with the red skins of tomatoes floating on the fatty water of the clogged sink. I didn't know how to reacquire the old confidence regarding the sticky remains of food that the kids left on the tablecloth, on the floor.'[23]

The equation of food with care, affection and ultimately empathy was a hallmark of Serao's narratives, but it is markedly absent in Ferrante's. Olga muses that it seemed her own mother *non le piacessi* (didn't like her).[24] As Olga battles the fever and delirium from the virus referenced earlier, she comforts herself with Neapolitan lullabies. However, it is not her mother whom she recalls. Instead, the image of a woman who lived in her apartment stairwell when Olga was a child, whom Olga's mother mockingly had dubbed *la poverella* (the pitiful woman) appears to Olga in quasi hallucinogenic visions. It is striking that in her hour of desperate need, her mind provides her with a proxy mother figure. In Olga's childhood, *la poverella* had been the embodiment of motherly love, always brimming with joy and surrounded by groceries as well as candies for her own children and for the neighbourhood children until her husband left her and she eventually drowned herself. In these fever-induced visions, however, *la poverella* gently but firmly chides Olga, in a strong Neapolitan accent, to get help from a neighbour for her sick child and for her dog who is dying: "'Go to Carrano", she advised me with a strong Neapolitan accent [. . .] "let him help you [. . .] he is the only one that can help. . . .You don't have much time. Otto is dying"'.[25]

The theme of estrangement between mother and daughter is even more pronounced in Ferrante's novel *La figlia oscura*, in which the protagonist Leda, a middle-aged woman with grown-up daughters, reflects on her decision fifteen years earlier to leave them for three years without any contact when they were small children. Ironically, her goodbye of sorts takes place in the kitchen, with her daughter Bianca trying to stall her departure:

> Bianca took an orange from the tray of fruit, opened a drawer, handed me a knife. Make us a snake, she asked, also in the name of Marta and Marta smiled at me encouragingly [. . . .] Fine, I said, took the orange, and began to cut the peel. The girls stared at me. I felt their gaze that wanted to calm me, but more strongly I felt the brilliance of life outside of them [. . . .] Ah, to make them invisible, to no longer feel the demands of their flesh like pressing questions [. . . .] I finished peeling the orange and I left. From then on, for three years, I no longer saw them.[26]

In the loveless and joyless domestic scene that Ferrante creates, the orange and its tray of fruit become props, useless objects rather than food. With this act, Ferrante also annihilates any trace of nurturing or motherly love from her character. Compounding the tragedy is the comparison drawn between Leda's lack of motherly instincts and the close bond between Nina and Elena, a mother and daughter she meets during her solitary vacation at the beach. Observing them initially from a distance, and then getting to know them closely, Leda becomes fixated on the boundless warmth and love that define the relationship between mother and daughter:

> She spoke to the little girl and her doll with a pleasing dialectal cadence, the Neapolitan that I love, the tender one of play and sweetness. I was enchanted. Languages for me have a secret poison that occasionally foams and for which there is no antidote. I remember the dialect in my mother's mouth when she lost the sweet cadence and would yell at us, intoxicated by discontent: I can't take it with you anymore.[27]

Leda's description of the Neapolitan dialect is more analogous to food than to language. In the mouth of her mother it is poisonous, in Nina's mouth it is sweet. Nina represents an idealized motherhood that Leda cannot approach. The contrast between Nina and Leda is further enhanced by the respective descriptions of food: Nina is part of an extended family that eats heartily and enjoys ice cream on the beach, while by contrast, the fruit in Leda's vacation kitchen is rotting. Leda's observations of, and interactions with, Nina cause her to reflect upon herself as a mother. Ultimately, she resigns herself to having been predestined to her fate as a 'madre snaturata' (unnatural mother), a conclusion that is supported by her recollection of being unable to nurse her daughter Marta: 'Marta, no, not at all, she wouldn't latch on, she would cry, and I would despair. I wanted to be a good mother [. . .] but the body refused.'[28]

The body as sustenance: Food and sex

As discussed earlier, breastfeeding is a quintessential aspect of the relationship between food and mothering in Serao's and Ferrante's works, yet their treatments of this act diverge significantly. The approach of each author towards this subject is influenced by their respective historical contexts, but also reveals their personal attitudes about mothering and food. For Matilde Serao, as I have mentioned previously, mothering was an instinct shared by all women and was a consistent theme in her fiction and journalistic pieces. For Serao, this maternal instinct was naturally connected to breastfeeding. In 1884, Matilde Serao penned the masterful study of Naples and its inhabitants, *Il ventre di Napoli*, to create a true account of the people in Naples – to present them as dignified, human souls who deserved to be acknowledged as such by the callous government of President Agostino Depretis. This government proposed that the most effective solution to the new cholera epidemic was to *sventrare Napoli* (to gut Naples).[29] In support of the dignity of her fellow Neapolitans, Serao stressed their compassion and humanity, particularly among the women: 'No woman who is eating and sees a child in the street stops to look without giving him immediately what she is eating; and when she doesn't have anything else, she gives him bread.'[30] This compassionate charity of providing food also extended to mothers sharing their own bodies to provide milk to babies of other mothers: 'A frequent case of compassion is this: a mother [who is] too weak [. . .] has a baby, but doesn't have milk. There is always a friend or neighbor or some compassionate stranger that will offer her milk; she will nurse two of them, what does it matter?'[31] The concept of wet nurses was not limited to Naples, but historically it has been a remunerative trade. Naples in the late nineteenth century was somewhat unusual in that there was a system of both 'mercenary' wet nurses, usually employed by the higher social classes, as well as 'voluntary' ones, such as the ones Serao discusses.[32] This tradition, whether done charitably or for compensation, continued into the twentieth century before modern sociological trends began to move away from breastfeeding and towards bottle feeding in many industrialized Western countries.[33]

Despite the historic and cultural precedents, Elena Ferrante's protagonists narrate their experiences with breastfeeding either as complete failures or in negative contexts tainted with revulsion and disgust. As I discussed in the previous section, Leda, the protagonist of *La figlia oscura*, laments her inability to nurse her daughter Marta. The representation of the body as food is even more powerful in *I giorni dell'abbandono*. More in line with the theme of the *madre snaturata* I discussed earlier, the protagonist of *I giorni dell'abbandono*, Olga, recalls bitterly her breastfeeding days. It is important to note that she is re-examining this process within the context of her new reality, as a woman abandoned by her husband for a younger woman. She stresses how her children sapped her of her vitality and sensuality, reducing her to an amorphous pulp:

> I would write, in the evening, in my notebooks [. . .] how I felt: [like] a lump of food that my children constantly chewed; a cud of living matter that continually amalgamated and softened its living substance to allow two voracious leeches to feed themselves, leaving on me the smell and taste of their gastric juices. Breastfeeding, how disgusting, an animal function [. . .] as far as I washed myself, that mother's odour didn't go away.[34]

This metaphorical reduction of Olga's body into a virtual food trough extended to her relationship with her husband at that time: 'Sometimes Mario [. . .] would take me when I was sleepy [. . .] without emotions. He did it by attaching to my almost absent flesh that tasted of milk, cookie.'[35]

This way, as Olga's body figuratively becomes food, her relationship with her husband transforms into something that is virtually asexual. This transformation is paralleled in the memory of *la poverella*, the motherly figure from Olga's childhood that I discussed in the previous section. Like Olga, *la poverella* had been left by her husband. Prior to that fateful episode, Olga recalls a woman who was maternal towards all the children in her stairwell, distributing candy to them that she kept handy in her dress pockets. *La poverella*, who is not identified by any name other than by the derisive moniker ascribed to her after she was abandoned, is a person whose flesh, bones and very being seem tied up with food. She is surrounded by foodstuffs and dispenses sweets essentially from her body. Later, her husband leaves and she loses that joie de vivre depicted earlier. Instead, she descends into a deep depression, becoming a shell of her former self. Olga's mother describes the woman as *un'alice salata* (a salted anchovy), a description that is solidified when 'la poverella' eventually drowns herself in the Bay of Naples. Throughout her childhood, Olga is haunted by images of this woman whom she now regards as *la donna in salamoia* (the woman in brine).[36] The dual nature of that term can suggest the salinity of *la poverella's* ocean grave, as well as the brine used to pickle vegetables. In this sense, the once cheerful figure of *la poverella* is stripped of her humanity and reduced to the status of a preserved food.

Ironically, Olga's fear of following the same path as the tragic Neapolitan woman from her youth leads her initially to make strong overtures to regain her husband's affection after he has left her, presumably for another woman. Rather than trying to seduce him sexually, however, she attempts to lure him back by preparing his favourite foods:

> I prepared a sauce with meatballs, he liked it very much [. . . .] But I didn't cook with pleasure, I was listless, I cut myself with the can opener, a bottle of wine slipped away from me, glass and wine splashed everywhere, even on the white walls.
>
> I forced him to have dinner with me [. . . .] I wanted him to see in that plate of pasta everything that, since he left, he would never again be able to look at, touch, caress, listen to: never again.[37]

Olga is using food, as a conduit to the senses, as a proxy to her body. However, the forced presentation of pleasure is disastrously exposed after Mario finally surrenders to her questions and confesses to having another woman in his life:

> He stared at the plate, then he looked me right in the face and said, 'Yes, there's another woman.' Then with an out of place ardour, he pierced the pasta in abundance with his fork and brought it to his mouth almost as if to silence himself, to not risk saying more than he needed to [. . . .] He had begun to chew [. . .] but all of a sudden something crunched in his mouth [. . . .] Now he was spitting the mouthful into the palm of his hand, pasta, sauce, and blood, it was truly blood, red blood [. . .] immediately, with eyes wide open, he put his fingers in his mouth and pulled out a shard of glass.[38]

The broken glass from the wine bottle, a direct result by Olga's own admission of her apathy and distractedness in preparing the meal, reinforce the connection of food and the body as tainted and unattainable.

The fusion of food and the body can also be seen in Ferrante's *L'amore molesto*, which I briefly mentioned at the beginning of this chapter. Throughout the storyline, Delia is deconstructing the identity of her mother, Amalia, and ultimately, herself. This process involves solving mysteries that are bound up in Delia's past, and that have now come to light with the death of Amalia. The greatest mystery that had cast a pall over the young Delia's life involved Caserta, a man believed to have had an adulterous affair with Amalia, which led to the eventual dissolution of Amalia's turbulent marriage to Delia's violent and abusive father. Caserta is not the actual name of Amalia's possible paramour, but a pejorative nickname given to him by Delia's family that is tied to the city itself. Delia reflects on the two Casertas that existed in her childhood memories, one of visits to the royal residence on Easter and the decadent foods associated with it, and the other, a vague and dark place existing on the threshold of the real and the imaginary:

> For decades, Caserta had been a city of haste for me. Not the actual city [where] I had gone as a child, the Monday after Easter [. . .] to eat salami [. . .] and eggs cooked in the shell inside a greasy and peppery dough [. . . .] Instead, my less verbalised emotions recorded under Caserta above all a motion sickness, a dizziness and a lack of air [. . . .] Caserta was a place I wasn't supposed to go. [. . . .] It had the flavour of sugared candies but it was forbidden to enter it. Not even my mother was allowed to enter or my father would kill her.[39]

Contrasted in this conflation of images and memories are the holiday treats of *salame* and what would appear to be the Easter bread *casatiello*, with the murky image of the liminal Caserta – a nauseating place with the deceptive odour of *confetti nelle bomboniere*. The aforementioned candies in Italian party favours are typically Jordan almonds. This is significant, given the dual nature of the treat: they are somewhat bitter by nature, but this bitterness is masked by the cloying sweetness of the candy coating. As the story unfolds, the sense memory of other sweet-smelling confections like the almonds reveal an acrid truth: Delia was molested as a child by Caserta's father in his candy store. The alleged affair between Amalia and Caserta was a story the young Delia concocted to suppress the horrific reality. The adult Delia endeavours to unearth the truth about her mother's relationship with Caserta post-divorce, particularly in the days leading up to her death. The evidence from Amalia's last days before her mysterious drowning suggests that theirs was a non-physical relationship: sumptuous restaurant dinners supplanted intimacy, and Caserta's daily gifts of fruit and *sfogliatelle*[40] to Amalia served as love tokens for their chaste relationship.

Ferrante effectively navigates the troubling subtexts of sexual misconduct and sexuality in general through food imagery. In this respect, food becomes a metaphor for sexuality. Sambuco discusses the metonymic link between dresses and the woman's body in Ferrante's narratives.[41] I believe the same could be said for food.

Conclusion: 'Boundary confusion' in the mother–daughter relationship

Post-Freudian psychologists and theorists have examined the uniquely close bond in the mother–daughter relationship with slightly different approaches. Psychologist Nancy Chodorow uses the term 'boundary confusion' to describe the symbiotic relationship between mothers and daughters in which the line between respective identities is often blurred. The result of this situation is that often the daughter's attempts to distance herself, if not sever this connection altogether.[42] Luce Irigaray maintains that the separation of mother and daughter is ultimately due to machinations of the patriarchal society.[43] Although many of Serao's and Ferrante's narratives convey the unique closeness of the mother–daughter bond, a significant tension between the two is revealed in Ferrante's novels that could be attributed to the 'chauvinistic' city of Naples itself. Returning to Sambuco's chapter on Ferrante that I referenced in the introduction, it is this atmosphere that creates the tension between mother and daughter. Sambuco specifies that Ferrante's descriptions of 'Naples as a sexist place where a woman's body is objectified by the male subject reveal the oppression that patriarchal society has imposed on mother and daughter and on the daughter's perception of her mother'.[44]

Regardless of how each author represents the mother–daughter relationship, food frames and defines women's identities in Serao's and Ferrante's narratives. Food reveals empathy and maternal love, but in its absence, it also reveals apathy and solitude. Food symbolizes the complexity of sexual relationships as well as supplanting physical intimacy altogether. Finally, food reveals the perceptions as well as the realities of different socio-economic classes in Naples in a way that no historian would be able to. In this way, Serao's and Ferrante's stories ultimately create a collective autobiography of Neapolitan women, their formation of self and their interaction with others – an oppositional history that reveals the truth not only about the disenfranchised lower classes but also about women within all classes.

6

Eros and Thanatos meet in the southern kitchens of Italy

Castaldi, Ferrante and Torregrossa

Giovanna Summerfield

Historically, yet controversially, in many cultures, it has always been women's main duty to prepare food for and serve it to others.[1] The author of *Women, Food, and Families* (1990), Nickie Charles, having interviewed women from a wide range of social backgrounds, states that women clearly see their role as 'one of refueling men with food so that they will be able to return to work well fed and full of energy',[2] prioritizing men's food preferences, and consequently feeling hurt and rejected if the food they offer to their partners is refused (69). Whereas the man is the food provider, the dependence of the woman on the resources provided should produce some cooking abilities, that at first prove her suitability to marrying, and later her willingness to manage her household, to include husband's and children's needs – a concrete expression of her position as server.

The first Italian cookbook intended especially for young housewives written by magazine editor and author Ada Boni, in 1929, and titled *Il talismano della felicità* (Talisman of Happiness), with 2,000 recipes, seems to imply that the household harmony lies in the hands of the woman and her talent in the kitchen. The book, that was later translated in other languages and became very popular in American and British kitchens in 1950,

> was implicitly addressed to the ancient regime notion of the woman's role, to being 'ladylike', which equated wedded harmony with the notion of true happiness: 'Many of you, dear ladies and girls, know how to play the piano well or to sing with exquisite grace; many others have very exalted titles for upper-level studies, know the modern languages, are pleasant writers or fine

painters .... But alas, certainly not all of you, if you examined your consciences ... could claim to know how to cook two soft-boiled eggs to perfection.'[3]

With the title of the book, subtle sexual innuendoes and opening remarks, the destined readers were informed that the 'modern woman' should give her husband, through the fruits of her hands (and body), and to the Italian country, under fascist regime, health and prosperity. And yet, during that complex and terrible period, cooking for a family was much more than that. The meagreness of the resources imposed a certain degree of creativity and dietary knowledge, not to mention physical fortitude for the long and early hour ration lines and financial savviness. In spite of (or because of) these challenges, women embraced new duties and assignments.[4]

As food becomes a way to set connections, create responsibilities, exert influence, exchange and reward, transmit memories, values and cultural norms[5] and as women continue to be involved in the food preparation of their household, they can employ a kind of 'selfless selfishness', that works as an expression of empowerment,[6] by choosing the ingredients and quantities and by selecting cooking methods. Teresa Desavahayam, author of 'Power and Pleasure Around the Stove' (2005),[7] contends that women, indeed, derive personal gains from cooking and serving food; such tasks become means for creating their identity and finding agency in the creation of personal recipes, according to their taste and context (3).

Contrary to tradition, and in spite of the limited space in which she might fulfil an unpaid position, a woman's presence in the kitchen represents action, reaction and subversion rather than submission: her culinary creations become the vehicles to verbalize her feelings, her wish for retaliation and her hidden or subdued hunger. The *angelo del focolare* (hearth angel) can turn into an angel of death or temptress, and often both at the same time. The feeding responsibility, within a space she has created from which she can defeat male authority in subtle ways, gives her power because she serves as a gatekeeper, controlling and taming other members of the family. The selection of the channels through which foods are purchased, prepared and consumed and the food itself are under the control of women within the domestic space; women are responsible for the environment to meet the family needs, and for providing consumption opportunities. Regardless of the men's possible financial control, thus the commonly held notion of 'separate sphere of power', women continue to be the chief decision-makers when it comes to food selection and preparation, through status production, labour, control over household technology and emotional or sexual manipulation and retribution.[8]

Looking at the domestic setting as an arena of power, well-known anthropologist David Gilmore reminds us that it is crucial to define the concept of 'domestic power'. Departing from the classic formulation of power according to Max Weber, for whom power lies in the probability that one actor can carry out her/his/own will within a specific social relationship against any resistance within that specific relationship, Gilmore outlines other important tenets of authority independently of sanctions to provide a broader formulation that shifts its focus from control to praxis, such as the sociologist Anthony Giddens' power that lies in a 'transformative capacity' from individual authority over others to one's own personal freedom of action.[9] This transformative capacity of women within the domestic sphere has also been the subject of creative writing. For example, in 1997, Arlene Avakian's anthology *Through the Kitchen Window: Women Writers Explore the Intimate Meanings of Food and Cooking* underscored the complicated relationship between food and women, with a diverse selection of memoirs, while the following year, Margaret Randall published a book of poems with actual recipes as both real literature and food preparation guidance. The term 'recipe', which according to Merriam-Webster was first used in the 1500s to describe medicine, began to be applied to cooking only in the eighteenth century. It is no surprise, then, that by cooking, women not only fed but also healed and poisoned their targeted consumers. Maria Giuseppina Muzzarelli, author of *Nelle mani delle donne. Nutrire, guarire, avvelenare dal Medioevo ad oggi* (In the Hands of Women. To Nourish, to Heal, to Poison from the Middle Ages to Today, 2013), focusing on the relation between food and women, dedicates an entire section to famous women who manipulated ingredients and their combinations to create dishes and potions, able to 'better' relationships, refuel the passions with their husbands and, in same hopeless cases, end those unbearable relationships and wrong marriages.

Sadly, with the socio-economic restrictions of the south, even our contemporary women struggle with shaking off the stereotypes of women relegated to roles of ladies of the house: 'The female employment rate between the ages of 15 and 64, in Sicily, Campania, Puglia and Calabria, is even lower than the French Guiana, the Spanish Extremadura, Thessaly and Macedonia in Greece, and even the Spanish enclave of Melilla in Morocco.'[10] According to the SVIMEZ report, seven women out of ten are still at home, confirming 'Questione femminile [come] altra faccia della Questione Meridionale' (the woman question [as] other facet of the southern question) (Moro). It continues to be crucial to define their role and affirm their determination through the control of what is available to them in their own private sphere; in individualized ways, women are able to shape the objects and areas they can control, to make decisions and to reinvent themselves. Just like Giovanna Bonnano or Giulia Trofana of centuries past, as recalled by Muzzarelli, they can become nurturers, seductresses, healers or (potential) murderers.

Contemporary women writers from southern Italy, such as Elena Ferrante and Marosia Castaldi from Naples and Giuseppina Torregrossa from Palermo, present in their works these trajectories of transformation, which are the focus of analysis in this chapter. Their protagonists have in common the south as geographical location but also the nature of their rapport with others and themselves; they are strong women who are alone by choice or by abandonment, and who cook for the survival not only of others but also of themselves and also because they are passionate about cooking they seek pleasure and independence through food (starting their own restaurant and their own sexual adventures). They are aware of their power and the power of food. Particularly intriguing are their characters' alterations of recipes in order to harm or to entice, presented in their writings as powerful ways of controlling others, while allowing the female protagonists to attain self-assertiveness and liberation, as illustrated in *I giorni dell'abbandono* (The Days of Abandonment, 2002) and *La fame delle donne* (The Hunger of Women, 2012), respectively, and *L'assaggiatrice* (The Taster, 2007), *Manna e miele, ferro e fuoco* (Manna and Honey, Iron and Fire, 2011) and *Panza e prisenza* (2012).[11]

In all these stories, pain and pleasure follow each other while the female protagonists ultimately regenerate themselves. Their sense of adaptability and profound capacity for resilience are substituted by a fully regained command of their lives, with all the flavours and smells of the beautiful but controversial social contexts in which they live and which they mirror. The analysis of the literary works presented here will follow this progressive pattern of lamentation, vengeance and regained independence. It is not coincidental that Torregrossa starts her novel *Manna e miele*, with a clear definition of *patimento* or suffering:

> Every woman experiences on her own skin the suffering that can temporarily tarnish the harmony of her features, undermine her certainties, make her forget her talents. But most of the time, deprivation can be the engine of a search that leads her to discover her true gift, and to give life to her best fruits in complete freedom. But you, gentlemen, be careful not to make your partner suffer too much: because then she will fructify, and among her sweeter fruits she may discover the forbidden one of freedom.[12]

The author compares this behaviour to that of plants, which, deprived of soil and water, foreboding death, become instead fortified and luscious; thus, like a phoenix, a woman may come back to life from the ashes of her own existence. In the kitchen of a Gangi's modest home, Maricchia, following the family traditions, had placed some manna and honey, respectively between the legs and the lips of her newborn baby girl, Romilda/Anna. When the time is deemed right, the mother teaches her daughter how to use those treasures that women have but do not use appropriately (171). Romilda, betrothed to don Francesco, withers away while cared for by servants and by her own parents who try to comfort her and restore her to life. Romilda needs to abandon her role of Baroness Ventimiglia, and returns to her natal kitchen in Gangi to regenerate. After the smell of *minestra, baccalà, arance* (soup, cod, and oranges) (337), it was 'a strong tomato smell . . . from her mother's bottles of sauce inside that kitchen'[13] that put her back on the path towards Castelbuono to become *mannaluora* (manna gatherer) and use her talent while serving others but mostly pleasing herself:

> All the pleasure that I feel while nicking
> Balances out all the other disasters.
>
> I never move away from this small grove of mine:
> This is my room, this is my palace.[14]

This newly found kingdom of pleasure and self-awareness is also ultimately attained in Torregrossa's bestselling first book, *L'assaggiatrice*. While the men are outside, and after having been welcomed into Anciluzza's prenuptial kitchen by the women in her family, we learn that they are self-reliant women, some widows or with a sick husband, others abandoned without pretext: a foreshadowing of the young bride's destiny. Anciluzza's own husband Gaetano, an insignificant 45-year-old man, has disappeared, leaving her with two young daughters, Amalia and Caterina, who are, in turn, helpless and of no assistance. Cooking becomes for Anciluzza, at first, a soothing pastime, and then her occupation: in her *putìa* (trattoria, tavern), she fights hunger and desire: 'I'm good in the kitchen, I can create things out of nothing, and in a flash, so that people remain astonished . . . . I like cooking, it makes me feel powerful, important.'[15]

As Carole Counihan underlines, there is a life-long connection between oral and sexual pleasure; both are essential for growth and existence itself, thus food and sex are often overlapping. The intimacy created while copulating or eating can be beneficial or threatening, depending on the circumstances, and in both realms, there could be a set of rules or stipulations that accentuates the power dynamic of the parties involved. One can withdraw or give food or sex to the other for personal gain, whether material or emotional, and relief or repentance can result from either act.[16]

Anciluzza's sexual fasting is broken by the arrival of customers that are, in turn, in need of tasting her delicacies together with her body. Readers and customers alike are presented not only with her personal thoughts but also with her personal culture, becoming witnesses to the unrepeatable exotic recipes of *caponata* (sweet and sour ratatouille), *pignoccata* (deep fried pastry dough covered with honey), and *scorzette* and *biancomangiare al latte di mandorla* (both almond-based desserts). Every dish, every ingredient, but also every movement during the food preparation, is an invitation, a promise (128). Her own body becomes food to enjoy, like the warm ricotta she denies her husband when he suddenly reappears while she is about to close her store for the winter break.

Anciluzza has graduated from the role of submissive consort: transformed from a mother and quiet homemaker to a woman with economic independence, she has experienced the solidarity of women, passion, pride in her own physical attributes and, most of all, initiative. She has not succumbed to the wishes of others who desired her, but she did make the first move on the most 'sought after' and well-endowed man of the village, Cicciu lu Sceccu. At this point in time, she has gained control over whom to accept or to reject: 'You cannot enter, you cannot enter the store, you cannot enter my life, when you decide.'[17] Bitter and unwilling, especially after being reminded of the power-holding expedients of her husband in and out of bed, Anciluzza mixes some oregano in the eggs for a frittata she is preparing for his return, knowing well that Gaetano is allergic: 'Not much so that he does not notice it, but enough to make him feel bad. Every abdominal pain will be a blessing for me.'[18]

She also leads the sexual encounter as to humiliate him, to make fun of his lack of prowess. With his frittata unfinished, Gaetano is 'kicked' out of the store while sneezing for having ingested oregano. Showing defeat and disgust, he does not recognize in his wife the woman he once knew and took for granted, the woman he abandoned carelessly, the woman with whom he thought he could reconcile. The readers are reminded by Anciluzza that, 'the wind has changed . . . the air becomes magnetic, the soul begins to hope again . . . life will come back.'[19]

The excuse of boredom, confusion and mere dissatisfaction Gaetano confesses to Anciluzza mirrors the circumstances of the protagonists of Elena Ferrante's *I giorni dell'abbandono*. During one of the tormented visits of Mario to see his children and clarify his decision to end the marriage, his wife Olga prepares for him one of his favourite dishes, a sauce with meatballs. Harbouring a suspicion of betrayal and sexual infidelity, her preparation seems now sloppy, passionless and almost automated, and yet a potential tool to reconnect with her spouse: 'I cut myself with the can opener, the bottle of wine escaped me, glass and wine splashed everywhere, even on the white walls. Immediately thereafter, with too abrupt a gesture while picking up a rag, I also dropped the sugar bowl.'[20]

She covers the *maccheroni* with a thick layer of sauce, hoping that he can see in that dish everything he has willingly given up but she insistently probes him to reveal the reason of his departure, while he tries to sample the hot pasta dish in front of him. Answering affirmatively that he has fallen in love with another woman, he starts to chew and spit at the same time:

> Pasta and sauce and blood, it was really blood, red blood. I looked at him his mouth stained without emotion . . . . Immediately, wide-eyed, he wiped his hand with his napkin, put his fingers in his mouth and pulled a splinter of glass . . . . He shouted at me that I was scaring him, putting glass in pasta, how could I do it.[21]

Whereas Mario is chasing his dreams with an eighteen-year-old woman, thus trying to put together the lost pieces of his youth, Olga has to shed her maternal role with both her partner and her children, learning how to know and please herself. This is a struggle because during her life as a mother and as a wife, she had annulled her true identity. With Mario gone, she is lost: she has no interest in taking care of herself or others; she uses a tone and language that are inappropriate, even obscene and sarcastic, because she does not care about hurting or offending. Subconsciously, she feels she needs protection and affection, which she had generously given but not fully received. The culmination of this mental state that is represented by apathy and digression is bluntly voiced by Gianni, Olga's son: 'I thought you were dead.'[22]

Through and due to this abandonment, Olga dies emotionally. She dies like the *poverella* (the poor soul) of her childhood, a middle-aged Neapolitan woman married to a red-headed man from Abruzzo, who lived in the same building of Olga's family. Abandoned by her husband, her despair disgusted the eight-year-old Olga, a feeling that turned into pity when the woman tried to kill herself: 'Women without love extinguished the light of their eyes, women without love died alive',[23] comments the narrator. Within the same context and living the same sad story the *poverella* chooses to live, Olga experiences a self-reappropriation, through a roller coaster of actions and reactions, both conscious and subconscious: the pieces of broken glass in Mario's favourite dish; the spontaneous assault during the causal meeting of Mario and his young lover, who is wearing Olga's earrings, passed on by his mother so as to reiterate that this girl has taken her place. She feels and expresses it in the after-death of Otto, Mario's dog, and in her advances to her neighbour, a musician, as if to declare that it is time not only to take her revenge but also to assert that she is still wanted and needed. If at first, Olga survives in a sense of emptiness (11), in an atmosphere of sickness and death (Gianni, Otto, herself and even the phones are malfunctioning), she slowly starts to react with 'a tense, overdriven self-control'.[24] As psychotherapist and author Susan Anderson claims, the journey of abandonment is similar to bereavement over death, but it is also a serious ego-draining experience. The abandoned party develops feelings of unworthiness. Rage is a crucial part of the healing process needed to assure not only survival but also the newfound self-empowerment and capacity for love (11–17). Olga's turning point is the *ramarro*, the green lizard, coming into the apartment and scaring her children: 'I had to start from there. . . . I was alone.'[25] She stays and she is finally able to kill the intruder.

This interweaving, as well as juxtaposition of death and life, subjugation and emancipation, isolation and sense of community, domesticity and worldliness are also the core features of Marosia Castaldi's *La fame delle donne*. Sensual pleasure and pain seep through the walls or, better yet, through the tables of kitchens past and present – recipes that reproduce the odours and flavours of motherly and regional affections, and recipes that are improvised to display interest and passion for individuals just met, longed for, stolen away with epicurean charm. Rosa, a widow with a young adult daughter, spends her days cleaning and cooking, like her neighbour Tina. Readers learn quickly that these two women, sharing recipes and dining by candlelight, are drowning their solitude into the objects of their homes and chats of years past. The loud noise of the vacuum cleaner of Tina, who cleans with maniacal manners, is conveyed by a torrential style of writing without punctuation but with lower and upper-case letters to indicate briskly where a sentence starts and where it ends. Simultaneously, Rosa reinstates the Mediterranean wisdom through food specialties, indelible imprints of the past. This formal, stylistic choice has a specific resonance: 'Life and death do not have doors or windows or even one end and not even a beginning. They move together in a space-time where everything revolves and repeats itself according to the law of chaos and universal repetition.'[26]

These profound concepts reveal the deeper truth carefully sealed in each of the recipes shared and unveiled by the fellowship of the women who populate Castaldi's narrative kitchens, the sweetness and savoury of their existence, and the images and heritage they bring along, because 'food preserves the nature of the centuries and the wisdom of God'.[27] The recipes speak of Rosa's beloved Naples:

> In the strufoli (honey clusters) and cathedrals of sweets and pasta and macaroni [live] the glories of the seventeenth and eighteenth centuries . . . when Voltaire

> and the Flemish and the Germans came down to paint Vesuvius . . . in the pizza lives Pulcinella and Queen Margherita and the goddesses, ancient mothers and black madonnas . . . in seasoned bread . . . and in pork sausages relives the orgy of the realist people and the madness of Masaniello.[28]

Here, like in her other literary works, Castaldi brings forth the duality of her natal city: a continuous cycle of death and rebirth, demolitions and rebuilding, historical past and present with all their challenges; Naples is portrayed as the mirror of a global reality, internal chaos and the need of identity reappropriation.[29] Naples, with its food, is the tie between the narrators, her family and herself, the comfort 'we seek as adults in times of frustration and stress':[30] 'Now that I relive that past I realize that I have resurrected, with my cuisine, the extreme folly of the southern landscape within the landscape of mists and crimes of Lombardy.'[31]

For an immigrant, such as the protagonist of *La fame delle donne*, who goes through a cultural and spatial transition, the familiarity of food consumption, and the (re)creation of familiar contexts, is of the utmost importance.[32] Bodies 'eat with vigorous class, ethnic and gendered appetites . . . articulating what we are'.[33] The old and popular saying 'we are what we eat' could be a quick reading key, insofar as identity involves not only our personal preferences and pleasures but also family and ethnic background, our values and ideas being extended to the practices of the community to which we belong. Even if removed from that community, we will continue to retain those values and ideas, and we will, on the other hand, associate our food preferences and customs with stories, people and places we have experienced, met and savoured while in the midst of that community.[34]

This (re)creation happens in a small kitchen, through the talented hands of a woman. In a space of isolation, the creative process is bridle-free. As Adalgisa Giorgio highlights, Castaldi's novels originate in loss and death and depict a 'wavering between being and non-being, life and after-life . . . together with an understanding of ourselves only through the words and gaze of the (m)other', and, in turn, the resilience and the capability of mothering a woman has, not only in the sense of creating and recreating a safe space, a community, but also in the 'need to reconstruct female genealogies'.[35]

Through food preparation as imparted by her mother, 'the only true love of her life' (85), Rosa attains a grain of eternity (8–9). Rosa's love of cooking reflects her mother's love of cooking. Through cooking (and eating), Rosa and her mother had a close bond. As Carole Counihan remarks, the love to serve others that counterbalances the need to be served, the isolation that becomes sociability within the walls of the kitchen may represent paths to overcome one's own fears and obsessions, and abate one's own hunger (161, 164), which seems evident in the experiences of both Rosa and her mother.

With a flashback to Amalfi, where Rosa's mother serves her lover freshly baked croissants, after passionate nights, we are introduced not only to the 'restlessness' of the cook but also to the sensual pleasure of the consumers. At first, this hunger surprises Rosa herself, as she claims that it was not her intention while cooking and she is unaware of the reason why her dishes have these effects on her customers; she then proposes the reason to be the southern opulence found in her culinary creations to seek and fulfil the total satisfaction of their senses (50), an outcome she ultimately enjoys, drawing her own personal benefits by 'luring' the fellow women of the restaurant, especially Tina, Caterina and Edna ('I handed her the best morsels: slices of meat, chicken thighs cooked in rum and wine with milk. It was a fat and inviting food').[36] Rosa becomes aware of the potency and importance of her talents to arouse the desires and pleasures in others. Rosa's trattoria becomes a sanctuary of pleasure (98) ('In my kitchen there were flashes of fire. It was inhabited by the infernal and angelic powers that govern the God of food')[37] that individuals and families yearn to visit ('In the village they waited to see the fires of my kitchen light up to feel the awaken instinct of extreme pleasure'[38]). As Rosa and her assistants serve the clients, they are voyeurs of the orgies that take place every evening, witnessing eyes shining as if belonging to the devil (56), women and men of Botero all sweating (56), children getting dirty (58), young girls who lifted the skirts to the warm scent that came from the fireplace and the kitchen while the young boys put their hands on their knees and under their skirts (59).

Amid a 'mixture of hate, love and folly',[39] while retracing her past and encountering resurfacing events, the protagonist finally confesses to herself and her readers her love for women, perhaps as simulacra of her mother or because of her need of 'free and total affection and to escape to my bed where I sleep alone'.[40] Whereas both her mother and Caterina, her gluttonous friend/lover, had covered all their bitterness with food, both by serving and by consuming it (97), the effect that food preparation and serving has on Rosa is completely different: 'I have fought with food my battle in life, I have raised cathedrals of puff pastry up to heaven and of short crisp pastries and of pleasure'.[41] Rosa is able to give pleasure and to elicit her repressed desires to infuse her dishes with her willingness to overcome the oozing of a soul abandoned to itself and to the care of a house (43).

A genuine and free-spirited display of affection is also present in Torregrossa's *Panza e prisenza* and the series of dinner invitations that *vicequestore aggiunto* (assistant chief of police) Maria Teresa Pajno, aka Marò, extends to her colleague, the *sostituto commissario* (vice police superintendent) Rosario Sasà D'Alessandro (titles that denote mere work connection between the two characters, but which will be transcended in the context of food preparation and consumption). All seven recipes that introduce the chapters of Torregrossa's book show off Sicilian gastronomy, the protagonist's skills as a cook and temptress, and of her conflicted love for her colleague. Unlike the Neapolitan recipes shared by Castaldi, which appear throughout her narrative, in Torregrossa's novel, the Sicilian recipes are given with full details of quantities and cooking instructions, as well as the addition of the historical or cultural peculiarities:

> 'Greetings Sasà but tonight I'll wait for dinner'/ 'What do I bring, Marò?'/ 'Nothing Sasà, only yourself and your appetite.'[42]

The detective story starts with a mysterious woman at the market, a curvaceous forty-year-old woman who is unmarried yet eager to purchase all kinds of goodies to prepare food for someone. She is a caregiver: we know that from her physical attributes and her shopping spree; yet she is also introduced by her professional titles, *vicequestore* and *dottoressa* (doctor). She delegates her sister, who accompanies her, to take home her shopping bags. We are forewarned by the first recipe that this character is going to be atypical: the *pasta con le pezze* is a summer soup dish that has to be consumed while very hot and with a combination of tomatoes and long zucchini, most specifically their vines' leaves.

We learn at the story's inception that Marò operates in a very misogynistic society where she has to prove her worth not only to others but also to herself. Torregrossa herself believes that Sicilian women are self-reliant and are the real protagonists in the development of society: they are strong and play an important role in the lives of their male partners, caring for them and guiding them; that is, even if their 'power' is publicly hidden, women exercise it in original and tangible manners (*Speciale Ritratti*). Marò, for example, investigates through her nose, *un naso importante* (an important nose) (31), and her perception of smells: 'She had become a formidable hound: she even managed to categorize people on the basis of the smell they emanated. She happened, for example, to smell a perfume and foresee the intentions of those who wore it.'[43]

While Marò waits for her *pasta alla Paolina* (with anchovies and breadcrumbs, a substitute to meat that was banned to monks at the time) to get ready, Sasà sits on the couch at a table overflowing with *antipasti* (starters) and 'all the junk he liked'[44] wondering about life with her as a married couple, with children playing and a dog crouched at his feet. Teasing Sasà's imagination while he looks at the sensual body of his colleague Marò (a body that he is not allowed to touch) is the smell of *basilico*, *zagara* and *pomelia* (basil, orange blossom and prumelia) emanating from her warm skin (35).

The next dinner appointment between the two is labelled by the recipe Marò has chosen for her beloved colleague: *pasta ch'i sardi a mari* (with 'runaway' sardines). As the author notes at the bottom of the recipe, this is such a poor dish that the fish itself is absent; the pasta is just embellished by wild fennel, salty anchovies, pine nuts, raisins, onions and olive oil. Their relationship had been one of affection and collegiality, but not of sexual desire or commitment up to that point, even though both characters had dreamt of being together. Even without making their desires explicit, the dining scenes speak for themselves, depicting rituals and typical occurrences of married couples and of effective/affective serving:

> When the plate was empty, Marò filled it with more pasta,
> and he willingly gave into her insistence:
> 'Take some more, I made it especially for you.'
> He swallowed a mouthful after another, rolling
> his eyes, as if he were making a physical effort.[45]

Research conducted by Miller et al. (1998) and by Sobal et al. (2002), and summarized by Hamburg et al. in the article 'Food for Love', concludes that 'food sharing and feeding are important non-verbal indicators of friendship and romantic involvement' while reiterating that these rituals are fundamental in the context of courtship behaviour, showing an increased establishment of intimacy and love (4). In 2006, a very controversial volume, imbued with patriarchal implications, and authored by marriage and family therapist, as well as popular radio talk show host, Laura Schlessinger, went so far as to remind women that preparing dinners and caring for their husbands without complaining could result in harmonious outcomes in their marriage: 'Give him direct communication, respect, appreciation, food, and good lovin' and he'll do just anything you wish' (xvii). The female characters penned by the three authors discussed here seem to comply with this frame of mind, coaxed as they are by the cultural mores and the context in which they operate. They are to be shaken up by some drastic circumstances to realize that this strategy does not work. The dishes they prepare do represent sexual enticements and gratification for both the preparer and the individual served.

The second part of Torregrossa's *Panza e prisenza* is introduced by the simple recipe of *spaghetti cu' l'ova di rizzi* (with sea urchin eggs), with a note from the author stating that male sea urchins are unusable in the kitchen (132). It seems as if Marò is looking for a miracle, both regarding her investigation and her unsettled relationship with Sasà: she is certain that this recipe will do the trick. Working hard in the kitchen on the aesthetics of the recipe execution, she prepares a warm bath and body lotions, anticipating the arrival of her friend, while releasing her anxieties and opting for a natural seductive look. With seafood on the table and wild memories of the beach in Favignana, she chooses that night to put into practice the exotic charms of a Sicilian woman in black attire.

Black is a colour with many connotations, which span from elegance, power and mystery to death. This novel opens with a death, a murder; midway we witness the passing away of *questore* Lobianco due to illness. At the end of the book, preceding a dinner date at Marò's, we are presented with a different kind of death: the sexual impotence of Sasà. In a tug of war of aggression and tenderness, confirming the power struggle and the mystery involved in an investigation but also of the relationship between the two characters, Sasà and Marò finally give in to their desire. It has taken many months of trial and error to finally bring this love game to its conclusion, just like it takes a long time for a brioche to leaven, as we see in the second recipe of the second part of the book. The warmth and softness of this wonderful dish is to be compared to the way Marò feels and looks after the sexual act of that night. She is filled with contradictory sentiments about the outcome, physically fulfilled but emotionally unsatisfied at the same time, ready to start preparing fresh brioches:

> She experienced one of the usual attacks that led her to cook furiously and untidily, only then to freeze and store [the food] in the fridge waiting for an adequate co-diner. Sasà was still asleep, it would soon be daylight, she dreamt of a breakfast consumed together in her bed . . . . She liked Sasà, he loved her . . . the ingredients were all there, it was only necessary to mix them with wisdom.[46]

The interaction between the two lovers is now juxtaposed with the act of preparing and eating (he savoured it; he tried to bite her, to devour; he smeared it; it satiated him, filled him with that scent of basil, salty flavour of sea urchin eggs, with a voracious hunger).[47] Marò and Sasà consume a rich breakfast, made of brioches, cannoli, a chocolate cake and various gelatines. With pangs of hunger, for having skipped dinner the night before, they engage in a professional conversation alongside a venial satisfaction, each hoping to conquer and change the other, under the banner of love and attraction. But there is no substitute for real love, just like the essence of cinnamon should not replace the real gelatine. The recipes mark progress in the investigation as well as in the seduction game, with different gains but equal perils. Torregrossa's Eros is the desire of life, the hunger appeased by others, by the loved one who has sacrificed all, and who has the talent to prepare and serve the desired delicacies. What we see over and over again in the Sicilian author's works is the cycle of Eros and Thanatos in the hot kitchens that are so familiar to her as a woman, wife, mother and writer.

Living and writing within the geographical and cultural boundaries of Naples and Palermo, Castaldi's, Ferrante's and Torregrossa's characters are expressions of the dualities of their contexts: on the one hand, they are the products of traditions, restrictions, solitude and separation; on the other, they are agents of creation, originality, determination and self-identity. As Giorgio reminds us, Italian writers like Neera, Matilde Serao, Sibilla Aleramo, Maria Messina, Grazia Deledda, Natalia Ginzburg and Dacia Maraini had already exposed the suffocating domesticity to include food preparation and serving, and the gap 'between externally imposed ideals and the reality of women's lives'.[48] The three southern authors discussed here use their characters' cooking talents to take control of the situation, to regain their memories, to communicate and to create; together with their culinary products, they use their bodies, giving them and withdrawing them to attest themselves.

Preceded by women writers like Clara Sereni, who in 1987 penned the well-known *Casalinghitudine*, a book that stressed the ambivalence of autonomy and dependence, between family recipes and social memories, in the attempt to take ownership of the past to (re)invent the future, all three southern writers discussed here – Castaldi, Ferrante and Torregrossa – take us not into a kitchen as a gendered space that symbolizes submission, but rather into an empowering enclosure that screams subversion instead. The kitchen is presented as a place of action and reaction. Through the deprivation and breaking of the mores and social constraints – jumping from pain to pleasure, from receiving to giving, applying authority and determination and shedding innate anxieties – all of their characters succeed in resurrecting hidden bursts of hunger (within themselves and others), passion and control. Turning their kitchens into powerhouses where it is possible to violate norms and acquire a sense of agency,[49] these women, whose bodies and minds have been imprisoned within places of objectifications, have now transformed themselves into the sources of their own pleasure, thanks to the creation of their own hands: their food.

7

The 'greedy southern woman' as a national Italian cliché

A preliminary proposal

Marcello Messina and Teresa Di Somma

Introduction

Unpacking the charged cliché of the 'greedy southern woman' involves analytical confrontation with some of the many axes of exclusion that characterize Italy, intended as a patriarchal, northern-centric and body-normative society. Furthermore, it involves a critical grasp of the violent modes of visualization that coordinate the exposure of bodies, practices and subjectivities that are considered anomalous within the ideal norms of the nation: on this premise, drawing upon the work of Perera[1] and Feldman,[2] we have previously deployed the concept of 'scopic regimes' to describe contemporary Italy.[3] Among other things, our work on Italy as a 'scopic regime' briefly suggests that laughter has a crucial function in facilitating audience acceptance and digestion of these violent visualizations. Although not discussed in that publication, this theoretical insight is connected to the Bakhtinian notion of 'ritual laughter',[4] intended as a powerful and ambivalent practice that has the function of forcing those who are laughed at to change.

In this study, we will combine the notions of 'scopic regime' with that of 'ritual laughter', analysing comic and frivolous representations, such as films, advertisements, TV shows and so on. In particular, we aim to unearth precisely the hidden violence embedded in these representations, commonly disguised as innocent spectacles by means of the ritual, cathartic power of laughter. We shall situate our critical position against each of the aforementioned axes of exclusion (i.e. northern-centrism, sexism and body-normativity) by also identifying and revealing the crucial points in which these axes intersect each other. Primarily, we subscribe to the theoretical contributions that have identified and criticized the forced positionality of the South as Italy's Other,[5] as the negation of the ideal, positive qualities that characterize the nation,[6] and as the racialized recipient of a continued, uninterrupted colonial violence, both physical and symbolic, perpetrated by Italy as a monoglossic, northern-normative country.[7] As we have shown in previous work,[8] the colonial subjugation of the South by the North of Italy is governed by a set of gendered metaphors that function both as triumphal allegories of the military conquest/annihilation of the southern territories and as literal *laissez-passers* for the continued, indiscriminate consumption/exploitation/humiliation/elimination of southern female subjects within the Italian national space.

In order to illustrate the intersection of these violent racio-gendered practices of visualization with the axis of body-normativity and food consumption, we take our cue from Francesca Calamita, whose seminal work on 'voracious dolls'[9] unearths the complex web of discourses embedded in Italian food advertisements portraying women. Calamita suggests that the adverts involving women and food, in addition to objectifying female bodies, are connected to a sexual hunger that eventually represents a menace for men. In addition, as argued by Livio Giorgioni,[10] from the late 1970s onwards, the obsession with food that had characterized post-war Italian cinema is supplanted, both in society and in visual culture, by a desire to lose weight, whereby weightiness and excessive appetite start being seen as markers of backwardness. The conflation of this backwardness, a characteristic that is constantly assigned to the South, with an anomalous voracity and exuberance that menaces the patriarchal, northern-centric order, is key to understanding the emergence, in the 1980s, of new southern female characters with noticeable relationships with food consumption, preparation and serving.

In this particular work, based on our subjective experiences as members of the audience, we will focus on a number of films, TV shows and advertisements that would literally be broadcast on television while we were having lunch or dinner with our families, especially between the 1980s and the beginning of the 1990s. We will then add a much more recent case study from 2016. Our analysis, however, is to be intended to cover a larger timespan than the one examined here: in particular, a separate essay on Leonardo Pieraccioni's films from the 1990s and the 2000s, involving critical discussion on Tosca D'Aquino and Anna Maria Barbera, is currently in progress.

Undesirable servants

The cinema and, in general, the visual culture of the early 1980s are characterized by several southern female characters that serve food and are excluded by the main love plot. In *Il tango della gelosia* (Tango of Jealousy),[11] Diego Abatantuono plays Diego, a southern bodyguard working in the mansion of a rich prince. While preparing breakfast for her landlord, the housemaid, another southern subject, asks Diego out: 'If you asked me: "let's go dance", I could even accept. At the end of the day I don't dislike you at all, does it make sense?'[12] Disgusted and offended by the maid's proposal, Diego responds by unleashing a series of racially loaded insults against her:

> Listen, hourly-paid maid, what are you fantasising about? Look, the magical dream that you had in your little brain is over. But seriously, do you really think that someone like me, 100% Milanese, can take someone like you, a filthy Southerner, *terruncella*, 1.20 m tall to dance? Out of my way, look for someone of your social level to go dancing with! Grab some countryside bumpkin, someone from Trani, Cerignola, Canosa maybe; they will immediately take you to dance. I like northern women, as they have a certain charm, so to speak. Not an African like you, southern women are anchored to a lot of bollocks: pride, shame, jealousy . . . . And carry that tray on your head, like Negro women, so that it doesn't slip off, Abdullah![13]

Diego's racist slurs against the housemaid summarize most of the discursive arsenal at the disposal of racist northern ontologies of the South: Abatantuono's character initially displays classist snobbery ('Listen, hourly-paid maid'), and then goes on to unleash an incredible amount of racio-gendered insults against the woman. Diego's tirade against short, backward and repulsive southern women is centred around the concept of 'Africa' as a nebulous and yet eloquent buzzword that evokes an entrenched colonial imagery upon which Italy as a country is heavily based. According to Joseph Pugliese,

> the deployment of the loaded signifier 'Africa', as the lens through which the South was rendered intelligible for Northerners, marks how the question of Italy was, from the very moment of unification, already racialised by a geopolitical fault line that split the peninsula and its islands along a black/white axis.[14]

In the 1980s, Apulian actress Gegia embodied the very same stereotype of subservient and gregarious southern woman. For instance, in a Lavazza advertisement, she appeared as a clumsy housemaid who prepared coffee for the popular Roman film and TV star Nino Manfredi, who called her a 'witch' in return. Similarly, in the 1982 film *Bomber*,[15] Gegia is Susanna, a restaurant-keeper who is mainly preoccupied with feeding the protagonist, boxing coach Bomber (Bud Spencer), for whom she has developed a crush. In this film, food is literally intended as the one and only possible means of seduction employable by such a subservient and markedly southern character. With her characteristic Salentinian accent, Gegia/Susanna prepares Bomber all sorts of delicacies. While Bomber is flattered by Gegia's gastro-erotic courtship, this love plot never takes off during the film, as the male protagonists are much more interested in pugilism.

By contrast, in *Acapulco, prima spiaggia . . . a sinistra* (Acapulco, First Beach . . . on the Left),[16] the male protagonists, comedy duo Gigi e Andrea, from Bologna, are interested precisely in erotic adventures at beach resorts. Gegia is Miranda, a manicurist who works at Gigi e Andrea's local barbershop. While serving the two young men, Gegia/Miranda, who has a crush on Andrea, listens to their plans to go on holiday to Acapulco and declares that she 'would like to go, too'.[17] Andrea replies: 'I'm sorry, but we already have dates',[18] but importantly, Gegia/Miranda here is not quite seen as an undesirable woman by the comedy duo. In fact, earlier in the barbershop scene, Gigi had found himself admiring her body: 'Andrea, Miranda's bum is not that bad, is it? Have a look!'[19] In his reply, Andrea lectures Gigi as to the reasons why they cannot consider Gegia/Miranda as a potential partner: 'Don't you see she's got a flat bum? Also, she's a Moroccan, come on!'[20] Gegia's categorical exclusion from the duo's erotic adventures is openly motivated by her positionality as a southern woman, and confirmed by the use of a racially loaded signifier ('Moroccan'), semantically co-extensive with the aforementioned term 'Africa'. The rustic flavour of Gegia's exuberant corporality and personality, is, in Gigi's words, 'healthy, genuine, reminiscent of my roots',[21] and, at the same time, constantly excluded from the collective erotic fantasies negotiated by the two characters as an indissoluble duo. Skinny and exotic bodies populate their homo-socially projected fantasies: a rich Englishwoman desperate to cheat on her husband, a local northern Italian tobacconist, and so on. Forced to give up Acapulco for the local beach resort of Cesenatico, where all their pick-up attempts fail, they return to a deserted mid-summer Bologna. Here, they see a woman walking from a distance, possibly a foreign tourist, and start chasing her, only to realize to their shock and surprise that it is Gegia/Miranda. Once again, Gegia can deploy her best means of gastro-erotic seduction, inviting Gigi and Andrea to a *Ferragosto*[22] lunch at her place. After finishing his meal, Andrea is finally seduced: 'We ate really well! Well done, bravo!'[23] While Gigi goes upstairs with Gegia's Sardinian friend Bonaria, Gegia/Miranda can finally fulfil her romantic dream with Andrea. Strikingly both Gegia/Miranda and Bonaria are violently constructed as southern female characters who are always available, patiently waiting for the return of the male, northern hero, ready to feed him and make love with him when he chooses to. Despite offering food, shelter and love to these two failed, wannabe playboys, both Bonaria and Gegia/Miranda are exposed to their cruel depreciation. Right after being introduced to Bonaria, Gigi calls her "*un cesso*" (literally, 'ugly like a toilet'), and then impudently asks her to show him her breasts. Moreover, before Bonaria's arrival, both Andrea and Gigi had tried to trick Gegia/Miranda into working as an escort:

> (Andrea): 'Take my advice, if I were you, I would put myself about more! [. . . .] Also, you're already a manicurist, you've got a nice little bum, if you give yourself away for money, you'll become rich' [. . . .]
>
> (Gigi): 'After all, we're in the North here, are you afraid you'll spoil it?'
>
> (Gegia): 'What are you talking about? You cheeky pair!'
>
> (Andrea): 'If you put an advert up on the papers . . . . Something like . . . Manicurist available . . .'
>
> (Gigi): 'With discreet, independent access'
>
> (Andrea): '. . . independent access, fellatio[24] expert, you need to say that.'
>
> (Gigi): 'Totally confidential.'
>
> (Andrea): '. . . totally confidential, getting it on and on and on.'
>
> (Gigi): 'and then you're done.'
>
> (Andrea): 'and there you have it.'[25]

This disgraceful exhortation to prostitution confirms the construction of these southern female characters as empty and deserted territories, *terrae nullius*, where the male protagonists can literally do and say whatever they want. Importantly, in this dialogue, Gigi literally uses his own northerness ('we're in the North here') to validate and defend the reasonableness of the proposal he and Andrea are making to Gegia. In a spasm of cultural pride, Gegia responds precisely by calling upon her southerness: 'Are you crazy? I am a real, serious manicurist, don't you know? [. . . .] And on top of that . . . I am a Southerner, and I would never give myself if there wasn't a lot of passion involved.'[26] Rejected, excluded, depreciated and only reconsidered as a last resort, Gegia/Miranda proudly voices her defiant agency against the racially charged intervention/manipulation manifested by Gigi and Andrea. Right after that, though, and in keeping with her subservient gastro-erotic character, she serves her two male guests a family home-made liquor.

In these same years, the cliché of the undesirable, female southern servant reaches its peak in *FF.SS. – Cioè: . . . che mi hai portato a fare sopra a Posillipo se non mi vuoi più bene?* (FF.SS. – Or: Why Did You Take Me Up to Posillipo If You Don't Love Me Anymore?).[27] While the film itself is originally meant as a parody of the traditional stereotypes of southern people, it often ends up reproducing the same clichés, or even adding up other problematic images. The protagonist Lucia Canaria (Pietra Montecorvino) is an aspiring singer who works as a toilet attendant in Naples, then moves with her manager to Milan, Rome and Sanremo in search of success in show business. Lucia is affected by the *napoletanite* (Neapolitanitis), a condition whereby she faints every time she sees or smells Neapolitan food. Lucia's refusal of her own local, identitarian food is counterpointed by her repeated relegation to repugnant and sickening settings: regardless of where she travels to, she immediately starts working in the local toilet, surrounded by sounds of excretions and flushing toilets, and exposed to filthy, if amusing, limericks written on cubicle walls. In between these various restroom experiences, she lands occasional showbiz jobs. Her first job in Milan for a toothpaste advert is formatted as the typical comparison between a person who uses the product and one who does not: Lucia appears with her teeth disfigured by black spots, whereby it is difficult to distinguish stains from actual food remnants. While the 'healthy' characters of the advert show their shining grins, Lucia starts weeping while still displaying her disfigured dentition, finally crying: 'Jatevenne!' (Neapolitan for 'Go away!'). The oral cavity must necessarily be intended as the access point of food in the body, and the filthy spots that disfigure Lucia's mouth are obvious references to modes and circumstances of food consumption that are always in excess of a perennially North-centric idea of normality and moderation. The fact that this immoderation is assigned to a subject that already refuses Neapolitan food retraces a collective 'assimilationist itinerary' that 'is shaped by the torsions of violent contradictions'.[28]

In the particular case of Lucia, the violent contradictions that mark this assimilationist itinerary draw attention to the potential development of eating disorders. Psychiatrists such as Giovanni Maria Ruggiero and Marcello Prandin,[29] as well as Ann M. Cheney,[30] drawing on personal and heteronomous ethnographic work,[31] associate eating disorders in southern Italy to the troubled relationship of closed, 'backward' communities with 'modernity' and social change. In disavowing these approaches, we want to critically unpack the concept of 'modernity' on which such analyses are predicated. Taking our cue from Enrique Dussel, we want to expose the 'myth of modernity'[32] as a set of fallacious assumptions and deliberate self-effacements on which the violence of Eurocentric coloniality is founded. Transposing this myth to the national boundaries of the Italian nation-state, what is persistent and resilient in ethnographic incursions in the South is the ambivalent role of the North, eternally acknowledged as a model of virtuous civilization, cooperation and civic cohesion, and eternally invisibilized in its role of continued perpetrator of both physical and symbolic violence over the South.

Returning to *FF.SS.* and to the toothpaste advert, the contrast between the normative whiteness of the teeth of the northern, healthy protagonists and the blackened, depreciated grin of Lucia functions as a powerful chromatic metaphor of the racialized violence that inscribes the North/South relations in Italy. Analyses of behavioural disorders in southern Italy should not overlook the multiple agency of the North of Italy in setting bodily norms and aspirations, determining situations of infrastructural imbalance and economic disenfranchisement and constituting violent regimes of visualizations that always involve the South as an eternally imperfect, repugnant, inferior appendix of the North. Against this violent scopic regime, singing at the Sanremo Festival, Lucia reclaims her unextinguished self-determination, accompanied by a choir of other southern subjects: 'South, South, we are from the South / We are short and black.'[33] This 'tactical blackening [. . .] in the face of a virulent and violent caucacentrism'[34] is complemented by an equipollent, proud and co-extensive reclamation of the same food Lucia had so far refused in the film: 'the tomatoes for the ragout, the pizza, the mozzarella [. . .] the macaroni to eat.'[35] By reclaiming and affirming her unextinguished southerness, Lucia, at least symbolically, comes to terms with her refusal of Neapolitan food.

Marisa Laurito as patient/undomesticable wife

The 1980s were also the years when Marisa Laurito, a Neapolitan actress who already had several years' experience in theatre, gained popularity within cinema and TV. In the national Italian imagination, Laurito embodies the perfect cliché of the *napoletana buongustaia* (Neapolitan female foodie), always preoccupied with the preparation and consumption of food. This characteristic feature of Laurito's persona determines, right from the start, her relegation to secondary, gregarious roles in films, whereby she can only act as the housewife that cares for the home while her husband is involved in the main film action. In slightly different terms, both *Mi faccia causa* (Sue me)[36] and *A tu per tu* (Face to Face)[37] relegate the character interpreted by Laurito to the same role.

The opening sequence of *A tu per tu* perfectly encapsulates the polarized domestic power relationship existing between the northern protagonist and his vigorous southern wife. At the start of an animated family quarrel, Gino (Paolo Villaggio) threatens to punch his wife Elvira (Marisa Laurito), who, in response, slaps him in the face and calls him to the kitchen to have breakfast. In the kitchen, while Gino eats the food Elvira has prepared, she continues to scold him. Annoyed by Elvira's tirade in Neapolitan, Gino unleashes his most stereotypical anti-southern hatred: 'Learn to speak Italian, *terrona!* You've been living here for twenty years now, and I still need a translator and the subtitles to understand you!'[38] Gino's racist insults do not silence Elvira, who continues by angrily listing to her husband all the bills they need to pay as soon as possible. This is one of the last interactions between Gino and Elvira, and soon after that he leaves for the adventure that constitutes the core of the film.

This scene exemplifies the cliché of the undomesticated, recalcitrant southern woman who represents a threat for the northern patriarchal order. Villaggio/Gino's remark on the fact that Laurito/Elvira still speaks Neapolitan despite twenty years spent in the North, deploys directly the trite narrative of unassimilability that has historically been used against diasporic southerners in various geographical contexts, associated in turn to a 'racio-gendered vision of southern Italian women as lawless, immoral, vindictive, violent and murderess'.[39]

Following the script, the 'immoral' Neapolitan woman, suddenly abandoned by her husband, happens to have an affair with a *carabiniere* (military police officer). Importantly, the love relationship is not shown by means of magniloquent, voluptuous images, but is suggested by means of a food scene: upon one of the rare phone calls from Gino, Elvira picks up while she and her lover, half-naked, are enjoying a generous portion of spaghetti. Once Gino hangs up, relieved, they complement their 'sinful bites'[40] with a glass of wine. In this way the unassimilable, undomesticable southern woman is constructed as an adulterous and voracious lover. Marisa Laurito literally came to embody Glória Anzaldúa's trope of the 'shadow-beast',[41] that is to say the undefeated, frightening woman that populates men's nightmares. For her screen husbands, Laurito is always potentially on the brink of a sexual and/or gastronomic rebellion. Christian De Sica, who plays Laurito's husband in *Mi faccia causa*, frightfully imagines her and her mother working as prostitutes to make ends meet, due to the huge expenses they incur by buying food.

In the same years, Laurito's TV persona presents her, if possible, as even more exuberant and voracious than the characters she interprets in films. Always keen to show her energetic body, she often performs *la mossa* (literally, 'the move', a Neapolitan breast/shoulder shimmy), while constantly chattering about her food preferences and her best cooking tips. In advertisements, she becomes the celebrity spokeswoman of Pasta Voiello. In 1989, she is one of the participants at the Sanremo Music Festival with the song *Il babà è una cosa seria* ('The *babà*[42] is a serious thing'):[43]

> What cheers me up / is the smell of tomatoes / [. . .] love comes and goes / But the macaroni stay [. . .] / I feel more good-hearted and beautiful, / I make gnocchi with mozzarella![44]

Laurito's floorshow persona is suspended between the toxic construction of a female character, that is derisible on account of her insatiability, and the proud affirmation of a southern woman who defiantly neglects body-normative regimes of skinniness in order to openly voice her willingness to attain pleasure from food.

Comedy impressions of Laurito have often ridiculed her relationship with food. In the TV programme *Fantastico* (1988), for example, Anna Oxa made fun of Laurito's habitual and gratuitous references to Neapolitan food:[45] 'the difference between good afternoon and good evening is the same that exists between the *pasta cresciuta*[46] and the *panzarotto*'.[47] In the 1991 edition of the comedy TV show *Avanzi*, Cinzia Leone imitated Marisa Laurito by appearing dressed in flamboyant outfits, adorned with food: most notably, in an episode of the TV show, she appeared with a fish stuck in her cleavage.[48] In the previous episode, when the presenter Serena Dandini introduced the mock-Laurito to the in-studio audience: 'I'm here [. . .] waiting for a very important person, a renowned woman from the TV, who has been . . .' (*Avanzi*, 1991a),[49] the audience members interrupt Dandini and break in a noisy, collective laughter, while we hear one of the spectators: 'Sure! A woman, [you must be joking], hahaha' (*Avanzi*, 1991a).[50]

The cruel carnivalization of Laurito's proud femininity contemplates and involves her de-feminization. Her exuberance, her marked southerness and her outspoken food indulgence are all elements that are signified as incompatible with a moderate, desirable womanhood. This decisive de-feminization anticipates the final, self-punishing retreat of Laurito from her exuberant, politically charged relationship with food. She features in a mid-1990s TV advert for diet food Slim Fast: in the first few seconds, we are shown a classical 1980s sequence of her performing *la mossa*; then the screen splits and we are shown the new, thin Laurito. The images are counterpointed by these words: 'Once I was dancing on TV, and all of a sudden . . . tra! My dress got ripped. Now I am perfectly slim: look! I've lost 10 kilos in the last two months with the Slim Fast plan!'[51] Through this advert, Laurito's political defiance against body-normativity and food restraints is totally emptied, and her persona is violently put back on the track of the constantly scrutinized, eternally domesticated feminine bodies.

Miss'Illude as greedy southern woman

In this section, we take a considerable chronological leap to the 2016 debut of Neapolitan comedian Rosaria Miele in the comedy TV show Made in Sud. In her stand-up performances, Miele interprets Miss'Illude, a 'curvy young lady who is outside the traditional standards for beauty contests'.[52] With her body 'not suited for beauty contests', Miss'Illude appears on stage running, dancing, shaking and shouting. Fatima Trotta, one of Made in Sud's presenters, punctually interviews her:

> (Trotta): 'Tell me about one of your best strengths.'
>
> (Miss'Illude): 'Every morning I go to the gym.'
>
> (Trotta): 'Tell me about one of your weaknesses.'
>
> (Miss'Illude): 'Once I'm out of the gym, I go to the restaurant'.[53]

Food consumption is in fact at the core of Miss'Illude's character, and Trotta continuously remarks on this aspect, scolding her about the fact that she can only think about food:

> (Trotta): 'You always think about food, miss. Why are you so . . . let's say . . . chubby? Have you always been like this?'
>
> (Miss'Illude): 'No, I was so thin I looked like a little bird, look at me' [shows photo of thin self].
>
> (Trotta): 'But . . . miss . . . you were so beautiful, what did you do to yourself?'[54]

By affirming that Miss'Illude *was* beautiful, Trotta explicitly implies that, due to her bodily weight, she is not beautiful anymore. Right from her stage name, after all, Miele articulates this exclusion from the discursive field of 'beauty': 'Miss'Illude' can be roughly translated as 'Miss Delusion', intended as Rosaria's delusion about winning beauty contests. Excluded from the phantasmagorical domain of beauty, Miss'Illude, who constantly brags about eating all sorts of things, eats her competitors under the special training devised by her fellow comedian Peppe Step:

> (Peppe Step): 'Thanks to my special training, Miss'Illude, despite ranking 3rd, won!' (Trotta): 'Sorry, but if she came third, how could she win?'
>
> (Miss'Illude): 'I ate the first two!'
>
> (Trotta): '[. . .] this one literally eats everything!'[55]

Trotta plays the role of the body-normative, desirable woman who commiserates, when she does not openly insult Miss'Illude. Overall, though, these comedy sketches convey a powerful political content, as they promote and dignify models of feminine beauty that are constantly relegated to public shaming and derision. In almost every sketch, in fact, Miss'Illude's vigorous and exuberant corporeality culminates in her flashing her knickers to the audience. This eloquent act of self-affirmation as a woman is usually addressed to Trotta, who embodies the normative model of woman. Even the reference to anthropophagy, we contend, must be intended in a political sense: that of absorbing, digesting and deconstructing received notions of womanhood and beauty in order to reformulate them in the context of a queer, peripheral, constantly neglected and belittled space of existence.[56] Miss'Illude proudly disavows colonial teleologies of thinness and physical domestication by sardonically flagging her willingness to remain as she is:

> If you're waiting for me to become beautiful, if you're waiting for me to become thin, and if you're waiting for me to become your nasty girl, you can keep waiting as much as you like, all you need is a miracle![57]

Conclusions

We have examined cinematic and televisual representations involving Southern Italian women and their relationship with food consumption, food preparation and body weight. In most of the cultural manifestations discussed here, these relationships with food and weight are also connected to specific temperamental attributes that, in the sexist and northernist mythologies on which Italy is predicated, construct these women as patiently waiting wives/partners to whom the male protagonist can always return, or as undesirable, unmanageable or even repugnant individuals who are straight off excluded from the adventures of the male (often northern) hero. Furthermore, in the specific case of the two films with Marisa Laurito examined in this chapter, that is, *A tu per tu* and *Mi faccia causa*, the image of the wife who waits at home conflates with that of the unmanageable woman who is always on the brink of disrupting the patriarchal domestic order.

Importantly, almost all the female characters presented in this analysis are at some point put on the spot, criticized or even insulted for something that has to do, directly or indirectly, with their southerness, and that is then linked back to any perceived anomaly in terms of behaviour, eating and/or weight. An important exception to this recurrent trend is the case of Miss'Illude: however, this exception is easily explained with the fact that pretty much all the characters that interact with Miss'Illude in Made in Sud are also southerners. This fundamental exception, we contend, tells us precisely that investigation of behavioural and eating patterns in the South of Italy cannot ignore the (symbolically when not physically) violent influence of the North in shaping southern lives and aspirations. Trite tropes of locally circumscribed endemic backwardness, recalcitrance to modernity and vertical patronage are not only offensive but also urgently inadequate and chronically insufficient to assess determinate phenomena – we say this without questioning the colleagues' scientific excellence and the importance of their fieldwork and findings.

In our analysis of the various toxic representations scattered around the various media products examined here, we have constantly attempted to identify, illustrate and dignify the spaces of disobedience that have been painstakingly and vigorously reclaimed by almost every one of the characters discussed in this work. Obviously, this does not mean denying the fundamental ambivalence of these screen personas, who, despite any possible spasm of rebellion, are partly complacent with the patriarchal, North-normative scopic regimes that inevitably shape their cinematic and televisual apparitions. For example, in celebrating the rebellion of Miss'Illude, we have overlooked the self-flagellating elements embedded in her character, who always directs attention to her contrast with the ethereal body-normativity of the presenter Fatima Trotta (whose southern accent is also much less marked than Miss'Illude's). By encouraging the national TV audience to laugh about her own body, Miss'Illude inevitably flags her acknowledgement of dominant northern-normative, patriarchal, body-normative female models. To most members of the audience, she might only signify as an overweight, markedly Neapolitan, bizarrely self-derisive woman – a paradigm that in the national common sense is to be avoided at any cost.

Miss'Illude, along with all the other characters that relate to the cliché of the 'greedy southern woman' that we tried to unearth in this work, is strongly marked by the aforementioned 'torsions of violent contradictions'[58] that inevitably characterize any southern, queer, Other, marginal project aspiring to national recognition. Overall, the 'greedy southern woman' is a fairly recurrent cliché in Italian popular culture, deeply anchored to a national imagery that, in different ways, perceives both women and southerners as potential anomalies to be constantly domesticated.

Part III

Food, gender and Italian identity

8

From *pizzaiola* to phenom

Viewing Sophia Loren through food

Niki Kiviat

After the Second World War, as Italy transitioned from fascism to a democratic, constitutional republic, the role of women in Italian society became quite blurred. When men left home to fight, women replaced men at work, leaving their posts in the domestic space to substitute men in factories and workshops. It was assumed that, with the war's end, women would seamlessly retreat from the public sphere and return to the kitchen, ready to birth, rear and feed new children. Historian Molly Tambor, however, describes the sociopolitical pushback in the late 1940s, as Italy welcomed women as new participants in the new democracy:

> Despite the motivation that the war and post-war may have offered Italian men for a backlash against women, however, this time women would not retreat from new rights in politics and new roles in public. The trope of the Italian mother, though under attack from some quarters, paradoxically served women's rights activists in a positive and effective way as they sought to reconcile Italians to women's suffrage, women's equal citizenship as proclaimed by the new Constitution, and women's role in the marketplace as both workers and, as reconstruction progressed, leaders of the transition to a consumer economy.[1]

I quote Tambor at length not only because her commentary vividly illustrates the beginnings of women's emancipation but also because she seeks to qualify the prowess of women in the marketplace. Despite women's entrance into the public workspace, and despite their engagement with the new commodities of Reconstruction, women's participation in the market – as regulated by the capitalist, democratic principles of 1946 onward – is not necessarily free.

Indeed, the 1950s witnesses the birth of a complicated socio-economic actor, the Mrs Consumer, or the phenomenon where women first explore both their accessibility to and limits within the consumer's domain. Women enjoyed new political freedoms and were exposed to consumer durables – such as the washing machine and refrigerator – that alleviated and even invigorated household duties. Some historians argue that these 'electric servants'[2] give new value to women's labour. However, a woman's positionality is continually read with respect to men, and to systems and institutions constructed and dominated by men; this technologization only raises the standards imposed on women, as women are expected to excel in these pursuits *and* do so in a way that pleases their families. Although women have entered the public domain, and although it appears that they are full-fledged participants in the post-war economy, containment presents itself in a new way, as institutions – the church, a conservative government, and so on – uphold the traditional roles of women, perpetuating the idea that a woman's place is in the kitchen, and in the kitchen alone.[3]

These limitations imposed on women are, however, certainly not exclusive to a washing machine or the bountiful aisles of a supermarket. Post-war aesthetics, too, reflect the tensions women faced in their permeations of the public domain, often encouraging them to reassume the role of the *donna madre* (mother woman), thereby rejecting the cosmopolitan, individualistic tendencies of the *donna crisi* (crisis woman).[4] Throughout the fascist period, domestic literature instructed women on how to 'make do' in the kitchen, stretching limited resources to concoct filling, even satisfactory, meals for her family; *minestra* (soup) comes immediately to mind. With the boom, however, domestic manuals continued to flourish but became a platform that also continued to limit feminist agency and discourage self-fashioning. In a comparison between domestic manuals and novels and films of the post-war period, film scholar Rebecca West notes that the manuals of the 1950s 'propose "ideals" toward which real people aspire and, in the case of women, I would suggest that many of the ideals are harmful in that they draw upon concepts of femaleness and femininity that often stifle agency and choice'.[5] These ideals, which West aligns with feminist theorist Adriana Cavarero's concept of 'whatness', project a set of norms detailing what women should represent, particularly with respect to the family unit. West proceeds: '*What* men and especially women were and should be; *what* the ideal family was; *what* normative sexual behaviour should be: these *whats* underlie much of the prescriptive material to be found in post-war domestic manuals'.[6]

Yet women began to question those ideals, banding together and utilizing their bodies in ways that transcended the grand expectation of motherhood, taking to public spaces and demonstrating their self-ownership and jurisdiction over corporeal, political and economic matters. I do not mean solely the waves of protests during the 1960s, although these manifestations deserve far more attention than I devote here. Instead, this chapter considers food as the way in which women challenged the norms that long contained them to the private realm, upending such traditional values by using the same products that they once bought to fill their families' bellies and uphold their reputation. And the subject of this chapter is not just any woman: Where does Italian superstar Sophia Loren fit into this narrative?

Today Sophia Loren is unanimously considered a star, but that was not always so. This chapter investigates precisely Loren's struggles to achieve stardom amid such radical socio-economic and cultural transformations such as those that occurred in post-war Italy. Working within a capitalistic, man-made star system, and facing harsh scrutiny for her early relations with producer Carlo Ponti, Loren had to fight to become an icon recognizable among all Italians. Loren's ascendance to stardom is, curiously, peppered with food. As food is purchased and prepared predominately by women, the use of food in Loren's cinema is certainly a poignant way to document the trajectory of women in the 1960s and the 1970s, as they fought against Catholic, heteropatriarchal norms and legislation for equal rights. Loren's public demonstrations of cooking and eating spoke volumes to the millions of women across the peninsula who had been long confined to private spaces, but who were becoming increasingly aware of their changing status. The interaction between food consumption, production and reproduction across Italy, as embodied by Loren between 1954 and 1971, the years of Italy's Economic Miracle, intersect significantly with the battle for gender equality. Close readings of Vittorio De Sica's *L'oro di Napoli* (The Gold of Naples, 1954) and *Ieri, oggi, domani* (Yesterday, Today, and Tomorrow, 1963), as well as Loren's own cookbooks, suggest that Loren's path to stardom reflects the stakes of ordinary Italian women, both inside and out of the kitchen, in a transitional period of their history.

Much like those of 1960s housewives, Sophia Loren's choices were, too, largely controlled by men: not only inspirational male figures in Loren's life, but also the men who wrote the laws that regulated Catholic Italian society. When one contemplates Loren's career, three men immediately come to mind: director Vittorio De Sica, her mentor of nearly twenty years; producer Carlo Ponti, her long-time husband and agent; and actor Marcello Mastroianni, a very frequent co-star. These three men were instrumental in moulding and bolstering Loren towards lasting, global stardom, but in accepting their guidance, Loren was implicitly subscribing to a male-dominated star system, as these men determined her roles and reputation on- and off-screen, based on specific social criteria. As a working woman whose body was becoming increasingly commercialized,

Loren was expected to meet the demands of four cultural networks that were the basis of Italy's patriarchy in the post-war years.[7] Italy's Catholic subculture was deeply entrenched in society, as was widespread attachment to the church and religious hierarchy. Boasting the largest communist party outside of the Soviet Union, Italy's Left was equally strong, upholding the values of the working class, while scorning the oncoming waves of American popular culture. Yet despite the general economic growth of the country, urban poverty was still pervasive in the underbellies of Rome and Naples, two cities that defined Loren's upbringing. Satisfying all four subcultures that defined post-war Italian culture proved a challenge for Loren, but thanks to her cinematic collaborations with De Sica, Ponti and Mastroianni, she demonstrated that she was more than just a 'mobile of miscellaneous fruits and melons'.[8] Through various food tropes within the texts that I will now analyse, by combining the pleasures of her body with the conviction and strength of her characters, Loren fought the criticisms of these different subcultures, all the while championing women hidden from the limelight, who too were striving to find their niche and define their identity within patriarchy.

Loren's career began to blossom in 1954, following the production of *L'oro di Napoli*: the first of her eight collaborations with De Sica. In this collection of six vignettes, adapted from Giuseppe Marotta's novel of the same name, De Sica had intended to paint a pre-war portrait of Naples: a beautiful and primitive world, still untouched by the overbearing influence of America and the rapid new Western industrialization. Indeed, over the course of *L'oro di Napoli*, audiences encounter some of the quintessential stereotypes of the Italian south: a family subservient to a local Mafia boss; a hopeless gambler; a prostitute whose life turns to shambles; and an earthy, sexy *pizzaiola* (pizza-woman). With 'his third eye, which was trained to discover the actor behind the appearances',[9] De Sica extracted Loren's autochthon, unearthing and projecting her Neapolitan roots to the world at large as his explosive, blowsy pizza girl. Loren related to A. E. Hotchner, '[De Sica] said I had a quality of spontaneity, an outgoing impulsiveness, typically Neapolitan, that he wanted to capture in this part [. . . .] It was a part made to order for me: an explosive, earthy Neapolitan woman, a type I knew so well; she was even called Sofia.'[10] In this role, Loren accrued the first of her fan-base: those living in the poor, urban south who immediately recognized De Sica's Naples, weary of the cultural marks left behind by the American GIs. She did so, naturally, with an Italian product as iconic as she was: pizza.

Pizza perfectly embodies Neapolitan culture. In a book dedicated entirely to this dish, food historian Carol Helstosky claims that pizza started as a street food consumed largely by the poor of Naples, eaten on weekdays (so as to save for a more lavish meal on Sundays) and paid on credit.[11] It makes sense, then, that De Sica's vignette, appropriately titled 'Pizze a credito' (Pizza on Credit), was shot mostly on a street, centred around the small, makeshift pizza stand managed by Rosario and Sofia, husband and wife. The episode is centred most specifically around Sofia, her body portrayed as more mouth-watering than her pizzas, and shapelier than the dough. The viewer is immediately mesmerized by her presence; through a series of long shots, we meet the tall, buxom woman, dressed in white, whose appearance commands the attention of her fellow street urchins. Despite Sofia and Rosario's egregious shouts of 'Come have a snack!' and 'Eat today and pay within eight days!', it soon becomes apparent that their clientele flocks to the stand not for the pizza, but rather to get a glimpse of Sofia. As she pummels and kneads more dough, her customers stand on the street and consume not only the fresh pizza, but also her voluptuous body; viewers, watching from within the male gaze,[12] eroticize both the pizza and the *pizzaiola*. When Rosario yells at her to cover up, we are reminded that Sofia's curves match the suppleness of the dough she shapes into pizzas, and she embodies the fertility of the yeasty dough with which she works. Loren's star power is strongly rooted in her body: hearty and rounded, like the iconic pizza. But her allure is also carnal and scandalous, as this episode underlines.

While De Sica chose to shoot most of the vignette outdoors, the scenes that take place indoors are far more revealing. The vignette begins not at the family pizza stand, nor at church as Sofia has her husband believe, but at Sofia's lover's house. Sofia is having an extra-marital affair, thereby living against the Catholic values long entrenched in Neapolitan society. Worse yet, she lies to her husband not only about her whereabouts but also about her ring, which she claims she accidentally misplaced in the dough. While intended to be a simple alibi, this scenario bears deep consequences. The pizza becomes the culprit; the quintessential Neapolitan snack becomes a sign of betrayal not only of Rosario but also of the city's values. The metaphor of the dough is expanded and further sexualized, suggesting the use of Sofia's hands on both her dough and her lover, as the emblem of her marriage gets lost, even forgotten, in the amorphous, sticky substance. And if we look back on Loren's budding career in the 1950s, we must remember her own scandalous, illegal romance with Carlo Ponti, producer of *L'oro di Napoli,* which subjected her to years of chastisement by the Vatican and by conservatives, men and women alike, across the country.

Ponti and Loren first met in 1950, when Loren was a contestant in a beauty pageant; Ponti was one of the jurors. What began as a platonic, even fatherly, relationship soon escalated into a secret, illicit romance, as Ponti was married to someone else. At the time of their affair, divorce was still illegal in Italy, but Ponti's lawyers found a loophole: a proxy marriage in Mexico, unbeknownst to Loren and Ponti. One morning in 1957, while enjoying breakfast together in Washington, DC, they were shocked to discover – in the newspaper, of all places – that they were married. While everything appeared to be in order for the supposed newlyweds, in Italy, both legal and social troubles ensued. The media had come to portray Loren as much of an unfaithful home-wrecker as the *pizzaiola* of three years prior: a stark contrast from the universally adored star we know today. Indeed, in the months that immediately followed their proxy marriage, conservatives attacked the budding starlet; among women in particular, Loren 'became the concubine and the home-breaker, the siren who had stolen a man from the breast of his family without regard for morality or the sentiments of others'[13] while Ponti, 'the stolen man', had faced more lenient criticism. From a wider perspective, the church condemned Loren much more seriously. Cultural historian Stephen Gundle notes: 'Sophia was not a practicing Catholic but, as she later said, "emotionally Catholicism was my heritage and ex-communication was a chilling threat" [23]'.[14] Despite obstacles and attacks that the couple had to endure, Loren and Ponti's marriage lasted a remarkable five decades; yet, Loren's reputation was tarnished by her off-screen choices, and her career wavered under the critical eyes of the church and its millions of congregants. She was not the traditionally chaste, virtuous wife, nor was she a mother: two aspects for which Italy's conservatives long chastised Loren the woman, but guided the actress in the many roles that followed – *Ieri, oggi, domani* among them.

Despite widespread criticism that the film is exceedingly saccharine,[15] *Ieri, oggi, domani* remains a cornerstone of Italy's comedic cinema, as well as of Loren's career. The film, composed of three vignettes based in Naples, Milan and Rome, respectively, illustrates a fundamental transition in Italian history: the disentanglement of Italian society from fascism, against a backdrop of secularization and economic revitalization, while progressing towards women's emancipation. Loren, as the star of all three chapters, is at the helm of this fictionalized work, embodying the collective spirit of Italian women on and beyond the screen: mothers, wives and economically independent free-thinkers alike.

The film begins in Naples, the *ieri* (yesterday) of the film, where we are immediately thrown not only into the black market but also into a world dominated by sex, food and procreation: fertility abounds. The premise of the film is as follows: there is a warrant out for Adelina's (Loren) arrest for selling black-market cigarettes. The announcement of her pregnancy, however, puts her punishment on hold. Come December, when she gives birth to her child, she almost immediately gets pregnant again. This cycle continues, and Adelina and her husband, Carmine (Mastroianni), ultimately welcome seven children into the world. When they fail to have an eighth child, Adelina is sent to jail, but she is soon released and happily reunited with her family.

The vignette speaks to the interference of civic offices in women's most private, intimate moments: the conception and gestation of a baby. In this episode, a woman's pregnancies are not only for public exhibition but also historicized. While Loren and Mastroianni dominate the screen, one could make the argument that history is in fact the greatest protagonist in this first vignette. The idea of bearing seven children – to avoid a prison sentence, no less – is the source of comedy in this vignette. This sort of behaviour, however, would have won the family prizes and great acclaim under Benito Mussolini's rule. How, then, do the government's once-fervent encouragements of fertility change – or not – in the 1960s? And how does Adelina take advantage of such a system to remain a 'free'[16] woman? To best explain the conditions that women fought to overcome in later decades, and to highlight the progress of women in the post-war period, it is important to refer to fascism, both in terms of economics and gender politics.

We can begin this discussion with the setting and mise en scene. This vignette takes place in Naples, a city of the south long criticized for its picturesque backwardness. However, it must be noted that, with the invasion of the Allies in 1943 and the requisition of foodstuffs by the Nazis, Naples quickly became the central hub of Italy's black-market economy, developed in strong collaboration with American GIs.[17] The black market is, of course, an economy of crime built in response to fascist autarky, but one that was hardly curbed. Contraband goods filled the homes of all Italians, but predominantly of Neapolitans. We see this plenitude in Adelina and Carmine's neighbourhood and apartment. De Sica fills these spaces with not only heaping amounts of colourful produce – watermelon rinds in a bowl, green grapes at dinner and a tumbling mountain of oranges – but also symbols of Americana – Lipton tea, canned chicken and, of course, the ubiquitous red and white of Coca-Cola. These choices have prompted critics to suggest that De Sica was viewing the 1950s with thick, rose-tinted glasses; film scholar Stephen Snyder writes: 'It is as though a large screen painting of overflowing fruit bowls has been placed in front of *Umberto D.*,[18] rendering the world of that film effectively invisible.'[19] While the fresh fruit is indeed a stark contrast from, say, the burning of ants in Umberto D.'s kitchen, I argue that these objects signify something more poignant: the promise and abundance of the boom, and the tumultuous birth of modern, mechanized, even Americanized Italy in the aftermath of fascism.

In connection with fruit, we may also begin to unpack the questions of fertility and virility: the heart of gender politics under fascism. Without a doubt, the germination of seeds is analogous to Adelina's booming family. The nut vendor outside Adelina's home even likens her 'get out of jail free' gestational periods to the seasons of commercialized produce:

He still tries to read; he's finally able to do so.

> **PASQUALE**: . . . *Sra, sga . . . sgravata . . . Ah, sgravata!*[20] October 20th, I was selling prickly pears . . .

He stops reading and counts on his fingers.

> **PASQUALE**: Six months of lactation: November, December, January, February, March, April . . . April, May, when the first cherries blossom, her immunity expires.
>
> **CARMINE** (*sure of himself*): Well, we're in January. There's still time . . .[21]

De Sica validates Pasquale's analogy in the following shot, by focusing his camera on the bright cherries of May. Pasquale is selling cherries to the passers-by, when it is announced that the police are camped outside Adelina's home, waiting to arrest her:

We follow Elvira, who reaches her husband's stand.

> **ELVIRA** (*excited*): The cops have arrived into lower 'Mellino. Carmine is alone, Adelina's not there. But the cops have said that they're waiting for her, that they're not leaving.
>
> **PASQUALE**: The devil with them! But look at the cherries . . .[22]

Nevertheless, Adelina dupes the officers once more, presenting them with yet another certificate of pregnancy. When asked how many more children she could possibly want, she responds matter-of-factly: 'As many that I can hang on to.'[23] Adelina's defiance of the law, and of the patriarchy represented by the police, is testament to the 'unruly woman' – an icon by which the protestors of the late 1960s strongly abided. Through consumption choices, women found a space and inspiration to fight for emancipation, and thus, it is only logical for Loren/Adelina to exude the qualities of the unruly woman by way of fruit: bearing fruit to fight the patriarchal law.

What exactly does it mean to be an unruly woman? Coined by Kathleen Rowe in her book, *The Unruly Woman: Gender and the Genres of Laughter* (1995), the unruly woman is 'a woman who disrupts the norms of femininity and social hierarchy of male over female through outrageousness and excess'.[24] Thriving on the power of her femininity, the unruly woman embarks on a life of independence, rebelling against traditional, oppressive gender structures. Instead of being tamed and subsumed into the greater patriarchy, the unruly woman resorts to body performance to achieve her goals, thereby fending off the *inetto*: the impotent, inept male. In her book *Beyond the Latin Lover: Marcello Mastroianni, Masculinity, and Italian Cinema* (2004), film scholar Jacqueline Reich unpacks this dynamic with respect to Mastroianni, the cinematic *inetto* par excellence, and Loren, his 'unruly' co-star. Reich writes:

> She [the unruly woman] consciously uses her body through masquerade and performance to get what she wants: independence from familial structures, a career, or freedom from the norms of femininity. The tools she employs are either speech, as a way of taking control of the narrative, or her body, through which she parades her desire in a controlled spectacle of feminine masquerade.[25]

Adelina's constantly pregnant belly, quite literally paraded around Naples, is a sign of the unruly woman in action. Adelina does not become a mother to assume the traditional tasks of wet nursing and childrearing; instead, Adelina utilizes maternity to defy the police (itself a signpost of the heteropatriarchy) and evade her prison sentence. The 'outrageousness and excess' to which Rowe refers are Adelina's six pregnancies of incredibly quick succession. Further inverting the traditional notion of 'father works, mother rears the children', it is Adelina who goes to work each day and Carmine who takes care of their several children; the unruly woman breaks into the public domain, long occupied by men alone, as the *inetto* retreats into the private sphere, once predominantly a woman's space.

The idea of the *inetto* also underlines sexual potency, or, rather, a lack thereof. Referencing the fieldwork of David Gilmore, Reich noted that the phallus is the most determinant sign of manhood; to 'be a good man' is to procreate. The *inetto* fails at this singular, yet fundamentally important, task – as we see in *Ieri, oggi, domani*. An exhausted Carmine drops a box of oranges on the street and ultimately is unable to sustain his family's growth. When Adelina fails to conceive an eighth child, not only does her cigarette enterprise come to a screeching halt with her imprisonment but we also question Carmine's manhood. The viewer is led to believe that, thanks to the impotency of the *inetto,* Adelina is imprisoned. Since

Adelina is arrested by the police (the 'Man') because of a man's shortcomings, one could even read this as a metaphor for women's subordination in general, which faced great challenges and resistance in this period. This said, despite Loren's increasing star prowess, combined with women's voluminous, vociferous protests against patriarchal laws, Loren received universal praise only when she became a mother herself.[26] After repeated miscarriages, Loren landed the new, long-coveted role of 'mother' in 1968. This dual struggle towards universally recognized stardom and motherhood will now be unpacked by way of Loren's first cookbook.

A critically acclaimed master of cinema, winner of numerous awards, recognizable star across the oceans and sultry pin-up, but until December 1968, 'mother' seemed but another fictional role. In her memoir, Loren lamented the two miscarriages she had suffered: 'I felt gutted. It was as if the world had been turned off forever. I tried, but I could see nothing ahead of me, nothing that could console me [. . . .] My life as a star was nothing compared to the happiness of the new mothers I'd glimpsed at the clinic, getting ready to breast-feed their new-born babies.'[27] For years, Loren had felt this void, and this struggle could be read as the missing component to Loren's universal acclaim. To win the hearts of all Italians – including and especially the Catholic conservatives who for decades had scorned Loren's illicit sexuality – Loren had to retreat, temporarily, from acting, and focus instead on becoming a mother. Through this sabbatical, Loren embraced cooking.

Once she had become pregnant for a third time, under the authoritative watch of Dr Hubert de Watteville, Loren took leave of Cinecittà and moved to Geneva, to be near her obstetrician and wait patiently to deliver her child. To curb her anxiety and distract herself, Loren started cooking. With Ines, her secretary, Loren recreated recipes both from her childhood and her recent travels around the world, all the while taking copious and meticulous notes on her experience. This compilation was published three years later: *In cucina con amore* [In the Kitchen with Love] (1971), Loren's first cookbook.[28]

At first glance, *In cucina con amore* is a typical cookbook of the 1970s. The table of contents outlines recipes for festive appetizers, soups, meat-based and seafood-based dishes, desserts and side dishes. Loren writes with the matriarch in mind, addressing women who are responsible for organizing parties and seeing to their guests' dietary needs, as she suggests recipes for *piatti sfiziosi* (hors d'oeuvres) such as eggplant-and-mayonnaise crostini, bruschetta and tuna meatballs.[29] These women are also expected to be at the service of their families, as Loren recommends preparing the mainstays of Italian gastronomy.

She suggests ways to enjoy pizzas in the comfort of one's home, and she also lists 'the eight commandments for preparing pasta', where Loren insists that one can determine that pasta is done only through taste, and she emphasizes the importance of adding a teaspoon of olive oil to the water before straining.[30] But, between the lines of her cookbook, lie two important takeaways. One is Loren's tone: extremely approachable, inviting novice and experienced cooks alike to embrace, above all, a love of food and conviviality. At the end of her preface, Loren writes: 'There's nothing left but for me to wish you well and advise you to pay the most attention, because I want you to have great success with my recipes. It's also a question of pride. I beg you, don't make me look bad. In opening this book, may you be welcome in my kitchen. Eat with me.'[31] As we gather from this preface, where she hopes in earnest for her readers' success in the kitchen and implores them to not embarrass her (as a mother asks of her children before any outing), this cookbook is the means by which Loren prepared for her biggest role yet. Indeed, more than any of her films, the cookbook holds tremendous weight, as it signifies the success of her pregnancy with Carlo Junior; it was cooking that carried Loren along to her long-awaited due date, and, even today, the cookbook stands as Loren's personal reminder of those days of expectancy.[32] But more generally, this cookbook achieves much more, both for Loren and for women overall. Throughout her cookbook, Loren not only underlines the sense of warmth, homeliness and nostalgia that the soon-to-be mother sought to embody but, as she commands her readers to 'eat with me', also expresses a conviviality that welcomes women to eating and the social pleasures of mealtimes. Encouraging women to actually enjoy the meals they have created is an unorthodox, yet deeply progressive, message for a cookbook to relay, at the time.

The cookbook's messages are amplified within the national arena. On one hand, only through Loren's miscarriages and relentless pursuit of motherhood did she win the favour of the church and of Italy's Catholics: the last cultural network to embrace Loren as a true icon. As Gundle comments, '[b]y spectacularising her struggle to become a mother, Sophia rendered herself more human and acceptable even to those who had long viewed her with distaste. As the large circulation Catholic weekly *Famiglia Cristiana* (Christian Family) acknowledged in 1967, "The misfortunes of Loren render her more human and bring her nearer to us. They make her poorer than she appears, simpler and therefore more worthy of compassion" [33].'[33] Loren's cookbook, an exposé of her very public struggles with pregnancy, transformed Loren from a godlike diva to a human star. Loren's acting credentials were, apparently, not enough, and she became at last iconic among all Italians once she became a mother, the traditional signpost of womanhood. Thus it seems that by satisfying the ultimate expectation of motherhood, and, in turn, the provision of food for her children and for readers worldwide, Loren remains inscribed in the patriarchy. Loren's remarks in *Women & Beauty* (1984), her manual on health and beauty regimens, only further such a problematic stance: 'When I became pregnant, my concern for my career evaporated. Nothing mattered to me but my baby. If necessary, I would have given up my work to have a child. If this means I am not modern, then I am not modern.'[34] Do Loren's steps to superstardom underline a regression, an immutable subscription to the patriarchy? Not necessarily.

While the cookbook signifies her paradoxical triumphs in motherhood and in placating steadfast conservatives, this text is Loren's commentary on the continuous struggle for emancipation for millions of women: the fight to cook and to be a mother by choice only, and to control their own bodies and lives. In the introduction to her book, Loren acknowledges that Italy's social arena has changed greatly, that 'equality between the sexes, even in the kitchen, has almost been reached'.[35] But, later in the cookbook, Loren takes a profound stab at her remaining conservative naysayers, most – if not all – of whom are male. In a digression titled 'I mariti ai fornelli' (Husbands at the Stove), Loren suggests that if men are so appalled at the idea of cooking for their wives and families, perhaps they could learn a thing or two from her recipes: 'Rather, it is them, with their inadequate ideas on the evolution of society, that would need this "culinary therapy", let's call it, the most.'[36] After decades of harsh scrutiny, Loren takes to her cookbook to suggest that these men could learn something from her, a 'poor, simple woman'. Thus, while Loren may, in her own pregnancy, accept this antiquated view of society, she does acknowledge the wide-scale oppression of women, utilizing the subjunctive mood to express her hope that women today choose cooking out of love, not by force: 'Anyway, since it is natural that most of my readers are women, to them I say: *may you like* cooking, and that *it is not* a bothersome routine.'[37]

After more than six decades in the public eye, Sophia Loren continues to shine: brilliant, dynamic and regal. Indeed, Loren has assumed countless roles, conjuring to life – by way of food tropes – some of the most beautiful characters to ever grace the screen, recognizable among several generations and across a web of cultural networks: Italy's south, an Americanized youth and, of late, Catholic conservatives. Her path to such iconicity, however, is a response to containment: not only Cold War containment but also the increasingly obsolete ideals of womanhood and housewifery in this period, in that women contest their binds to the kitchen. Food was the tool of choice to challenge such norms, and what allows Loren to carve a space into the heteropatriarchy in which her stardom could blossom, unchecked, and where she may be a working mother of two.

In that position of 'working mother', Loren demonstrates that motherhood is far from the sole determinant of a woman, echoing the protests of her fellow 'unruly' women outside the theatre. Squashing the backlash, Italy's foremost icon expressed the fundamental notion of a woman's choice. Loren's work puts forth a vision that promotes independence from the multidimensional governance of men, where women are to actively fight for their beliefs, to get married, to give birth and, certainly, to enter the kitchen to cook an enjoyable meal, only if they want to. This does remain a vision: I must acknowledge that the systems within which Loren functions and perpetuates her fame are ones that continue to be dominated by men. Nevertheless, these food tropes remain powerful images along the winding path to universal emancipation.

9

Women's eccentric and nomadic cooking in Fabrizia Ramondino's *Althénopis*

When food tastes good and subversive

Rossella Di Rosa

In the last two decades, Fabrizia Ramondino's debut novel *Althénopis* (1981) has received much attention by critics and scholars both inside and outside Italy.[1] This novel, like many other works by Ramondino, revolves around the female characters' sense of exclusion from society, the mother–daughter relationship, the complexity of the coming of age process and the protagonists' experience of Naples.[2] However, *Althénopis* also contains conspicuous references to food, which I aim to investigate in this chapter.

Cooking and recipes, as well as manners and rules that regulate food consumption and its preparation in the kitchen, reveal the author's original critique of the social and cultural constrictions of patriarchy. In this chapter, I propose a re-reading of *Althénopis* through the food present within the work, in order to draw new conclusions about the novel's historical setting, the characters' social class and their family relationships. I will argue that the protagonists of the novel, specifically the anonymous grandmother and granddaughter (who is also the narrator in the novel), are endowed with what Annie Hauck-Lawson and Jonathan Deutsch call a 'food voice', that is to say a particular language system that expresses meaning through food.[3] Indeed, food, as many anthropologists, sociologists and semiologists have proven, functions as a language, with structures and codes that are as complex as verbal ones. But perhaps, unlike many verbal languages, it has the ability to convey messages that sometimes go beyond what words can say.[4] Roland Barthes, for instance, in *Toward a Psychosociology of Contemporary Food Consumption* (1961), describes food as 'a system of communication, a body of images, a protocol of usages, situations and behaviour'; and more specifically as a 'sign' that communicates different meanings.[5] Food conveys not only dietary preferences or habits but also class differences, religious restrictions, power relationships, desires, hopes and ambitions, which are not strictly nor necessarily related to the edible sphere.[6]

Hence, I contend that through their food voices – that is, the nexus between the food they cook, consume, avoid and no longer eat – the grandmother of *Althénopis* and her favourite granddaughter describe what Barthes calls the 'social environment' in which they live.[7] At the same time, I will also argue that the characters' food voices reveal their nomadic identities and their material conception of reality. Specifically, I propose that the grandmother as well as her granddaughter epitomize the nomadic consciousness theorized by Rosi Braidotti in *Nomadic Subjects* (1994). Braidotti refers to the image of the nomad – a person who always lives in transition and outside the normative apparatus of the state – that 'resists settling into socially coded modes of thought and behaviour'.[8] According to Braidotti, the nomadic state has 'the potential for positive renaming, for opening new possibilities of life and thought'.[9] This is exactly what the grandmother and her granddaughter accomplish in the novel.

Recently, scholars have identified several features that are distinctive of a nomadic consciousness both in Ramondino's biography and in her characters' existences, often the former's alter egos. For instance, Monica Farnetti and Franco Sepe have underlined how Ramondino's erratic existence during her childhood, and her ability to speak different languages crucially affected her ideas of 'homeland' and 'mother tongue'.[10] Stefania Lucamante emphasizes that the young protagonist of *Althénopis* experiences a form of 'displacement' that does not entirely possess negative valences, but allows her to experience and know the world.[11] Similarly, Adalgisa Giorgio considers the young protagonist of *Althénopis* 'a woman in exile from herself and from the maternal'.[12] Moreover Giorgio, who has been a trailblazer in interpreting Ramondino's works in light of Braidotti's nomadism, illustrates how in several of her novels, Ramondino challenges the idea of a fixed place, a steady identity and a monolithic language, while instead privileging movements, blurred borders and precarious subjects in search of their own selves.

Although according to Giorgio the novel *In viaggio* (Travelling, 1995) is where Ramondino configures the prototype of the nomad, it can be argued that in the earlier *Althénopis* also the author sketches the main characters' nomadic posture for a number of reasons.[13] To begin with, even though they are part of a community, the grandmother and granddaughter live at the margins of society and of the family, often outside the laws of the patriarchal order and almost without maternal guidance. Similarly, they are somewhat immune to the normative power of common institutions. The grandmother, for example, follows her intimate form of religiosity that does not conform with the dictates of the Catholic Church. Furthermore, the female protagonists challenge the accepted codes of class structure. Indeed, on many occasions, Ramondino shows the characters directly confront the system of values of the bourgeoisie, the class they belong to. Lastly, in *Althénopis*, Ramondino fully shares Braidotti's project of looking for a different and more inclusive form of thought to counteract the fundamental dichotomies and exclusive binaries of Western philosophy. The character of the grandmother in particular, as I will discuss later, challenges the supremacy of reason, elaborating a thought that does not focus exclusively on rationality, but that creatively combines medicine and gastronomy.

Indeed, it can be argued that the grandmother significantly exemplifies Braidotti's figuration of the nomadic subject, and it is crucial that her responses to the patriarchal hierarchies, to the masculine *logos* and to fixed social codes of the bourgeoisie are expressed through food. Similarly, the granddaughter displays several features that are typically distinctive of nomadic subjectivities. For instance, her tactile experience of preparing some food, particularly vegetables, allows her to feel the produce's materiality and to discover the traces that minerals, starches and other nutrients – especially contained in aubergines and potatoes – leave on her hands. She realizes that food is not made of inert matter and that it interacts with its surroundings, including her own body. Such experience triggers numerous associations with and discoveries about the materiality of the food she cooks and of her own body, but most of all the realization that these are interconnected and ultimately inseparable from one another. In other words, she perceives her own body in a nomadic way, as a 'surface of intensities and an affective field in interaction with others'.[14]

Furthermore, the granddaughter's experience conforms in general terms to the thesis expounded by Stacy Alaimo's *Bodily Nature* (2010), according to which human bodies are not fixed entities and closed systems, but rather should be seen through the perspective of 'trans-corporeality', that is to say as intermeshed with both environment and non-human matters, including food.[15] Indeed, Alaimo argues, food is 'the most palpable trans-corporeal substance': eating food implies that 'peculiar material agencies [. . .] reveal themselves during the route from dirt to mouth' and inevitably affects and transforms the eating subject.[16] This principle, which represents one of the tenets of food studies, remains an unduly overlooked aspect of Ramondino's *Althénopis*.

From the very start of the novel, food plays an essential role, reflecting what Gian-Paolo Biasin in *Flavors of Modernity* defines as its 'narrative function':

in this case, it introduces the characters on the scene of the narration.[17] The grandmother's first appearance is specifically linked to a place, a room in her house, located in a remote village of the Campania region, called Santa Maria del Mare, where the granddaughter (first alone and then with her whole family) takes refuge from the bombings during the Second World War.[18] Significantly, she is portrayed both socially and psychologically through the dishes she prepares and consumes or cooks for others.

The grandmother is a meek, middle-aged widow, who lives a simple and retired life regulated by daily prayers and chores. Her religiosity emerges in different occasions, and the narrator also emphasizes her lineage, mentioning that she had a sister who joined the Poor Clares religious order and that her family descended directly from Saint Clare. It is her nutrition, more than her prayers, that reveals her mystical inclination. She prefers to cook frugal meals for herself based primarily on *pancotto*, a simple soup traditionally made 'with stale bread, cooked in water or broth, seasoned with herbs and garlic, and enriched with olive oil'.[19] This dish, a cornerstone of farmers' diets in several regions of Italy, is one of the most emblematic examples of peasant cooking and culture, which never wastes the ingredients available in the kitchen, but rather transforms them into tasteful dishes.

For several reasons, the *pancotto* appears as the exclusive repast of the grandmother's diet. First, she considers it an ideal food to eat during the war, since bread is nutritious, inexpensive and made with a large variety of grains, which were available even in the period of penury and destitution characteristic of the Second World War. Second, and most significant for this discussion, she refuses to eat the delicious dishes that she cooks for her grandchildren. The grandmother's primary rationale behind abstaining from these dishes is based on her desire not to deprive her grandchildren of a greater quantity of food and her preference to let them have her own portion as well. Although her choice to eat very little and very poorly herself in order to feed her grandchildren seems to fall in line with the patriarchal idea of self-sacrifice that women of her generation were expected to embrace, what emerges from the novel is quite the opposite. Her decision to eat only her *pancotto* as a natural remedy for her stomach problems and, above all, as a purifying food may recall a specific behaviour typical of the anorectic subject. As Susie Orbach has illustrated, the anorectic's choice of refusing food and the need of purging the body can express not only a way to 'symbolically cleanse herself' but also the 'relief of being in control' of others, who have shaped her and tried to 'fit herself in their projections'.[20] Like the anorectic, the grandma's refusal to eat can reveal an attempt to resist normative attitudes, behaviours and thoughts, a challenge to patriarchal culture and a protest against her daughters, especially the granddaughter's mother, who have marginalized and divested her from the power she originally enjoyed in the house.[21]

Furthermore, the old lady's state of isolation and her nutritional habits remind us of some women saints and the diet they used to follow, as those described by Cristina Mazzoni in her essay on the relationship between female sainthood, food and writing.[22] Mazzoni claims that such saints were able to establish, through the food they ate – and especially with the bread they consumed every day – a 'bond between the earthly and the heavenly spheres, between corporeality and spirituality'.[23] It can be claimed that such union between body and soul is what the grandmother achieves through her *pancotto*, whose spiritual quality is acknowledged by her favourite granddaughter. In her narrator's voice, she describes her grandmother's *pancotto* as a 'miracle'[24] both for its taste, despite its plain and inexpensive ingredients, and for the surprising outcome of the recipe, where bread is no longer bread and water has been transformed into broth.

The holy aura that surrounds the grandma acquires dramatic importance in light of the 'sacrifices' she makes in her diet in order to save precious ingredients and cook something tasty for others, especially for the little granddaughter. During the war, parsimony ruled the family's pockets and the house budget in general, including the kitchen. Hence, the grandmother's efforts to procure some extra sugar to prepare a dessert for her granddaughter become key moments associated with food in the narrative: the ingenious woman gives up the daily sweetening of her coffee in order to save enough sugar to prepare for the young girl a sort of custard 'just for me, from a drop of tinned milk and thirty grams of sugar spared from her coffee in those days of wartime and scarcity'.[25] What the grandmother does not eat is therefore as revealing as what she does eat, since what she refuses to consume attests to the exclusive and exceptional nature of her relationship with her granddaughter.

The young girl sees her grandma as a holy and mythical figure as well as a mysterious woman capable of achieving extraordinary, sometimes even magical, results. The kitchen, where the woman spends the majority of her time preparing scrumptious dishes, appears to her like an enchanted place, *un antro fiabesco* (a fairy-tale cave),[26] where the rest of the family cannot enter as it would leave them disgusted due to what they see as the grandmother's unreasonable way of cooking, with its waste of food, money and energy. Similarly, the food the grandmother assembles in the kitchen possesses wonderful and alluring qualities as claimed by the granddaughter and her siblings who, unlike the adults, are allowed to taste such foods and are admitted into the magical reign.

More interestingly, the grandmother is able to show her nomadic attitude in the kitchen. In assembling the ingredients in different ways, she finds alternative recipes to the traditional dishes suggested by her daughter and provides her grandchildren with new and creative dietary choices in spite of food's short supply. For example, she uses chestnuts, which due to their inexpensive and bountiful presence throughout the war are always present at her table, to obtain a flour that she can use instead of wheat flour. These nuts become delicious and scented desserts, much like the *castagnaccio*, a chestnut flour cake that the grandma prepared as a welcome gift for her granddaughter when she arrived for the first time in Santa Maria del Mare.

Another special ingredient that appears in the novel is 'the white bread got from the Americans'[27] that arrived in Naples, and the rest of the peninsula, with the American troops that liberated Italy. This special white bread, usually given by the soldiers to the children and families that helped them, existed during and right after the war also in its Italian variety, but as Karima Moyer-Nocchi has noted, only rich people could afford its overinflated price.[28] By contrast, the Italian government implemented a fixed rationing at two hundred grams per day per family of wheat bread known as 'pane unico' ('common bread').[29] Hence, white bread became special for ordinary Italians, and the American variety is perceived by the children of *Althénopis* as an exotic food that breaks up their dietary routine. Their grandmother never serves the American white bread simply as it is, but she fries it and sprinkles it with a thin layer of sugar and cinnamon, one of the most fragrant and exotic imported spices that she received as a gift from the village priest, who in turn obtains it from the Americans. Her cooking methods not only crucially enrich the taste of the bread but also reveal one of her peculiar, and nomadic, culinary preferences, namely, transforming the primary ingredients of the recipes she serves in a creative fashion, with the exception of some fresh herbs used in salads. The granddaughter's depiction of her grandmother, described in one of her moments of culinary creativity, is emblematic:

> When this urge came over Grandmother and she came out of the kitchen in her great white apron, my mother would make a dash to stop her, and not succeeding, would then try to contain the impetus in the kitchen. Grandmother went straight ahead with whatever the urge prompted, all sweaty and stained from the rising smoke and oil, red in the face, her sleeves rolled up, having a go at washing the pans in soda to avoid clashing headlong with Mother and the grumbling maid.[30]

The granddaughter refers to the passion that her grandma employs in her cooking as *estro* (urge), a term that refers both to artistic inspiration and to eccentricity or whim.[31] By contrast, her culinary creativity is perceived as mere oddness by her daughters who cannot tolerate it in a woman of her age, especially in those dramatic years of war. However, neither the family's prohibition nor the war can prevent the grandmother's 'oddities' (*stramberie*)[32] that occur in the kitchen.

Both the food that the grandmother prepares and her kitchen's organization provide crucial examples of her nomadic way of cooking. The layout of the grandma's kitchen, for example, differs significantly from a traditional one. She removes all utensils from the shelves and cupboards without respecting the original use of each tool, but inventing a new one for every meal she cooks. For instance, she prefers to use sewing scissors rather than kitchen ones for food preparation, and submerges pots and pans in baking soda to clean them, even though other detergents were popular and available in Italy at that time; this, of course, infuriates her daughters.

The grandmother works with food in an iconoclastic and revolutionary way, which 'had nothing to do with penny-pinching or modern rules of health and diet, but only with the imagination',[33] which the narrator's mother attributes to the grandmother's arteriosclerosis, responsible, in her opinion, for the old woman's bizarre cooking and for her apparent lack of rationality. The grandmother's way of cooking is 'eccentric' due to the creativity both in its preparation and presentation, and, in Teresa De Lauretis's words, for being at the periphery of the accepted bourgeois social norms that the family follows faithfully. She assumes, therefore, a position typical of the 'eccentric subject', an alternative form of subjectivity similar to that elaborated by Braidotti. According to De Lauretis, such eccentric perspective is 'a position attained through practices of political and personal displacement across boundaries between sociosexual identities and communities, between bodies and discourses'.[34] Hence, in the grandmother's hands, food becomes a crucial tool to debunk the moral and cultural codes of the Italian middle class during and in the immediate aftermath of the Second World War, as well as a powerful means to express her subjectivity.

A key way in which the grandmother challenges Italian mores of the time is by her refusal to pay special attention to the narrator's father as would be normally expected by virtue of his male gender, especially at the table. The few times the father shares a meal with the family, he is neither the first person to be served nor does he receive the most bountiful portion, as often happens in other families, especially the families of the granddaughter's friends. Only a few habits are adopted for the sake of the father's status when he dines with his family: kids are required to eat together with the adults in the living room, where the kids would normally sit only on rare and special occasions, and they are excluded from the kitchen. This means that they have to wait for their meal to be brought to the table in special trays, as in the case of the *sperlonga* (a big plate originally used to serve fish but also other meals), where food is elegantly placed but soon becomes cold and unappealing. By contrast, when the father is absent, the family does not gather in the living room for their meals, and the children sometimes do not even eat at the table. The grandmother allows them to eat in the kitchen, often while she is still cooking. She does not eat with them, but she chooses to leave the children to consume their food alone, while she concentrates on their needs and culinary desires.

Another way the grandmother challenges bourgeois codes and expectations is with her cooking: even when the father eats with the family, the grandmother often ignores the amount of daily proteins, the appropriate food portions and the equilibrium of carbohydrates and vitamins, thereby flouting both the guidelines that ensure healthy nutrition and her daughter's prohibitions about the children's diets. Moreover, the grandmother does not respect mealtimes and fixed budgets for grocery shopping, nor the quantities indicated in recipes. By doing so, she undermines the social manners followed by the family and, more significantly, she challenges the logic of the patriarchy, using food to express both her dissent against society and her feelings for the grandchildren.

A further example of the grandmother's intolerance of fixed norms and bans, and particularly of bourgeois table etiquette, is apparent when she gives her grandchildren permission to eat food with their hands. Such a habit, which the narrator's mother considers a repulsive practice detrimental to her children, is completely tolerated by the grandmother, and almost encouraged for certain foods, as in the case of French fries. Indeed, she is happy when the grandchildren burst into the kitchen and take the fries with their hands while they are still hot and crispy. Only by doing so, she argues, can they fully taste and appreciate the flavour, which would be completely lost if the children waited to eat the fries at the table with silverware. Furthermore, the eating-by-hand is sorely missed by the children when the young girl's family, including her grandmother, spend Easter at aunt Celeste's, one of the grandmother's sisters, all of them longing to come back to Santa Maria and eat without cutlery: 'we were able to stuff ourselves with custard, only regretting that we had to use fork and spoon, for our pleasure would have been multiplied had we been able to use hands and mouth and feel ourselves fuse with the sweet into a single substance.'[35] Eating the dessert with their hands not only would allow them to experience a contact between two different materialities, that is to say, between their kid bodies and the dessert, but it would also allow them to take part in a phenomenon of 'trans-corporeality', to perceive movement across different types of matter. Furthermore, their desire to eat dessert with their fingers can be read as an attempt to enact and prolong the osmosis between materialities, as though they are aware of the food's impending disappearance from their bodies.

Another instance where the experience of 'trans-corporeality' is evoked in the novel occurs when the granddaughter prepares some vegetables. The interaction between different matters leaves a tangible trace in the granddaughter's fingers, which turn blackish and wrinkled after peeling an aubergine. When she looks at her fingertips, she realizes that her 'adolescent integrity'[36] has been affected and that something has changed in her life. The granddaughter thus concludes that her body is not an impermeable container but made of porous matter. She feels her fingers pruning after contact with the vegetables, and she sees that her skin has absorbed, released and interacted with the produce's particles and nutrients. Such a discovery causes a significant shift in the way she perceives her subjectivity, which appears not as a 'final or finished product as in the case of the Cartesian automaton'[37] but as an unstable entity. The idea of a malleable identity, which Ramondino vividly describes in *Storie di Patio* (*Patio Stories*, 1983) with the image of an elastic and amorphous dough,[38] is created in *Althénopis* through a similar material image when the first-person narrator (the granddaughter) describes her own cooking:

> Even more I liked to fry aubergines and the courgettes, and my vague, wispy, never-ending lack of consistency seemed to condense and become substance, though formless still, in the heavy vapour of the frying oil; and when it spat and a scalding drop fell on my hands, arms, and neck, at last I seemed to have hands, arms and a neck.[39]

In these moments, when contact takes place between the materiality of her skin and that of the food, the narrator perceives and discovers her body as well as her future. The frying pan, indeed, becomes a sort of mirror where the young girl can prefigure herself as a woman and a mother, cooking for her own family. The kitchen, therefore, becomes for the granddaughter a warm place, not only for the heat of the stove but also for the warmth of relationships, affections and feelings that originate in this place, where secrets are revealed, and instincts disclosed. Moreover, the kitchen, which was once her grandmother's realm, becomes the granddaughter's safe place too, especially when she moves to her aunt Callista's house in Naples after the grandmother's death.[40]

The granddaughter discovers in aunt Callista's kitchen the same allure and fascination she experienced when she was a child in Santa Maria del Mare. When several years have passed and the war feels like a recently healed scar, the granddaughter works in the kitchen from early morning, even though she is not the little girl she used to be anymore. She helps her aunt's maids with cooking, assisting in their meal planning, participating in their conversation and often helping them to do the dishes:

> I liked to do the washing-up and dip my voluptuously busy hands into the water, greasy and slippery with soda. I liked feeling the grease melt, and in that grey malodorous water, I seemed to glimpse the turbid secrets of life. It was my way of interpreting the mystery of the resurrection of the dead, for in the vapours, the acrid smells, the sweat of the kitchen, I saw the semblance of Grandmother appear.[41]

Once again, the importance of tactile experience becomes clear for the granddaughter. The experience of touching the traces of filth that remain attached to the flatware and of feeling with her hands the oil and greasy particles dissolve in the water enables her to perceive the fluidity of life, its secrets, rhythms and cycles. The washing process, where the matter (the dirt) transforms from material to vaporous state, provides the granddaughter with a suitable metaphor for understanding the deterioration of bodily flesh caused by death. Also, she finds in the kitchen vapours, fumes and bitter odours a way to describe the phenomenon of the resurrection of the soul. Hence, in the kitchen, she undergoes both a material and a metaphysical experience, which inevitably brings to her memory her loving grandmother. The physical contact with the dirty dishes, and with the water and bicarbonate soda, in which the dishes have been submerged, becomes for the granddaughter an important way to cultivate the vital bond she shared with her grandmother during her childhood. The granddaughter also recognizes that it is thanks to her grandmother that she learned the importance of food, the difference between pleasure, taste, desire for food and the urgency of nutrition, as well as food's curative power.

The grandmother firmly believes that food plays a pivotal role in human beings' health and well-being. Indeed, the elderly woman frequently uses food in order to cure diseases, alleviate pains and remedy bodily infections. She employs different ingredients and herbs according to symptoms and ailments, such as sliced potatoes for wounds, lettuce leaves for bumps, fig milk for warts or vinegar for headaches. As the narrator explains, the other family members consider this practice a 'wicked art',[42] closer to superstition than to medicine.

However, when analysed in light of Braidotti's theory of the nomadic subject, the grandmother's medicinal use of food, ultimately, discloses a noteworthy alternative to mainstream medical practices.

Her special knowledge, one that significantly revolves around medicine and gastronomy, and which instantiates Hippocrates' lesson of 'let food be thy medicine',[43] embodies the type of alternative epistemology described by Braidotti in her call for a nomadic form of thought that questions and challenges patriarchal authority: 'highly phallogocentric and antinomadic; it maintains a privileged bond to the domination, power, and violence and consequently requires mechanism of exclusion and domination as part of its standard practices.'[44]

Braidotti explicitly aims at placing human subjectivity outside the hegemonic sphere of patriarchy, and at identifying categories of thought that supersede the binary masculine/feminine, where the latter is always considered inferior and subjugated to male authority. This task applies equally well to the sphere of discourse. Her theory emphasizes the urgency to reform the *logos* and to challenge the supremacy of reason. Crucially, in *Althénopis*, the grandmother introduces her alternative approach to Western, male-centric conceptions of knowledge: her *arte malefica* combines reason, superstition, imagination and food. It is particularly significant that it is the grandmother, an uneducated woman considered unable to act reasonably by her daughters, who possesses this gastronomical and medical knowledge, which she passes on to her granddaughter, thereby contributing to the formation of the younger woman's food voice.

As discussed so far, in Ramondino's *Althénopis*, food does not simply exist as a principle of nutrition, a social good or an object of desire, to name only a few of the categories listed by David Kaplan,[45] but rather as a 'voice' that communicates eaters' tastes, habits and lives, and above all as what Massimo Montanari calls 'a system [that] contains and conveys the culture of its practitioner', as well as a crucial component of one's personal and social identity.[46]

What is at stake in *Althénopis* is food as a powerful tool for female characters to react, more or less overtly, against the dynamics of patriarchal culture imposed upon them. This does not mean that the female protagonists of the novel, and especially the grandmother and her granddaughter, act heroically and ultimately defeat patriarchal ideology.[47] Rather, it proves that the grandmother and the granddaughter are able to find alternative ways to express their choices, personalities and even their creativity (the famous *estro* mentioned earlier) with respect to patriarchy and bourgeois culture; to increase awareness of their bodies; and to experience trans-corporeal phenomena based on interchanges between substances and the materiality of the body.

In *Althénopis,* denying food, as scholars have suggested, appears as emblematic as consuming it. Francesca Calamita thoroughly describes how an apparent loss of appetite can often disclose a covert act of disobedience as well as a complex discomfort, or even a serious pathology.[48] As mentioned earlier, there are a few moments in the novel where the grandmother's attitude towards eating approximates anorexia. For instance, the fact that the grandmother does not eat what she cooks for her grandchildren represents a typical practice of the anorectic. Another clue of the grandmother's eating disorders can be identified in her need to consume food in private and her refusal to sit at the family's table (Orbach XII). Although the grandmother does not allude to her desire to lose weight or to any discomfort with her body, it is undeniable that her eating habits and her diet reveal a problematic relationship with food and its preparation becoming, in Calamita's words, an 'instrument of her inner rebellion' and 'a powerful weapon to express her deepest feelings'.[49]

Hence, food in Ramondino's *Althénopis* tastes good and subversive. Readers of the novel find in the grandmother and her granddaughter's food voices pragmatic examples of gastronomic identities, which show how they define themselves or relate to others through the food they eat or cook, and how ultimately food and its preparation inevitably affect the characters' development and perception of their subjectivities.

10

Feeding the body, feeding the language

Nourishment as a metaphor of writing in Igiaba Scego's literary works

Laura-Marzia Lenci

While studies on food and representations of alimentary diseases in literature originated primarily from Anglophone and Francophone women and gender, and postcolonial studies, for a long time Italian studies focused on philological–historical analysis, and for decades, Italian colonialism was not considered a subject of research, either from a historical or from a social perspective. Only in the last twenty years have investigations on food partially moved in a different direction,[1] and included authors and works that present a multicultural background.

In this chapter, I would like to highlight the poetics that underpin the writings of the Somali–Italian author Igiaba Scego (Rome, 1974), putting them in relation to different food narratives that have their roots in African postcolonial contexts like Amara Lakhous' novel *Scontro di civiltà per un ascensore a Piazza Vittorio* (Clash of Civilization Over an Elevator in Piazza Vittorio, 2006), Chohora Nassera's novel *Volevo diventare bianca* (I Wanted to Become White, 1993) and Tsitsi Dangarembga's novel *Nervous Conditions* (1988). In particular, I will focus on the short stories 'Salsicce' (Sausages), winner of the Eks&tra prize in 2003 but published in 2005, and 'Dismatria' (Exmatriates, 2005), as well as some scenes of the novels *Rhoda* (2004), *Oltre Babilonia* (Beyond Babylon, 2008) and *La mia casa è dove sono* (My Home Is Where I Am, 2010).

Scego's stories are characterized by a constellation of female *personages* who deal with meals management, and live in conditions of visible discomfort. The narrators of the short stories 'Dismatria' and 'Salsicce' struggle to understand who they are; *Rhoda*'s protagonist is very sick and dies at the beginning of the novel; and finally, the four female voices in *Oltre Babilonia* are not satisfied with their bodies, sexuality and life and have also not reconciled with the past of their family. Scego's characters are often victims of different kinds of injustice: they are denied a legitimate role in society; it is impossible for them to acquire citizenship in a country such as Italy where the law is still based on *ius sanguinis* (Italian citizenship law);[2] they are marginalized in political and economic decision-making; and they still have limited access to education and have castrated sexual rights. Nonetheless, men are completely excluded from food scenes, since Scego voices the difficulty of being a woman in a society that still conceives of women as objects of sexual desire or keepers of the family. At the same time, these women represent a specific community inside Somali culture. They are custodians of stories, songs, lullabies and recipes that are passed on from mother to daughter. All of this knowledge, usually transmitted orally, feeds into women's ability to preserve and perpetuate stories. Scego's characters invite us to consider some behaviours as being symptomatic of a caring loss: not necessarily caring for others, but rather caring for oneself. Buying, touching, cooking, smelling and eating food often have a therapeutic function.

This is the case of the tea scene that appears in Scego's short story 'Dismatria'. The female narrator, who lives in a matriarchal family where all women hold their belongings in suitcases instead of wardrobes, wants to overcome the sense of precariousness she experiences in her life. She would like to move from her family's home and find her own place, but she worries about offending her mother and betraying her nomadic Somali roots. After long internal conflicts and with a sense of guilt, the young woman decides to confront her mother by inviting a friend for tea. The mother of the protagonist is the only person who immediately understands that this invitation has a particular meaning for her daughter. In fact, the table is not only rich with every sort of food and beverages but also compared to a Christmas banquet or a dinner table set up at the end of the day during Ramadan. Food clearly marks the uniqueness of the event, something that requires particular care. The description of the table that all family female members have contributed to prepare not only shows the respect and devotion that Somali culture has for guests but also symbolizes the different conceptions of time, space and social hierarchies hidden behind a tea ceremony. The richness of the ingredients, which is exotic to the modern Italian reader (at least more exotic than for our ancestors who went to Somalia and Eritrea as colonizers), places the reader's self in an unfamiliar situation. This is exactly the same uncomfortable condition experienced by the protagonist and expressed in the short story with the metaphor of Angélique's nature as a transsexual woman: she appears woman and man at the same time, fascinating and extraneous in the eyes of the protagonist's family. Despite their contradictory feelings towards the new friend, the narrator's family, who lives a painful displacement due to their emigration from Somalia to Italy after Siad Barre's coup in 1969, perfectly understands the in-betweenness of Angélique's identity. Like her, they also feel as if they existed in between two realities: they love both Rome and Mogadishu, Italian and Somali culture, food and language, but they feel suspended between the idealized time and space of memory, and the time and space of every day.

For all these reasons, and to make a good impression on their guest, they have prepared a perfect tea party:

> I surveyed the table [. . . .] The table was groaning with good things. With every delight known to East and West. It looked like a cross between Christmas dinner and the evening meal that breaks the fast during the holy month of Ramadan. Every inch of the table was taken up. Three sorts of herbal tea, two kinds of coffee, one flavoured, one not. Fruit juice galore, various sweets, various salads, various pickles. A feast for the eyes. Zainab had made her great speciality too: having lived for years in Egypt she had prepared a meat and chickpea stew, something guaranteed to make you hear angels carolling. A shame, though, that no one took the initiative to start the banquet [. . . .] Clearly, everyone was waiting for Angélique to make the first move.[3]

There is no free space on the table, like in a neo-baroque scene, as if emptiness reminded the characters of the gap left by migration. Homesickness is replaced by objects that neutralize the sense of loss through their concrete presence. When the narrator describes the food, she does so to postpone the dreaded moment when she will make her request to leave the maternal house. This narrative strategy works like a magnifying glass that produces an anamorphic effect and prepares the protagonist, as well as the reader, for the *climax* of the story. The protagonist, in fact, is reluctant to speak alone with her mother, who represents the authority within the family, and her decisions are consequently irrefutable.

Nonetheless, the beginning of the banquet is depicted as a scene of conflict, since the protagonist expects a negative reaction from her mother. On the contrary, the narrative expansion of time produced by the lengthy description of the food on the table allows both women to navigate the conflict, and maybe reach an agreement. This expansion, in fact, creates a sort of hiatus in the communication between the two women, which is suspended, and they have the time to consider how to manage their conflict.

> The hand shot out and Angélique's jaws went straight into action [. . . .] Angélique had relished the booty, her palate revelled in the meat packed inside that little

> fold of puff pastry. It wanted a second shot at that little fortress of savouries [. . . .] I surveyed the table that had been so neat and orderly. A tornado had torn through it. Every inch of the table had been plundered. The three sorts of tea had been drained, the two kinds of coffee gulped down, the fruit juices sucked up. And what can I say about the various sweets, the various salads, and the various pickles? Destroyed in the maelstrom of various jaws in action. Chewed, enjoyed, digested [. . . .] In short, the food had done itself proud. Only that in all that bedlam of chatter and munching one crucial sound had been missing: the sound of the voice (and jaws) of my mum. She had not uttered a word and had not tasted a thing. She had confined herself to sipping a traditional coffee with no sugar. In other words, the city had been conquered but not the citadel . . . only then could victory be declared.[4]

Unlike what happens in the African novel written in English by Tsitsi Dangarembga, *Nervous Conditions* (1988), where the cultural discomfort of the female protagonist is represented by her inability to stomach any food, the uneasiness experienced by Scego's characters is resolved on a semantic level, through the use of a lexicon of war: spoils of war, conquer, raid, fort and triumph. After the reception, there are no crumbs left on the table: food is not perceived as an obstacle to communication, but rather it is intentionally used as a facilitator of interaction. In 'Dismatria', eating together is accepted by the characters for its intrinsic function of socialization: this works well, with the exception of the narrator's mother who does not partake in the food. It is Angélique's inappropriate intercultural behaviour that forces the conflagration of the non-verbal rules followed by the family; for instance, while starting banqueting or when later in the story she overturns Muki's suitcase and lets its contents spill. Angélique in fact does not know that for the narrator family, suitcases represent the entire life and emotions of each member. Therefore, in doing so, she puts all women in front of their existential lies.

Also in Scego's short story 'Salsicce', which is the most concerned with identity, the role of food reveals an existential conflict: there is no recipe that can describe how we become who we are. In a process similar to the list of things stored in the 'Dismatria' suitcases, the narrator of 'Salsicce' enumerates when and for what reasons she identifies both as a Somali and an Italian. But different from another, albeit geographical, list that Scego compiles in *La mia casa è dove sono*, this listing does not help to clarify the question of identity. Identity, in fact, escapes a concrete and precise definition and remains something abstract, like Scego shows through the use of irony and strategy of listing. Also, the image of buying sausages serves as a metaphor to reinforce the paradox of buying an identity just like we buy a pair of shoes, a duty stamp needed for the permit of stay application, the tax we pay to receive a valid passport or any identity document. If this is possible in an institutional context, since this is what we do to show our citizenship, it ceases to be so simple once the protagonist, who is a Muslim woman, after buying sausages, must eat them. Some questions immediately come to the protagonist's mind: How must they be cooked? How do people become Italian after receiving a permit of stay? How is integration or assimilation possible? Which 'recipes' are there for cooking identity?

To prepare food, within the extended metaphor of 'Salsicce', means to prepare the individual to 'be' in the world. However, the protagonist of the short story needs to confront some issues: first of all, that she does not know who she "is". In fact, her urgency to buy sausages is dictated by her need to be considered Italian. Despite sausages being a food broadly present in all of Italy, and as common a food as pasta or pizza, the narrator does not consider the latter two for her transformation from a Somali Cinderella to an Italian princess (i.e. what she aspires to be). The problematic identity of the protagonist is reflected within her desire to consume sausages, which become idiosyncratic within this context: sausages are an Italian food; however, they are made of pork. The two elements perfectly convey the protagonist's identity crisis since, as a Muslim woman, the protagonist cannot resolve the ambiguity of her identity by eating *haram* (impure) food. The major conflict created by Igiaba Scego brings to the reader's attention the ambiguity of one's identity and the impossibility of substituting it with another. As in the already mentioned novel *Scontro di civiltà* by Lakhous, Scego's protagonists are also overwhelmed by the host culture and have no other choice than to accept the European model. They are culturally too young to understand that assimilation comes at a very high price, as exemplified in this passage from 'Salsicce':

> And then disaster struck: that vile question on my damned identity! More Somali? More Italian? Perhaps you are three-quarters Somali and one-quarter Italian? Or, perhaps, just the exact opposite? I don't know what to answer! I had never 'fractioned' myself before – and, besides, in school I always hated fractions (they were unpleasant and inconclusive) [. . . .] I am not a 100% anything. I never have been, and I don't think I can be now. I think I am a woman with no identity. Better yet, a woman with several identities [. . . .] Let's see: I feel Somali when 1) I drink tea with cardamom, cloves and cinnamon; 2) I pray five times a day facing Mecca; 3) I wear my *dirah*; 4) I burn incense and *unsi* in my house [. . . .] I feel Italian when: 1) I eat something sweet for breakfast; 2) I go to art exhibitions, museums and historic buildings; 3) I talk about sex, men

> and depression with my girlfriends; 4) I watch movies with the following actors: Alberto Sordi, Nino Manfredi, Vittorio Gassman, Marcello Mastroianni, Monica Vitti, Totò, Anna Magnani, Giancarlo Giannini, Ugo Tognazzi, Roberto Benigni and Massimo Troisi; 5) I eat a 1.80 euro ice cream: chocolate chip, pistachio, coconut without whipped cream.[5]

The strategy of listing things helps the narrator to explain that identities are not static. The concept of identity involves many aspects of life and it is primarily based on singular preferences that are the result of the stratification of the past: the history of the motherland and one's own family, the mother tongue and other languages individuals have been exposed to, culinary culture of the family and countries, sense of morality and truth, religious education, education itself, and so on. The addition of experiences, in fact, that the Italian–Arbëreshë writer Carmine Abate theorizes in his writings, modifies the nature of an identity during the entire life-long process.

If at a first reading, 'Salsicce' seems to be focused on the consumption of some impure food, implying the rejection of the protagonist's mother culture, a more careful analysis shows that it is more concerned with the process of cultural integration. Scego chooses to approach this topic through the lightness of irony, and emphasizes the process of storytelling creating an original *mise en abîme*. The story has some light-heartedness, as if the mixture of the two meats, human and pork, really assured a corporal metamorphosis, together with a new identity.

However, the question moves to a different level encompassing not so much 'what' is Italian, but rather 'how' to become Italian. The diverse recipes on how to cook sausages present new evidence to her. There are many ways of 'being', as well as there are many ways of eating. Eating is not just an act that allows the individual to feed him or herself. In fact, the lexicon of food consumption employed by Scego in her writings includes a wide variety of terms: *divorare*, *masticare*, *ingoiare* (devour, chew, swallow), but also *vomitare*, *sputare*, *rosicchiare*, *frantumare*, *insaporire*, *assaggiare*, *annusare*, *presentarsi alla bocca* and *assaporare* (vomit, spit, gnaw, crush, flavour, taste, sniff, show up at the mouth and savour). The relationship with food is a metaphor for the experience of life, which reserves sweet and bitter bites.

At the same time, food preparation and consumption are strictly related to the activity of telling stories. Both actions activate characters' memories and let the narrative process begin, which passes again through the experience of the body and becomes the linguistic body of the narration. Both Scego and Lakhous make use of similes, metaphors and proverbs that come from their other cultures and often refer to food semantics. They, however, do not serve an ornamental function, but a narrative contingent function instead. Unlike the migrant literature published in Italy in the early 1990s, when there was a lure for the exotic, I contend that the heteroglossia of these two authors is the tentative realization of an integration of their respective cultures in the form of art: a work of literature. It becomes clear that this is possible only thanks to a reciprocal understanding between these cultures. At the same time, their diglossia, and sometimes polyglossia, represent the reality of modern Italian society where, despite the recent political negationism, cultures and languages coexist.

The understanding of Algerian and Italian, Somali and Italian history, language, habits, the role of women and, yes, food culture is the starting point for considerations on the aesthetic production of both authors. Through a critical use of the Italian language, alternated with the competent use of Italian dialects (Lakhous) and slangs (Scego), and the insertion of words and expressions from the respective African languages and cultures, both writers operate a hybridization of literary Italian that creates for readers a sense of *Verfremdungseffekt* (estrangement) and awakens in them a critical response.

However, beside the irony and sarcasm that make the text linguistically and stylistically very enjoyable, 'Salsicce' discusses more aesthetic questions: In relation to the concept of identity, is it true that language represents the form only? Why is Scego's character looking for a different kind of bodily substance? Are Ferdinand De Saussures's considerations about *langue* and *parole* not clear enough to explain this complexity?[6] In her narrative, Scego creates a paradox to embody all these questions that her character has not yet realized. For Scego, language is the most *essential substance* of the 'I'. Her narrative style is typified by a language that expresses the uniqueness of the writer, as highlighted by Daniela Brogi (2011). The Italian scholar underlines that Scego's Italian is correct from a morpho-syntactic point of view, but intentionally moves away from the language of canon Italian literature. Her choice to rely on a language that is the expression of the dominant culture depends not only on the complicated relation between Italy and its ex-colony Somalia, but also on the urgency for Scego to represent herself as a woman, and as a black female writer in a world that still perpetrates injustices and violence against women.

Talking about a female character of *Oltre Babilonia* who tries to understand who she is, Scego writes: 'Memories must be neither politically correct, nor the destination of humanitarian vacations.'[7] Literature, as an instrument of testimony, needs to shake and take the readers out from their bourgeois sleep. This, for Scego, is possible only when history becomes flesh. In *Oltre Babilonia*, the author manifests her perspective on history and identity: bodies are signs that attest historical truth. Bodies bear the stamp of history and confirm with their presence that the attribution of a meaning is possible 'only if memory becomes flesh'.[8] Scego's narrative strategy allows her to give substance to the subject for whom the food is intended, since food is the substance of which the 'self' is moulded. Scego names food elements as a generative act that passes through the listing of food. Not only is this functional to the representation of the plural identity of Scego's characters but it is also fractioning, classifying and enumerating that remind us of a bigger and painful fragmentation that, in all of Scego's and African Horn narratives[9] is represented by the communal diaspora experienced after the fall of the colonial domination.

In *La mia casa è dove sono*, for example, the female narrator enjoys a memorable dinner in Finland at her brother's house. Here, over a tasteful chicken meal, the narrator sits with her family. In this novel, Scego uses the image of fractions not only to discuss the multifaceted nature of her character but also to speak about the history of Somalia. The dinner allows the family to feel united again, albeit for a short time. The convivial table creates a peaceful atmosphere. Nura's chicken awakens the homesickness that the family members have overcome and the dinner is especially delicious not only because it offers solace in a country where language, climate, and gastronomic culture are a million miles away but also because it embodies the emotional stability and the cohesiveness among family members. A box of cookies shared at the table is the starting point for the storytelling. However, unlike the male characters, who grab cookies by the handful, the young narrator takes only one. In doing so, Scego stages a contrast between the compulsiveness of the male world, willing to immediately recompose the mosaic of their lost identity, and the more meditative female approach. Not only does food awaken the past and move memories to a deeper substrate, but it also embodies the writing process. However, writing is not only the act of drawing a line on a piece of paper. The writing process is also seen as a metaphorical birth-giving, something that again goes necessarily through and beyond the body. Food is introduced into the body and serves as a mediator for the direct experience. The body represents, in fact, the first space where the 'I' locates itself, but it also represents the space where the food of the emigrated country is ingested. This duplicity of the body allows the past to connect to the present: in the stomach, food is reprocessed, and the digestion and revision of the past transform the life experiences into a story. In the novel, starting from the drawing of the pre-war Mogadishu map, the narrator feels the need to explain the geography of the city that looks to her like a body, 'Maka al-Mukara [. . .] was the pulsing heart of Mogadishu, its backbone', and word by word, line after line, the protagonist and her family members 'blended them in with their memories, like eggs in a mixture'.[10]

The introjection or rejection of food recalls the learning process and its digestion, its acquisition. Therefore, the impact of food on the body is strictly related to these experiences. If food can be seen as the linguistic component of all of our discourses, literary writing must then be seen as the nourishment of the individual through language. This happens from the moment of birth, as both Scego and Lakhous agree. In *Oltre Babilonia* one of the two protagonists, Zuhra, says:

> Mom speaks to me in our mother tongue. A noble Somali where every vowel makes sense. Our mother tongue. Foamy, unfriendly, daring. In Mom's mouth, Somali becomes honey. I wonder if the language of my mother can be a mother for me. If in our mouths the Somali language sounds the same. How do I speak this our mother tongue? Am I as good as she is? Perhaps not, certainly not [. . . .] Unsure I stumble on my confused alphabet. The words are all twisted. They smell of paved roads, concrete and suburbs. Every sound is contaminated. But I still try to speak with her that language that joins us. In Somali I found comfort in her womb, in Somali I heard the only lullabies she sang to me, in Somali I certainly made my first dreams. But then, every time, in every speech, word, sigh, the other mother peeks out. The one who suckled Dante, Boccaccio, De André and Alda Merini. The Italian I grew up with and at times I also hated, because it made me feel a foreigner. The sour Italian, which taste is like vinegar at the local markets, the sweet Italian of the radio speakers, the serious Italian of the lectiones magistrales. The Italian I write.[11]

Languages are compared to breast milk, honey and sweet tastes, and also to vinegar and other sour tastes, but the narrator cannot avoid using language to express herself. This process, however, does not consist in a simple translation from one language to another: it takes an entire lifetime, in fact, for Scego's character to solve her internal conflict. After many years, she still feels unsure; she stumbles on sounds and words, and her language is described as contaminated. *Oltre Babilonia*'s epilogue paraphrases Derrida's invitation to use languages as creative instruments to represent our subjectivity.[12] Languages are composed by morphology, syntax and lexicon, but the way through which we use structures and rules to express ourselves is necessarily unique, since each individual has a different personal story and a different style to express himself or herself. The intrinsic flexibility of the linguistic system promotes the resilience of the subject who can amalgamate languages, sounds, words and imaginaries to draw his or her 'self'. Scego's nourished body brings to the world a written body, a place that hosts an identity that arises from the linguistic trace. *Matria* is not just the country idealized in the memories of 'Dismatria's' characters. It is more than a place, it is the linguistic body to which each individual belongs, and which is enriched by experiencing themselves into the world.

Scego's writings embody Spivak's contention that it is in the text that we witness the 'wordling' of the world – and in this particular case of the female world. It is the process of verbal symbolization that allows for reality to be in the world as a representation, and not only as a description. The act of writing, in fact, is far from being a simple rhetorical or aesthetic exercise, and it represents not merely the legitimation of a specific voice into the canon of the dominant culture. Scego's writings offer themselves as the expansion capability of the language to touch the entire variety of emotional situations and existential events, including the events that still do not have a shape or cannot be constrained into the verbal language. Scego, in fact, intentionally forces the language over the consuetudes. By doing this, she is able to return to the language its poetic function and allows it to become a politically aware gesture through which the value of the writer, woman and citizen are affirmed.

Part IV

Food, family and politics

11

Writing food

Issues of female identity and gender politics in Dacia Maraini's novels

Maria Morelli

By her own admission, Dacia Maraini's 'obsession' with food dates back to her traumatic experience of the Japanese concentration camp for anti-fascists where she was interned with her family during the Second World War, an experience she has recounted in her autobiographical account of her childhood years, *La nave per Kobe: diari giapponesi di mia madre* (The Boat to Kobe: My Mother's Japanese Diaries, 2001).[1] The hunger she suffered then, as a small child, inevitably shaped her aesthetic and literary imagination. Food – or lack of it – has become a quasi-ubiquitous motif in her writings.[2]

Women's predilection for food imagery and symbolism in literary works has been a growing interest for scholars at least since the 1980s. For Hélène Cixous, food is central to women's relationship with their corporeality, as well as with their culture. Taking the 'scene of the apple' as recounted in Genesis as a starting point for her argument, in 'Extreme Fidelity' (1988), Cixous contends that Eve's story is that of every woman, constantly negotiating the cultural taboos that the patriarchal law has inscribed onto the surface of her body. Albeit addressing the relationship between women and food in strictly psychoanalytical terms, in *The Hungry Self: Women Eating, and Identity* (1985), Kim Chernin reaches a similar conclusion, positing eating habits – and conformance to, or denial of, maternal teachings about them – as the most obvious factor in shaping women's identity. This connection between food and what it entails (housework, childbearing and childrearing) and female identity became all the more obvious with the women's movement, when expectations about domesticity and foodwork were challenged by the feminist critique of the myth of the 'happy housewife'.[3] Women began to question their role as nurturers – food purveyors, that is – and to explore the implications of conforming to a traditional, patriarchal script.

In this chapter, I will analyse the recourse to food imagery in a number of Maraini's works belonging to what critics have usually identified as her most explicit feminist phase: *Donna in guerra* (Woman at War, 1975), *Lettere a Marina* (Letters to Marina, 1981), *Il treno per Helsinki* (The Train to Helsinki, 1984), all texts where images of food, or what it stands for, are too pervasive to be merely coincidental. Looking at both levels of representations – the literal and the symbolic – I will argue that in these writings, the act of preparing, presenting or consuming meals, while reaffirming food as central in the shaping of the female experience, also bespeaks the author's preoccupations with an essentialist model of female identity that casts women in the role of carers, the very same preoccupation that feminism had for the first time brought to the fore.

Donna in guerra tells the story of a meek and compliant primary school teacher, Vanna (Vannina) Magro, and her path towards self-awareness and emancipation from patriarchal expectations and a constrictive marriage. Heralded by many as Maraini's most overt feminist novel, it reflects the author's concern towards domesticity against a backdrop of changing cultural values.[4] Written in the form of a fictitious diary covering only five months, *Donna in guerra* opens with the monotonous holiday routine of Vannina and her husband, Giacinto, while they are vacationing on the imaginary southern island of Addis, off the Neapolitan coast. The first entries appear as a mere listing of household chores that Vannina performs in a mechanical manner that suggests she has interiorized the patriarchal script of the subservient wife: 'I cleaned the house thoroughly from top to bottom. I washed and scrubbed everything: the floor, the toilet, the walls, the sink, the windows. I took down the thick black curtain that separates the bedroom from the kitchen. I soaped it and washed it and rinsed it' (*Woman at War*, trans. Benetti and Spottiswood, 144).[5] The detail of the curtain separating the kitchen from the bedroom is a significant one within the economy of the novel. Despite being described as 'thick', the curtain is no wall; it foregrounds a spatial contiguity between the realm of domestic chores and that of marital duties that is metonymic of the treatment of the female protagonist for most of the novel as functional to satisfy her husband's needs – in the kitchen as well as in the bedroom – and as an objective correlative for a suffocating daily and matrimonial routine. To compensate for the size of the small apartment is a beautiful courtyard, of which Vannina is quite fond: 'To make up for it we have a beautiful courtyard, enclosed by a ten foot wall, as secret as an Arab garden' (*Woman*, trans. Benetti and Spottiswood, 4).[6] What she fails to realize, however, is that, as acutely observed by Giancarlo Lombardi, her secret Arab garden is but a spatial extension of the household, 'a claustrophobic corner designed to act as yet another stage of her domestic duties' since it is but 'an orchard where vegetables grow, the same vegetables which constitute basic components of the meals she is expected to prepare'.[7]

Confined within the prison-like walls of her holiday home, Vannina is mostly busy cooking for her husband or making coffee for the men who often come round – be they friends of Giacinto's or the fellow members of the leftist political group *Vittoria proletaria*.[8] The protagonist's fixation with cooking reveals the author's concern towards the enslavement of women within the domestic walls. Food becomes an alibi for domesticity and the emblem of a distorted value system whereby woman is thought of in utilitarian terms as a carer and a provider. In her retrospective analysis of the position of women in society in 1970s and 1980s Italy collected in the volume *La bionda, la bruna e l'asino* (The Blonde, the Brunette and the Donkey, 1987), Maraini approaches the question of domestic work in materialistic terms to denounce the exploitation of women as a means of production and, at the same time, a source of unpaid labour. In arguing, as she does, that 'without women's unpaid housework [. . .] the whole economic system would implode',[9] the author is superimposing a markedly feminist outlook onto the hotly debated question of the unwaged labour of housework, acknowledging that women are not exploited as a class – as a Marxist socio-economic perspective would have it – but as a sex. This viewpoint is emphasized later in the narrative during an animated exchange between the militant feminist Suna, Vannina's friend and mentor in the matter of women's rights, and Vittorio, the founder of *Vittoria proletaria*. When Suna enquires about his mother's sexual life, Vittorio, utterly outraged, retorts sharply that 'this mother of mine is an old hag, she isn't a woman' (*Woman*, trans. Benetti and Spottiswood, 73).[10] This response stresses the incompatibility of a woman's wifely and maternal duties with any sexual desire she may have – she is, above all, the one who 'makes your dinner, she makes your bed, she washes your dirty underwear, she irons your shirts, she does your shopping, she cooks for you, she washes your dishes' (*Woman*, trans. Benetti and Spottiswood, 73).[11] Thus dehumanized, woman as 'mother' is envisaged, in Vittorio's distorted value system, as a mere provider attending to her husband and sons' primal needs – among which, of course, is food intake.

Fish plays a major role in the foodscape of *Donna in guerra*, contributing to the demarcation of female and male roles: it is the men who hunt, and it is the women – who, incidentally, are often associated with fish and, as such, metaphorized as prey – who cook the catch.[12] It follows, then, that 'woman, *fish* comes to symbolise the Lacanian phallus, that which all men are bound to try and regain through their relationships with women, quintessential bearers of the phallus itself'.[13] Significantly, Giacinto takes pride in his fishing trips, which he recounts in painstaking detail to an unimpressed Vannina: 'I've discovered a grouper fish, and a murena, where they live, I mean. Tomorrow I'll start stalking them, but I'll have to be patient: the sea-bed's clear and the rocks go down a sheer hundred feet, but they're cautious, the bastards, they're afraid' (*Woman*, trans. Benetti and Spottiswood, 7).[14] In flaunting his trophies-to-be, Giacinto seeks to validate his manhood, with hunting becoming a symbol of masculinity because of its associations to wilderness and the primitive. Giacinto's engagement with typically masculine activities notwithstanding, the character's fluctuation between normative masculine and feminine behaviours, coupled with his closeted desires for his fishing buddy Santino, inevitably casts some doubt over his virility. In this regard, his obsession with fishing serves also to underline the degree of violence that a regime of compulsory heterosexuality exerts not only upon women but also upon men, aiming at reinforcing 'the myths and fantasies about masculinity that have ensured that masculinity and maleness are profoundly difficult to pry apart'.[15]

Food in the novel works as a benchmark for the gendered functions traditionally associated with it and, as such, it serves as a powerful reminder that, in the end, both sexes are at the mercy of a patriarchal system whereby their respective roles are established *a priori*. Vannina spends most of her holiday behind the kitchen counter cooking her husband's catch, thereby sanctioning the correspondence between femininity and a 'natural' – both in the sense of innate and biological – predisposition to act as caretaker and nourisher. Giacinto, on the other hand, is also a victim of patriarchy, for he feels compelled to adhere to 'masculinity's iconicity',[16] understood as a set of inherently masculine habits he is expected to perform so as to guarantee a perfect adherence between his biological nature (male) and the gender thus assigned (masculine) – habits of which fishing is but an illustrative example.

That *Donna in guerra* is set in 1970s Italy, at a time when women were questioning their subordinate role, in the public as well in the private sphere, is not coincidental. The protagonist is entrapped within an anachronistic idea of domesticity, which makes the contrast between her condition and the cultural changes in the background all the more striking. Through her character, Maraini is denouncing a system that, despite granting women entry into the labour force, has not freed them from the work they are expected to do at home (such as household chores and childrearing, to which men fail to contribute their fair share).[17] As anticipated by the book's title, however, Maraini's Vannina is a 'woman at war'; one of the battles she will have to face is escaping her marital and domestic routine, and emancipating herself from the idea of woman as functional to men's needs, a goal she will achieve after undergoing a gradual process of awakening and subsequent empowerment. And it is indeed significant that, concomitantly with the protagonist's emancipation, the food imagery employed in the narrative no longer serves to pattern the gendered functions associated with it, as we have seen with regard to fish, but becomes instead a symbol of feminist liberation. In one of the concluding passages of the novel, Vannina has a revealing dream. She sees herself soaring above the city's roofs and falling to the ground; she is then handed a pair of crutches by her physically impaired and sexually non-conforming friend Suna and, in an unexpected queer act of breast feeding, she starts drinking milk from Suna's vulva: 'I drank some of that milk which tasted of seaweed, and as I drank it I felt it was filling me up with strength, with courage' (*Woman*, trans. Benetti and Spottiswood, 280).[18] Thus invigorated, Vannina is ready to get back on her feet – literally and metaphorically – and to gather the strength she needs to flee a constrictive marriage that is symptomatic of a larger societal, patriarchal apparatus. By the end of the novel, she has learnt to define herself in terms other than those applied to her by her husband, which coincides with her disillusionment with marriage when this translates into subjugation and loss of individuality, foregrounded by her initial confinement in the tiny kitchen of their rented holiday home. Vannina's choice to leave Giacinto is a feminist statement about the need for women to seek fulfilment outside the domestic walls, rather than settling for traditional norms that debase and enchain them.

Maraini wrote *Lettere a Marina* at the beginning of the 1980s, at a time when feminists' demands for equality and social advances had given way to more ideological concerns such as, *in primis*, the (re)creation of a new female symbolic, that is, a new system of representation for women. Written in a stream-of-consciousness manner and with minimum punctuation, the book consists of seventy-eight unsent letters that Bianca, the protagonist and first-person narrating voice, writes to Marina, who is also her ex-lover. This unilateral correspondence is, in fact, but a pretext for the sender to delve into her own past in order to try and make sense of her previous love affairs, her non-normative sexuality and her inability to finish the book on which she is working as a professional writer.

Credited with the representation of the taboo subject of homosexual love, Maraini's epistolary novel challenges societal sexual proscriptions by staging non-binary practices that break down the normative, heterosexual ideal. One way that the novel achieves this is by eroticizing the relationship between the two women through the use of food metaphors. The passages recounting their sexual encounters are dense with oral imagery that are suggestive of sexualized cannibalistic fantasies: 'Suddenly you bare one of my breasts and you take it in your mouth with awkward grace. I don't dare to breathe. I know that to refuse you at that moment would be like giving you poison. "Marina please don't. Let's stop!"' (*Letters to Marina*, trans. Kitto and Spottiswood, 16).[19] As in *Donna in guerra*, milk is also used here to signify an act of queer breast feeding, although in this case it is less about empowering the other than it is about satisfying one's sexual fantasies. Although, in the passage recalled earlier, it is Marina who initiates the sadomasochist seduction game, Bianca herself is not immune to impulses of carnal violence: 'Like the time when I smeared your neck and tummy and thighs with honey [. . . .] I was trying to change your smell and taste . . . . No – I wanted to cut you in pieces and then as a penance I would have drunk the familiar over-sweet honey of your blood' (*Letters*, trans. Kitto and Spottiswood, 24).[20] The two women cannibalize each other in turns, in a non-polarized relationship whereby the traditional dichotomy between male activity and female passivity is displaced by both the deconstruction of gender hierarchies and the plasticity of the masculine and feminine roles played by the two lovers, oscillating between masochistic fantasies and maternal tenderness.

In *Lettere a Marina* the sensory depiction of food images, both literal and metaphorical, also serves the narrative function of inscribing the relationship between the two lovers within the psychoanalytical pattern of incestuous fusion with the maternal. This is achieved through images of orality associated with food incorporation ('milk') and gustatory and olfactory sensations ('sweet'), which, in turn, are replicated by evocative physical details that, condensing maternal subtext, recall the generative potential of women's bodies ('breast'). This stress on oral pleasure is highly suggestive of what Freud identifies as the first stage of psychosexual development in infancy, the mouth being the child's primary erogenous zone that hints at a desire of regressive semiotic fusion with the mother: 'Can I drink your milk? You were lying curled up in my arms and you began to suck my breasts. It was the mother and daughter game. You told me how it was such good sweet creamy milk and it seemed as if you were really swallowing it. You said it was like condensed milk but even better' (*Letters*, trans. Kitto and Spottiswood, 54).[21] Here, milk becomes the signifier for a wished-for infantile state: 'And I stroked your hair as if I were fondling a little child' (*Letters*, trans. Kitto and Spottiswood, 54).[22] Bianca herself refers to her love-making with Marina as a mother–daughter role play, a maternal fusion that replicates the semiotic unity while also eroticizing it through the staging of sexual games of quasi-murderous undertones, where the sexual act is dramatized through disturbing desires of 'tearing into pieces' or 'swallowing up' the other. Thus eroticized, the maternal metaphor comes to symbolize a challenge to the incest taboo,[23] a looming threat to the symbolic order. The socio-cultural origin of incest is explicitly evoked in the novel through re-appropriation of the apple scene: 'Which tree the apple comes from isn't very important: I don't know – and anyway it's not significant – how much the conditions for transmitting cultural taboos matter in comparison with the exquisite and tender kernel of the human condition' (*Letters*, trans. Kitto and Spottiswood, 86).[24] Bianca's defiant eating of the forbidden apple – here metaphorized as incest – is paradigmatic of her rebellion against a system premised upon a regime of 'compulsory heterosexuality', understood as the societal coercion of the individual to adopt pre-established, clear-cut gender positions alongside the feminine/masculine divide, positions that Bianca boldly challenges by not fitting into the cultural ideals of her gender category.[25]

In Maraini's 1981 novel, the busy housewife of *Donna in guerra* has given way to an unmarried woman whose love life oscillates between homosexual and heterosexual affairs. Bianca would at first come across as an independent and self-asserted woman seeking self-fulfilment through writing. On a closer look, however, we realize that Vannina's self-effacement is replicated in Bianca's excessive dedication to others – to her mother, her sister and, not least, strangers. One day the activist brother of a friend of hers shows up unannounced at her door looking for a place to hide for a couple of days and ends up staying for much longer. Unable to send him away, Bianca finds herself taking care of her unsolicited guest in the same way a mother would with her child: 'I put the squids on the table. I seasoned them with oil mustard lemon and parsley. There was a tomato and celery salad yoghurt and some strawberry tart [. . . .] Or probably it's just the anxiety of a mother who sees her son in danger and wants to fill him with herself stuffing him with love and security' (*Letters*, trans. Kitto and Spottiswood, 143).[26] A decade after feminism had begun to advocate for alternative models of female identity, in the 1980s, women are still thought of as the ones who bear the responsibility of providing meals, for, as Maraini tells us, deep-seated cultural beliefs are extremely difficult to uproot. Bianca herself concedes that 'I can't get away from my feeding instinct when I have a guest' (*Letters*, trans. Kitto and

Spottiswood, 143),[27] thereby sanctioning the equation between 'woman' and 'food' (woman *is* food) that, deriving from the Judeo-Christian tradition, has permeated Western philosophical thought for centuries.[28]

Despite never denying women's 'natural' – in the sense of innate – nurturing abilities, Maraini proves sceptical of a culture of care when this becomes a pretext for an essentializing definition of woman that identifies her with the patriarchal female role of the feeding mother. Within such a limiting and oppressive paradigm, the author is nevertheless able to forge alternative spaces for female solidarity that take place within the domestic walls, of which the sisterhood that Bianca develops with her next-door neighbour is a case in point. With a name that can be derived from 'basil' and, as such, is itself evocative of domesticity, Basilia is the embodiment of the self-effacing mother, devoured, so to speak, by her sons and husband – the cannibalistic imagery here becoming emblematic of submission to a feminine code of self-abnegation.[29] As noted by Virginia Picchietti in her study of the 'relational spaces' in Maraini's writings and films, it is thanks to Basilia that Bianca can restore her former relationship with her mother and situate herself within a female genealogy.[30] This is rendered in a climactic moment when Basilia's massaging of Bianca's shoulders is linked to the kneading of 'her peasant mother [. . .] while she prepare[s] the bread and the pasta and the pizza dough' (*Letters*, trans. Kitto and Spottiswood, 119),[31] thereby sanctioning the passing down onto the (symbolic) daughter of a system of inherently female values and traditions, here exemplified as food-making.[32] Bianca also acts as a catalyst for change for Basilia in allowing her to develop a sense of self outside of her marital and parental role,[33] as in the restaurant scene when the two women are out dining together, thus abdicating their domestic chores and carving out of a space where meals can be enjoyed and shared, rather than just prepared for others.

Decrying the denigration of kitchen culture among feminists, Barbara Haber argues for the possibility for domestic life to be 'acknowledged and even celebrated without buying into an oppressive value system'.[34] In *Lettere a Marina*, Maraini does just that. She (re)thinks the relationship between women and the kitchen in terms other than coercion and subservience, instead presenting food preparation and consummation as a source of female solidarity and an opportunity to resist patriarchal oppression.

In the last of Maraini's novels to be discussed here, *Il treno per Helsinki*, food frames the narration and serves as a ruse for the reconstruction of the protagonist's past, told in a flashback, but also as a compelling metaphor for her as a way of filtering and processing – digesting, so to speak – her lived experiences.[35] The story begins with Armida peeling a potato. The voice she hears on the radio – that of her ex-lover and now politician Miele – is the catalyst for a Proustian *recherche* into her past eighteen years, a reminiscence that provides the narrative material of the book's 264 pages, before finally returning to the initial kitchen scene, at which point the narration ends. The image of the potato thus serves as a narrative prop sustaining the story, tying up beginning and ending in a circular fashion that mirrors the lack of evolution in the psychological development of the narrator–protagonist. *Il treno per Helsinki* is Maraini's 1980s look back at the 1968 movement in Italy and, partially, the author's historical reflection on its shortcomings. The train recalled in the title is the one taking Armida and her leftist friends to the Finnish capital to attend the Youth Festival alongside fellow activists from all over the continent. Thus, Armida's personal recollections – her marital crisis, her love story with Miele and her pregnancy – coexist alongside the account of a particular historical period marked by the questioning of the institutions, with the personal and the political merging together.[36]

Food functions not just as a mere narrative expedient to compress the recounted events to the peeling of a potato, but also as a link to memory, a cognitive tool to come to grips with one's past and make sense of it, in a move that has aptly been captured by Tommasina Gabriele as a travelling 'backward to go forward'.[37] But in order for Armida 'to go backward' it is necessary that she first 'goes downward',[38] that is, metaphorically speaking, down to her bowels so as to 'digest' the memories that are now starting to resurface.[39] Miele's voice on the radio triggers a return of the repressed, metaphorized as an intestinal journey: 'The past has the consistency of a soup. Years since I've come down this road. From my throat to my bowels' (*Il treno per Helsinki* 7).[40] Armida's digestive system becomes the enchanted mirror of *Alice in Wonderland*: 'I eat Alice's mushroom [. . . .] I enter the looking glass [. . .] with its soft walls that push me down towards the roots of my bowels towards the corridors of my twisting anus and there I come out, shat out by myself' (*Il treno* 7).[41] Philosopher Julia Kristeva interprets the physiological act of food elimination as purging one's body of what was once ingested (and has thus become part of the self) in order for it to become other from what it was. She proceeds to claim that identity boundaries (self/other; subject/object) are threatened by 'that ambivalence, duplicity, or permanent or potential compound between same and other that all nourishment signifies'.[42] Returning to the image of Armida's self-generation (excretion) in light of Kristeva's paradigm, we can read it as the expression of the protagonist's desire to become *self*, which she can only attain by coming to terms with what still lingers from her past, that is, by piecing together the reasons for her personal and historical disenchantment. And so begins the chronological recollection of the crisis of her marriage with Paolo, her love affair with the charming liar Miele, her excruciating pregnancy that ended in miscarriage and her journey to Helsinki.

Armida is attracted to Miele whose 'unusually sweet' name (*Il treno* 12–13), literally translating as honey, clashes with the deceitful personality of this Machiavellian philanderer. Miele's name takes on an antiphrastic connotation when Armida remembers him instructing her on polygamy, just before announcing that he is going to marry a Guatemalan refugee for alleged political reasons. The ambiguity intrinsic to his persona is well encapsulated in the image of the birthday cake he brings home for Paolo. Armida stores it in the fridge and from time to time checks on it, as if to learn more about Miele by doing so: 'I wait for it to tell me something more about him' (*Il treno* 16).[43] Her hope to find answers, however, is thwarted by a sugary icing that hides what is inside ('But the white icing hides the cake's interior'; *Il treno* 16),[44] which, metonymically, functions as a visual reminder of the man's deceitfulness. The motif of the birthday cake reminds us of *The Edible Woman* (1969), the internationally renowned first novel of Canadian feminist author Margaret Atwood, where the protagonist, Marian, bakes a cake in the shape of her own image and offers it to her fiancé on his birthday, thus symbolically renouncing her former passive self and refusing to be manipulated any longer, providing him with a substitute to consume instead. For both Maraini's and Atwood's protagonists, the sweetness of the cake symbolizes a sugar-coated version of reality of which they are victims (Armida) or from which they are trying to emancipate themselves (Marian). Invariably, both novels end full-circle, back to where they began.[45] Despite making some steps towards emancipating themselves from toxic relationships, neither Atwood nor Maraini provide us with the certainty that either Armida or Marian have really evolved at the end of their personal journeys – thus making us question whether true emancipation for women is really possible as long as patriarchal structures persist.[46]

In the same way as Vannina and Bianca before her, Armida too is often busy making food for others, mostly for her husband and his disabled brother who lives with them. Sharing abundant meals accompanied by good wine is a recurrent motif in the novel and, overall, a prerogative of Armida's activist friends. Food seems to be the glue that holds together the group, otherwise marred by a Shakespearean web of unrequited loves: 'Nico loves Dida who is in love with Cesare who in turn loves you who are in love with Dida' (*Il treno* 26).[47] There are several scenes depicting the cohort gathering around a table, at someone's house or in some trattoria. But food works also as a benchmark for the ideological contradictions inherent in these young anarchists, contradictions that they manifest while en route to Helsinki. Emblematic in this respect is the episode of the stopover in Vienna when, treasuring the lessons they have learnt on the train, Armida's cohort mobs a hot-dog stall to beat all their fellow travellers to it. Rather than being a convivial moment, as one might expect, given the shared ideology fuelling the group's activism, eating turns into food-hunting, with grotesque undertones: 'We spend our days keeping an eye of the sentinels, followed by running, ambushing, planning' (*Il treno* 161).[48] Not without a note of irony on Maraini's part, once in Helsinki, Armida and the rest end up spending all their money on a luscious dinner, thereby buying into the very same capitalist logic they supposedly oppose. It is only under the uninhibiting effect of the vodka given to her by the radical activist Asia that Armida is able to speak her mind at the festival. As a playwright, she is invited to give a talk on the clash between social classes in theatre, but she denounces instead the contradictions that she has witnessed during her ten-day train journey, thereby provoking the rage of Miele, for whom political activism does not necessarily mean that one ought to be always truthful.

Pregnancy proves to be a traumatizing experience for Armida. Unable to come to terms with an inevitable miscarriage, her mother-in-law arranges for a five-hour ambulance ride to a private clinic in Milan so that she can receive better care. At the hospital, she is fed an excessive amount of food: 'I eat like an ogre: rare steak pasta cheese sweets' (*Il treno* 69).[49] Lapsing into a state of apathy and acquiescence, Armida resigns herself to such therapeutic obstinacy and eats everything, 'without thinking without smelling pushing down my throat the overcooked meals drinking liters of milk' (*Il treno* 69).[50] Inevitably, she swells up, just like Alice in Lewis Carroll's fantasy novel, except that the clinic is no Wonderland, but rather a dystopian setting. Reasoning over the patriarchal enforcement of motherhood, Adrienne Rich denounces the tendency to over-idealize pregnancy, and to depict it as an idyllic state and a natural feminine instinct, a 'sacred calling'[51] that reduces woman's worth to her capability of generating life, namely, to the purpose of her existence.[52] This stance is reflected also in *Il treno per Helsinki*, which Maraini wrote after reading Rich's seminal book and which may have struck a chord with her.[53] The treatment that Armida receives at the hospital, as well as her husband and mother-in-law's sole concern for the health of the baby above that of its mother, resonates with Rich's idea that '[a]s long as birth – metaphorically or literally – remains an experience of passively handing over our minds and our bodies to male authority and technology, other kind of social change can only minimally change our relationship to ourselves, to power, and to the world outside our bodies'.[54]

The writing of *Donna in guerra* (1975), *Lettere a Marina* (1981) and *Il treno per Helsinki* (1984) spans through the period in which theories and practices of sexual difference were central to Italian feminism. Yet, across the three novels, there is little change in terms of what is expected of women in a patriarchal ideology where kitchen culture is but a manifestation of a larger controlling apparatus, confirming Maraini's assertion that we should never forget what it took to gain ground during several decades of feminist battles and how little it takes to lose it all.[55] As a politically engaged writer, though, Maraini does not limit herself to provide a social commentary. Rather, through her works, she addresses the question as to whether women are empowered or subjugated by their role as food providers. Eschewing facile generalizations, she answers this question by resorting to tropes of (queer) breast feeding, metaphorical cannibalism, food-making and forced eating to foreground complex issues of female identity and gender power dynamics that are just as relevant today as they were some fifty years ago. Food plays a crucial role in shaping not only the subjectivity of Maraini's female protagonists and their relationship with, and position within, family and society, but also the (re)telling of their personal stories. Each in her own way, Vannina, Bianca and Armida, keep 'diary fiction[s]' where they religiously annotate the food they consume or prepare for others. In their hands, writing food becomes a means to create a new subjectivity premised upon intrinsically and traditionally female values[56] – a reclamation, rather than demonizing, of women's practices, which is less a return to nature than it is the affirmation of a female genealogy premised upon non-hierarchical and homosocial (or homosexual) forms of relationships between women. Recourse to culinary imagery allows, in their first-person writings, Maraini's protagonists, and the author with them, to problematize the implications of conceiving woman in functional terms and to prompt us to confront how we think about the roles between the sexes, with food being deployed both literally and symbolically as a suggestive and convincing tool for sociological and critical enquiry.

12

Around the table

Gender and generational conflict in Clara Sereni's autobiographical writing

Maria Grazia Scrimieri

In contemporary Italian women's writing, Clara Sereni's narrative work is certainly among the richest in food references and food-related activities. Born in Rome in 1946 in an intellectual middle-class Jewish family, the author fully experienced the years marked by the union movement, feminism and terrorism, as well as pro-divorce and pro-abortion activism. The daughter of Emilio Sereni – a prominent scholar and an influential figure of the Italian Communist Party's political establishment – she experienced those years of profound social change through a constant process of conflict and negotiation. Her literary career – from her first novel *Sigma Epsilon* (1974), which went almost unnoticed compared with her successful food memoir *Casalinghitudine* (1987) and her family novel *Il gioco dei regni* (The Game of The Kingdoms, 1993), to her last autobiographical novel, *Via Ripetta 155* (Ripetta Street 155, 2015) – brings to light her views on women's relation not only to food but also to identity, society and gender.[1]

In Sereni's narrative work, personal conflict arises from inner contradictions and from the overlapping of multiple roles. As a result, the writer attempts to reinvent her self-image, aware that her entire life can be considered a 'mosaic' and sometimes 'a badly cut mosaic piece'. In this context, she consciously chooses to use food as a means to describe and analyse the pieces and fragments of her identity in her writing. From a cultural perspective, the redefinition of female subjectivity operated by Sereni involves conflict; it also requires her, to quote the philosopher Rosi Braidotti, to work 'through the stock of cumulated images, concepts and representations of women, of female identity'.[2] The subject 'woman' in fact is not a monolithic block defined once and for all, but rather a group of multiple experiences, complex and often contradictory, and it's a process that forms the basis of 'female nomadism' – a concept coined by Braidotti to refer to the construction of the subject, which is a positive expression of the female desire to represent and redefine subjectivity in its diverse and singular forms. Braidotti gives great importance to this process and this redefinition, emphasizing the importance of identity as a place of differences; to analyse the conditions and terms of this redefinition, Braidotti draws a map of female subjectivity that comprises of three different but interconnected levels: 'the difference between man and woman', 'the differences among women' and, finally 'the differences within each woman'.[3]

In this perspective, it is appropriate to revisit Sereni's autobiographical production *sub specie culinaria*[4] – including her last novel, which encapsulates this conflict on multiple levels including around the table. Previous essays on Clara Sereni have focused mainly on the relation between food and subjectivity, on food as a language of the fragmentation of the 'self' or food as a tool to represent Italian political history.[5] This chapter adopts a different approach by analysing the role of food in Sereni's writing not only as a representation of social activity but also as a metonymy for cultural and social belonging in the context of gender and generational conflict.

According to Sereni, writing means 'putting [her] world in order, establishing a fixed point; writing means a moment of balance, it means bringing the reality into focus through pathways that cannot be explored through any other tools'.[6] In her narrative work, multiple identities emerge and intersect: Sereni presents herself as daughter, a young Jewish woman, an activist, a writer, a wife and a mother who chooses to confront complex, contradictory and personal conflicts through the table and the kitchen, and to write about these experiences in a style saturated with food images.

As the daughter of Emilio Sereni – a historian, parliamentarian and one of the most important figures of the anti-fascist movement and of the Italian Communist Party – Sereni described her relation to politics and political activism as complicated. She came to consider cooking as an act of rebellion when she realized that at home food was perceived as a merely functional way of providing sustenance, and therefore associated with austerity and severity, as she recounts in *Casalinghitudine*. In the novel, for the first time after leaving her parents' home, the narrator is invited by her father to a very fancy Roman restaurant. Over the course of the meal, she becomes aware of different issues in their relationship:

> That lunch was a revelation about my relationship with my father, not only for the terrible things he was saying to me, but also about his relationship with

> the outside world, for the poise with which he moved about the high-class restaurant, for the haughtiness that he showed in the selection of wine (at home we didn't drink any), for the ease with which he paid the bill.[7]

Clara Sereni reflects on the two different sides of her upstanding and demanding father, who imposed flavourless and monotonous meals at home while enjoying elaborate and expensive food outside. She begins to cry into her pea soup, a soup she does not eat at that moment, but that she will recreate on her own a year later. Two other dishes, the bean soup and the Neapolitan sauce, give her a further chance to re-evaluate her father. The approach towards these two recipes is very different because the narrator faces the inherent conflict in foods that relate to her father and to her family. In the first dish, the bean soup, she successfully takes on the new challenge of cooking pasta with beans, a dish traditionally considered a symbol of the narrator's struggle for personal independence, as noted by David Del Principe:

> The dish 'pasta e fagioli', then, prepared at a time when the narrator was contemplating living on her own, comes to symbolize the narrator's struggle for independence, itself a subject of the power struggle. Spoken by the narrator's brother-in-law, the maxim 'Vai, vai a vivere da sola, tu non sai cosa significhi campare di pasta e fagioli' ('Go, go ahead, go live by yourself: you don't know what it means to live on *pasta e fagioli*') concretises the relation between female independence and sustenance with the message that the narrator cannot survive either on 'pasta e fagioli' or on her own.[8]

The conflicting paternal relationship is narrated in absentia: the father is not present in the event told, but he emerges as a memory and link with the recipe. Thanks to her good friend Enrico, who is always there to help even when Clara is faced with the possibility of getting an abortion, the author finds the courage to recreate this bean soup, although this dish is loved by her father. This meal represents the generation gap as well as individuality and unconventionality, because Clara decides to ignore the family recipe – which requires garlic and rice – and to instead follow Enrico's memories and desires, to use the food available in her home and more importantly to trust her own culinary instinct: in doing so, she demonstrates that not only does she indeed know how to survive on *pasta e fagioli* but she is also able to create her own bean soup – with tomatoes, onion, bacon and broken spaghetti – and to make it better than others.

Concerning the second dish, the first-person narrator seems unable to deal with the memory of the Neapolitan sauce. The father sometimes crosses into the kitchen, while Sereni wants this to be an area that she can keep all to herself, especially to stand out from him, as the 'room of one's own' mentioned by Virginia Woolf. The confrontation with the strong paternal personality is hard, and the conflict is far from being resolved. On the contrary, he is stigmatized by this recipe, because it is the only recipe her father was able to cook, about which he always bragged and with which the narrator admits that she has not yet reconciled. For Sereni, 'cooking is a form of action' that can provide important moments of reflection and autonomy, and since she uses food to reflect on the generational and personal conflict with her father, it is no coincidence that she decides not to share the recipe for this sauce that he appreciated so much.

Although this has rarely been discussed by scholars of Sereni's work, her identity as a daughter is also defined by her relationship with two mother figures: Xenia Silberberg, her biological mother who died when Clara was only six years old, and her stepmother Silvana Pelori. In an interview with Iaia Caputo,[9] Sereni reveals how the construction of a female genealogy played a fundamental role in her sense of identity. She lost her mother when she was only a child, but she explains that, because of her mother's absences caused by her illness, 'when my mother died, she had long been dead for me, and my early childhood was set on a track that did not anticipate her presence'.[10] Sereni then goes on to disclose the effects of growing up without a maternal role model.

The narrator of *Casalinghitudine* regrets that she has no significant personal memories of Xenia Silberberg, and that most of the things she knows have been reported by other members of the family. Xenia does not have a reputation for having ever been a great cook but in the book the narrator associates her with a stuffed cabbage recipe, although her memory of this connection remains vague: 'I like to think that the stuffed cabbage leaves – a Slavic tradition I believe – come from her, but that doesn't really mean that it is so. It is uncertain, like all the other things about her life that have come down to me.'[11] In *Casalinghitudine*, the mother is not a character who fills a relevant space, and Sereni attempts to recreate her through recipes. As critics have noted, in this novel, an egocentric point of view of the storyteller who considers the death of the mother almost as a betrayal highlights what Adalgisa Giorgio defines as a 'difficult process of elaboration of the loss of the mother's body'.[12] Not even in the novel *Il gioco dei regni* – the autobiographical work that is more about family relations but in which food is less used – is there a real reconnection to the mother figure: on the one hand there is no reflection in the mother – which leads to positivity – but on the other there is not even a negative loss of identity. This is because the storyteller makes the mother assume a symbolic connotation and creates her own genealogy thanks to previous generations.

As we have seen, Sereni uses food and meals to describe and reveal her role within the family, describing them according to diverse situations: these elements can be considered as symbols of her troubled relation with her father and they can also become moments that allow the writer to elaborate on the relationship with her two mothers and with other strong female presence in Sereni's patriarchal family. Her writing highlights other important maternal figures such as aunt Ermelinda and grandmother Alfonsa, two sisters very different from each other. In *Casalinghitudine*, Sereni describes their opposite personalities, which are connoted through their manners and ways of cooking, and from which Sereni learns two different aspects of culinary practice. The former did not cook much, but she agreed to prepare one important dinner every year for Yom Kippur. Having lived in a royal court during her youth, Aunt Ermelinda considered elegance and decoration important, with a special inclination for setting the table and selecting special foods:

> For Yom Kippur, Aunt Ermelinda, who almost never cooked, prepared an excellent dinner. There had to be several delicacies, but it was the olives that held the greatest fascination for me: black, very big [. . . .] Seated at the head of the table in her most elegant dress, Aunt Ermelinda proceeded to surround herself with big plates, little plates, glasses, and silverware in great quantities; our normal dinner was brightened by her rituals, and there were always a few olives set aside for me.[13]

For Ermelinda, food – its preparation and consumption – takes on great value only during religious festivities; from her, Clara learns gestures and absorbs the rhythms of cooking, symbols and rituals, the importance of some gestures of the kitchen and the accuracy of the details of the table, which are also an instrument of care and attention to the other. On the other hand, grandmother Alfonsa, who lived in Israel where she bred chickens and only came to Italy to help her son's family, is described as a strong and strict woman, realistic and practical, especially in the kitchen:

> The golden rule in the kitchen was very simple: 'you eat what is put on the table'. [. . . .] Fortunately, the food was generally simple and without flights of fancy; not even kosher cuisine was represented among Grandmother's dishes, which were chosen mostly on the basis of nutritional value and low cost [. . . .] Grandmother Alfonsa was capable of recycling everything: leftover stew went into meatballs, pieces of dry cod into fritters.[14]

In *Casalinghitudine*, in addition to evoking recipes and memories of her grandmother and her aunt, the narrator also reveals echoes of what she assimilated and absorbed during her childhood: the foods and practices, routines and culinary procedures that she rediscovered and revisited as an adult woman in her kitchen. Sereni highlights their importance in defining her identity and breaking free from the past: it is precisely from Alfonsa that the protagonist feels the need to move away, and she does so through the recipe of *crostini* (bread croutons) – a snack much appreciated in childhood in the 1950s. Unlike her grandmother Alfonsa, the narrator grants herself the use of fresh bread, and that freshness contains a promise of renewal and novelty, a sort of liberation from the past: 'When I started to make *crostini* in my own home, for a while I used fresh bread instead of stale bread, a conscious act of waste in order for me to cut the umbilical cord.'[15] Food, recipes and cooking thus acquire the significance of tools in the narrator's quest for independence. In her path towards adulthood, seventeen-year-old Sereni decided to leave her father's house and live alone. This significant life change, only briefly described in *Casalinghitudine*, is the focus of the writer's final book, *Via Ripetta 155*. This work provides an excellent example of gender and generational conflicts emerging through the redefinition and negotiation of several levels of identity, because the historical context in which the story takes place is intrinsically hostile and coincides with the most contradictory years in the narrator's life. In this book, Sereni describes the struggles she faced between 1967 and 1977 in the context of Italy's political and social conflicts: this context was marked not only by the union movement, the pro-divorce referendum and the feminist movement, but also by the wider challenges faced by young people and students in their search for new role models, as they gradually rejected old world views and the society created by their fathers. In *Via Ripetta 155*, Sereni's personal change, growth and development, and her reflections and achievements, intersect with her conflicts with society, family and her own identity, in the kitchen. In particular, it is through her writing about food that Clara Sereni reveals her contradictory feelings and reflections on being an independent and politically active woman both in politics and in literature, and on her desire to connect with her male 'comrades' without giving up on her feminist ideals. The break from tradition that characterized the crucial years of the sociopolitical movements marked a turning point for women's thinking and is at the centre of Sereni's narrative. The narrator is shown as she confronts different ideas of womanhood and women's inherited social roles, even within the left-wing political movement. For example, she reflects on her comrade Cesare De Michelis: 'He had seen me type and cyclostyle, he had brought me some sandwiches when I just could not stop and I was exhausted: I was afraid of not being able to shake off this role as the angel of the mimeograph machine.'[16]

Later, she writes: 'We woke up early [. . .] I rushed to make hot drinks, fearing recriminations that would rightly rain on my head.'[17] And also:

> [Stefano] could have used the table in the dining room, but maybe he did not use it because he wanted to avoid the steam of the pasta and tomato sauce that I kept preparing for crowds of people, the greasy pots for which I invented cheap recipes, the thousand different omelettes I made to escape the routine, or my sautés of very few mussels on very many slices of toast.[18]

Although the ideals of the youth and student movements proclaimed gender parity and equality, within these groups, women struggled to eradicate the old and established attitudes that kept them trapped in the role of the 'angel in the house' – only to make them the 'angel of the mimeograph'.[19] Their male comrades expected them to participate in occupations, marches, sit-ins and protests, but also – consciously and subconsciously – to prepare meals for the whole group, with care and creativity. Sereni's narrator does not want to be relegated to the kitchen just because she is a woman, but she does not want to give up on this activity either. She is torn by the awareness that as a feminist and an activist, she should leave the kitchen, which historically has been the place and the symbol of women's oppression and constraints. Despite this inherent contradiction, the narrator does not hide her personal passion and interest in food practices, and the importance they have in her life. A significant turning point in her independent life in *Via Ripetta* is the arrival of an electric burner, which marks – as the author ironically highlights, borrowing the expression from Lévi-Strauss – the transition from 'the raw to the cooked'.[20] Her diet then evolves from salads to cooked and more elaborate meals. Some months later, the arrival of a three-burner stove with an oven allows her to fully display her skills in the culinary arts, the ancestral knowledge of women who with imagination and commitment have been able over the centuries to make enough food for the table: for example, by putting into practice some tricks to water down a sauce or a dressing that was not enough for all her guests. In *Via Ripetta 155*, besides the redefinition of the autobiographical narrator's identity as a young adult woman, Clara Sereni also explores another path in female self-definition through the kitchen. The book evokes the tension between a strong sense of duty as an older sister, and an equally strong desire for liberation and emancipation. This conflict emerges most acutely in an episode related to family life. The narrator's mother and her little sister are forced to take a long trip to England for health reasons, and the narrator feels duty-bound to go back home to play her role as the elder daughter – that is to say, the only person who can run the house and the kitchen. The narrator is especially concerned about the culinary aspect of this task because her younger sister wants to eat only pasta with butter and parmesan cheese, milkshake and hamburgers, while her father wants only broccoli.

In *Via Ripetta 155*, the representations of food once again become functional to a better understanding of the difficult relationship with the father, the construction of a female genealogy and even the political dimension. The protagonist would like to reconcile all her identities, 'reassemble' them, and give space to all the contradictory moments and uncertainties that arise during her life without ever considering them as defeats, but thinking of identity as something complex and multifaceted, in constant conflict and ever-changing because – as Braidotti wrote – 'speaking "as a feminist woman" does not refer to one dogmatic framework but rather to a knot of interrelated questions that play on different layers, registers and levels of the self'.[21] In her latest work, Sereni therefore reworks in particular the last level of Braidotti's scheme, which concerns the conflicts within each woman, since she recognizes herself as not unique, but as a subject who from time to time negotiates the inner dynamics and micro-conflicts inherent in the individual roles.

The narrator, in fact, relapses into her role as a daughter: after two months living in her father's house, fully immersed in her 'casalinghitudine',[22] she needs to go back to her independence and her autonomy, but she expects her family, and in particular her mother, to reward her with a gift. In this contradiction between chosen and endured roles, the narrator's inner conflict becomes evident. The different parts of her identity force the narrator to reflect on the idea of herself that she has started piecing together in her adult life. In this path towards knowledge and personal development, the arrival of a partner plays a crucial role as this new presence provides the narrator with the opportunity to examine the implications of political activism, feminism and relationships. In *Via Ripetta 155*, Clara Sereni admits, via her narrator's voice: 'And as I was in love and absorbed by the construction of a couple and of everything around it, I didn't see many things that were happening not too far from me: feminism for example, which changed me as well, even though I did not realise it. Always with this arrogant idea that I was "new" already.'[23] In her relationship, the narrator of *Via Ripetta* experiences a conflict between the feeling of being a new, modern and emancipated woman and the necessity of modifying her habits and practices – including in the kitchen – around her lover's needs. Once she enters a relationship with Stefano, for example, the long and lazy Sundays of the past, with plenty of sleep and no regular meals, become less frequent: they become sparser due to the guilt caused by having internalized the ancestral, historical and cultural link between women, food and the responsibility of caring for others.

As Gian-Paolo Biasin points out, 'the discourse on food inevitably becomes a discourse on pleasure and power'[24] and in Clara Sereni's autobiographical novels, food is, as we have seen, the focal point of a twist in the public and private spheres. Since food provides a precise parallel language, Clara Sereni describes meal scenes that also denote gender issues in the context of her characters' political life. As a matter of fact, it is important to remember that, after her early years of activism in the 1970s, Clara Sereni was also elected deputy mayor of Perugia from 1995 to 1997 – a significant experience that she refers to in some of her books and articles, in particular the novel *Passami il sale* (Pass the Salt, 2002). For Sereni, food and meals provide the opportunity for a subjective reconsideration of historical and social events, while also becoming the narrative *loci* around which similarities and differences emerge. During a dinner among friends, the protagonist of *Casalinghitudine* observes that food can also be a social metaphor: 'In Aldo and Maria's home there was a fixed menu: overcooked pasta and ascetic, bland omelettes, maximum frugality, minimum time spent in the kitchen. To be able to serve the "people" meant that one had to adjust to their lowest and most uneducated standards, a norm that the group never dared to challenge.'[25] On the one hand, Aldo defines Clara's way of cooking as 'bourgeois' because her preference for fancy wines or French cheeses is considered incompatible with left-wing activism; on the other hand, Maria represents a new wave of women who became involved with political movements that professed the need for social equality, but without practising it: Maria is implicitly required to have basic culinary skills to adapt to the demands of activism.

To quote Biasin again, food defines and assigns power. In Sereni's novel, we see this literally become a political issue. As French sociologist Pierre Bourdieu writes in *La Distinction. Critique sociale du jugement* (1979), food was – and still is – an essential tool to highlight social differences, reinforcing and strengthening identities: this appears clearly when the narrator of *Casalinghitudine* articulates her amusement about the relation between food and 'left-wing' activists. This 'group' of militants 'is represented as being dogmatic and patriarchal, just like the traditional left whose policies it opposes'.[26] To quote Mirna Cicioni again, 'Clara understands that in order to become like them (and to be liked by them) she must suppress her love of cooking', because the enjoyment of good food and wine is condemned as not only bourgeois but also dangerously individualistic.[27] Sereni ironizes on left-wing militants, for whom food takes on a political meaning and meals must necessarily adapt to the needs of activism. Similarly, in *Passami il sale*, the narrator describes her activity as a deputy mayor, writing not only about her commitment and responsibilities but also about the difficulty of reconciling her public role with her private life as a wife, and above all, as a mother. These conflicts too are narrated through food-related scenes and episodes.

According to Mirna Cicioni, 'the food of public life – consumed in the time of politics, between a city council, a session and a meeting with members of various parties – is poorly cooked, indigestible, swallowed quickly'.[28] Like a parallel language, this bad or poorly cooked food represents and symbolizes political life, in particular the Italian political scene of the mid-1990s: fast and gaudy, possibly rich and abundant, but not nourishing. Sereni's deputy mayor narrator struggles to find time to spend with her family, for whom lunch and especially dinner were significant shared moments. Unlike the food of politics and public life – flavourless bread, salmon canapés and unhealthy sandwiches – all the dishes that the protagonist of *Passami il sale*, a wife and a mother, is able to prepare for her family in her spare moments are to be considered 'little domestic miracles'. One dish in particular, the zucchini soup prepared by her son Tommaso, 'warms the soul'.[29] Tommaso, who suffers from a mental disability, can be very aggressive, and cooking is one of the very few activities his mother can share with him. Sereni does not define her autobiographical narrator simply as a mother, but as a 'handicapped mother' – an expression that defines her role as the mother of a son with a serious psychological illness, which affects her maternal identity. As the narrator explains her long and difficult path towards becoming and being this mother, she tells us how food and cooking have helped her to find her way. In this conflict too – 'in the context of the search for "meaning" between the narrated self and the son'[30] – cooking reveals itself as a language, a tool that the mother–narrator needs to understand her son's behaviour and to create a connection with him: food discloses its power of negotiation and communication. In Sereni's own words:

> Many things have changed over the years in my kitchen [. . . .] It was my son who changed what we eat at home: because cooking together was one of the few languages that I managed to share with him, and because his dislike of some of my purchases forced me to invent recipes that gave meaning to the shopping and to the dialogue between us.[31]

As we have seen, food can have a resonance far beyond its superficial meaning. In Sereni's autobiographical writing, food, cooking and meals are not just so many meaningful elements but also represent indispensable moments of aggregation, social identification and self-awareness. They reflect memories, human and family relations, and they also strongly resonate with the semantic dimension of food analysed, among others, by Roland Barthes, who highlights the link between language and food.[32] Barthes defines food as a communication system, a protocol of habits, situations and behaviours, and seeks to recognize its grammar – or rather its grammars. Food means something other than itself because it indicates and represents a certain situation, it conveys messages and systems of value and it acquires meaning when it is utilized in a society, in a community.

Food and cuisine, and their connection with the female experience, are recurring themes in the narrative works of Clara Sereni. They are at the heart of a generation gap and are a source of conflict between public and private life. Through food and culinary practices, the reader can understand the cultural construction of the conflict created by gender identity. In her writing and through the voices of her narrators, the author finds a way to redefine and bring together the pieces of her different experiences of identity, as explained by Giuliana Menozzi: 'The awareness, gained through food, of others and herself occurs in many narratives. It marks her relationship with the members of the political group to which she belongs, the different men she loves, her family, her mother-in-law, children and female friends.'[33]

The language of food and its signifiers serve to communicate the notions of devotion, dedication, care and attention, but also the relation between the self and 'the Other' – in other words, the 'difference within' described by Rosi Braidotti under the three levels of female subjectivity. The representations of food and meals that Sereni often incorporates into her narratives are described in order to amplify and develop their significance in the text. They are functional to understanding and explaining the narrator's difficult family relationships (in particular between father and daughter), the construction of a female genealogy, the political dimension and the discovery and difficulties of motherhood. For these reasons, food becomes a key to read change, and meals become the tools for a subjective reassessment of diverse social, family-related and personal circumstances, while remaining the core around which differences arise; as Elisa Gambaro recently stated: 'What Clara Sereni cares most about is a notion of food as an encrypted device used to talk about herself.'[34]

The author allows space for her contradictory moments, and for all her greatest uncertainties and unsolved questions, without considering those as a failure but rather as complex and multifaceted concepts in perpetual conflict with one another. In her representation of the most intimate form of conflict – internal conflict – Clara Sereni recognizes her autobiographical characters (and herself) as not-unequivocal: they are subjects who must gradually negotiate internal conflicts in every new role, while remaining aware that gender identity is not set and fixed by convictions, beliefs or stereotypes, but rather constantly changing and evolving, through social relations and human connections over the course of specific circumstances. As Stephen Kolsky points out:

> The notion of fragmentation has been much exploited by feminist writers to stress that women's lives are subject to male prerogatives and usually shaped by forces more powerful than themselves. In Sereni's case, the nature of the fragmentation is such that many details about central events in her life are omitted, and the reader is left only with powerful images of moments that she considers crucial to her development.[35]

Gender identity is not definite, but is renegotiated according to social relations and confrontations. Moreover, as the generational rupture of the late 1960s has changed the places and characters of conflict and debate, food has been reconfirmed as a communication tool that comes where a more conventional language does not always succeed in doing so. As Francesca Calamita affirms: 'The food taken, prepared or refused by Sereni's autobiographical protagonist intersects with her human experience and inevitably with her socio-cultural condition as a woman.'[36] For this reason, paying attention to the presence of food in literature can thus provide a way of better understanding narrative works and their interpretations of the world: '[w]riting to put the world in order'[37] as we already pointed out, but also '[re]inventing is the only possible way to escape our boundaries, reinventing so as not to tread over the same ground, reinventing so as not to eat one's heart out'.[38]

13

Beyond size and weight

Gianna Schelotto's 'La ragazza che mangiava la luna'[1]

Francesca Calamita

Food, feminism and self-injury

In 2011, Michela Marzano, a well-known Italian philosopher, essayist and academic, wrote an autobiographical novel on her anorexic experience, thereby sharing with her audience her deepest fear, frustration and hopes.[2] 'I convinced myself', she wrote in *Volevo essere una farfalla* (I Wanted to Be a Butterfly, 2011), 'that if I could become as light as a butterfly, everything would work out.'[3] By metaphorically transforming into a butterfly, a symbol of lightness, grace and beauty par excellence, and therefore losing most of her body weight, the young autobiographical protagonist believes that she will be able to achieve happiness and emotional fulfilment. Thus, her desired body shape becomes for her not only the visible proof of the numbers displayed by her weighting scale but also a tool by means of which she can reach something else: love, admiration and academic success.

Other present-day Italian women writers, such as Alessandra Arachi in *Briciole* (Crumbs, 1994) and more recently in *Non più briciole* (No More Crumbs, 2015) as well as Nadia Fusini in *La bocca più di tutto mi piaceva* (The Mouth I Like the Most, 2004) and Margherita Da Bac in *Per fortuna c'erano i pinoli* (Fortunately There Were Pine Nuts, 2014),[4] have portrayed a series of anorexic and bulimic characters whose shape and weight perception is related to their emotional fulfilment and to the construction of female identity in contemporary Italian society; by refusing food and trying to shape their bodies, all these young women attempt to change their existence. Among these texts is also Gianna Schelotto's 'La ragazza che mangiava la luna' (The Girl Who Ate the Moon), a short story published in Schelottos's own collection *Una fame da morire* (Starving to Death, 1992),[5] one of the first Italian narrative books to analyse the epidemic of women's pathological relationships with food. By decoding the meaning of the protagonist's anorexic and bulimic struggles and by relating her paradoxical behaviours towards food and body to women's socio-cultural position in contemporary Italian culture and society, my chapter will provide a reflection on how disorderly eaters can split up their mental desires from their corporeal bounds. I will frame my argument along Susie Orbach's understanding of eating disorders and other feminist readings of anorexia and bulimia that see these pathological behaviours as controversial, yet powerful answers to patriarchal dictates in women's lives. Orbach's feminist readings of eating appeared in the 1980s, just a few years before the publication of *Una fame da morire*, and considers issues of gender and identity in the development of anorexia, bulimia and binge eating that Schelotto also narrates in her stories. Furthermore, in the same years, Italian scholars in the area of women's studies did not work extensively on eating disorders, hence the necessity to frame my argument in Orbach's well-known texts.

In the development of anorexia nervosa and bulimia nervosa as well as other food-related disorders, such as binge eating and orthorexia, the body plays a key role: first, it becomes the focus of attention of those who suffer from these pathologies; second, it is regarded by sufferers as something to be venerated, feared and hated at once. According to the latest edition of the *Diagnostic and Statistical Manual of Mental Disorders* (DSM-5), published by the American Psychiatric Association in 2013, one of the criteria for identifying anorexia nervosa is a 'disturbance in the way one's body weight or shape is experienced'.[6] Similarly, the influence of body shape and weight perception as an instrument of self-evaluation is one of the conditions present in the diagnosis of bulimia nervosa.[7] 'Disorderly eaters'[8] engage in a series of self-harming behaviours that help them to achieve the fictional figure that they dream of inhabiting. They include – but are not limited to – decreasing their daily food intake drastically, using laxative products inappropriately and exercising excessively. While attempting to isolate themselves from their real bodies, anorexic and bulimic women try also to change their existence, as the autobiographical protagonist of *Volevo essere una farfalla* reveals explicitly and how Sara, the protagonist of Schelotto's 'La ragazza che mangiava la luna', attempts to do, as we will see shortly. The slimness they pursue is not related to the achievement of bodily perfection or to vanity, but rather it is a means to gain control over their lives.[9] Eating disorders, therefore, become an answer to the family and socio-cultural problems these women face. Furthermore, the body often also acts as an indicator of the illness for family members, friends and acquaintances, who can see the physical outcome of the obsessive–compulsive behaviour towards food displayed by those who suffer from eating disorders.

Eating disorders are also complex instruments of communication employed by women in order to say what they cannot express explicitly in words. They are self-destructive languages where the words starvation, binging and purging often recur. As the young protagonist of *Volevo essere una farfalla* reveals: 'Anorexia is the symptom of a word that cannot be spoken in a different way.'[10] This interpretation echoes feminist understanding of anorexia and bulimia, developed in the late 1970s, when scholars of women's studies began to engage in the debate on eating disorders at the same time, significantly, as feminists were beginning to question traditional notions of gender and the female body. Since then, feminist researchers have highlighted the important link between anorexia and social context as well as its interpretation as a language to communicate with others; indeed, Susie Orbach's *Fat Is a Feminist Issue* (1978) and *Hunger Strike* (1983), Kim Chernin's *The Hungry Self* (1986), Marylyn Lawrence's *The Anorexic Experience* (1981), Morag MacSween's *Anorexic Bodies* (1993), Helen Malson's *The Thin Woman* (1998) and more recently another analysis by Orbach, *Bodies* (2009)[11] emphasize the link between the hierarchical aspects of the social structure and eating disorders, tracing the evolution of the close relationship between anorexia, bulimia, binge eating and social contexts across decades. In doing so, they also remind us about psychiatric studies published at the same time, such as Mara Selvini Palazzoli's *L'anoressia mentale* (Mental Anorexia, 1963),[12] that sees the origin of these pathologies in societal expectations and cultural norms placed on women by patriarchal authority.

From different disciplinary perspectives and with different approaches, all these scholars suggest that women's troubled relationship with food and body do not fall into the category of traditional illnesses, but rather that they should be considered complex pathologies where sickness, cultural context and women's psychology come together. In Lawrence's words: 'anorexia is a problem crucially related to women's psychology, which is related in turn to women's way of being in the world.'[13] As Susan Bordo reminds us, in the past, clinicians did not consider feminist readings of eating disorders in their diagnosis, as their aim was to create a 'dividing line between pathology and normality',[14] thus partially taking into account in their diagnoses the significant socio-cultural factors involved in the development of eating disorders claimed by feminist scholars. Today, however, the situation has changed: as more men experience eating disorders, psychologists are encouraged to re-rethink feminist cultural arguments in a broader context and the significant relationship between body image, socio-cultural context and identity and anorexia, bulimia and binge eating.[15] In her autobiographical novel, Marzano briefly touches this point by referring to her father who does not understand the complex socio-cultural mechanism that shapes the development of eating disorders: '[he] believes that anorexia is like a cold that you catch it outside if you are not covered up enough [. . . .] But when will this battle end?'[16] Just as in many feminist scholars' readings of eating disorders, Marzano's anorexia is not a conventional disease, as her father believes, but a fight against herself, her family environment, those who do not feed her constant hunger for love, her socio-cultural circle and the expectations placed on women by contemporary society. In Orbach's words, 'the anorexic is in protest at her conditions';[17] and the protagonists of Italian women's writing of the 1990s and the 2000s, such as Schelotto's Sara, Marzano's Michela and Arachi's Elena, are in protest at their socio-cultural role.

Sara's obsession with food: 'A recipe for binging and hurting'

Schelotto introduces the young protagonist of 'La ragazza che mangiava la luna'[18] by emphasizing her addictive behaviour towards food: 'Did you eat some chocolate? [. . .] Where was it? Where did you find it?'[19] In this passage, Sara, a 24-year-old bulimic, and her mother are arguing in front of an embarrassed shop assistant who is helping the protagonist to find a new nice shirt. Frustrated by her daughter's lack of self-control, Sara's mother believes that humiliating her in public will have a positive effect on her eating habits; however, the protagonist's self-esteem is regularly undermined by these episodes. As Orbach suggests in *On Eating* (2002), a collection of bite-size statements to self-help: 'denying yourself particular foods is a recipe for binging and hurting. If you banish or forbid yourself a particular food, you crave endless amount of it' (44). This is precisely how Sara feels; unable to eat chocolate when her family does, she devours it secretly, away from humiliating gazes. The confrontation between her mother and the protagonist is just one example of her suffocating daily routine. Indeed, the young character's decisions are often questioned, predominantly by her mother, who constantly and publicly denigrates her curvaceous silhouette and her disordered eating habits, but also by her lover, who desires obsessively Sara's fat body. Overwhelmed by her toxic family environment, Sara has found a way to escape. She believes herself to be Livia, an imaginary alter-ego who is as thin and light as a butterfly: 'Livia is a very beautiful name, very light. You can say it in one breath, this is why I chose it for the thin girl hiding inside myself.'[20] According to a young disorderly eater, interviewed by the British sociologist Morag MacSween, 'inside every bulimic is an anorexic trying to get out.'[21] This mechanism is precisely what Sara experiences every day. Sara suffers from her relationship with her mother in the family environment as well as from the social stigma every fat woman endures in contemporary society. Imagining herself to be Livia, a name that the protagonist considers appropriate for an elegant woman, therefore helps her to relieve the pain temporarily, although this relief is not sufficient and gorging becomes her default mode to cope with her unhappy existence.

Psychological research considers the symptoms of anorexia an attempt to accomplish the social construction of femininity, while those of bulimia are read as unconventional. In the collective imaginary, anorexics are perceived to be women with self-control towards food, while bulimics are those who lack it and indulge constantly in eating. Since the nineteenth century, indeed, middle-class women have been formally constructed in the medical discourse as unstable creatures whose nature should be regulated by following a series of rules, including diets that could control their nervous nature.[22] Currently in Western cultures, it is still considered more traditionally feminine to lack appetite, rather than to eat too much; consequentially, it is more feminine to have a thin body shape rather than a voluptuous one. As Maree Burns has demonstrated in an article on the perception of eating disorders in New Zealand, anorexia and bulimia revolve around a 'dualistic logic',[23] which in turn relates to the social construction of femininity. Anorexia is equated with self-control and supremacy, while bulimia is equated with a lack of willpower and shame. Like other obsessive-compulsive disorders and addictions, a bulimic loses control in front of food and, in doing so, she experiences the social stigma of being shamed for her habits. In contrast to these traditional perceptions, in *Volevo essere una farfalla*, Marzano suggests that 'anorexic women and bulimic women do not exist, but rather many people who use food to say something.'[24] Similarly, for Sara, food is a language, and it is not important to focus on the means – starving, binging or a mix of them – employed to voice this protest, but rather on the meaning of that particular protest.

Coping with an eating disorder: Anxiety and excellence

Sara is aware of her troubled relationship with food and she attempts to control it. When her father suggests that he would buy the moon for her if he could only see her happy, for example, she replies sagaciously: 'Do not do that dad [. . . .] I am sure that one day or another I would eat it.'[25] She knows that her eating habits are not natural acts of nourishment but a way to relieve her anxiety temporarily. It is significant that she speaks in these terms to her father, who emerges as the most permissive between her parents, thus admitting that she needs help and protection to overcome her addiction. She also realizes that her fat body acts as a shelter to protect her fragile ego: "It protects me from almost everything. By losing weight I would enter into a world that my organs and senses would not recognize."[26] In *Fat Is a Feminist Issue*, Orbach makes strikingly similar statements to those pronounced by Sara, suggesting that fat is used to 'provid[e] space and protection for the feelings. Without fat a woman might worry unconsciously that her feelings will be exposed. There would be no difficulty in getting thin if the competitive feelings could find no place to hide and just disappeared.'[27] Sara experiences these mixed feelings every day, and she believes that everyone perceives her as a failure. Similarly, in 'La mamma in un boccone' (Mom in one bite), the other short story published by Schelotto in *Una fame da morire*, anorexics are labelled as 'diabolically smart patients'[28] who are aware of their troubled relationship with body and food and who try to hide it from their psychotherapists; Schelotto's Sara, Arachi's Elena in *Briciole* and the unnamed protagonist of Fusini's autobiographical novel *La bocca più di tutto mi piaceva*, as well as the young Michela in *Volevo essere una farfalla*, are all extremely smart women who excel at high school, university and work. Parents and relatives decode their illness only when it becomes visible through their bodies since these women are often able to hide their secret binges and daily purges from them and their doctors. For example, in Arachi's book, Elena's endless cycle of binging and purging is accompanied by four hours of running every day and long afternoons at her desk to study to become 'the pride of the institute'[29] as her school principal and teachers expect of her. While Elena is studying to fulfil her role as the school's best student, she dreams about food all the time: 'on each page, on each line, tonnes of puddings and chocolate cakes would appear';[30] however, only when her body drastically shrinks, people around her acknowledge her eating disorder. Elena also refuses professional help because, like many disorderly eaters, she does not trust her therapist:

> I already knew it: those visits would become four sessions per week, for almost two, three or even four or five years . . . . I convinced myself that psychoanalysis could do nothing for me. I wanted Massimiliano back, I wanted to be as beautiful as Sofia Loren. As clever as Marie Curie [. . . .] How could Dr Costantino Bricaro's useless therapy couch give me back all these things?[31]

Like Arachi's Elena, Schelottos' Sara believes that several hours per week with a therapist will not help her to find any happiness; rather, trying to reach her unachievable goals will bring some form of satisfaction. Therefore, she decides to visit a dietician rather than a psychologist who will help her to get back in shape and therefore find some happiness. In search of her true self, Sara's attitude is similar to Sheila McLeod, who in the introduction to her memoir about her battle with eating disorders, *The Art of Starvation*, declares:

> I have decided to meet the phenomenon in meeting my former self and attempting to recall what was actually going on before the onset of the disease and during the time that it was taking its course. I was trying to resolve something, trying to prove something and, through the language of my symptoms, to say something. Whether she knows it or not, and however obliquely metaphorical the language of her symptoms may appear, the anorexic is trying to tell us something, and something quite specific about herself and the context in which she exists.[32]

Like McLeod, Sara's attempt to embody a new person through her diet is a clear attempt to change her life: by following her dietician's suggestions, she tries to meet another version of herself. McLeod has overcome her illness and therefore talks about her 'former self', while Sara, who is fully affected by the pathology, is looking for her desired self: Livia. Eating disorders for Sara and Sheila are a tool of expression that is both powerful and self-destroying; they allow Sara to communicate her deepest feelings, exactly as McLeod does. Her symptoms are, therefore, material outcomes of her innermost self, a non-verbal language by which she attempts to speak about herself.

Stigma, love and attempts to create a new self

In accordance with Orbach, who argues that contemporary society places cultural stigma upon overweight individuals – because 'everyone knows that fat women can't win, in fact aren't even in the same game'[33] – I suggest that this situation is exactly what Schelotto describes in a passage where her character Sara deals with similar circumstances. When Laura, Sara's best friend, takes her to a meeting with one of their professors, with whom both girls are infatuated, she believes that bringing Sara with her will be harmless; with her curvaceous body shape, Sara does not reflect a contemporary ideal of femininity and beauty. Laura considers Sara to be almost asexual and therefore 'out of the game', to use Orbach's language. When the professor – who will become Sara's lover – gives his whole attention to Sara, Laura thinks: 'Ugly fatty.'[34] She does not address the protagonist directly with these words, but Sara intuits correctly that this is precisely what her best friend is thinking about her in that moment. Sara trusts food more than her best friend who, as we have just seen, is not honest with her about her feelings.

The relationship with the young professor Giorgio Turro, which is central to Schelotto's short story, increases Sara's self-esteem only partially. Sara was infatuated with him since the start of her university studies, and while Giorgio is not in love with her, he is obsessed with her, and particularly with her fat body. The author does not address explicitly his psychopathology, but his sexual deviance emerges clearly page after page.[35] Giorgio displays an egocentric, narcissistic personality and also, as is true of many individuals affected by borderline disorders, has a very fragile self-esteem that needs constant attention. At the start of their relationship, Sara decides to follow a new diet and for the first time in her life she is able to lose weight. She follows her new regime diligently because she feels loved by someone and therefore does not feel the need to fill the emotional empty space anymore. Nevertheless, this blissful scenario ends as soon as Sara feels forced to eat what Giorgio pushes her to ingest. Giorgio does not want her to become thinner; their sexual encounters are characterized by sharing of chocolates, pastries and desserts. Giorgio feeds Sara in a desperate attempt to feed his selfish ego; he forces the young woman to devour numerous high-calorie desserts, thus satisfying his perverse sexual needs.

Anorexics and bulimics' relationship with food is paradoxical: they love and hate it at the same time. Their favourite recipes for themselves are usually those that require a quick preparation and do not involve too many ingredients; by contrast, they love feeding others. Orbach notes of this dichotomy that the anorectic

> shows concerns for the food needs of those close to her. She cooks and shops for them, and discusses recipes, dinner party menus and the latest restaurants [. . . .] She gives to others what she so craves herself. Her need for food is converted into satisfying those needs in others.[36]

In satisfying Turro's behaviour, Sara follows this mechanism and satisfies his need rather than taking care of herself.[37] However, once she understands that her lover is manipulating her, she refuses to play his game. This refusal is an evident sign of her growing awareness concerning her own illness and a way to protect her fragile ego from further disappointments.

Initially seen as positive, the start of a new relationship that could potentially boost her ego becomes a further suffocating liaison. Sara is obsessed by food, Giorgio by sexual encounters with fat women: they both suffer from compulsions that are different and similar at the same time. Trapped in this obsessive–compulsive scenario, Sara decides to leave Giorgio and ironically informs him about her decision when he is waiting for her at his house with some pastries ready on the table. Sara runs away from her perpetrator while he desperately cries: 'Sara! Sara!' Feeling highly self-empowered, Sara thinks: 'But he is not calling me! I am Livia.'[38] Giorgio's sexual compulsion for fat women acts as a mirror for Sara; by decoding his obsessive behaviour, she understands the complex mechanism she employs with food. His lust is similar to her gluttony: 'this is how you managed to stop it',[39] says her dietician, psychoanalysing her new attitude towards food. Paradoxically, a toxic relationship with a man who is scared of intimacy with thin women and is only able to enjoy sexual encounters with fat women helps Sara to understand her illness. At the end of the short story, she has lost some kilograms along with a man who used her to satisfy his sexual deviance. Furthermore, she has gained the confidence to embrace a new existence. In this short story, bulimia is a self-destructive illness, but it also becomes an empowering solution, however, allowing Sara to escape from her body shape, to find her desired self, Livia, and to be on the right path to fully incorporate her new self.

Bulimarexic routines

Schelotto's short story focuses mostly on the dynamics of the toxic relationship between Sara and Giorgio, while Arachi's first novel, *Briciole*, depicts the bulimarexic routine that Elena follows religiously every day, sharing numerous details about her binging–purging cycle. If Schelotto privileges the psychological aspects in her short story and therefore focuses on Sara's daily eating habits only partially, Arachi, like many other contemporary writers on this subject, describes regularly Elena's routine with food. In order to vomit, Elena experiments with the ways to do it and spends hours in her toilet pushing her fingers deeper and deeper into her throat: 'That day I was firm: with two fingers in your throat you can vomit, all first aid manuals said it.'[40] In this pathological process, Elena loses weight daily, thereby entering another realm where she is able to separate her mind from her body: 'To disappear slowly into my clothes would have pushed me out of the real world. More and more each day.'[41] Leslie Heywood uses the expression 'anorexic logic' to explain the separation of body and mind in the development of eating disorders; this logic represents 'a set of assumptions that values mind over body, thin over fat'.[42] As Heywood suggests, this legacy affects not only women who suffer from anorexia and bulimia but also those who are at war with calories and food.[43] This split between the real body and the imagined one is precisely what Elena is experiencing, exactly as Sara does while she imagines to be her alter-ego Livia.

In her study on eating disorders in Italian women's writing of the 1990s and the 2000s, Grazia Menechella suggests that Elena experiences a troubled relationship with her mother, which is one of the factors involved in the development of her eating disorder. Indeed, at the beginning of the novel, Elena is able to vomit three meatballs in tomato sauce, a gesture that represents her rejection of her mother.[44] The meatballs are synonymous with her mother's affection: a kind of love that she rejects. Elena does not want to be fed with food but rather with feelings, but both her mother and her husband do not understand this need. Elena sends constant messages to her loved ones, but exactly as it happens with Schelotto's Sara, who attempts to gain attention from Giorgio and her mother, these emotional memos are not decoded. If her closest friends and members of her family are not available, Elena tries to satisfy her emotional need by meeting new men, exactly as Sara does with food. As Menechella notes, Elena's bulimic phase coincides with an obsessive–compulsive attitude towards sex that paradoxically may help her to fill the void.[45] However, throughout her bulimarexic experience Elena meets several men who do not satisfy her hunger for affection and protection.[46] They are absent lovers and often self-centred, and they do not pay attention to her needs: Saverio is addicted to heroin, Osvaldo is self-absorbed, Giorgio is a narcissist and Franco, her future absent husband, is more devoted to his work than to her. Elena understands that her problematic relationship with food is related to her need to feel loved and desired by others, similarly to Sara who does not feel happy with Turro. Elena, like Sara, persistently sends verbal and non-verbal messages about her feelings to all of her lovers and her family members, but as intimacy-disablers, they are unable to understand her struggle with food. Both characters starve and binge, under the distracted eyes of their families and lovers who cannot see the self-destructive reality these women are experiencing. Both 'La ragazza che mangiava la luna' and *Briciole* are autobiographical texts: Schelotto retells a story of one of her patients, including personal observations as a woman and comparing Sara's vicissitudes with her own life experience, while Arachi's novel is explicitly autobiographical, thus confirming that *bulimanografie*[47] often uses personal circumstances as a starting and focal point for the narrative.

Conclusion

The protagonist of Schelotto's *Una fame da morire* attempts to transform her body into a utopian silhouette that will allow her to partake of the illusion that she has separated herself from her real self, thereby finding some illusory happiness. Becoming Livia, her imaginary alter-ego, is a way to create a new Sara who has left behind her problematic relationship with her mother as well as her toxic partner, albeit she does not find a permanent solution to her struggles. Anorexia, bulimia, binge eating and other atypical relationships with food are problematic, paradoxical, harmful instruments of self-empowerment in Schelotto's short story, similar to other Italian women's writing of the same time, such as Marzano in *Volevo essere una farfalla* and Arachi in *Briciole* and *Non più briciole*. On the one hand, they are depicted as complex diseases where several factors contribute to their development; on the other hand, they play into a process of self-discovery and transformation, thus fitting into the categories of the paradoxical diseases that are at the same time harmful and empowering, as feminist scholars of the 1970s to 1990s frame them. Self-injuring through food becomes a metaphorical language that helps Sara to find a way to question the social constrictions and cultural contradictions inherent in Italian women's position in contemporary, yet patriarchal, culture, which she experiences at the hands of her family. Through a self-destructive, yet arguably self-empowering, path, Sara, like Michela and Elena, looks for her real self in a quest motivated by her hunger for love, affection and protection, thus deconstructing her past identity and trying to shape an alternative persona.

14

Happy hours

Food, politics and female friendship in Silvia Ballestra's *Amiche mie*

Claudia Bernardi

Introduction

Political engagement is a constant theme of Silvia Ballestra's (b. 1969) literary production, but her ongoing reflection on the possibilities, forms and spaces available for political action in contemporary Italy, as well as the role that writing should play in this, have found their most convincing expression in *Amiche mie* (My Friends, 2014).[1] In this novel, food appears prominently as a subject around which the characters' political discussions and actions revolve, as well as a subtle signifier of the female protagonists' personal and social anxieties linked to the persistence of gender expectations regarding meal preparation and consumption. Throughout the narrative, Ballestra weaves together many of the motifs that have appeared in her work since her debut in the early 1990s, including her generation's disillusionment with engagement in civil society, women's growing discontent about the limited platforms available for their activism and the tension experienced by experimental writers who wish to express such concerns through innovative forms while still being able to communicate the urgency of the country's political crisis.[2] In food, Ballestra finds a theme that allows her to connect her political, feminist and literary concerns in an immediate way, by denouncing political corruption in the context of the very relatable matter of healthy nutrition for children, but also by presenting food-related activities as emblematic of a culture that continues to cast women in the role of nurturers, whether they like it or not.

The politics of food and the relationship between politics and food in Italy have been the subject of important studies, but for the most part these have been guided by historical, sociological and anthropological perspectives, with a focus on issues of national and regional identity.[3] The link between political engagement, food and eating habits has received, until recently, far less attention, and most of the research conducted on this nexus has focused on issues of food ethics and activism prompted primarily by the Slow Food movement.[4] In this context, Carole Counihan has addressed specifically the role of gender in food activism, remarking on the strong participation of women at grassroots level, while institutional roles remain dominated by men.[5] However, there has been little discussion of the connection between political engagement and food in literary representations of and by women, despite the fact that studies grounded in feminist scholarship have gone a long way to address the relationship between food, women and different forms of cultural production in Italy, variously emphasizing representations of food preparation or consumption both in personal and social contexts. From an interdisciplinary perspective, for example, Maria Giuseppina Muzzarelli, Lucia Re and the other contributors to their volume,[6] have argued that food and eating appear in books, media and other cultural artefacts as emblematic of the patriarchal social structures that at different times have positioned women as nurturers or starvers, voracious or puritanical, or have cast them as edible or devouring bodies. More recently, and with a focus on literary writing, Francesca Calamita has offered readings of literary representations of food and female eating habits by Italian women writers as attempts to communicate women's anxieties and discontent about their lives and social roles otherwise impossible to verbalize, whether due to social constraints or to personal circumstances.[7]

As we shall see, in *Amiche mie*, food certainly functions as a cultural signifier for worries and anxieties of middle-class, middle-aged, white Italian women from different regional, religious and ideological backgrounds, with occasional mentions of eating disorders as manifestations of those anxieties (not exclusive to women), but, on the whole, it mainly plays out as an opportunity for political reflection and activism against the backdrop of school canteens run by corrupt conglomerates, the source of guilt for the many pre-cooked meals served and eaten by women in the interstices of their frenetic Milanese lives and a scathing critique of the 'Milano da bere' (Milan to drink) culture harking back to the 1980s, its bars dominated by happy hours where it has become impossible to order a simple coffee.[8] While it still appears in the text as, to quote Calamita's title, a 'language of the female experience', in Ballestra's novel, food is also presented as the very concrete source of ethical concern, the political significance of which needs to be unpacked, fully verbalized and challenged in the social sphere by her protagonists. This discussion intends to do exactly that, unpacking and discussing the way food gradually reveals itself to the protagonists and to the readers of *Amiche mie* as a multilayered cultural signifier of female traditions, constraints and expectations, but also as a tangible locus of social conflict and therefore an opportunity for public participation for women who, for a combination of gender politics and historical circumstances, have been excluded from other platforms of social engagement.

Women, politics and engaged writing: Ballestra's long-standing commitment

In an interview about *Amiche mie*, Ballestra was asked whether supermarkets had a meaningful presence in literary writing. Ballestra framed her reply in wider-ranging terms, preferring to speak about food in general:

> I don't know about supermarkets, but food certainly [plays an important role in literature], and not only in recent times! (Madeleines, tomato soups, Montalbano's delicacies, the investigation-expose-thrillers of so many writers [. . .]). Every discourse has to do with food, food is something people talk about a lot [. . . .] Here [in *Amiche mie*] I talk specifically of 'public' food [. . .] therefore food that is somehow 'administered, politicised, participated' as well as fed to young citizens who are sensitive to its quality [. . . .] I was also interested in measuring the gap between 'dream' food of television [. . .] and real everyday food (canteens, drinks and nibbles, frozen foods for the family) and the re-positioning of women in relation to the preparation and knowledge of this food.[9]

Ballestra's words point not only at the centrality of food culture and consumption in literary writing in general and in *Amiche mie* in particular but also at how these are presented in the novel as belonging to both the public and the private spheres, with women forced to bridge the gap between the two in a historical moment where gender expectations in relation to food appear to be changing, but perhaps not as quickly as the technology of its production and the practices of its consumption. Either way, whether presenting the flawed economy of mass food production and distribution in public schools or the changes in women's personal experiences of domestic meals, the novel's focus on the gender dynamics that govern the characters' relationship with food is consistent with Ballestra's effort to draw a political link between all aspects of contemporary Italian life, in this case the lives of women from white, middle-class, urban families living in northern Italy in the aftermath of the global financial crisis.[10] Through her increasingly bleak portrayal of four women in their forties and fifties, and some of their friends, as they navigate personal and social crises in a Milanese winter and spring, while also trying to fight corrupt catering companies and feed their families, the novel ultimately offers female friendship as an important resource for solace to personal and political disillusionment, as well as a motivation to remain engaged in society, even when this engagement is limited to fighting so that children can eat safe and nutritious meals. In doing so, Ballestra adds a new, mature chapter to her socially committed literary output that began in the 1990s.

In Ballestra's first three books – the collection of short stories *Compleanno dell'iguana* (The Iguana's Birthday, 1991), the novel *La guerra degli Antò* (The War of the Antòs, 1992) and the second short-story collection *Gli orsi* (The Bears, 1994)[11] – political engagement took the form of a post-modern satire of the ineffectual attempts of young university students to effect social change in the Italy of the 1990s, marked by the unstoppable ascent to power of media magnate and billionaire Silvio Berlusconi.[12] In those early books, the stylistic focus was on the creation of an innovative language that could represent the voice of that generation. After publishing her interview/biography of woman writer and activist from the Marche region, Joyce Lussu (1912–98),[13] however, Ballestra reconsidered the effectiveness of her early experimental emphasis, finding it ineffective when trying to describe the lives of ordinary women in a country that was increasingly challenging the political and social gains of the previous decades, including their rights regarding sexual and reproductive choices.

From the end of the 1990s, we see a stylistic shift towards realism in Ballestra's narrative production. In *La giovinezza della signorina N.N. Una storia d'amore* (The Youth of Miss N.N. A Love Story, 1998), *Nina* (2001) and *Il compagno di mezzanotte* (The Midnight Friend, 2002),[14] key moments of women's coming-of-age process, such as first heterosexual love, female friendship and childbirth/motherhood, are presented as both private and social experiences, with inescapable political reverberations. With *Tutto su mia nonna* (All About My Grandmother, 2005), Ballestra returns to the experimental modes of her early books but reframes them within the tradition of communication among women, arguing for a specifically female language passed on from generation to generation, from grandmothers to mothers to granddaughters, along with family recipes.[15] Only one year later, her historical novel *La seconda Dora* (The Second Dora, 2006) shows Ballestra again adopting realist narrative conventions to tell in a lyrical but linear style the story of a young, Jewish woman, Dora, under fascist rule and during the Second World War (1922–45), and her life of quiet moral resistance as a school teacher in the post-war years.[16] The tension between the desire to experiment with narrative language and structure and the need to adopt more mainstream forms in order to communicate effectively the urgency of her subject matter is also evident in Ballestra's second historical novel, *I giorni della Rotonda* (The Days of the Rotunda, 2009),[17] which interweaves the history of the failures of the alternative Left of the 1970s and the subsequent disenchantment and political involution of the 1980s.

Ballestra's belief in the political responsibility of writers and intellectuals, especially in the portrayal of women's lives and experiences, a belief reflected in the careful negotiation of content and form in her fiction, also inspired her to write non-fiction works: in *Contro le donne nei secoli dei secoli* (Against Women across the Centuries, 2006),[18] she discusses the misogynistic backlash against women in Italian society, institutions and media during the years of Berlusconi rule, while in *Piove sul nostro amore. Una storia di donne, medici, aborti, predicatori e apprendisti stregoni* (It Rains on Our Love: A Story of Women, Doctors, Abortions, Preachers and Sorcerer's Apprentices, 2008) she argues for the need to uphold the Law 194 that guarantees women's reproductive rights in Italy.[19] In the same vein, she contributed in the role of screenplay supervisor to Alina Marazzi's *Vogliamo anche le rose* (We Want Roses Too, 2007), a film on women's lives and the feminist movement of the 1960s and 1970s. And to counter the indifference of Italian intellectuals to the tradition of women writers, Ballestra also published her first book for children, *Christine e la città delle dame* (Christine and the City of Ladies, 2015),[20] based on the life of fifteenth-century Italian–French writer Christine de Pizan.

It is with *Amiche mie* however, that Ballestra's decades-long reflections on political commitment, the existential and social condition of women in Italian society, and the role of writing in exploring this connection find their most articulate expression. This is due in great part to the use of food both as a central theme and as a metaphor that encompasses multiple layers of discourse. As already mentioned, this is not the first time that food features in Ballestra's writing, and in the acknowledgements at the end of *Amiche mie* she explains that the relationship between women, children and food has 'obsessed' her since writing *Tutto su mia nonna*. In the same note, she also mentions her contribution to a collection of short narratives about food published on the occasion of the international expo held in Milan in 2015, *Storie di cibo, racconti di vita* (Food Stories, Life Stories).[21] In *Amiche mie*, this theme is brought to the fore and is tied to the core political, feminist and writerly preoccupations of her overall production. Through a subtly experimental structure that gives voice to multiple, diverse experiences of family life and matrimonial disillusion, the novel reveals a world of women who are unable or unwilling to cook like their mothers and grandmothers used to do, and who nevertheless identify in the commitment to feed themselves and others an intellectual and emotional resource, as well as an encouragement for social participation.

A spiral pattern: Food and gender roles between guilt and nostalgia

The four chapters of the novel are presented in chronological order, each showing a shift in focalization, alternating between first-person and third-person narrators. Sofia and Norma are the main characters and first-person narrators of the opening and third chapter respectively: Sofia's chapter is entitled 'Novembre' (November), while Norma's chapter is called 'Primavera' (Spring). The second chapter, 'Dicembre–Gennaio' (December–January), is focalized through Carla's perspective, but it is narrated in the third person, as is the fourth and final chapter, 'Maggio' (May), devoted to Vera. Ballestra explained the use of alternating narrators as a strategy to create 'effects of closeness and distancing according to the things that must be told',[22] a statement that links back to Ballestra's long-standing preoccupation with choices of narrative form, style and language discussed earlier. Layered with multiple and intersecting personal, social and political reflections, these 'things that must be told', are, on the surface of the plot, quite mundane. In November, Sofia guides us through the fight undertaken by the parents' committee at her younger son's school against the company that provides sub-par meals to the school canteen, while developing an obsession with all matters related to food. In December and January, we witness Carla's marriage falling apart due to the growing absence from home of her successful husband, while Carla herself continues to be frustrated by her own unemployment. In early spring, Norma narrates in the first person her divorce from her husband, who has left her for a much younger woman, as well as her baffling post-divorce life. Finally, in May, Vera's story, foretold in the preceding interconnected chapters, is brought to its conclusion as the third-person narrator re-focalizes through the character's perspective the events leading to her husband's sudden death and its aftermath.

The structure of the novel, articulated through different characters with intersecting lives, shows women at different stages of similar crises that become progressively darker and more dramatic, as reflected in the gradual shift from the ironic, outward-looking and overall optimistic tone of the first chapter to the increasingly more serious, inward-looking and pessimistic ones of the next three parts. Ballestra described this progression as 'a spiral [. . .] pattern, starting from the public and moving on to the private'.[23] But while it is true that, as we move from Sofia to Carla to Norma and to Vera we witness an increasing focus on the characters' interior lives and their progressive retreat into private spaces, the friendship between the four protagonists and other women, invigorated by their commitment to the case of the school canteen, ensures that public and private spheres remain connected throughout the narrative. Parallel to this, the spiral structure with its ever-decreasing circles from public to private also reminds us that personal disappointment, failure and pain impact on the quantity and quality of public participation, including women's participation in local food politics, or more simply on their ability and willingness to produce family meals.

Food and gender roles between guilt and nostalgia

Food is indeed the dominant theme of the first part of the novel, conveyed by Sofia's first-person obsession with the subject. The primary school attended by her youngest child has been shaken by the scandal of the *lasagne pelose* (hairy lasagna), after a piece of beef rind was found in a portion of lasagna served at the school canteen. The moniker of *il caso delle lasagne pelose* (the case of the hairy lasagna) has since been used to refer to the substandard and corrupt practices of food production and distribution on the part of GustaMi (TasteMi, 'Mi' standing for both me and Milan), the publicly subsidized company that delivers meals to many of the city schools. Sofia and other parents challenge the company and the local administration that supports it, which is equally lacking in honesty and transparency. The parents refer to their action as *lotta* (struggle) and they describe themselves as being *sul piede di guerra* (on the warpath),[24] a language that invests their campaign with the passion and dedication of a true political fight. As this fight unfolds, Sofia and the other characters find themselves reflecting on their past political commitment to various causes: from the anti-corruption movement that followed the Tangentopoli scandal in the early 1990s[25] to women's rights activism born to contrast the misogynistic backlash of successive right-wing governments in the 1990s and 2000s to a more general engagement in social issues that waned as the bleak Italian political landscape and the characters' fatigue of their married and family lives became more prominent. The case of the hairy lasagna allows them not only to develop their friendship but also, to different degrees, to rekindle their past engagement.

In the meantime, Sofia's personal obsession with healthy eating leads her family to tease and accuse her, jokingly, of showing symptoms of orthorexia nervosa, the obsessive preoccupation with healthy food that some psychologists have controversially classified as an eating disorder.[26] The narrator fights back against her family's assessment, reminding them and the readers that her preoccupation is not a pathology, but a consequence of her role as a mother, and that this role is also based on social expectations placed on her gender:

> What did they know? What did they know about how of my worries had started! Did their father know? No, he wasn't the one who had been expected to feed the two little ones since they were born.
>
> Feed them, give them milk, wean them, raise them.
>
> [. . . .]
>
> After a while the children wouldn't remember. Their fathers would rarely take on these responsibilities. Therefore, those who knew were the mothers and the grandmothers, the baby-sitters and the teachers.
>
> In short, those who knew were the women.[27]

While reclaiming what Counihan calls the 'emotional ties' women have with food that may encourage their activism in this area,[28] Sofia accepts both the role of nurturer assigned to her, conflicted between her nostalgia for her own mother's Sunday lasagna – 'the most classic of all Italian comfort foods, the food of memory'[29] – and her grandmother's *maccheroncini* (an oven-baked pasta dish), and her guilty resentment for coming up short of those unattainable models of female culinary expertise and maternal care. The notion of the tangible, measurable care provided by home-cooking is reiterated later in the novel when Sofia, Carla and Norma attend the funeral of Vera's husband and, upon saying goodbye, Vera asks them to thank their friend Lorenza for the trays of lasagna and *parmigiana di melanzane* (oven-baked aubergines) she had sent after Piero's death: 'It had been important for her to receive that cooked food, as a sign of affection and practical help to overcome those moments when she felt completely lost, a break from the small responsibilities of daily life. Eating, holding herself together.'[30] Yet Sofia cannot help but feel conflicted. Her older son mocks her cooking skill when she prepares frozen gnocchi, and she speculates that her relationship with food is far more theoretical than practical: she enjoys the research, the history and the analysis of how it can be used as a weapon for murder or as television entertainment, but this rarely triggers in her a desire to cook. This ambivalence between nostalgia for home-cooking as a cherished act of caring and rejection of the traditional expectation that women should cook remains unresolved within the space of the narrative (as does the fight against GustaMi), but it helps Sofia, in her role as first narrator, to frame her and her friends' political participation in the case of the school meals as an alternative act of nurture and care.

If Sofia's apprehensions are expressed through an obsession with food that she reclaims as a necessary form of engagement born out of gendered responsibility for her children, Carla's personal and social unhappiness takes the form of an irrational fear of hidden pockets of dirt in her seaside home, fear that she defines *incubi immobiliari* (real estate nightmares).[31] Her anxieties are a manifestation of her deep dissatisfaction with her condition of unemployment, broken by rare periods of precarious work, accompanied by her resentment towards her husband Fabrizio, whose career seems to thrive despite the global financial crisis. Carla's long history of precarity, like that of Sofia, Norma and many other women of their social class and education,[32] has become a justification for all domestic responsibilities falling on them, pushing them back by stealth into the roles of unpaid home-makers and care-givers traditional of their gender. Carla laments specifically the double standard by which her cooking is taken for granted, while when in the past her husband Fabrizio prepared the occasional meal, his efforts were considered admirable, the manifestation of a new, enlightened generation of men: 'Once upon a time he used to cook and when he cooked, then everyone was always expected to say "how delicious!" How amazing this man who cooks! Don't you see what a favour he was doing us? What a big concession? Nobody cares that now I am the one who always cooks, every lunch and every dinner'.[33]

Counihan's anthropological research confirms that in Italy 'even as social roles change and women are increasingly working outside the home for wages and men are increasingly involved with food preparation at home, culturally women are identified with cooking and feeding and expected to manage if not carry out these tasks; women's food work is taken for granted whereas men's is celebrated'.[34] In *Amiche mie* we see that the responsibilities of care, of nurturing, are still firmly placed on women's shoulders despite their relatively privileged white, middle-class status, their modern urban lives and regardless of their financial contribution to the household. This is made explicit in the final part of the novel, when we find out that, after his sudden redundancy, Vera's husband Piero plunges into such a deep depression that Vera cannot count on his help for the domestic tasks, while, as the sole earner for the family, she must take on more paid work, thus doubling her role as both material and emotional nurturer.

Food plays again a major role in this dynamic. As Piero lets himself go, he also eats less and less ('like a little bird'),[35] triggering a response of guilt and extra care on Vera's part, who starts preparing special meals for him and encourages him to eat at the table using plates and cutlery: 'try to keep up some decorum, if you prefer I wash them later, but please at least use plates, a table cloth, eat some fresh bread.'[36] Her pleas come to nothing, leaving Vera stuck in her traditional nurturing role with her depressed, unemployed husband, as Carla is with her successful, career-driven one, both male and female members of these modern heterosexual couples being defined by the persistence of culturally constructed gender expectations.

For Carla and for Vera, as well as for Norma, whose husband has left her for a younger woman and whose divorce has caused her both emotional pain and financial hardship, the consequences of global, matrimonial and personal crises are entirely interconnected, forcing the protagonists to become financially and socially self-reliant while also remaining for the most part the main providers of care and nurture for their families. It is therefore significant that defiance of such expectations also comes in the form of refusal to cook, menu challenges and unusual meals. Carla responds to her husband's growing absence from home by sabotaging his dinners: 'maybe I throw a focaccia and two pieces of cheese on a plate, and sometimes I won't give him any bread, which is his greatest fear.'[37] If Vera does not fully abdicate her nurture of Piero, it is noteworthy that in what will turn out to be the night of his death she orders sushi for his dinner, while she joins her work colleagues for a restaurant meal: a gesture that still shows care (the sushi platter is carefully selected from a high-end caterer), but that also challenges the expectation that she should cook and eat with him. Symbolically, this act of defiance and independence also coincides with Piero's last meal.

Happy hours: Conclusion

Although food does not play such a central role in the other parts of *Amiche mie* as it does in Sofia's opening chapter about the case of the hairy lasagna and the subsequent political fight, feeding responsibilities and rituals continue to provide a commentary to the problems and turmoil faced by the protagonists throughout the narrative. Carla and Fabrizio's crumbling marriage, for example, reaches breaking point at a pre-Christmas cocktail party with some of Fabrizio's colleagues. Food and drink offerings, a casual combination of nibbles and *panettone* (traditional Milanese Christmas cake), Japanese whisky and *prosciutto di Parma* (Parma ham) mirror the superficiality of the conversation and embody everything that Carla despises about the current cultural and political climate in Italy: the effort to appear cosmopolitan and sophisticated indicated by a combination of traditional and imported products, randomly mixed together, in a shallow pretension of urbanity and modernity. She berates her husband and his friends for wanting to send their children to study in English-speaking countries while prestigious Italian universities give up teaching their courses in Italian altogether, chasing after half-baked ideas of internationalization: 'Carla told them that believing they could become less provincial, they were thinking in the most provincial way.'[38] And while Carla's marriage seems inevitably destined to fall apart in a sequence of sabotaged meals and sad drinks and nibbles soirées, Norma navigates her newly divorced status by trying to avoid the approaches of men who share drinks and dinners under the guise of friendship but then are terribly wounded when their sexual overtures are turned down. Finally, as we have seen, it is again food that opens Vera's eyes when her suddenly unemployed husband Piero not only rejects any notion of taking on domestic responsibilities, including the preparation of his own meals, but also becomes increasingly dependent on Vera to care for him.

The support of female friends in the face of death, divorce, loneliness, precarity and financial crisis is presented in Ballestra's novel not only as the one stable source of consolation for personal disappointment but also as an encouragement to step outside of oneself. If the spiral pattern of the novel curls from Sonia's political activism towards the personal heartbreak of Carla's and Norma's failed marriages and of Vera's husband's death, the cafes and bars where the friends meet remain spaces of mediation between public and private throughout the narrative. Sofia is particularly scathing about the culture of *aperitivi* or *apericena* (finger food and drinks) that has come to replace proper dinners in Milan, calling it 'a degenerate type of meal'[39] that exemplifies not only a regrettable loss of culinary tradition but also the wider cultural impoverishment of the country: 'With its closed factories, its failed business, its unappealing universities, all that the city had been able to produce, recently, were bars. Little watering holes. Big cocktails, in order to forget.'[40] Yet, it is in some of these bars and cafes that Sofia and her friends continue to meet, talk, plan possible futures, discuss the news and occasionally engage in politics, helping each other out of the spiral. Indeed, while the characters fall very well short of becoming a feminist collective, Ballestra's emphasis on their moving in and out of their personal and shared experiences through their reciprocal relationships echoes the new practices of women's movement groups, with their distrust for institutionalized organization and their 'continuum of individual-collective', which scholars have identified as characteristic of women's resistance to misogynist culture and policies in the Berlusconi years.[41]

By choosing to open her novel with a chapter that focuses on the fight of a group of parents and friends against a profit-focused and corrupt catering company and on the narrator's obsession with healthy food, Ballestra invites her readers to pay attention to the more discreet presence of cooking and meals in the next three chapters. In doing so she weaves a unifying theme across a narrative that is deliberately polyphonic, off-setting mainstream reading expectations for a single consistent narrator or focalizer, in the same way as she frustrates expectations for a central plot carried to a clear conclusion by not indicating a definitive outcome for Sofia's fight against the school caterers, for Carla's marriage, for Norma's dating and working life or for Vera's life as a widow. The structure of intersecting plots and multiple voices moving in a spiral pattern from public to private ultimately portrays a group of Italian women who are still expected to cook for their families or are forced to reflect on their failure to do so. At the same time, food and eating/drinking spaces provide these characters with the opportunity to bond in friendship and, to different degrees according to their individual stories, to engage in the social sphere, including through political activism, thus challenging the same gender expectations and historical circumstances that would see them pushed back into the kitchen.

Notes

Introduction

1 Maria Giuseppina Muzzarelli and Fiorenza Tarozzi, *Donne e cibo: una relazione nella storia* (Milan: Mondadori, 2003).

2 Maria Giuseppina Muzzarelli and Lucia Re (eds), *Il cibo e le donne nella cultura e nella storia. Prospettive interdisciplinari* (Bologna: CLUEB, 2005).

3 See Anna Colella, *Figura di vespa e leggerezza di farfalla. Le donne e il cibo nell'Italia borghese di fine Ottocento* (Florence: Giunti, Firenze 2003).

4 'Il fatto è che ingrasso'. Marchesa Colombi, *Un matrimonio in provincia* (Milan: Galli, 1885), 195.

5 Giuliana Morandini, *La voce che è in lei. Antologia della narrativa femminile italiana tra '800 e '900* (Milan: Bompiani 1980), 16.

6 Susie Orbach, *Fat Is a Feminist Issue: The Anti-Diet Guide to Permanent Weight Loss* (New York: Paddington Press, 1978), 25.

7 See, for example, Kim Chernin, *The Hungry Self: Women, Eating and Identity* (London: Virago, 1986); Marilyn Lawrence, *The Anorexic Experience* (London: Women's Press, 1984); Morag MacSween, *Anorexic Bodies: A Feminist and Sociological Perspective on Anorexia Nervosa* (London: Routledge, 1993); Susie Orbach, *Hunger Strike: The Anorectic's Struggle as a Metaphor for Our Age* (London: Penguin, 1993).

8 Francesca Calamita, *Linguaggi dell'esperienza femminile: disturbi alimentari, donne e scrittura dall'Unità al Miracolo Economico* (Padua: Il Poligrafo, 2015); Petra Bagley, Francesca Calamita and Kathryn Robson (eds), *Starvation, Food Obsession and Identity: Eating Disorders in Post-1968 Women's Writing* (Oxford: Peter Lang, 2017).

Chapter 1

1 The quotes in this chapter are my translations from the original Italian unless otherwise indicated.

'Artusi's importance is remarkable, and it is necessary to recognize that *Science in the Kitchen* accomplished what *The Betrothed* could not for national unification. Artusi's *gustemes* were, in fact, able to create a code for national identification, precisely where Manzoni's stylemes and phonemes failed.'

'L'importanza dell'Artusi è notevolissima e bisogna riconoscere che *La Scienza in cucina* ha fatto per l'unificazione nazionale più di quanto non siano riusciti a fare *i Promessi Sposi*. I gustemi artusiani, infatti, sono riusciti a creare un codice di identificazione nazionale là dove fallirono gli stilemi e i fonemi manzoniani.' (Pellegrino Artusi, *La scienza in cucina e l'arte di mangiar bene*, introduzione di Piero Camporesi [Torino: Einaudi, 2007], xvi)

2 See Daniele De Feo, *Olindo Guerrini: Aesthetics, History, and an Italian Gastrosophy* in *Italian Foodways Worldwide*, ed. Roberta Iannacito-Provenzano and Gabriele Scardellato (Welland: Soleil Publishing, 2019), 67–86.

3 'un concerto d'armonia e di melodia del gusto . . . che viene poi portato alla massima perfezione dal genio dell'artista' (*Fisiologia del piacere* [The Physiology of Pleasure, 1880], 65).

4 'fra tutte le arti che si dicono belle, perché intese a soddisfare l'intelligenza e gli affetti, questa si dovrebbe chiamare bellissima, perché mira ad appagare e la mente e il cuore e il senso, e perfino il ventre' (Giovanni Rajberti, *L'arte di convitare* a cura di Giovanni Maffei [Salerno Editrice, 2001], 103).

5 'tanto di forza nelle vene di tutto il popolo italiano' (Mantegazza, *Piccolo dizionario della cucina* [The Small Dictionary for Cuisine, 1882], 100).

6 Laura Solera Mantegazza (1817–1873), mother of Paolo and one of the many notable women who espoused the cause of independence, was well known for her political activism and for her promotion for women's and children's rights. Rajberti had vivid correspondence with Laura and Paolo, who wrote a book detailing her heroism, *La mia mamma* (My Mother, 1866). Mantegazza also honours his mother's friend for the festivities to be held in his honour. His contribution is found in the volume *Onoranza a Giovanni Rajberti* (A Tribute to Giovanni Rajberti, 1875), held in the Berlin State Library in Germany.

7 Artusi, *La scienza in cucina e l'arte di mangiar bene*, 51.

8 'allevare delle giovani cuoche le quali, naturalmente più economiche degli uomini e di minore dispendio, troverebbero facile impiego e possederebbero un'arte, che portata nelle case borghesi, sarebbe un farmaco alle tante arrabbiature che spesso avvengono nelle famiglie a cagione di un pessimo desinare' (Ibid., 51–2).

9 See: June di Schino and Furio Luccichenti, *Il cuoco segreto dei papi*: *Bartolomeo Scappi* (Rome: Grangemi editore, 2011).

10 For example, see: *Il cuoco piemontese perfezionato a Parigi* (1766) and *L'economia della città e della campagna ovvero il nuovo cuoco italiano secondo il gusto francese* (1772).

11 Recipe books such as the Neapolitan *Il cuoco galante* by Vincenzo Corrado (1786), *Il cuoco maceratese* (1779) by Antonio Nebbia and the Roman *L'Apicio moderno ossia l'arte di apprestare ogni sorta di vivande* (1790) by Francesco Leonardi are

all works that leave a significant imprint demonstrating the germs of provincial cuisines, while introducing gastronomy to a new audience: the bourgeoisie.

12 Rosmini was a theologian and philosopher who garnered much success and controversy during his day. He was later beatified in 2007, mainly for his work in creating the religious community The Institute of Charity.

13 'timida dolcezza, graziosa debolezza, attenta docilità: [la donna] è delicata, tranquilla, casalinga, paziente.' (Rosmini in Re 171).

14 'lo rendono atto a comandare, coraggio, forza, attività, mente ferma o certo più sviluppata.' (Ibid).

15 Gabriella Turnaturi, *Signore e signori d'Italia. Una storia delle buone maniere* (Milan: Feltrinelli, 2011), 76.

16 'il dietro le scene del teatro domestico' (L*o spirito del galateo – il galateo dello spirito*, 108). This notion is also in Turnaturi (*Signore e signori d'Italia*, 81–2).

17 'bisogna darsi l'aria di non usar le regole e fingere' (Ibid).

18 Rajberti, *L'arte di convitare* a cura di Giovanni Maffei, 73.

19 'non vi è solo nella donna la poesia e la bellezza, dei vezzi, dello spirito, ma v'è anche quella di padrona di casa che noi convitati vogliamo immaginarci seduta in sala e occupata in opere gentili, e non ai fornelli a lavorare' (*L'arte di convitare*, 212).

20 Stia pure in cucina tutto il giorno, se abbisogna: faccia anche il desinare colle proprie mani: ma non ce lo racconti, perché queste sono cose che noi non dobbiamo saperle' (Ibid).

21 'L'elogio delle vivande conduce facilmente a descrizioni sul modo di cucinarle; e non è raro che la padrona di casa si spoetizzi enumerando gli ingredienti d'un intingolo o di una pasta' (211).

22 'la dissimulazione è poesia, e prosaccia la verità' (124). Other comments about dissimulation include: 'dissimulation [is] the perpetual and indispensable arm of living together' ('la dissimulazione [è] arma perpetua e indispensabile della convivenza') (123); 'it is necessary to hide art with art' ('Bisogna nasconder l'arte coll'arte') (123); and 'dissimulation, hiding a thousand disgusting truths, is the maximum virtù of civility' ('la dissimulazione, celando mille disgustose verità, è la virtù massima dell'incivilmento') (125).

23 The term *sprezzatura* originates from Baldassare Castiglione's *Il Cortegiano* (*The Book of the Courtier*; 1528) and can be defined as the ability to disguise one's true feelings and thoughts behind a certain nonchalant guise for the sake of good etiquette. For an interesting analysis of *sprezzatura,* see: Peter D'Epiro and Mary Desmond, *Sprezzatura: 50 Ways Italian Genius Shaped the World* (Anchor Books, 2001), 201–9.

24 'Raccomanda poi alle tue donne che, se necessitano loro alcune assenze, queste sieno brevi e rare: che infine non si mostrino seriamente occupate che di noi' (*L'arte di convitare*, 288).

25 'le parve sempre cosa strana e inconcepibile come a questo mondo si debba aprire bocca per quella trivialità tanto prosaica del mangiare e bere' (132).

26 Similarly, Patricao McEarhern examines French novels of this period where anorexia nervosa becomes symbolic of non-verbal discourse: *Deprivation and Power: The Emergence of Anorexia Nervosa in Nineteenth-Century French Literature* (Westport: Greenwood Press, 1998).

27 See J. Brumberg, *Fasting Girls: The History of Anorexia Nervosa* (Cambridge: Vintage Books Press, 2000) and J. Moorey, *Living with Anorexia and Bulimia* (Manchester: Manchester University Press, 1991).

28 Ibid.

29 See Brumberg, *Fasting Girls: The History of Anorexia Nervosa*, 213–23. For a study of women writers and eating disorders within the Italian context, see Francesca Calamita, *Linguaggi dell'esperienza femminile. Disturbi alimentari, donne e scrittura dall'Unità al miracolo economico* (Verona: Il Poligrafo, 2015).

30 Turnaturi, *Signore e signori d'Italia*, 76.

31 'l'uomo fu anche un questo privilegiato dalla natura . . . . La donna, quantunque sia più sensibile del maschio, pure è troppo poco egoista per analizzare e prediligere questi piaceri sensuali. D'altronde la delicatezza de' suoi organi digerenti e le tante specialità dei suoi gusti bizzarri le precludono il più delle volte i piaceri più intensi' (*Fisiologia del piacere*, 62).

32 'La donna, vana per eccellenza, studia se stessa in tutti i suoi movimenti ed in tutti i lineamenti esterni della sua persona, cercando di trarre l'interesse più alto dei capitali a lei concessi dalla natura, e di nascondere con tutti gli artifici i difetti' (Ibid., 169).

33 'Essa nelle sue forme generali rassomiglia a un uomo giovinetto . . . che anche psicologicamente gli si avvicina . . . [con] un carattere infantile e soprattutto atavico' (*Fisiologia della donna* [The Physiology of Women, 1893], Vol. 1, 93, 292).

34 'La fronte della donna ha quasi sempre (almeno nelle razze superiori) debolissime o mancanti arcate sopraccigliari, è stretta ed ha marcate le gobbe frontali; tutti caratteri del cranio infantile' (*Fisonomia e mimica* [Physiognomy and Expression], 43).

35 Mantegazza was one of the main proponents of Darwinism in Italy. See, for example, *Commemorazione di Carlo Darwin. Discorso di Paolo Mantegazza.* Coi Tipi Dell'arte della Stampa, 1882. In turn, Darwin cited Mantegazza in various texts (e.g. *The Origin of the Species*, 1859; *The Descent of Man*, 1871).

36 Jerry Bergman, in his article 'The History of Teaching Human Female Inferiority in Darwinism', demonstrates how Darwin and his followers contended that 'female evolution progressed slower than male evolution'. The link between female and the young is therefore seen in other Darwinist authors that Bergman cites. One such example is Carl Vogt (a professor of natural history from Geneva) who contended

that women, in both intellect and personality, were closer to 'both infants and the lower races'. See 'The History of the Teaching of Female Inferiority in Darwinism', *CEN Technical Journal* 14, no. 1 (2000): 117–26.

37 *Misoneismo* is a term attributed to Lombroso that is used to describe a certain refusal towards anything new or innovative. Here, it is used to denote a certain placated conservative thought of women who fear a change in their routine. See Paul Knepper and Per Jorgen Ystehede, *The Cesare Lombroso Handbook* (New York: Routledge, 2013), 51.

'La donna, come il bimbo, è, notoriamente, infatti, misoneica; conserva gli abiti, i costumi' (*Il delitto politico e le rivoluzioni* [Political Crime and Revolutions, 1890], 221).

38 'L'impulsività che si nota nella donna si riscontra anche nei fanciulli' (Ibid., 232).

39 'in complesso la donna [normale] è più infantile dell'uomo' (48). Lambroso analyses the differences in taste between men and women, concluding by quoting the above-cited judgement of women being *too selfless to analyse and prefer the pleasure of taste* (54).

40 'i piaceri del gusto e della gola sono più sentiti dal maschio che la femmina' (38).

41 Many of the examples are difficult to read; however, I provide two in order to further establish the viewpoint of women found in Darwinism and in Mantegazza: 'Woman, among savages, is a workhorse; in the East, furniture; in Europe a poorly raised male child – Melhan' ('La donna, presso i selvaggi, è una bestia da soma; in Oriente un mobile; in Europa un fanciullo male allevato – Melhan') (267); 'according to Montequieu, [woman is] a pleasant child' ('secondo Montesquieu, [la donna è] un fancuillo piacevole') (449).

42 'Si trovano dei grandi rapporti fra il sesso femminino e l'infanzia mascolina: hanno tra loro dei punti comuni di sensibilità e passioni in tutto somiglianti. La tessitura dei loro organi è ugualmente molle ed umida; le loro membra sono delicate e tondeggianti; i loro cuori sensibili e mutabili; lo spirito d'osservazione poco profondo . . . la donna è un fanciullo adulto, ed ha bisogno dell'aiuto morale e materiale dell'uomo' (112, 363).

43 *Nervine foods* are a category of foodstuffs that Mantegazza indicated as stimulants for the mind and the intellect. According to the author, man makes a conscious choice to arouse his mind through their use instead of living 'without enthusiasm'. See: *Igiene d'Epicuro* (Società Editrice Partenopea, 1910), 11–19, *Igiene della cucina. Igiene della casa* (Casa Editrice Madella, 1912), 29–48, and *Elementi di igiene* (Gaetano Brigola Editore, 1871), 59–63 and 138–85.

44 'Alcoholic inebriation is more dangerous in children, in women, and in brutes . . . and only he who has a strong will can try them without letting themselves fall into vice' ('L'ebrezza alcoolica è più pericolosa, nel fanciullo, nella donna, e

nell'uomo selvaggio . . . e solo chi ha una volontà di ferro può provarli senza correre sull'irrestibile china verso del vizio.') (*Fisiologia del piacere*, 125).

45 'Essa mangia meno di noi, ma preferisce mangiar più spesso . . . . Anche questo un carattere della dietica infantile' (Ibid).

46 'Nella femmina abbiamo la tendenza di ricomporsi delle molecole, cioè una corrispondente inattività o passività. Il maschio spende l'energia, la femmina la accumula' (*Fisiologia della donna*, Vol. 1, 104).

47 'La donna è un angelo o un demonio? – Né l'uno né l'altro: essa è la femmina dell'uomo' (Ibid., 1).

Gabriella Armenise appropriately summarizes Mantegazza's view of women: 'Mantegazza has a vision of society where women take care of the materiality of the home and where she has to obey her husband and abide by their every need, she is almost never free, and cannot do what she wants' (94) ['Mantegazza ha una visione della società dove la donna si occupa della materialità della casa che deve ubidire al marito e tenersi intorno alle loro mille esigenze, che è quasi mai libera, che non può e non deve fare quello che vuole' (94)].

48 Mantegazza is famous for founding the first professorship of anthropology in Italy in addition to the National *Museo Nazionale di Antropologia ed Etnologia* [Museum of Anthropology and Ethnology] and its subsequent periodical and society in Florence. This is aside from his numerous anthropological studies, which see Mantegazza travel to Latin America in 1854 (Paraguay, Chile, Bolivia and Brasil), Lapponia (1879) and India (1882). See Sandra Puccini, 'I viaggi di Paolo Mantegazza: Tra divulgazione, letteratura e antropologia', in *Paolo Mantegazza e l'Evoluzionismo in Italia*, ed. Chiarelli and Pasini (Firenze University Press, 2010).

49 Lucia Re, 'Passion and Sexual Difference: The Risorgimento and the Gendering of Writing in Nineteenth-Century Italian Culture', in *Making and Remaking Italy*, ed. Albert Russell Ascoli and Krystyna von Henneberg (Oxford: Berg, 2001).

50 Ibid.

51 Hollows Ashley, Steve Jones and Ben Taylor, *Food and Cultural Studies* (London and New York: Rouledge, 2004).

52 In Denise Gigante, *Taste: A Literary History* (Yale University Press, 2005), 57.

53 See Katharine Mitchell's discussion of the 'private' versus the 'public' and the 'official' sphere (63).

Chapter 2

1 Craig Seligman, 'Warped, Battered, Torn and Stained', *Salon*, 27 December 1999. https://www.salon.com/1999/12/27/warped/.

2 Craig Claiborne's brief profile of Hazan, the first instance in which she gained wide recognition and published before she had written any cookbooks, portrays her

instead as warm and points to her maternal instincts through a description of her son's school lunches. In Craig Claiborne, 'There Was a Time She Couldn't Cook', *New York Times*, 15 October 1970. http://www.nytimes.com/1970/10/15/archives/there-was-a-time-she-couldnt-cook.html.

3 Scott Simon, 'Marcella Hazan: Italian Cooking with a Master', *NPR*, 8 January 2005.

4 Davis Sipress, 'Marcella Hazan Changed My Life', *New Yorker*, 30 September 2013. https://www.newyorker.com/culture/culture-desk/marcella-hazan-changed-my-life.

5 Mark Bittman, 'Remembering Marcella', *New York Times*, 6 November 2013. http://www.nytimes.com/2013/11/10/magazine/remembering-marcella.html. In his review of her autobiography, Seligman reiterates this idea more explicitly, stating that Marcella and Victor Hazan 'weren't ambitious', and that her career/their combined success was 'foisted upon them' (Craig Seligman, 'Classic Italian', *New York Times*, 3 October 2008. http://www.nytimes.com/2008/10/05/books/review/Seligman-t.html).

6 Female reviewers also repeat this trope, as in the recent example of Domenica Marchetti who notes that Hazan's last book, published post-mortem, contains her 'sometimes-cranky' 'full-throated opinions' (Domenica Marchetti, '3 Years Gone, Marcella Hazan Speaks to us Still through New Book "Ingredienti"', *Chicago Tribune*, 22 July 2016. http://www.chicagotribune.com/dining/recipes/ct-marcella-hazan-book-ingredienti-food-0727-20160722-story.html). The most widely read coverage of Hazan's writings is by male reviewers, hence the selection provided here. On gender and language, and the coding of direct language as male in contrast with indirect, female language – and the labelling of women who use direct language as 'bitchy' or 'bossy' – see the classic study by Robin Lakoff, 'Language and Woman's Place' along with several more recent contributions on the subject and updated reflections from the author in Robin Lakoff, *Language and Woman's Place: Text and Commentaries*, ed. Mary Bucholtz (Oxford: Oxford University Press, 2004).

7 For an overview of approaches and sources, see Barbara Ketcham Wheaton, 'Cookbooks as Resources for Social History', in *Food in Time and Place: The AHA Companion to Food History*, ed. Paul Freedman, Joyce E. Chaplin and Ken Albala (Berkeley: University of California Press, 2014). Allen Grieco has also outlined the challenges and scholarly potential of using specifically Italian cookbooks as sources and provides an important case study as an example in his essay, 'From the Cookbook to the Table: A Florentine Table and Italian Recipes of the Fourteenth and Fifteenth Centuries', in *Du manuscrit à la table: essais sur la cuisine au moyen âge et répertoire des manuscrits médiévaux contenant des recettes culinaries*, ed. Carole Lambert (Montreal: Université de Montréal, 1992), 29–38.

8 Hazan frequently observed that she was basically uninterested in food, and only learned to cook after she married and moved to New York (see for example Marcella Hazan, *Marcella Cucina* [New York: HarperCollins, 1997], 2).

9 See, for example, the episode of *The Mind of a Chef* where April Bloomfield, internationally renowned chef and restaurant owner, cooks with Marcella Hazan and is moved to tears when she receives Hazan's approval: 'Italian', *The Mind of a Chef*, dir. Michael Steed and Claudia Woloshin, [TV programme] PBS, 23 November 2003.

10 Henry Notaker, *A History of Cookbooks: From Kitchen to Page over Seven Centuries* (Berkeley: University of California Press, 2017), preface.

11 Ibid., 62. In Italy in particular, this shift is only notable in the late nineteenth century, following unification, as witnessed in Artusi, discussed further.

12 In addition to the work by Anna Martellotti and the crucial overview provided by Capatti and Montanari, both cited further, there has been significant work especially on the *Opera* of Bartolomeo Scappi: June Di Schino and Fabio Luccichenti, *Il cuoco segreto dei papi: Bartolomeo Scappi e la confraternita dei cuochi* (Rome: Gangemi, 2007); Terence Scully, *The* Opera *of Bartolomeo Scappi*: L'arte et prudenza di un maestro cuoco (Toronto: University of Toronto Press, 2011); and most recently Deborah Krohn, *Food and Knowledge in Renaissance Italy: Bartolomeo Scappi's Paper Kitchens* (New York: Routledge, 2017).

13 Alberto Capatti and Massimo Montanari, *Italian Cuisine: A Cultural History*, trans. Aine O'Healy (New York: Columbia University Press, 2003), 155–6.

14 Grieco, 'From the Cookbook to the Table', 29.

15 See for example Allen J. Grieco, 'The Social Politics of Pre-Linnaean Botanical Classification', *I Tatti Studies: Essays in the Renaissance* 4 (1991): 131–49 and Allen J. Grieco, 'From Roosters to Cocks: Italian Renaissance Fowl and Sexuality', in *Erotic Cultures of Renaissance Italy*, ed. Sara F. Matthews-Grieco (Surrey: Ashgate, 2010), 110–22.

16 Anna Martellotti, *I ricettari di Federico II: Dal "Meriodionale" al "Liber de coquina"* (Florence: Olschki, 2005).

17 Cristoforo Messisbugo, *Banchetti, compositioni di viuande et apparecchio generale* (Ferrara: Giouanni de Buglhat et Antonio Hucher compagni, 1549), 2.

18 Krohn, *Food and Knowledge in Renaissance Italy*, 12.

19 Ibid., 83–107.

20 Pellegrino Artusi, *La scienza in cucina e l'arte di mangiar bene* (Florence: Landi, 1891). On Artusi as a 'culinary Manzoni' see Piero Camporesi's introduction to Pellegrino Artusi, *La scienza in cucina e l'arte di mangiar bene* (Turin: Einaudi, 1970), lv; and Luigi Ballerini, 'Introduction: A as in Artusi, G as in Gentleman and Gastronome', in Pellegrino Artusi, *Science in the Kitchen and the Art of Eating Well*, ed. Luigi Ballerini, trans. Murtha Baca and Stephen Sartarelli (Toronto: University of Toronto Press, 2003), xv–lxii (esp. xx–xxiv).

21 For more on Artusi's work see again Capatti and Montanari, *Italian Cuisine.*

22 Artusi, *Science in the Kitchen*, 19.

23 Ibid., 13–24; the glossary of standardized Italian terms is not included in the translation but only in the original, Artusi, *La scienza in cucina*, 29–31.
24 Ballerini, 'Introduction: A as in Artusi, G as in Gentleman and Gastronome', xxix.
25 Notaker, *A History of Cookbooks*, esp. 28–46.
26 As Capatti and Montanari point out, towards the end of the early modern period, increasing numbers of cookbooks appear in Italy with non-specific female chefs in their titles (e.g. *La cuciniera Piemontese*, 1771; *La regina delle cuoche*, 1882) that are more explicitly directed at a female audience and introduce the presence of a woman in the kitchen, but they do not ascribe authorship of the recipes to the female cook, in Capatti and Montanari, *Italian Cuisine*, 158–9 and 164–6.
27 Ada Boni, *Il talismano della felicità* (Rome: Colombo, 1929), prefazione. Though the text is translated in Ada Boni, *The Talisman Italian Cookbook*, trans. Matilda La Rosa, intro. Mario A. Pei (New York: Crown, 1950), Boni's original introduction is omitted.
28 Piero Meldini, 'A tavola e in cucina', in *La famiglia italiana dall'ottocento a oggi*, ed. Piero Bairati and Lucetta Scaraffia (Rome: Laterza, 1998), 443.
29 Marcella Hazan, *Amarcord: Marcella Remembers* (New York: Penguin, 2008), 58.
30 Ibid., 82.
31 Hazan citing herself, *Amarcord*, 73.
32 Hazan relates her difficulty conversing in standard Italian with Italian–American owners of local shops, and then reflects, 'If there was another good reason to learn English, it was to speak to those oafish men in a language they could understand'. In *Amarcord*, 81–2.
33 Seligman, 'Classic Italian'. As noted earlier, in the same article, Seligman also suggested that the success of Hazan's work was imposed upon her rather than consciously sought out.
34 Hazan, *Amarcord*, 137.
35 Hazan, *The Classic Italian Cookbook* (New York: Harper's Magazine Press, 1973), 393–4.
36 Hazan, *More Classic Italian Cooking* (New York: Knopf, 1978), xi.
37 Ibid., ix.
38 Ibid., 459–67 and 469–71.
39 Hazan, *The Classic Italian Cookbook*, 394.
40 See, for example, the work by Marvin Harris, *Good to Eat: Riddles of Food and Culture* (Long Grove: Waveland Press, 1998) that offers practical explanations of global gastronomic taste evolution. Regarding the Italian context specifically, Serventi and Sabban have noted that the development of pasta does not follow a clear path from need to taste, and its appearance can only be explained as taste-driven in many cases. In Silvano Serventi and Françoise Sabban, *Pasta: The Story of a Universal Food* (New York: Columbia University Press, 2002), 12.

41 Cited in Bill Daley, 'The Legacy of Marcella Hazan', *Chicago Tribune*, 12 September 2014. http://www.chicagotribune.com/lifestyles/sc-food-0912-giants-hazan-20140912-story.html.
42 Hazan, *Marcella Cucina*, 19.

Chapter 3

1 'La British Airways della dedica è proprio la compagnia aerea britannica. A un ritardo del volo Palermo-Londra del 2 settembre 2000 devo l'"illuminazione' che mi ha condotto a questo romanzo. E per ciò – ma forse anche per quel filo 'aereo' che mi consente di mantenere un legame fra i miei due paesi – la British Airways figura lì dov'è.' Simonetta Agnello Hornby, *La Mennulara* (Milan: Giangiacomo Feltrinelli Editori, 2002), 202.
2 Gisela Ecker, '*Zuppa Inglese* and *Eating up Italy*', in *Performing National Identity*, ed. Manfred Pfister and Hertel (Amsterdam and New York: Rodopi, 2008), 34.
3 For an analysis of *Il Mulino Bianco* in the context of branding strategies and food consumption habits in Italy in the 1970s and the 1980s, see Federico Chiaricati, 'Economia e cultura dei consumi alimentari degli anni Ottanta', *Storia e Futuro* 27 (2011). Online: http://storiaefuturo.eu/economia-e-cultura-dei-consumi-alimentari-degli-anni-ottanta-le-fonti/ (accessed 22 February 2019).
4 Andreas Huyssen, *Present Pasts: Urban Palimpsests and the Politics of Memory* (Stanford: Stanford University Press, 2003), 25.
5 Stephanie Malia Hom, 'Italy without Borders: Simulacra, Tourism, Suburbia and the New Grand Tour', *Italian Studies* 65, no. 3 (2010): 367–97 (377).
6 Huyssen, *Present Pasts*, 5.
7 Sharon Haar and Christopher Reed, 'Coming Home', in *Not at Home*, ed. Christopher Reed (London: Thames and Hudson, 1996), 258, cited in David Morley, 'The Gender of Home', in *Home Territories: Media, Mobility and Identity* (Oxford and New York: Routledge, 2000), 56–85, 59.
8 Jean Duruz, 'Home Cooking, Nostalgia, and the Purchase of Tradition', *Traditional Dwellings and Settlements Review* 12, no. 2 (2001): 21–32 (24).
9 Ibid., 26.
10 'Percorrendo le corsie dei supermercati mi accorgo che il ciclo delle stagioni è scomparso' (*Il pranzo di Mosè*, 54). All translations my own.
11 'Dovunque in Europa oggi si trova tutto e sempre; rimpiango la scomparsa della stagionalità nei mercati e la sua perdita nella dieta. Per settimane a Mosè si mangiano gli stessi prodotti, maturati tutti assieme; si conservano sotto sale, sott'olio, sotto aceto, e si elaborano, si cucinano, si surgelano. Tutto a un tratto sulle piante non ce ne sono più. Altri prodotti prendono il loro posto. C'è un'antica

bellezza nell'aspettare che inizi la stagione dei finocchi; è confortevole fare pentoloni di marmellata di albicocche pensando che basteranno per l'intero anno, e ha un no so che di sensuale fare scorpacciate di arance, e una panzata di fichi, sapendo che non ce ne saranno altri per più di otto mesi.' (*Il pranzo di Mosè*, 54).

12 Jennifer Burns, *Migrant Imaginaries: Figures in Italian Migration Literature* (Oxford: Peter Lang, 2013), 102.

13 'Non riuscii mai a capire perché a Mosè la nostra dieta fosse tanto diversa da quella di Agrigento [. . . .] Papà andava ad Agrigento o nei paesi vicini ogni giorno: avrebbe potuto comprare tutto ciò che ci serviva oltretutto, gli piaceva. Invece, ritornava a mani vuote. I primi giorni desideravo molto il pesce, che in città ci veniva servito ogni sera, e i formaggini che non mancavano mai alla nostra tavola. Quando chiedevo a papà di comprarli, ricevevo sempre la stessa risposta, lapidaria: 'In campagna mangiamo quello che si produce, come i contadini' (*Un filo d'olio*, 49–51).

14 '"Simonetta, eccola, la guardiola di Mosè!"' Ma io l'avevo già avvistata, e il cuore mi batteva forte. Sapevo che dietro la guardiola, il terreno si piegava in colline coperte di ulivi e più giù, e metà collina, nascosta agli occhi degli automobilisti, c'era la nostra casa. Non vedevo l'ora di raggiungerla. Quello era Mosè. Un posto "nostro"'. (*Il pranzo di Mosè*, 17).

15 'Papà ripeteva quelle parole ogni volta che passava da lì, le sapevo a memoria'. Ibid.

16 'Nell'aia spizzuliavano galline e pulcini; le corna a torciglione delle capre girgintane spuntavano alte dallo steccato della mandria. Mamma raccontava che Rosalia, la moglie di Luigi, il campiere, a cui lei e zia Teresa volevano molto bene, aveva offerto loro 'u caffè du parrinu e del pane ancora tiepido, cotto nel forno a legna' (*Il pranzo di Mosè*, 19).

17 'Se dovessi immaginare la ninfa protettrice di Mosè sarebbe proprio lei, Rosalia' (*Un filo d'olio*, 28).

18 'Rosalia si occupava di tutti con energia straordinaria e generosità'. Ibid.

19 Sara Ahmed, 'Killing Joy: Feminism and the History of Happiness', *Signs* 35, no. 3 (2010): 571–94 (591).

20 Ibid., 580.

21 'Il compito delle donne di famiglia era di badare al marito e ai figli, di essere brave padrone di casa e, quando si ricevevano visite, di occuparsi della felicità dell'ospite, dal momento in cui costui arrivava fino al commiato' (*Il pranzo di Mosè*, 28).

22 'sempre pronta al sorriso' (*Un filo d'olio*, 31).

23 Duruz, 'Home Cooking, Nostalgia, and the Purchase of Tradition', 24.

24 See for example the work of Louise DeSalvo, especially *Vertigo: A Memoir* (New York: Dutton, 1996), and *Crazy in the Kitchen: Food, Feuds and Forgiveness in an Italian American Family* (New York: Bloomsbury, 2005); and Edvige Giunta and Louise DeSalvo (eds), *The Milk of Almonds: Italian American Women Writers on Food and Culture* (New York: The Feminist Press at CUNY, 2003).

25 Margherita Sprio, *Migrant Memories: Cultural History, Cinema and the Italian Post-War Diaspora in Britain* (Bern: Peter Lang, 2013), 19.
26 'dava conto a tutte, grandi e piccine' (*Un filo d'olio,* 31).
27 'Avrebbero potuto evitare l'intera discussione se avessero chiesto fin dall'inizio che c'era in cucina; inoltre Raimondo aveva ragione: le melanzane a quaglia devono essere piccine. Non lo dissi perché avrei potuto sciupare il divertimento e, forse, la parvenza di riavvicinamento tra marito e moglie: era noto che Raimondo aveva un'altra famiglia nascosta chissà dove' (*Il pranzo di Mosè*, 47).
28 'Rosalia era la prima a venirci incontro a baciarci, sempre. Quell'incontro, caloroso e informale perché tra noi c'era vero affetto, aveva una propria ritualità tutta femminile' (*Un filo d'olio,* 28).
29 'legava le donne della famiglia di mamma a quelle della famiglia di Rosalia, che da sette generazioni abitava a Mosè', Ibid., 31.
30 'Ogni ninfa ha il suo rito, e quello di Rosalia era il caffè d'u parrinu, celebrato soltanto all'arrivo di mamma e a quello di zia Teresa. La cuccuma del 'caffè speciale' come lo chiamava Giuliana brontolava sul fornello, il coperchio ben chiuso, ma dal beccuccio sfuggiva un profumo speziato, anticipo del pieno aroma, e ci raggiungeva sottile sottile, penetrava nelle narici e poi invadeva la stanza: un misto di cacao, vaniglia, chiodi di garofano, caffè e cannella'. Ibid., 30.
31 'presi dalla voglia di emulare Rosalia'. Ibid., 73.
32 'Le labbra ormai sottili increspate dallo stesso sorriso limpido, e tuttora bella, Rosalia non disse né sì, né no. Mi elencò i sette ingredienti e spiegò che il caffè d'u parrinu, fatto come si doveva, richiedeva una lunga preparazione, ribollitura, 'e poi deve arripusari'. Non mi diede la ricetta, ma per il resto del mio soggiorno a Mosè me ne portò una caffettiera intera a metà mattina, ogni giorno. Ricetta niente. Sua figlia Antonia mi disse anni dopo che la madre, benché avida lettrice di libri e riviste di argomento religioso, scriveva di rado: tutte le sue ricette le sapeva a memoria e temeva di non riuscire a scriverle per bene. Antonia e, ora, Chiara lo preparano esattamente come lei. Ma il loro caffè d'u parrinu, benché ottimo, non è la stessa cosa – manca il tocco magico di Rosalia'. Ibid., 32.
33 As the author explains in the prologue, the finished text is the work of four hands or six, counting the advice of the Agnello sisters' cousin, Silvestro.
34 'un buon punto di partenza perché si trasformi in un'altra ricetta mi sembra il miglior risultato che potessi ottenere' (*Un filo d'olio,* 194).
35 'far rivivere la cultura della tavola di casa nostra attraverso le sue ricette, fotografie d'epoca e alcune pagine "narrative"'. Ibid.
36 'Il pranzo di Mosè', *RealTime,* 11 September 2014–13 December 2014. http://www.realtimetv.it/programmi/il-pranzo-di-mose/ (accessed 22 February 2019).
37 Edvige Giunta, 'Memoir as Cross-Cultural Practice in Italian American Studies', *Assay: A Journal of Nonfiction Studies* 5, no. 1 (2018). Online: https://www.assayjournal.com/uploads/2/8/2/4/28246027/__5.1_giunta.pdf (accessed 22 February 2019).

38 On entrenched positive cultural stereotypes of England and 'Anglophilia' in Italy, see Robert J. Blackwood and Stefania Tufi, *The Linguistic Landscape of the Mediterranean: French and Italian Coastal Cities* (London: Palgrave Macmillan, 2015), 179–83.
39 See Morley, 'The Gender of Home', 56–85 for a comprehensive review of scholarship on the home as a gendered space.
40 Micaela di Leonardo, 'The Female World of Cards and Holidays: Women, Families, and the Work of Kinship', *Signs* 12, no. 3 (1987): 440–53.
41 Ibid., 442.
42 'Mi piace tagliare i rametti di allora e di rosmarino, disporre i biscotti sui vassoietti di cartone, avvolgerli nel cellophane e infiocchettarli con nastri di seta riciclati o perfino comprati a posta, riempire i sacchetti con pistacchi e mandorle, facendo attenzione a scegliere soltanto quelli sani, e annodarli per bene, pensando alla persona a cui andranno' (*Il pranzo di Mosè*, 42).
43 Terry Lovell, 'Thinking Feminism with and against Bourdieu', in *Reading Bourdieu on Society and Culture*, ed. Bridget Fowler (Oxford: Blackwell Publishers, 2000), 41.
44 'dispongo le fette fritte a disegni geometrici, a zigzag, a spina di pesce, verso la salsa di pomodoro come stendessi pennellate di tempera' (*Il pranzo di Mosè*, 52).
45 'Il lavoro umile'. Ibid., 50–2.
46 'compiango coloro che non cucinano e che non sanno cucinare. Perdono piaceri e occasioni di riflessione molto belle'. Ibid., 49.
47 Anne Allison, 'Japanese Mothers and *Obentōs:* The Lunch-Box as Ideological State Apparatus', in *Food and Culture: A Reader*, ed. Carole Counihan and Penny Van Esterick (New York and Oxford: Routledge, 2013), 165.
48 'un lavoro di gruppo faticoso, ed era 'cosa' di donne' (*Un filo d'olio*, 52).
49 'La sua approvazione era accompagnata dai sospiri di sollievo delle altre'. Ibid., 59.
50 'Con il dorso della mano Rosalia si asciugava il sudore dalla fronte, poi, a gambe larghe, la schiena leggermente inarcata all'indietro, dava l'ordine e controllava le donne che con la pala tiravano fuori i pani dal forno'. Ibid.
51 'Quando erano fuggiti dalla fattoria con i bambini, Rosalia s'era portata la livatina, la pagnottella di pasta lievitata che si conserva ad ogni impastina di pane, per farla inacidire e trasformarsi nel lievito per le successive panificazioni. La livatina di Mosè proveniva da una pasta madre mantenuta in vita dalle femmine della sua famiglia sin dal 1870. Scappando, Rosalia se l'era messa adosso, sotto le vesti, a diretto contatto con il proprio corpo per proteggerla e mantenerla calda' (*Il pranzo di Mosè*, 19–20).
52 Beverley Skeggs, *Formations of Class and Gender: Becoming Respectable* (London: SAGE Publications, 1997).
53 Ahmed, 'Killing Joy', 592.
54 Ibid.
55 Duruz, 'Home Cooking, Nostalgia, and the Purchase of Tradition', 24.

Chapter 4

1 Italian quotes from *La virtù di Checchina* refer to the 2000 edition of the text, *La virtù di Checchina* (Lecce: Piero Manni, 2000). English translations (by Tom Kelso) refer to the 2006 edition of 'Checchina's Virtue', in *Writing to Delight: Italian Short Stories by Nineteenth-Century Women Writers*, ed. Antonia Arslan and Gabriella Romani (Toronto: University of Toronto Press, 2006), 19–57.

2 Matilde Serao, *La virtù di Checchina* (Catania: Giannotta Editore, 1884).

3 Serao moved from Naples to Rome after her mother's death in 1879 and started her collaboration with the magazine *Capitan Fracassa* in 1880. In Rome she met Edoardo Scarfoglio, whom she married in 1885.

4 Matilde Serao, *Fantasia* (Turin: Casanova, 1883).

5 Matilde Serao, *Il ventre di Napoli* (Milan: Treves, 1884).

6 Matilde Serao, *La conquista di Roma* (Florence: Barbèra, 1885).

7 See Antonio Ghirelli, *Donna Matilde* (Venice: Marsilio, 1995), 78.

8 Ibid. 91.

9 Anna Banti, *Matilde Serao* (Turin: UTET, 1965).

10 Matilde Serao, *La virtù di Checchina*, ed. Natalia Ginzburg (Milan: Emme Edizioni, 1974).

11 Arslan and Romani, *Writing to Delight*, 7.

12 Katharine Mitchell, *Italian Women Writers: Gender and Everyday Life in Fiction and Journalism, 1870-1910* (Toronto: University of Toronto Press, 2014), 7.

13 Arslan and Romani, *Writing to Delight*, 4.

14 Marchesa Colombi (Maria Antonietta Torriani), *Un matrimonio in provincia* (Milano: Galli, 1885); Neera (Anna Zuccari), *Teresa* (Milano: Galli, 1886).

15 Arslan and Romani, *Writing to Delight*, 10.

16 Mitchell, *Italian Women Writers*, 115.

17 The Geodetic Conference of Rome (which took place in October of 1883, the month before the publication of *La virtù di Checchina*) was extensively reported in Italian newspapers and paved the way for the resolution on World Standard Time, approved at the Meridian Conference of Washington in 1884.

18 Aldo Palazzeschi, 'La passeggiata', in *Tutte le poesie*, ed. Adele Dei (Milan: Mondadori, 2002), 295.

19 Gistucci refers to Serao's penchant for food: 'this spontaneous, almost animal, interest [. . .] is the point of departure of a minor theme, which is permanent throughout her entire work' (Martin Gistucci, *L'ouvre Romanesque de Matilde Serao* (Grenoble: PUG 1973), 309).

20 Neera (Anna Zuccari), *L'indomani* (Milao: Galli, 1889). Carlo Collodi, *The Adventures of Pinocchio. Le avventure di Pinocchio*, trans. Nicolas Perella (Berkeley and Los Angeles: University of California Press, 1991).

21 Mitchell, *Italian Women Writers,* 60.

22 As confirmed by Francesca Calamita, 'Italian women writers of late nineteenth and early twentieth century, such as Neera (1846–1918), Marchesa Colombi and Matilde Serao (1856–1927), often portray female protagonists who employ the nonverbal language of food as a powerful weapon to express their feelings, mirroring in their fiction its social meaning.' Francesca Calamita, Wellington 2013 – 'Tastefulness: Fashion, Food, Lust and Domesticity in Matilde Serao's *La Virtù di Checchina* (1884)', *Altrelettere* (2015): 9.

23 Serao, 'Checchina's Virtue', 19. 'Strofinaccio puzzolente'; 'grembiule tutto sporco di grasso'; 'fazzoletto, tutto profumato di *Jockey-club*'. Serao, *La virtù di Checchina*, 2000, 13.

24 Serao, 'Checchina's Virtue', 49. 'Allora Susanna tirò fuori qualcosa di bianco, una carta, una lettera che si era bagnata e macchiata di sugo rosso'. Serao, *La virtù di Checchina*, 2000, 55.

25 Serao, 'Checchina's Virtue', 22. 'mi sarà utile'. Serao, *La virtù di Checchina*, 2000, 17.

26 Serao, 'Checchina's Virtue', 22. 'ci voleva una padella nuova'. Serao, *La virtù di Checchina*, 2000, 19.

27 My translation. 'a una vendita, da Stella'. Serao, *La virtù di Checchina*, 2000, 19.

28 Serao, 'Checchina's Virtue', 22. 'appunto la settimana prima Bianchelli aveva fatto una grande esposizione di macchinette, tutte lucide, fiammanti, che parevano di oro e di argento'. Serao, *La virtù di Checchina*, 2000, 20.

29 Serao, 'Checchina's Virtue', 24. 'la torta con la conserva di amarena? Quante uova metteva, allora, con un chilo di fior di farina, mezzo chilo di zucchero finissimo e mezza libbra di burro?'. Serao, *La virtù di Checchina*, 2000, 19.

30 Serao, 'Checchina's Virtue', 25. 'li sapresti fare, Susanna, i riccioli sulla fronte?' Serao, *La virtù di Checchina*, 2000, 21.

31 Serao, 'Checchina's Virtue', 25. 'aveva il viso rosso, due placche di fuoco sulle guance, tanto la vampa del fornello le aveva mandato il sangue alla testa'. Serao, *La virtù di Checchina*, 2000, 21.

32 Serao, 'Checchina's Virtue', 25. 'quattro volte si era lavate le mani per paura che avessero il sito di pesce e macchinalmente le fiutava, come in un sonnambulismo'. Serao, *La virtù di Checchina*, 2000, 21.

33 Serao, 'Checchina's Virtue', 25. 'un pranzetto alla buona'. Serao, *La virtù di Checchina*, 2000, 22.

34 Serao, 'Checchina's Virtue', 25. 'un profumo molle e dolce [. . .] come un sapore di zuccherino'. Serao, *La virtù di Checchina*, 2000, 22.

35 Serao, 'Checchina's Virtue', 26. 'disinvoltura da gran signore'. Serao, *La virtù di Checchina*, 2000, 23.

36 Serao, 'Checchina's Virtue', 26. 'grossa allegria di medico'. Serao, *La virtù di Checchina*, 2000, 22.

37 Serao, 'Checchina's Virtue', 26. 'una bottiglia di *vieux cognac,* che gli aveva regalato un suo cliente di Francia'. Serao, *La virtù di Checchina*, 2000, 23.
38 Serao, 'Checchina's Virtue', 26. 'per corrispondere, bevve un bicchierino di *cognac,* liquore che non aveva mai bevuto, di un fiato solo'. Serao, *La virtù di Checchina*, 2000, 23.
39 Mitchell notes, in reference to this trope in contemporary women's literature: 'at night, the relative privacy of the bedroom provides a space for adolescent girls and married women to let their minds wander without being caught off guard. This is apparent in Serao's "Checchina's Virtue". While the protagonist's husband sleeps, snoring profoundly, Checchina visualizes the route to the marquis's apartment, to which she has been invited, unbeknown to her husband and friends'. Mitchell, *Italian Women Writers*, 72.
40 Serao, 'Checchina's Virtue', 42. 'esaltamento della fantasia nella notte [. . .] assoluta mancanza di volontà nel giorno'. Serao, *La virtù di Checchina*, 2000, 44.
41 Serao, 'Checchina's Virtue', 40–1. 'sarà stata la braciola di maiale che t'ha fatto male, Checca mia. Se ti senti male, perché non prendi del citrato di magnesia effervescente? È una bibita piacevole e ti spazza lo stomaco come una scopa. Checca mia, più ti guardo e più mi pare che tu debba avere della coprostasi: perchè non ti decidi addirittura per un po' di olio di mandorle? Fresco, spremuto, da Garnieri, è una bellezza'. Serao, *La virtù di Checchina*, 2000, 43.
42 Mitchell, *Italian Women Writers*, 5.
43 The relationship between new technologies and accessibility to different flavours and tastes is exemplified in Checchina's imagination of coffee consumption by noble people: 'these nobles with their nimble, vivacious air – it's clear that they take coffee prepared with a coffee machine on the stove'. Serao, 'Checchina's Virtue', 24. 'questi nobili, con la loro aria sempre svelta e vivace, è chiaro che prendono il caffè fatto con la macchinetta'. Serao, *La virtù di Checchina*, 2000, 20.
44 Anna Colella's monograph *Figura di vespa e leggerezza di farfalla. Le donne e il cibo nell'Italia borghese di fine Ottocento* (Florence: Giunti, 2003) portrays the diet of Italian bourgeois women and remarks that red meat and spices, as well as caffeinated or alcoholic drinks were not conceived as part of what a woman could consume.
45 Serao, 'Checchina's Virtue', 20. 'un piattino di frutta artificiali, anche questo in marmo, dipinte vivacemente, il fico, il pomo, la pesca, la pera e un grappoletto di ciliegie'. Serao, *La virtù di Checchina*, 2000, 13.
46 Serao, 'Checchina's Virtue', 42. 'vi soffiava dentro, scotendole, per farne andar via la polvere'. Serao, *La virtù di Checchina*, 2000, 45.
47 For more information about the theme of *rovina*, see Francesco Orlando, *Gli oggetti desueti nelle immagini della letteratura. Rovine, reliquie, rarità, robaccia, luoghi inabitati e tesori nascosti* (Turin: Einaudi, 2015).

48 Serao, 'Checchina's Virtue', 26. 'sguardo serio, pensoso'. Serao, *La virtù di Checchina*, 2000, 23.

49 Serao, 'Checchina's Virtue', 26. 'mani benedette'. Serao, *La virtù di Checchina*, 2000, 22.

50 Serao, 'Checchina's Virtue', 26. 'mezza voce, con una *erre* molto lieve, quasi aspirate, e una *esse* infantile, molto dolce'. Serao, *La virtù di Checchina*, 2000, 23.

51 Serao, 'Checchina's Virtue', 26, 29. 'larghi fogli che putivano di acido fenico come tutte le cose che Toto toccava'. Serao, *La virtù di Checchina*, 2000, 26–7.

52 Francesco Bruni notes that the word *virtù* 'never appears in the novel, even though the title in this case is an integral part of the text'. Francescao Bruni, 'Nota Introduttiva', in *Il romanzo della fanciulla. La virtù di Checchina*, ed. Francesco Bruni (Napoli: Liguori, 1985), I–XXXVI.

53 Ibid., XXX.

Chapter 5

1 See Meredith Abarca, *Voices in the Kitchen: Views of Food and the World from Working-Class Mexican and Mexican American Women* (College Station: Texas A & M University Press, 2006), 54–5.

2 Patrizia Sambuco, *Corporeal Bonds: The Daughter-Mother Relationship in Twentieth Century Italian Women's Writing* (Toronto: Toronto University Press, 2012), 7.

3 The title 'Terno secco' does not translate well into English. A lottery term, to score a 'terno secco' is to choose three winning numbers.

4 Armando Pappalardo, 'Matilde Serao, la più grande scrittrice del secolo, la fondatrice e direttrice del "Giorno", si è spenta ieri', *Il Giorno*, 17 July 1927. Available online: http://www.identitainsorgenti.com/il-documento-90-anni-fa-ci-lasciava-matilde-serao-cosi-la-ricordavano-i-suoi-giornalisti-sul-giorno/ (accessed 19 October 2019). All translations in this chapter, unless otherwise noted, are mine.

5 Marie-Gracieuse Martin-Gistucci, *L'Oeuvre Romanesque de Matilde Serao* (Grenoble: Grenoble University Press, 1973), 15–21.

6 Victoria A. Goddard, *Gender, Family, and Work in Naples* (Oxford: Berg, 1996), 213.

7 Ida Baccini, *La mia vita. Ricordi autobiografici* (Rome: Società Editrice Dante Alighieri, 1904), 181.

8 Ibid.

9 For more on the motif of motherhood in late nineteenth-century and twentieth-century Italian literature, see Laura Benedetti, *The Tigress in the Snow: Motherhood and Literature in Twentieth Century Italy* (Toronto: Toronto University Press, 2007).

10 'O mamma, tu mi porti. . .' 'Ma tu mi sostieni, piccola'. Matilde Serao, 'Terno secco', in *All'erta Sentinella!* (Milan: Baldini & Castoldi, 1914), 117–64 (86).

11 Serao, 'Terno secco', 83, 84.

12 'Su, piccola, su'. Serao, 'Terno secco', 83.
13 Serao, 'Terno secco', 84.
14 'Aveva [. . .] una testa troppo piccola sopra un corpo molto magro'. Matilde Serao, *Piccole anime* (Naples: Libreria Economica, 1907), 18.
15 'Ciccotto bello, Ciccotto mio [. . .] dove stai? [. . . .] Se non ti porto a casa, mamma Pasqualina non mi dà da mangiare'. Serao, *Piccole anime*, 17.
16 'Aveva fame anche lei come Ciccotto [. . . .] Non pensava neppure più: aveva semplicemente e unicamente fame'. Serao, *Piccole anime*, 18.
17 Elena Ferrante, *L'amore molesto* (Rome: Edizioni e/o, 1999), 139.
18 'Era la lingua di mia madre [. . . .] Non un dialetto gioioso o nostalgico: un dialetto senza naturalezza, usato con imperizia, pronunciato stentatamente come una lingua straniera mal nota [. . . .] Adesso che era morta e che avrei potuto cancellarlo per sempre insieme alla memoria che veicolava, sentirmelo nelle orecchie mi causava ansia. Me ne servii per comprare una pizza fritta imbottita di ricotta. Mangiai con gusto dopo giorni di quasi digiuno'. Ferrante, *L'amore molesto*, 21–2.
19 Emily Brady, 'Smells, Tastes, and Everyday Aesthetics', in *The Philosophy of Food*, ed. David M. Kaplan (Berkeley: University of California Press, 2012), 69–86 (81).
20 'Ero insomma in una condizione di labilità, a cui reagivo con un teso estenuato autocontrollo. Avevo la testa tutta occupata da Mario, dalle fantasie su di lui e quella donna, dal riesame del nostro passato, dalla smania di capire in che cosa ero stata; insufficiente e d'altra parte vigilavo disperatamente sulle mansioni d'obbligo: attenzione a salare la pasta, attenzione a non salarla due volte, attenzione alla scadenza dei cibi, attenzione a non lasciare acceso il gas'. Elena Ferrante, *I giorni dell'abbandono* (Rome: Edizioni e/o, 2002), 28.
21 'il gesto diventava così meccanico, così distante e indipendente, che il metallo mi tagliava le unghie, la pelle dei polpastrelli'. Ferrante, *I giorni dell'abbandono*, 153.
22 'Ripresi a cucinare sforzandomi di invogliarli al cibo con nuove ricette. Ricominciai ad affettare, rosolare, salare. Mi misi persino a fare dolci, ma per i dolci non avevo vocazione, non avevo abilità'. Ferrante, *I giorni dell'abbandono*, 152–3.
23 Provavo una nausea che mi era stata sempre estranea per le chiazze verdi di prezzemolo mescolate alle pelli rosse dei pomodori, a galla sull'acqua grassa del lavandino otturato. Non sapevo riacquistare la vecchia disinvoltura verso i resti appiccicosi del cibo che i bambini lasciavano sulla tovaglia, sul pavimento. Ferrante, *I giorni dell'abbandono*, 153.
24 Ferrante, *I giorni dell'abbandono*, 54.
25 '"Va' da Carrano," mi consigliò con un forte accento napoletano [. . .] "fatti aiutare da lui [. . .] è l'unico che ti può aiutare [. . . .] Hai poco tempo. Otto sta morendo"'. Ferrante, *I giorni dell'abbandono*, 114.
26 'Bianca prese un'arancia dal vassoio della frutta, aprì un cassetto, mi porse un coltello [. . . .] Ci fai il serpente, chiese allora lei anche a nome di Marta, e Marta

mi sorrise incoraggiante [. . . .] Va bene, dissi, presi l'arancia, cominciai a tagliare la buccia. Le bambine mi fissavano. Sentivo i loro sguardi che volevano ammansirmi, ma più forte sentivo il fulgore della vita fuori di loro [. . . .] Ah, renderle invisibili, non sentire più le richieste della loro carne come domande [. . .] pressanti [. . . .] Finii di sbucciare l'arancia e me ne andai. Da allora, per tre anni, non le ho viste né sentite più.' Elena Ferrante, *La figlia oscura* (Rome: Edizioni e/o, 2006), 100.

27 'Parlava alla bambina e alla sua bambola con una cadenza dialettale gradevole, il napoletano che amo, quello tenero del gioco e delle dolcezze. Ero incantata. Le lingue per me hanno un veleno segreto che ogni tanto schiuma e per il quale non c'è antidoto. Ricordo il dialetto nella bocca di mia madre quando smarriva la cadenza dolce e ci strillava, intossicata dallo scontento: non ce la faccio più con voi'. Ferrante, *La figlia oscura*, 16–17.

28 'Marta, no, per niente, lei non si attaccava, piangeva, e io mi disperavo. Volevo essere una buona madre [. . .] ma il corpo si rifiutava'. Ferrante, *La figlia oscura,* 110.

29 Luca Torre provides a succinct and informative historical background to this crisis in his introduction to Matilde Serao, *Il ventre di Napoli* (Naples: Torre editrice, 1992), XLIII.

30 'Nessuna donna che mangi, nella strada, vede fermarsi un bambino a guardare, senza dargli subito di quello che mangia: e quando non ha altro, gli dà del pane'. Serao, *Il ventre di Napoli*, 73–4.

31 'Un caso frequente di pieta è questo: una madre troppo debole [. . .] ha un bambino, ma non ha latte. Vi è sempre un'amica o una vicina o qualunque estranea pietosa, che offre il suo latte; ne allatterà due, che importa?' Serao, *Il ventre di Napoli*, 72.

32 See Anna-Maria Tapinen, 'Motherhood through the Wheel: The Care of Foundlings in Late Nineteenth Century Naples', in *Gender, Family, and Sexuality: The Private Sphere in Italy 1860-1945*, ed. Perry Willson (London: Palgrave Macmillan: 2004), 57–70.

33 For more information on the more recent history of breastfeeding in Italy, see Elizabeth Dixon Whitaker, *Measuring Mamma's Milk: Fascism and the Medicalization of Maternity in Italy* (Ann Arbor: Michigan University Press, 2000).

34 'Scrivevo, la sera, nei miei quaderni [. . .] come mi sentivo: un grumo di cibo che i miei figli masticavano in continuazione; un bolo fatto di materia viva che amalgamava e ammorbidiva continuamente la sua sostanza vivente per permettere a due sanguisughe voraci di nutrirsi lasciandomi addosso l'odore e il sapore dei loro succhi gastrici. Allattare, che disgusto, una funzione animale [. . .] per quanto mi lavassi, quel malodore di mamma non se ne andava'. Ferrante, *I giorni dell'abbandono*, 91–2.

35 'A volte Mario [. . .] mi prendeva stringendomi assonnata [. . .] senza emozioni. Lo faceva accanendosi sulla mia carne quasi assente che sapeva di latte, biscotti'. Ferrante, *I giorni dell'abbandono*, 92.

36 Ferrante, *I giorni dell'abbandono*, 52.

37 'Preparai un sugo con le polpette di carne, gli piaceva molto [. . . .] Ma non cucinai con piacere, ero svogliata, mi tagliai con l'apriscatole, mi sfuggì di mano una bottiglia di vino, vetro e vino schizzarono da ogni parte, anche sulle pareti bianche.

Lo costrinsi a cenare con me [. . . .] Volevo che vedesse in quel piatto di pasta tutto ciò che, andandosene, non avrebbe più potuto sfiorare con lo sguardo, o lambire, o accarezzare, ascoltare, annusare: mai più'. Ferrante, *I giorni dell'abbandono*, 18.

38 'Lui fissò il piatto, poi mi guardò diritto in faccia e disse: "Sì, c'è un'altra donna." Quindi con una foga fuori luogo infilzò con la forchetta maccheroni in abbondanza e si portò la pasta alla bocca quasi per mettersi a tacere, per non rischiare di dire più del dovuto [. . . .] Aveva cominciato a masticare [. . .] ma all'improvviso qualcosa gli era scricchiolato nella bocca [. . . .] Ora si stava sputando il boccone nel palmo della mano, pasta e sugo e sangue, era proprio sangue, sangue rosso [. . .] lui subito, a occhi sbarrati [. . .] si infilò le dita in bocca e si tirò via dal palato una scheggia di vetro'. Ferrante, *I giorni dell'abbandono*, 19.

39 'Da decenni per me Caserta era una città della fretta [. . . .] Non la città reale [. . .] ero andata da piccola, il lunedì dopo Pasqua [. . .] a mangiare salame di Secondigliano e uova cotte col guscio dentro una pasta grassa e pepata [. . .] Invece ciò che le mie emozioni meno verbalizzabili registravano sotto la voce Caserta, custodiva soprattutto una nausea da girotondo, il capogiro e la mancanza d'aria [. . . .] Caserta era un posto dove non dovevo andare [. . . .] Aveva il sapore dei confetti nelle bomboniere ma era vietato entrarci. Nemmeno mia madre doveva entrarci altrimenti mio padre la uccideva.' Ferrante, *L'amore molesto*, 34.

40 *Sfogliatelle* are Neapolitan pastries with flaky layers of crust, and a dense filling of ricotta and usually candied orange or citron.

41 Sambuco, *Corporeal Bonds*, 12.

42 Nancy Chodorow, *The Reproduction of Mothering* (Berkeley: University of California Press, 1999), 109.

43 Luce Irigaray, *Thinking the Difference* (New York: Routledge, 1989), 112.

44 Sambuco, *Corporeal Bonds*, 7.

Chapter 6

1 'The standard kitchen work surface height of 36 inches (91 cm) is based on the dimensions of the average woman.' (Gardner Soule, 'The New Kitchen Built to Fit Your Wife'. *Popular Science*, September 1953).

2 Nickie Charles and Marion Kerr, *Women, Food and Families* (Manchester: Manchester University Press, 1990), 83.

3 Marina Balina and Evgeny Dobrenko, *Petrified Utopia: Happiness Soviet Style* (London: Anthem Press, 2011), 87.

4 For a detailed historical and social context, consult *Le donne e la cucina nel ventennio* by Luisella Ceretta (2008).

5 Carole Counihan, 'Female Identity, Food and Power in Contemporary Florence', *Anthropological Quarterly* 61 (1988): 53, 56.

6 Lesa Lockford, *Performing Femininity: Rewriting Gender Identity* (Walnut Creek: AltaMira Press, 2004).

7 Teresa Desavahayam, 'Power and Pleasure around the Stove: The Construction of Gendered Identity in Middle-Class South Indian Hindu Households in Urban Malaysia', *Women's Studies International Forum* 28, no. 1 (2005): 1–20.

8 Wm. Alex McIntosh and Mary Zen. 'Women as Gatekeepers of Food Consumption: A Sociological Critique', in *Food and Gender: Identity and Power*, ed. Carole Counihan and Steven L. Kaplan (Amsterdam: Harwood Academic Publishers, 1998), 128–32.

9 David Gilmore, 'Men and Women in Southern Spain: "Domestic Power" Revisited', *American Anthropology* 92 (1990): 953–5.

10 'Il tasso d'occupazione femminile tra 15 e 64 anni, in Sicilia, Campania, Puglia e Calabria, è addirittura più basso della Guaiana francese, dell'Estremadura spagnola, della Tessaglia e della Macedonia in Grecia, e perfino dell'enclave spagnola di Melilla in Marocco.' This and all translations in this chapter are mine.

11 The title is a Sicilian idiomatic expression normally used to describe when someone turns up to a dinner or a party without bringing or contributing anything.

12 'Ogni donna sperimenta sulla propria pelle il patimento che può temporaneamente offuscare l'armonia delle sue fattezze, minare le sue certezze, farle dimenticare i suoi talenti. Ma il più delle volte la deprivazione può essere motore di una ricerca che la porta a scoprire il suo vero dono, e a dar vita ai suoi frutti migliori in piena libertà. Ma voi, signori, state attenti a non far patire troppo la vostra compagna: perché poi fruttificherà, e tra i suoi frutti più dolci potrebbe scoprire quello proibito della libertà' (10).

13 'Un forte odore di pomodoro . . . [delle] bottiglie di sugo [di] sua madre dentro a quella cucina' (339).

14 'E lu piaciri chi 'ntaccannu provu
tutti l'autri disastri mi compensa.

Di stu miu luchiceddu mai mi movu:
chist'è la stanza mia, lu miu palazzu' (379).

15 'In cucina sono brava, riesco a fare certe cose con niente, e in un viriri e sviriri, che la gente resta ammammaluccuta . . . . A me cucinare piace, mi fa sentire potente, importante' (57).

16 Carole Counihan, *Anthropology of Food and Body* (New York: Routledge, 1999), 9–10.
17 'Non puoi entrare, non puoi entrare nel negozio, non puoi entrare nella mia vita, quando lo decidi tu' (140).
18 'Non molto in modo che non se ne accorga, ma abbastanza per farlo stare male. Ogni suo mal di pancia sarà per me una benedizione' (143).
19 'Il vento è cambiato . . . l'aria si fa magnetica, l'anima riprende a sperare . . . tornerà la vita viva' (149).
20 'Mi tagliai con l'apriscatole, mi sfuggì di mano una bottiglia di vino, vetro e vino schizzarono da ogni parte, anche sulle pareti bianche. Subito dopo, con un gesto troppo brusco che doveva servire a prendere uno straccio, feci cadere anche la zuccheriera' (16–17).
21 'Pasta e sugo e sangue, era proprio sangue, sangue rosso. Gli guardai la bocca macchiata senza partecipazione . . . . Lui subito, a occhi sbarrati, si pulì la mano col tovagliolo, si infilò le dita in bocca e si tirò via dal palato una scheggia di vetro . . . . Mi gridò che gli facevo paura, mettergli il vetro nella pasta, come avevo potuto' (18–19).
22 'Ho pensato che fossi morta' (37).
23 'Le donne senza amore dissipavano la luce degli occhi, le donne senza amore morivano da vive' (47).
24 'Un teso, estenuato autocontrollo' (29).
25 'Dovevo cominciare da lì . . . ero sola' (30).
26 'La vita come la morte non hanno porte e nemmeno finestre e nemmeno un fine e nemmeno un inizio Si muovono insieme in uno spazio tempo dove tutto ruota e si ripete secondo la legge del caos e della ripetizione universale' (184–185).
27 'Il cibo conserva la natura dei secoli e la sapienza di Dio' (12).
28 'Negli strufoli e le cattedrali di dolci e pasta e maccheroni i fasti del Seicento e Settecento . . . quando Voltaire e i fiamminghi e i tedeschi scendevano per dipingere il Vesuvio . . . nella pizza vive Pulcinella e la regina Margherita e le dee madri antiche e le madonne nere . . . nel pane condito . . . e nelle salsicce di maiale rivive l'orgia del popolo realista e la follia di Masaniello' (16–17).
29 Adalgisa Giorgio, '"Allegorie" di Napoli. Marosia Castaldi e Giuseppe Montesano tra tradizione e innovazione', *Nuova Corvina* 19, no. 6 (2007): 133–6.
30 Gina Almerico, 'Food and Identity: Food Studies, Cultural, and Personal Identity', *Journal of International Business and Cultural Studies* 8 (June 2014): 5.
31 'Ora che rivivo quel passato mi accorgo che ho risuscitato con la mia cucina la follia estrema del paesaggio del sud dentro il paesaggio di brume nebbie e delitti della Lombardia' (76).
32 Mustafa Koc and Jennifer Welsh, 'Food, Identity, and the Immigrant Experience', *Canadian Diversity* 1, no. 1 (2002): 46–8.
33 Arlene Avakian and Barbara Haber, 'Feminist Food Studies: A Brief History', *Feminist Studies* 40, no. 2 (2014): 16.

34 Warren Belasco, *Food: The Key Concepts* (Oxford: Berg, 2008), 8, 16.

35 Adalgisa Giorgio, 'Writing Versions of Home: Marosia Castaldi's *Per quante vite* and the Poetics of the Visible', *Journal of Romance Studies* 10, no. 2 (2010): 80, 86, 92.

36 Le porsi i bocconi migliori: fettine di carne, coscette di pollo cotte nel rum e nel vino col latte Era un cibo grasso e invitante (84).

37 'Dalla mia cucina si levavano lampi di fuoco Era abitata dalle potenze infernali e angeliche che governano il Dio del cibo' (60).

38 'Nel paese aspettavano di vedere accendersi i fuochi della mia cucina per sentirsi risvegliare l'istinto del piacere estremo' (62).

39 'Misto di odio, amore e follia' (83).

40 'Affetto gratuito e totale e per fuggire al mio letto dove dormo sola' (82).

41 'Ho combattuto col cibo la mia battaglia nella vita. Ho elevato fino al cielo cattedrali di paste sfoglie e di paste frolle di brame e di piacere' (184).

42 'Ti saluto Sasà ma questa sera ti aspetto per cena.
E che ti porto, Marò?
Niente Sasà, panza e prisenza' (28).

43 'Era diventata un formidabile segugio: riusciva persino a catalogare le persone sulla base dell'afrore che emanavano. Le capitava per esempio di annusare un profumo e prevedere le intenzioni di chi lo portava' (46).

44 'Tutte le schifezze che piacevano a lui' (33).

45 'Quando il piatto era vuoto, Marò lo riempiva di altra pasta, e lui volentieri si piegava alla sua insistenza: 'Prendine ancora un pò, l'ho fatta apposta per te.' Buttava giù un boccone dietro l'altro strabuzzando gli occhi, come se facesse uno sforzo fisico' (56).

46 'La colse uno dei soliti attacchi che la spingevano a cucinare furiosamente e disordinatamente, per poi congelare e riporre nel frigo in attesa di un commensale adeguato. Sasà dormiva ancora, tra poco sarebbe stato giorno, fantasticò di una colazione consumata insieme sul suo letto . . . . Sasà le piaceva, lui la amava . . . gli ingredienti c'erano tutti, si trattava di mescolarli con sapienza' (173).

47 Lo assaporò, provò a morderla, divorare, spalmò, lo saziava, si riempì di quel profumo di basilica, sapore salino di uova di riccio, da fame vorace (174–5).

48 Giorgio, 'Writing Versions of Home', 78.

49 Lockford, *Performing Femininity*.

Chapter 7

1 Suvendrini Perera, 'Dead Exposures: Trophy Bodies and Violent Visibilities of the Nonhuman', *Borderlands-e-journal* 13, no. 1 (2014): 1–26.

2 Allen Feldman, 'Violence and Vision: The Prosthetics and Aesthetics of Terror', *States of Violence* 10, no. 1 (2006): 425–68.

3 Marcello Messina and Teresa Di Somma, 'Unified Italy, Southern Women and Sexual Violence: Situating the Sexual Assault TV "Prank" against Emma Marrone within the Dynamics of Contemporary Italy as a Scopic Regime', *Tropos* 6, no. 1 (2017): 1–18.

4 Mikhail Bakhtin, *Problems of Dostoevsky's Poetics* (Minneapolis: University of Minnesota Press, 1984).

5 John Dickie, 'The South as Other: From Liberal Italy to the Lega Nord', *The Italianist*, no. 14 [Special Issue – Culture and Society in Southern Italy: Past and present] (1994): 124–40.

6 Gabriella Gribaudi, 'Images of the South: The Mezzogiorno as Seen by Insiders and Outsider', in *The New History of the Italian South: The Mezzogiorno Revisited*, ed. Robert Lumley and Jonathan Morris (Exeter: University of Exeter Press, 1997), 83–113.

7 Joseph Pugliese, 'Whiteness and the Blackening of Italy: La Guerra cafona, Extracommunitari and Provisional Street Justice', *PORTAL Journal of Multidisciplinary International Studies* 5, no. 2 (2008): 1–35.

8 Marcello Messina, 'Matteo Garrone's Gomorra: A Politically Incorrect Use of Neapolitan Identities and Queer Masculinities?', *Gender/Sexuality/Italy*, no. 2 (2015): 179–87; Marcello Messina, 'Gendered Metaphors of Territorial Subordination, Theologies of Independence and Images of a Liberated Future: Sodaro & Di Bella's Làssami as a Sicilian Decolonial Allegory', *Muiraquitã* 5, no. 2 (2017): 91–143.

9 Francesca Calamita, 'Voracious Dolls and Competent Chefs: Negotiating Femininities and Masculinities in Italian Food', *Gender/Sexuality/Italy*, no. 1 (2014): 1–13.

10 Livio Giorgioni, 'Pane, amore e fantasia: il cibo nel cinema italiano dal dopoguerra ad oggi', in *La grande abbuffata: percorsi cinematografici fra trame e ricette*, ed. Livio Giorgioni, Federico Pontiggia and Marco Ronconi (Cantalupa: Effatà Editrice), 28.

11 *Il tango della gelosia*, directed by Steno (Ypsilon Cinematografica, 2015).

12 'Se tu mi dici: "ci venghi a balla?", Io potrei sempre accettare. Insomma tu non mi dispiaci affatto, me so' spiegata?' Ibid.

13 'Senti, ragazza a ore, che stai fantasticando, guarda che il magico sogno che hai vissuto nel tuo cervelletto, è finito, cara. Secondo te, ti pare che uno come me, milanese al 100%, può portare al ballamento na schifezza di meridionale, terruncella, alta un metro e venti come te? Ma levati di mezzo, cerca qualcuno della tua stazza sociale p'andà a ballà! Ciappa qualche bifolco di paese, qualcuno di Trani, di Cerignola, di Canosa magari, ti portano subito a ballà quelli. A me piace la donna settentrionale, con un certo, diciamo, fascino. No africana come te, la donna meridionale è ancorata ad un sacco di puttanate, a tutta la tradizione della famiglia, appesa all'albero come le scimmie, aggrappata ad un sacco di stronzate: l'orgoglio,

la vergogna, la gelosia . . . e mettitelo in testa sto vassoio, come fanno le negre, così almeno non ti scivola, Abdullah!' Ibid.

14 Pugliese, 'Whiteness and the Blackening', 3.

15 *Bomber*, directed by Michele Lupo (Elio Scardamaglia, 1982).

16 *Acapulco, prima spiaggia . . . a sinistra*, directed by Sergio Martino (Cinematografica Alex, 1983).

17 'Mi piacerebbe venire anche a me ad Acapulco'. Ibid.

18 'Eh mi spiace, siamo impegnati'. Ibid.

19 'Andrea, mica male il culo di Miranda, eh? No, dico, guarda lì!' Ibid.

20 'Ma non vedi che è basso? E poi è una marocchina, dai!' Ibid.

21 'È sano, genuino, mi ricorda le mie radici'. Ibid.

22 A public holiday celebrated in Italy on the 15th of August.

23 'Abbiamo mangiato proprio bene! Brava, brava!' Ibid.

24 The original Italian is '*arte bolognese*', literally 'Bolognese art', a coded term for phallic oral sex, deriving from the horrendous cliché according to which women from Bologna are allegedly more inclined than other Italian women to perform fellatio.

25 Andrea: 'Io la darei via di più! [. . . .] E poi tu, manicure sei già, hai un bel culetto, se la vendi per dei soldi diventi ricca!' [. . . .] Gigi: 'Tanto qui siamo al Nord, hai paura che si consumi?' Gegia: 'Ma che discorsi fate? Siete due bricconcelli!' Andrea: 'Se tu metti un bell'annuncio sul giornale . . . AAA manicure offresi . . .' Gigi: 'Ingresso indipendente.' Andrea: '. . . ingresso indipendente, esperta arte bolognese, che ci vuole quello.' Gigi: 'Massima riservatezza.' Andrea: '. . . massima riservatezza, che ci dà, che ci dà, che ci dà.' Gigi: 'Hai risolto.' Andrea: 'E via!' Ibid.

26 'Ma che sei scemo? E poi io sono una manicure sul serio sai? [. . . .] E poi . . . io sono una meridionale, e non mi darei mai se non ci fosse di mezzo un bel po' di sentimento'. Ibid.

27 *FF.SS. - Cioè: ...che mi hai portato a fare sopra a Posillipo se non mi vuoi più bene?*, directed by Renzo Arbore (Eidoscope Productions, 1983).

28 Joseph Pugliese, 'Assimilation, Unspeakable Traces and the Ontologies of Nation', in *Asian and Pacific Inscriptions: Identities, Ethnicities, Nationalities*, ed. Suvendrini Perera (Victoria: Meridian, 1995), 229–54.

29 Giovanni Maria Ruggiero and Marcello Prandin, 'Tradition, Transition, and Social Cognition in Italy: Are They Correlated with Eating Disorders?', *Eating Disorders in the Mediterranean Area: An Exploration in Transcultural Psychology*, ed. Giovanni Maria Ruggiero (New York: Nova Biomedical Books, 2003), 127–39.

30 Ann M. Cheney, 'Emotional Distress and Disordered Eating Practices among Southern Italian Women', *Qualitative Health Research* 22, no. 9 (2012): 1247–59.

31 For example, Ruggiero and Prandin draw upon highly controversial work, such as Edward Christie Banfield, *The Moral Basis of a Backward Society* (Glencoe: Free

Press, 1958); and Robert D. Putnam, *Making Democracy Work: Civic Traditions in Modern Italy* (Princeton: Princeton University Press, 1993).

32 Enrique D. Dussel, 'Europe, Modernity, and Eurocentrism', *Nepantla: Views from South* 1, no. 3 (2000): 471–3.

33 'sud sud, nui simmo ro sud / nui simm curt e nir'. *FF.SS.*

34 Pugliese, 'Whiteness and the Blackening', 2.

35 'e pummarole po' ragu / a pizza 'a muzzarella [. . .] / e maccarune pe' magna'. *FF.SS.*

36 *Mi faccia causa*, directed by Steno (Fulvio Lucisano, 1984).

37 *A tu per tu*, directed by Sergio Corbucci (Adige Films, 1984).

38 'E impara a parlare italiano, terrona! È vent'anni che vivi qui, e ci vuole l'interprete e i sottotitoli per capirti!' Ibid.

39 Lara Palombo, *The Racial Camp and the Production of the Political Citizen: A Genealogy of Contestation from Indigenous Populations and Diasporic Women* (PhD thesis, Sydney: Macquarie University, 2015), 194.

40 Calamita, 'Voracious Dolls'.

41 Glória Anzaldúa, *Borderlands/La Frontera* (San Francisco: Aunt Lute Books, 1999), 39.

42 Neapolitan soft bun, soaked in liquor and filled with cream or custard.

43 Salvatore Palomba and Eduardo Alfieri, *Il babà è una cosa seria* (Fonit Cetra, 1989).

44 'A me quello che mi consola / È l'addore d'a pummarola / / [. . .] l'ammore viene e va / Ma il maccherone resta [. . .] / Io mi sento più buona e bella / Facci' o gnocco c'a muzzarella'. Ibid.

45 Anna Oxa, 'Imitazione di Marisa Laurito', *Fantastico 1988*, 1988. 'La differenza che passa tra un buon pomeriggio e una buona sera è la stessa che passa tra la pasta cresciuta e o panzarotto'.

46 *Pasta cresciuta*, or *zeppole*, are traditional Neapolitan fried pastry balls.

47 While the word *panzarotto*, or *panzerotto*, indicates a different dish in almost each Southern Italian region, in the Neapolitan tradition the word refers to fried croquettes of mashed potatoes.

48 Cinzia Leone as Marisa Laurito, *Avanzi*, 18 March 1991.

49 'Sono qui [. . .] in attesa di un carico molto importante, una primadonna della TV che è stata . . .' Cinzia Leone as Marisa Laurito, *Avanzi*, 11 March 1991.

50 'Sì, donna, hahaha'. Ibid.

51 'Una volta stavo ballando in TV, e a un certo punto . . . tra! Si è rotto il vestito. Adesso sto in linea perfetta: guarda qua! Sono dimagrita 10 chili in due mesi col piano Slim Fast!'. Slim Fast, *Spot con Marisa Laurito*, n.d.

52 'Una formosa signorina che non ha i canoni classici per un concorso di bellezza.' Fatima Trotta cit. in Alessia Di Raimondo, 'Fatima Trotta, l'intrattenimento innato di una donna Made in Sud'. *Il giornale digitale*, 29 February 2016.

53 (Fatima): 'Un suo pregio?' (Miss'Illude): 'Tutte le mattine vado in palestra.' (Fatima): 'Un suo difetto?' (Miss'Illude): 'Appena esco vado al ristorante.' Miss'Illude, *Made in Sud*, 4 April 2016.

54 (Trotta): 'Signorina, ma lei pensa sempre al cibo. Ma perché lei è così . . . diciamo così in carne? È sempre stata così?' (Miss'Illude): 'No, io ero talmente magra che sembravo un uccellino, guardate com'ero!' [. . . .] (Trotta): 'Ma signorina, ma era bellissima, ma che ha combinato?' Miss'Illude and Peppe Step, *Made in Sud*, 12 April 2016.

55 (Peppe Step): 'E grazie ai miei allenamenti, Miss'Illude, ad un concorso di bellezza, nonostante sia arrivata terza, ha vinto!' (Trotta): 'Scusate, ma se è arrivata al terzo posto, come ha fatto a vincere?' (Miss'Illude): 'Me so magnata e pprimme roje!' (Trotta) '[. . .] ma magna qualsiasi cosa questa!' Peppe Step, Miss'Illude and Nonno Moderno, *Made in Sud*, 30 May 2016.

56 Cf. Larissa Pelúcio. 'Traduções e torções ou o que se quer dizer quando dizemos queer no Brasil?'. *Revista Periódicus* 1, no. 1 (2014): 68–91.

57 'Se aspetti che divento bella, se aspetti che divento magra, e se aspetti che divento una monella, hai vuogli'e spettà, ci vuò no miracolo'. Miss'Illude, *Made in Sud*, 4 April 2016.

58 Pugliese, 'Assimilation', 243.

Chapter 8

1 Molly Tambor, 'Mothers, Workers, Citizens: Teresa Noce and the Parliamentary Politics of Motherhood', in *La mamma: Interrogating a National Stereotype*, ed. Penelope Morris and Perry Willson (New York: Palgrave Macmillan, 2018), 54–5.

2 Victoria De Grazia describes the mass influx of electric appliances in the decades following the Second World War: 'The new household's center of operations was the kitchen. Here the battery of machinery was located – the set defined from the mid-1950s and 1960s as the stove, refrigerator, washing machine, vacuum cleaner, together with assorted automatic mixers, blenders, and coffee grinders; from the 1970s it included dishwashers and television sets as well; and from the 1980s microwave ovens, toasters, and electric steamers and fryers. The kitchen's manager was the modern homemaker, a Mrs. Consumer who worked solo or with her "electric servants"'. De Grazia, *Irresistible Empire: America's Advance through Twentieth-Century Europe* (Cambridge, MA: Harvard University Press, 2005), 418–19.

3 American historian Elaine Tyler May underlines that the consumer novelties of the 1950s could be read as ploys to lure women back into the kitchen; whether in America or in Italy, there was the underlying objective to contain women to the domestic space, in line with the containment policies budding from the Cold War. May, *Homeward Bound: American Families in the Cold War Era* (New York: Basic Books, 2008), 166.

4 *Donna crisi,* or 'crisis woman', is a propagandistic term developed and publicized by the fascist regime that denounced the women of the 'roaring' 1920s who favoured watching movies, smoking cigarettes, playing sports and American-style fashions over starting a family. The family policies of the regime instead prized the *donna madre,* 'mother woman', who was charged with birthing and raising multiple children: future soldiers servicing the regime. For further reading on the *donna crisi,* see Natasha V. Chang's *The Crisis-Woman: Body Politics and the Modern Woman in Fascist Italy* (2014), or, as the first historical undertaking of this kind, Victoria de Grazia's *How Fascism Ruled Women: Italy, 1922-1945* (1992).

5 Rebecca West, '"What" as Ideal and "Who" as Real: Portraits of Wives and Mothers in Italian Postwar Domestic Manuals, Fiction, and Film', in *Women in Italy, 1945-1960: An Interdisciplinary Study,* ed. Penelope Morris (New York: Palgrave Macmillan, 2006), 22.

6 Ibid., 23. The italics are West's.

7 These networks are elegantly described in Stephen Gundle, 'Sophia Loren: Italian Icon', *Historical Journal of Film, Radio, and Television* 15, no. 3 (1995): 368.

8 As Loren was described by *TIME* magazine in 1962 (Gundle, 'Sophia Loren: Italian Icon', 376).

9 Sophia Loren, *Yesterday, Today, Tomorrow: My Life* (New York: Atria Books, 2014), 63.

10 A. E. Hotchner, *Sophia: Living and Loving* (New York: William Morrow and Company, Inc., 1979), 96.

11 Carol Helstosky, *Pizza: A Global History* (London: Reaktion Books, 2008), 23.

12 For further reading on the male gaze, please consult Laura Mulvey's essay 'Visual Pleasure and Narrative Cinema' (1975).

13 Réka Buckley, 'Marriage, Motherhood, and the Italian Film Stars of the 1950s', in *Women in Italy, 1945-1960: An Interdisciplinary Study,* ed. Penelope Morris (New York: Palgrave Macmillan, 2006), 39.

14 Gundle, 'Sophia Loren: Italian Icon', 377.

15 Stephen Snyder describes De Sica's late work as 'miles away from his neorealist art', pointing out how these films have not 'occasioned interesting commentary'. Critics argue that De Sica sold out to the demands of the filmmaking industry, acquiescing to producers like Carlo Ponti and Dino De Laurentiis who wanted to emulate the prowess of Hollywood. De Sica himself, in a 1972 interview with Charles Thomas Samuels, lamented of having been ruined by money. Snyder, 'Hiding in the Light: De Sica's Work in the 1960s', in *Vittorio De Sica: Contemporary Perspectives,* ed. Howard Curle and Stephen Snyder (Toronto: University of Toronto Press, 2000), 235.

16 I write 'free' in quotation marks to suggest the notion that although Adelina's pregnancies keep her out of jail, her maternal responsibilities grow as she bears more children. However, as I explain, it is Carmine, not Adelina, who bears the weight of childcare.

17 For a more detailed reading of GI crimes in the south, see Isobel Williams, *Allies and Italians under Occupation: Sicily and Southern Italy, 1943-1945* (Basingstoke: Palgrave Macmillan, 2013).

18 This is a reference to Vittorio De Sica's neorealist masterpiece, *Umberto D.* (1952), in which a retired pensioner debates whether to commit suicide when he and his dog, Flike, are threatened with eviction from their Roman apartment. The film underscores the vast social injustices against marginalized groups – in this case, the elderly – in the years following the Second World War. Vittorio De Sica, dir., *Umberto D.*, prod. Rizzoli, 1952.

19 Snyder, 'Hiding in the Light', 235.

20 The term *sgravata* is left untranslated to leave the double meaning of 'pregnant' and 'unburdened'.

21 Tenta ancora di leggere; alla fine ci riesce.

PASQUALE: . . . Sra, sga . . . sgravata . . . Ah, sgravata! Il 20 ottobre. Io vendevo i fichi d'India . . .

Smette di leggere, si fa i conti con le dita.

PASQUALE: Sei mesi d'allattamento: novembre, dicembre, gennaio, febbraio, marzo, aprile . . . Aprile, maggio, quando escono le prime primizie delle ciliegie, scade l'impunità.

CARMINE (*sicuro di sé*): E mo' stammo a gennaio. Il tempo ci sta . . .

Cesare Zavattini, et al. Sceneggiatura di *Ieri, oggi, domani.* Excerpt from *Ieri oggi domani di Vittorio De Sica: Testimonianze, interventi, sceneggiatura*, a cura di Gualtiero De Santi e Manuel De Sica (Rome: Associazione Amici di Vittorio De Sica, 2002), 142.

22 Seguiamo Elvira, la quale raggiunge la bancarella del marito.

ELVIRA (*concitata*): So arrivate 'e guardie into' basso 'Mellino. Carminello sta solo, Adelina nun ce sta. Ma 'e guardie hanno detto che l'aspettano, che non se ne vanno.

PASQUALE: Mannaggia 'o diavolo . . . Guardame 'e cerase. . .

Zavattini, et al., *Ieri oggi domani di Vittorio De Sica*, 143.

23 Ibid., 144.

24 Jacqueline Reich, *Beyond the Latin Lover: Marcello Mastroianni, Masculinity, and Italian Cinema* (Bloomington: Indiana University Press, 2004), 105.

25 Ibid., 108.

26 We could make the argument that since Loren's children are both male, these are two more men (following De Sica, Ponti, and Mastroianni) who have shaped Loren into the woman she is today.

27 Loren, *Yesterday, Today, Tomorrow*, 170.

28 Besides numerous reprints, Loren published a second cookbook in 1997, *Sophia Loren: Recipes and Memories.*
29 Sophia Loren, *In cucina con amore* (Milano: Rizzoli, 2013 reprint), 18–23.
30 Ibid., 40.
31 'Non mi resta che farvi gli auguri e raccomandarvi la massima attenzione, perché voglio che con le mie ricette abbiate un grande successo. E' anche questione di orgoglio personale. Vi prego, non mi fate fare brutte figure. Aprendo questo libro siate le benvenute nella mia cucina. Mangiate con me' (Loren, *In cucina con amore,* 13).
32 Loren, *Yesterday, Today, Tomorrow*, 175.
33 Gundle, 'Sophia Loren: Italian Icon', 380.
34 Sophia Loren, *Women & Beauty* (New York: William Morrow and Company, 1984), 184.
35 Loren, *In cucina con amore,* 10.
36 'Anzi sono proprio loro, con le loro idee inadeguate all'evolvere della società, che avrebbero più bisogno di questa, diciamo, terapeutica culinaria' (Loren, *In cucina con amore,* 213).
37 'Comunque, poiché è naturale che il maggior numero dei miei lettori siano donne, a loro dico: la cucina *vi piaccia, non sia* una fastidiosa routine'. The italics are mine to highlight the subjunctive mood (Loren, *In cucina con amore,* 213).

Chapter 9

1 Among the studies on Ramondino's *Althénopis*, see Monica Farnetti, *Il centro della cattedrale. I ricordi d'infanzia nella scrittura femminile. Dolores Prato, Fabrizia Ramondino, Anna Maria Ortese, Cristina Campo, Ginevra Bompiani* (Mantua: Tre Lune, 2002); Adalgisa Giorgio (ed.), 'Non sto qui a Napoli sicura di casa', in *Identità, spazio e testualità in Fabrizia Ramondino* (Perugia: Marlocchi Editore, 2013); Paula Greene, 'Writing Home to her Mother: Fabrizia Ramondino's *Althénopis*', in *Across Genres, Generations and Borders. Italian Women Writing Lives*, ed. Susanna Scarparo and Rita Wilson (Newark: Newark University Press, 2004), 117–39; Stefania Lucamante, '*Teatro di guerra*: Of History and the Fathers', in *Under Arturo's Star: The Cultural Legacies of Elsa Morante*, ed. Stefania Lucamante and Sharon Wood (West Lafayette: Purdue University Press, 2006), 221–56; Franco Sepe, *Fabrizia Ramondino – rimemorazione e viaggio* (Naples: Liguori, 2011); Rita Wilson, 'Personal Histories: Fabrizia Ramondino', in *Speculative Identities: Contemporary Italian Women's Narrative*, ed. Rita Wilson (Leeds: Northern University Press, 2000), 83–98.
2 Naples, as Ramondino reveals in a note, appears transfigured in 'Althénopis' (meaning 'old woman's eye'), an epithet used by German soldiers during the

occupation of Italy to indicate the city's decline, and which contrasts with its mythological name Parthenope (meaning 'virgins' eye'), from the name of the nymph who gave birth to the city. Fabrizia Ramondino, *Althénopis* (Turin: Einaudi, 1981), 10. All quotations in Italian are from this novel and edition. English quotations are from Fabrizia Ramondino, *Althénopis*, trans. Michael Sullivan (Manchester: Carcanet, 1988).

3 For the concept of food voice, see Annie Hauck-Lawson, 'When Food Is the Voice. A Case Study of a Polish-American Woman', *Journal for the Study of Food and Society* 2, no. 1 (1998): 21; and Annie Hauck-Lawson and Jonathan Deutsch (eds), *Gastropolis. Food and New York City* (New York: Columbia University Press, 2009), XIV.

4 I refer to the milestone reflections of Claude Levi-Strauss, Pierre Bourdieu, Roland Barthes and Mary Douglas, as discussed by Maria Giuseppina Muzzarelli and Lucia Re in the introduction to their edited book, *Il cibo e le donne nella cultura e nella storia. Prospettive interdisciplinari* (Bologna: CLUEB, 2005), 11.

5 Roland Barthes, 'Toward a Psychosociology of Contemporary Food Consumption', in *Food and Culture: A Reader*, ed. Carole Counihan, and Penny Van Esterik (New York: Routledge, 2008), 22–4.

6 Ibid., 21.

7 Ibid., 23.

8 Rosi Braidotti, *Nomadic Subjects: Embodiment and Sexual Difference in Contemporary Feminist Theory* (New York: Columbia University Press, 1994), 23–5.

9 Ibid., 29.

10 According to Sepe, the protagonist of *Guerra di infanzia e di Spagna* (War of Childhood and Spain, 2001) cannot count on the idea of a 'homeland' but on its 'linguistic simulacrum'. Sepe, *Fabrizia Ramondino,* 74. Similarly, Farnetti observes how the protagonist in *Guerra* is able to move among different languages, much like the nomad: Italian spoken by her mother, Spanish spoken by the inhabitants of Majorca where she is living and the Spanish dialect of her nurse. Farnetti, *Il centro della cattedrale,* 81–2.

11 Lucamante, '*Teatro di guerra*', 232.

12 Adalgisa Giorgio, 'Moving Across Boundaries: Identity and Difference in the Work of Fabrizia Ramondino', *The Italianist* 18 (1988): 176.

13 As Giorgio argues, '[f]rom exile in *Althénopis*, to migrancy in *Taccuino Tedesco,* to unease about stability in "Star di casa", we move to representation of a new condition in *In Viaggio*, that of a permanent migrant, the nomad'. Giorgio, 'Moving Across Boundaries', 177.

14 Braidotti, *Nomadic Subjects*, 25.

15 Stacy Alaimo, *Bodily Natures: Science, Environment and the Material Self* (Bloomington: Indiana University Press, 2010), 2–3.

16 Ibid., 12.
17 Gian-Paolo Biasin, *The Flavors of Modernity: Food and The Novel* (Princeton: Princeton University Press, 1993), 13.
18 Massive bombing raids, mostly from Allies, destroyed Naples during 1940 and 1944. The city suffered the destruction of strategic places (port, rail, churches and hospitals) as well as heavy losses of civilians. See Gabriella Gribaudi, *Guerra totale. Tra bombe alleate e violenze naziste. Napoli e il fronte meridionale 1940-44* (Torino: Bollati Boringhieri, 2005). As Ramondino herself documented, people used to take shelter in the basement of their buildings or other anti-aircraft refuges of the city. The luckiest, instead, could leave their homes in Naples and seek refuge in other villages of the region. Ramondino, *Althénopis*, 66–7, and 165.
19 Gillian Riley, *The Oxford Companion to Italian Food* (Oxford: Oxford University Press, 2007), 357.
20 Susie Orbach, *Hunger Strike: Starving Amidst Plenty. 1985* (New York: Other Press, 2011), 94.
21 The girl's mother's frequent invectives against the older woman who is guilty of being extravagant and irresponsible, especially given her poor management of the inheritance she received from her parents and from her dead husband. See Ramondino, *Althénopis*, 11.
22 Cristina Mazzoni, 'Cucina, donne e santità: dalla pratica alla scrittura', in *Il cibo e le donne*, 67–81. Quotations in English are mine.
23 Ibid., 68.
24 Ramondino, *Althénopis*, 16.
25 Ramondino, *Althénopis*, trans. Sullivan, 13; 'un po' di latte in scatola, in piccoli tegami solo per me, con trenta grammi di zucchero sottratti al suo caffè, in quei tempi austeri di guerra'. Ramondino, *Althénopis*, 7.
26 Ramondino, *Althénopis*, 16.
27 Ramondino, *Althénopis*, trans. Sullivan, 23; 'il pane bianco degli americani'. Ramondino, *Althénopis*, 17.
28 Karima Moyer-Nocchi, *Chewing the Fat: An Oral History of Italian Foodways from Fascism to Dolce Vita* (Perrysburg: Medea, 2015), 24.
29 Italians could buy this wheat bread by showing their shopkeeper their ration book released by the city halls. Pierpaolo Luzzatto Fegiz, 'Alimentazioni e prezzi in tempo di guerra: 1942-43', *Annali triestini* 18, no. 2a (1948): 94.
30 Ramondino, *Althénopis*, trans. Sullivan, 22; 'Quando alla nonna veniva quell'estro e usciva dalla sua stanza col grande grembiale bianco, nostra madre cercava di correrle dietro, di fermarla [. . .] la nonna continuava ad andare avanti, laddove l'estro la spingeva, tutta sudata e macchiata, nei vapori di fumo e olio, arrossata, con le maniche rimboccate, cercando di lavare qualche stoviglia nella soda per

non incorrere nelle furie di nostra madre o nel borbottio della serva.' Ramondino, *Althénopis*, 16.

31 For the meaning of the word *estro* in Italian, I refer to the following definition from the Treccani Italian dictionary: 'Among the Greeks, the word [estro] was used to indicate the reaction of prophetic and poetic enthusiasm of the mortal to the divinity's action; the word acquires then other meanings, such as warlike fury, inspiration, passion, tantrum, whim, and sudden fantasy.' http://www.treccani.it/vocabolario/estro/. (accessed 28 August 2019). The English translation is mine.

32 Ramondino, *Althénopis*, 15.

33 Ramondino, *Althénopis*, trans. Sullivan, 21; 'mai misurata sul risparmio o su moderne regole igienico-dietetiche, ma sulla fantasia.' Ramondino, *Althénopis*, 15.

34 Teresa De Lauretis, 'Eccentric Subjects: Feminist Theory and Historical Consciousness', *Feminist Studies* 16, no. 1 (1990): 145.

35 Ramondino, *Althénopis*, trans. Sullivan, 118; 'si sarebbe moltiplicato quel piacere se avessimo potuto servirci delle mani e della bocca, per sentirci col dolce fusi in unica sostanza.' Ramondino, *Althénopis*, 115.

36 Ramondino, *Althénopis*, 176.

37 Alaimo, *Bodily Natures*, 13.

38 Fabrizia Ramondino, *Storie di Patio* (Turin: Einaudi: 1983), 206.

39 Ramondino, *Althénopis*, trans. Sullivan, 177; 'Ancor più mi piaceva friggere le melanzane e le zucchine, e mi pareva che la mia vaga, esile, iterativa inconsistenza si addensasse e diventasse sostanza, seppure informe, nei pesanti vapori dell'olio fritto; e quando qualche goccia bollente mi schizzava le mani, le braccia, il collo, mi pareva finalmente di avere delle mani, delle braccia, un collo.' Ramondino, *Althénopis*, 176–7.

40 We can infer that the granddaughter was fourteen years old when she moved to Callista's house in 1950. See Ramondino, *Althénopis*, 174–6.

41 Ramondino, *Althénopis*, trans. Sullivan, 177–8; 'Mi piaceva lavare i piatti e immergevo [. . .] le mani nell'acqua unta e scivolosa di soda. Mi piaceva sentire il grasso che si scioglieva, e in quell'acqua, grigia e maleodorante, mi pareva di intravvedere i torbidi segreti della vita. Era quello il mio modo di interpretare la resurrezione dei morti, ché tra i vapori, le acredini e i sudori della cucina vedevo comparire le sembianze della nonna [. . .]' Ramondino, *Althénopis*, 177.

42 Ramondino, *Althénopis*, 17.

43 The famous motto attributed to Hippocrates is quoted by Micheal Pollan in his *In Defense of Food: An Eater's Manifesto* (New York: Penguin, 2008), 29.

44 Braidotti, *Nomadic Subjects*, 33.

45 David M. Kaplan (ed.), *The Philosophy of Food* (Berkeley and Los Angeles: University of California Press, 2012), 3–4.

46 Massimo Montanari, *Food Is Culture* (New York: Columbia University Press, 2006), 133.

47 Indeed, there are few crucial examples in the novel that allude to a world that is not completely free from male authority. See Ramondino, *Althénopis*, 6, 14, and 17.

48 Francesca Calamita, *Linguaggi dell'esperienza femminile: disturbi alimentari, donne e scrittura dall'Unità al miracolo economico* (Padua: Il Poligrafo, 2015), 18–20.

49 As Calamita argues for the protagonist of Matilde Serao's short story. Francesca Calamita, Wellington 2013 – 'Tastefulness: Fashion, Food, Lust and Domesticity in Matilde Serao's *La Virtù di Checchina* (1884)', *Altrelettere* (2015): 9.

Chapter 10

1 See Gian-Paolo Biasin, *I sapori della modernità, cibo e romanzo* (Bologna: Il Mulino, 1991); Silvana Ghiazza, *La funzione del cibo nel testo letterario* (Bari: Wip, 2011); Gian Mario Anselmi and Gino Ruozzi, *Banchetti letterari. Cibi, pietanze e ricette nella letteratura da Dante a Camilleri* (Rome: Carocci, 2011); Ilaria Crotti and Beniamino Mirisola, 'A tavola con le Muse', *Italianistica* 8 (2017). On representations of food diseases, see Sarah Sceats and Francesca Calamita's remarkable researches cited in bibliography. On Italian migrant literature: Vera Horn, 'Assaporare la tradizione. Cibo, identità e senso di appartenenza nella letteratura migrante', *Revista de Italianistica* 19-20 (2010): 156–75; Silvia Camilotti, 'Saperi e sapori d'altrove: le scrittrici (si) raccontano', *Questioni di Cibo. Scienze e Ricerche Special Issue* (2015): 84–7; Fulvio Pezzarossa, *Cibi dei migranti*, in Anselmi and Ruozzi (eds), *Banchetti letterari. Cibi, pietanze e ricette nella letteratura italiana da Dante a Camilleri*, 100–7 and 377–8.

2 The Italian citizenship based on the geographical place of birth (*ius soli*) is given in the cases in which the parents of the person born on Italian soil are unknown.

3 Igiaba Scego, 'Exmatriates', in *Rome Tales*, ed. Helen Constantine, trans. Hugh Shankland (Oxford: Oxford University Press, 2011), 248–9. Original Italian: 'Guardai la tavola [. . . .] La tavola era imbandita di ogni ben di Dio. Di ogni leccornia presente in Oriente e in Occidente. Sembrava qualcosa tra il pranzo di Natale e il pasto serale che rompe il digiuno nel mese sacro di Ramadan. Ogni centimetro del tavolo era occupato. Tre tipi di tè speziato, due tipi di caffè, uno speziato e uno no. Succhi di frutta a volontà, avariati dolci, svariati salati, svariati agrodolci. Era una festa per gli occhi [. . . .] Peccato però che nessuno prendesse l'iniziativa di cominciare il banchetto [. . . .] Era evidente che tutti si aspettavano una mossa di Angélique'. Igiaba Scego, 'Dismatria', in *Pecore nere. Racconti*, ed. Emanuele Coen and Flavia Capitani (Rome/Bari: Laterza, 2005), 15. When no published translation is available, English translations of Scego's works are by Brandon Breen, unless otherwise indicated.

4 Scego, 'Exmatriates', 250–2. 'La mano partì e le mascelle di Angélique si misero subito in movimento [. . . .] Angélique aveva gradito il bottino di guerra. Il suo

palato si beava della carne che faceva da ripieno a quel fagottino di pasta sfoglia. Volle anche fare il bis e conquistare definitivamente quell'est di fagottini ripieni [. . . .] Guardai la tavola che un tempo era stata imbandita. Ci era passato sopra un tornado. Ogni centimetro del tavolo era stato saccheggiato. I tre tipi di tè speziato prosciugati, i due tipi di caffè tracannati, i succhi di frutta aspirati. E che dire poi degli svariati dolci, svariati salati e svariati agrodolci? Dissolti nel gorgo di varie mascelle in attività. Mangiati, gustati digeriti [. . . .] Insomma, il cibo aveva fatto il suo dovere. Solo che in quella bagarre di suoni vocali e suoni mascellari mancava un suono decisivo: il suono della voce (e della mascella) di mamma. Lei non aveva pronunciato verbo e non aveva assaggiato nulla. Si era limitata a sorseggiare un caffè tradizionale senza zucchero. Ecco, la città era stata conquistata, ma mancava la fortezza . . . solo allora si sarebbe potuto parlare di trionfo'. Scego, 'Dismatria', 17.

5 Igiaba Scego, 'Sausages', *Metamorphoses*, trans. Giovanna Bellesia and Victoria Offredi Poletto, 13, no. 2 (Fall 2005). Available online: http://www.warscapes.com/retrospectives/food/sausage (accessed 7 July 2018). 'E poi il patatrac! Quella domanda odiosa sulla mia identità del cazzo! Più somala? Più italiana? Forse ¾ somala e ¼ italiana? O forse è vero tutto il contrario? Non so rispondere! Non mi sono mai "frazionata" prima d'ora, e poi a scuola ho sempre odiato le frazioni, erano antipatiche e inconcludenti (almeno per la sottoscritta) [. . . .] Non sono un cento per cento, non lo sono mai stata e non credo che riuscirò a diventarlo ora. Credo di essere una donna senza identità. O meglio con più identità [. . . .] Vediamo un po'. Mi sento somala quando: 1) bevo il tè con il cardamomo, i chiodi di garofano e la cannella; 2) recito le 5 preghiere quotidiane verso la Mecca; 3)mi metto il *dirab*; 4) profumo la casa con l'incenso o l'*unsi* [. . . .] Mi sento italiana quando: 1) faccio una colazione dolce; 2) vado a vistare mostre, musei e monumenti; 3) parlo di sesso, uomini e depressioni con le amiche; 4) vedo i film di Alberto Sordi, Nino Manfredi, Vittorio Gassman, Marcello Mastroianni, Monica Vitti, Totò, Anna Magnani, Giancarlo Giannini, Ugo Tognazzi, Roberto Benigni, Massimo Troisi [. . .]. Igiaba Scego, 'Salsicce', in Coen and Capitani (eds), *Pecore nere. Racconti*, 29.

6 De Saussures's distinction between structure and content of a language is appropriate to explain the idiosyncrasy concerning the concept of identity. The exterior aspect, language, religious faith or sexual preferences do not necessarily reveal the identity of an individual. Scego's character in this case is struggling between her identity and the identity given to her by others.

7 'La memoria non dev'essere politically correct, né tantomeno una meta per una vacanza umanitaria'. Igiaba Scego, *Oltre Babilonia* (Rome: Donzelli, 2008), 96.

8 'solo se la memoria si fa carne'. Scego, *Oltre Babilonia*, 97.

9 We mention, among others, Cristina Ali Farah, Erminia Dell'Oro, Kaha Mohamed Aden and Gabriella Ghermandi.

10 'Maka al-Mukara [. . .] era l'arteria pulsante di Mogadiscio, la sua colonna vertebrale'; 'li amalgamava[no] ai [loro] ricordi, come le uova in un impasto'. Igiaba Scego, *La mia casa è dove sono* (Turin: Loescher, 2010), 24–5.

11 'Mamma mi parla nella nostra lingua madre. Un somalo nobile dove ogni vocale ha un senso. La nostra lingua madre. Spumosa, scostante, ardita. Nella bocca di mamma il somalo diventa miele. Mi chiedo se la lingua di mia madre possa farmi da madre. Se nelle nostra bocche il somalo suoni uguale. Come la parlo io questa nostra lingua madre? Sono brava come lei? Forse no, anzi sicuramente no [. . . .] Incespico incerta nel mio alfabeto confuso. Le parole sono tutte attorcigliate. Puzzano di strade asfaltate, cemento e periferia. Ogni suono di fatto è contaminato. Ma mi sforzo lo stesso di parlare con lei quella lingua che ci unisce. In somalo ho trovato conforto nel suo utero, in somalo ho sentito le uniche ninnananne che mi ha cantato, in somalo di certo ho fatto i primi sogni. Ma poi, ogni volta, in ogni discorso, parola, sospiro, fa capolino l'altra madre. Quella che ha allattato Dante, Boccaccio, De André e Alda Merini. L'italiano con cui sono cresciuta e che a tratti ho anche odiato, perché mi faceva sentire straniera. L'italiano aceto dei mercati rionali, l'italiano dolce degli speaker radiofonici, l'italiano serio delle lectiones magistrales. L'italiano che scrivo'. Scego, *Oltre Babilonia*, 443.

12 In *Monolingualism of the Other or, The Prosthesis of Origin*, trans. Patrick Mensah (Stanford: Stanford University Press, 1998), Jacques Derrida postulates that it is not possible to consider the native language in terms of possession. On the contrary, even when more individuals build enunciates that respect the rules of the same linguistic system, each individual expresses him or herself differently.

Chapter 11

1 On 28 February 2014, Dacia Maraini visited Wheaton College for a 'Conversation with the Author' event, which I organized for my Italian literature students at the time. On that occasion, I had the opportunity to talk with her about her experiences in the concentration camp and the constant hunger she suffered there. She conceded that this memory has since played a major role in her relationship with food both in her life and in her writing.

2 Although food generally tends to abound on the tables of Maraini's works, it is worth noticing (and it would certainly deserve more attention in future studies) that a few of her writings centre on the scarcity of nourishment. Significant in this respect, besides the already cited *Diari giapponesi*, are *Memorie di una ladra* (Memories of a Female Thief, 1972), a picaresque account of the vicissitudes of Teresa Numa, a thief whom Maraini met during her inquiries in the Roman women's penitentiary of Rebibbia; *I digiuni di Santa Catarina* (The Fasting of

Catherine of Siena, 1995), a one-act play recounting the life (and fastings) of St. Catherine of Siena, an influential Italian Catholic mystic and writer; and *Chiara D'Assisi* (Chiara of Assisi, 2013), which vividly recounts the ascetic life of the famous Italian saint.

3 The formulation of the 'happy housewife' is drawn from Betty Friedman's seminal text *The Feminine Mystique* (1963), where she used it to criticize a formulation of woman as biologically programmed for attending to man's needs with regard to food.

4 On the feminist stance of the novel, see for instance Sumeli Weinberg's description of *Donna in guerra* as a seminal text on the woman's cause (*Invito alla lettura di Dacia Maraini* [Pretoria: University of South Africa Press, 1993], 62). Diaconescu-Blumenfeld's introduction to her monograph on Maraini argues the following: '1975 saw the publication of *Donna in guerra* (*Woman at War*), her first major feminist novel' (*The Pleasure of Writing: Critical Essays on Dacia Maraini* [West Lafayette: Purdue University Press, 2000], 5). This is a position with which the author herself concurs, as confirmed by an interview released the same year of the publication of the novel, where she stated: 'Questo è il mio romanzo più coscientemente femminista' ('this is my most overt feminist novel', *Il Resto del Carlino* 1975). The connection between Maraini's text and the feminist movement, as well as between Vannina and her literary precursor, the protagonist of Sibilla Aleramo's *Una donna,* is pointed out also by Augustus Pallotta ('Dacia Maraini: From Alienation to Feminism', *World Literature Today* 58, no. 3 (1984): 359–62). Similarly, Ursula Fanning notes that 'it is remarkable that Aleramo's *Una donna* (*A Woman*, 1906), written at the very beginning of the twentieth century, should find as many echoes and parallels as it does in Maraini's late-twentieth century output' ('Generation through Generation: Maternal and Paternal Paradigms in Sibilla Aleramo and Dacia Maraini', in *Women's Writing in Western Europe: Gender, Generation and Legacy*, ed. Adalgisa Giorgio and Julia Waters [Cambridge: Cambridge Scholars Publishing, 2007], 248).

5 'Ho pulito la casa da cima a fondo. Ho lavato, strigliato, sgrassato ogni cosa: pavimenti, cesso, pareti, lavello, finestre. Ho staccato la grossa tenda nera che separa la stanza da letto dalla cucina. L'ho insaponata e sciacquata' (*Donna in guerra* 140–1). Hereafter referred to as *Woman.*

6 'In compenso abbiamo un bellissimo cortile, chiuso dentro un muro alto tre metri, segreto come un giardino arabo' (*Donna in guerra* 4).

7 Giancarlo Lombardi, *Rooms with a View: Feminist Diary Fiction, 1952-1999* (Madison: Fairleigh Dickinson University Press, 2002), 96.

8 *Vittoria proletaria* is the name of the revolutionary, Marxist-oriented political group of which Vannina becomes a member, before distancing herself from it after witnessing the kidnapping (and violent beating) of a corrupt governor.

9 'Senza il lavoro gratuito delle donne in casa [. . .] tutto il sistema economico esploderebbe'. Translations from the Italian are my own unless otherwise stated (*La bionda, la bruna e l'asino* [Milan: Rizzoli, 1987], 31).

10 'Quella mia madre è una vecchia, mica è una donna' (*Donna in guerra* 73).

11 '[Quella che] ti prepara il pranzo, ti rifà il letto, ti lava la biancheria, ti stira le camicie, ti va a fare la spesa, ti cucina, ti lava i piatti' (*Donna in guerra* 72). 'She makes your dinner, she makes your bed, she washes your dirty underwear, she irons your shirts, she does your shopping, she cooks for you, she washes your dishes' (trans. Benetti and Spottiswood 73).

12 An instance of the equation of women and fish in the novel is provided by the episode recounting the rape of an English tourist perpetrated by the older Pizzocane brothers, who disparagingly describe their victim as 'a dead fish' (*Donna in guerra* 33).

13 Lombardi, *Rooms with a View*, 110; Lombardi's emphasis.

14 'Ho scoperto una cernia e una murena, dove abitano dico, domani comincia la caccia, mi toccherà aspettare, il fondale è pulito, le rocce vanno giú a picco per una trentina di metri' (*Donna in guerra* 7).

15 Jack Halberstam, *Female Masculinity* (London: Duke University Press, 1998), 2.

16 Ibid., 3.

17 Looking back at the 1970s, Maraini writes: 'it seems clear to me that the old belief according to which extradomestic work automatically implies emancipation is wrong, even though work can help women develop a better understanding of themselves' ('mi sembra chiaro che la vecchia idea secondo cui il lavoro extradomestico significherebbe automaticamente emancipazione sia da considerarsi un falso, anche se il lavoro può aiutare le donne ad acquistare una maggiore consapevolezza di sé', *La bionda*, 41–3).

18 'Ho bevuto di quel latte che sapeva di alghe marine e bevendo sentivo che mi riempiva di forza, di coraggio' (*Donna in guerra* 266).

19 'Improvvisamente mi denudi un seno e lo prendi in bocca con grazia infelice. E io non oso fiatare. So che un rifiuto in quel momento sarebbe veleno. Marina per favore smettiamo. Ma tu non parli più ingolli il mio latte e ti ubriachi ingordamente' (*Lettere a Marina* 14). Hereafter referred to as *Letters.*

20 'Come quella volta che ti ho spalmato di miele la pancia il collo le natiche [. . . .] Volevo cambiarti odore sapore volevo farti a pezzi e il miele era il tuo sangue troppo dolce e conosciuto che avrei inghiottito come un castigo' (*Lettere a Marina* 22).

21 'Posso bere il tuo latte? Ti sei accucciata fra le mie braccia e hai preso a succhiarmi il seno. Era il gioco della mamma e della figlia. Dicevi che era un latte buonissimo denso e dolce e sembrava che inghiottissi davvero. Come il latte condensato Nestlé sai ma più buono dicevi' (*Lettere a Marina* 53). On the pre-cultural, maternal semiotic, see Kristeva (*Revolution in Poetic* Language, trans. M. Waller [New York: Columbia University Press, 1984]).

22 'E io ti accarezzavo i capelli come si accarezzano a una neonata' (*Lettere a Marina* 53).

23 Beverly Ballaro, 'Making the Lesbian Body: Writing and Desire in Dacia Maraini's *Lettere a Marina*', in *Gendered Contexts*, ed. Laura Benedetti, Julia L. Hairston and Silvia M. Ross (New York: Peter Lang, 1996), 182.

24 'Da quale albero sia nata questa mela non ha molta importanza: condizioni per la trasmissione della cultura modo per passare dalla endogamia alla esogamia che sia il nocciolo squisito tenero della condizione umana' (*Lettere a Marina* 86).

25 The term is Adrienne Rich's coinage who used it for the first time in the homonymous essay 'Compulsory Heterosexuality and Lesbian Existence' (1980).

26 'Ho messo in tavola i calamari conditi con olio mostarda limone e prezzemolo l'insalata di pomodoro e sedano lo yogurt fatto da me un pezzo di torta alle fragole [. . . .] Probabilmente invece sono solo le ansie di una madre che vede il figlio in pericolo e vuole riempirlo di sé ingozzarlo d'amore e sicurezza' (*Lettere a Marina* 142).

27 'Non riesco a sottrarmi a questo spirito di nutrice quando ho un ospite in casa' (*Lettere a Marina* 142).

28 Maria Giuseppina Muzzarelli and Lucia Re, 'Introduzione', in *Il cibo e le donne nella cultura e nella storia. Prospettive interdisciplinari*, ed. Maria Giuseppina Muzzarelli and Lucia Re (Bologna: CLUEB, 2005), 13.

29 Virginia Picchietti offers another interpretation of Basilia's name, linking it to the word *basiliare*, in the sense of 'fundamental' and 'basic', which would allude to the character's function in fulfilling the needs of her husband and sons (Picchietti, *Relational Spaces: Daughterhood, Motherhood, and Sisterhood in Dacia Maraini's Fiction and Films* [Cranbury: Associated University Press, 2002], 166, n. 49). The association between Basilia's emaciated looks and her sons' metaphorical cannibalism finds textual confirmation in Bianca's words: 'Although she knows they are selfish to the point of murder in their desire to suck her life-blood and trample on her she loves them passionately and she is willing to let herself be *eaten up* without uttering a word of complaint' (*Letters*, trans. Ditto and Spottiswood 162) ['Pur sapendo che sono egoisti fino all'omicidio che vogliono succhiarla e pestarla li ama furiosamente ed è disposta a farsi *divorare* da loro senza un lamento'; *Lettere a Marina* 160, emphasis added].

30 Picchietti, *Relational Spaces*, 133.

31 'Sua madre contadina mentre prepar[a] il pane o le tagliatelle o la pizza bianca' (*Lettere a Marina* 120).

32 Picchietti reads Maraini's novel as providing a space for the investigation of the models of feminist practice put forward by feminist groups in the late 1970s and the early 1980s, which are collectively referred to with the name of *affidamento* (entrustment) (2002). For more on this practice, developed especially by the Milanese *Libreria delle Donne*, see Paola Bono and Sandra Kemp *Italian Feminist Thought: A Reader* (Cambridge, MA: Blackwell, 1991).

33 Picchietti, *Relational Spaces*. 133.

34 Barbara Haber, 'Follow the Food', in *Through the Kitchen Window: Women Writers Explore the Intimate Meanings of Food and Culture*, ed. Arlene Voski Avakia (Boston: Beacon, 1977), 68.

35 Tommasina Gabriele contests the applicability of 'flashback' to describe the narrative strategy of Maraini's novel, preferring instead '*prolepsis*'. For more on this, see Gabriele, *Dacia Maraini's Narratives of Survival: (Re)Constructed* (Madison: Fairleigh Dickinson University Press, 2016), 2.

36 The merging of private matters (relationships with men, sexuality, family and so forth) with the political (the public sphere) has traditionally been one of the most established standpoints of Italian feminism. Maraini's own writings are a testimony to this well-known feminist stance, attesting to the fact that 'the personal *is* political'.

37 Gabriele, *Dacia Maraini's Narratives of Survival*, 4.

38 Ibid.

39 The digestive analogy is used explicitly in the text with regard to Paolo, Armida's ex-husband, and his inability to 'digest' his family's wealth (*Il treno per Helsinki* 8).

40 'Il passato ha la consistenza di una minestra. Anni che non percorrevo questa strada. Dalla gola alle viscere.' Hereafter referred to as *Il treno*.

41 'Mangio il fungo di Alice [. . . .] Entro nello specchio [. . .] dalle pareti molli che mi cacciano in fondo in fondo verso le radici degli intestini verso le strettoie dell'ano che si torce e plof esco cacata da me stessa.'

42 Julia Kristeva, *Powers of Horror: An Essay on Abjection*, trans. Leon S. Roudiez (New York: Columbia University Press, 1982), 76.

43 'Aspetto che mi dica qualcosa di piú su di lui'.

44 'Ma la glassa bianca nasconde l'interno del dolce'.

45 Unsurprisingly, the birthday cake metaphor in Atwood's novel has received many, at times dissimilar, interpretations. In response to those who have read it in an optimistic vein, however, the author has clarified that the tone of her novel is 'pessimistic' and that the story 'is a circle' (Arnold E. Davidson and Cathy N. Davidson, eds, *The Art of Margaret Atwood: Essays in Criticism* [Toronto: Anansi, 1981], 124).

46 Although, admittedly, Maraini knows and appreciates the work of Margaret Atwood, she did not have *The Edible Woman* in mind when writing *Il treno* (personal conversation with the author, 12 September 2019). From a transnational perspective, the two authors' shared (and unconscious) use of the birthday cake as a metaphor for women's relationship to men and society is remarkable, for it reveals connections between 'writing woman' and 'writing food' in international feminist literature.

47 'Nico ama Dida che invece è innamorata di Cesare che a sua volta ama te che a tua volta ami Dida'. The debt to Shakespeare's masterpiece *A Midsummer Night's Dream* is openly acknowledged in Maraini's novel (*Il treno* 28).

48 'Le giornate consistono in un continuo guatarsi dei gruppi all'erta seguito da corse appostamenti strategie'.
49 'Mangio come un orco: bistecca al sangue pasta asciutta formaggio dolci'.
50 'Senza pensare senza annusare spingendo a forza nell'imbuto della gola i cibi stracotti bevo litri di latte'. The doctors' inappropriate overtreatment is made evident in Armida's account of the invasive practices to which she is subjected (*Il treno* 74).
51 Adrienne Rich, *Of Woman Born: Motherhood as Experience and Institution* (New York: W. W. Norton & Company, 1976), 43.
52 Here is another resonance with Atwood's writings, this time with her dystopian novel *The Handmaid's Tale* (1985), a bleak fictionalization of (bio)political control over women's body that still strikes a chord today in the light of a worrisome conservative turn of certain Western governments (among which is Italy) in matters of reproduction and women's rights. Atwood's novel was adapted into an award-winning Hulu television series in 2017.
53 Maraini was not only a reader of but also a reviewer for Rich's most famous book. Her review appeared in *Signs* (Dacia Maraini, 'On *Of Woman Born*', trans. Mary Jane Ciccarello, *Signs* 4, no. 4 (1979): 687–94.
54 Rich, *Of Woman Born*, 185.
55 Paola Gaglione, ed., *Conversazione con Dacia Maraini: Il piacere di scrivere* (Rome: Omicron, 1995): 22.
56 Patrizia Sambuco, 'Immaginario alimentare e femminismo in Dacia Maraini', in *Femminismo e femminismi nella letteratura italiana dall'Ottocento al XXI secolo*, ed. Sandra Parmegiani and Michela Prevedello (Florence: Società Editrice Fiorentina, 2019), 178.

Chapter 12

1 Of Clara Sereni's novels, only *Casalinghitudine* has been translated into English under the title *Keeping House: A Novel in Recipes* (only the translation has this subtitle) by Giovanna Miceli Jeffries and Susan Briziarelli (New York: State University of New York Press, 2005), the edition from which I quote in this chapter. For the original Italian, I quote from Clara Sereni, *Casalinghitudine* (Turin: Einaudi, 1987). All other translations from Italian are mine unless otherwise stated.
2 Rosi Braidotti, 'Becoming Woman: Or Sexual Difference Revisited', *Theory, Culture & Society* 20, no. 3 (2008): 31.
3 Rosi Braidotti, 'Embodiment, Sexual Difference, and the Nomadic Subject', *Hypatia* 8, no. 1 (1993): 5.
4 Gian-Paolo Biasin, *The Flavors of Modernity: Food and the Novel* (Princeton: Princeton University Press, 1993), 31.

5 Giuliana Menozzi, 'Food and Subjectivity in Clara Sereni's Casalinghitudine', *Italica* 71, no. 2 (1994): 217–27; Mirna Cicioni and John Gatt-Rutter (eds), 'Il cibo come linguaggio nella narrativa di Clara Sereni', in *Quaderni dell'Istituto Italiano di Cultura (2003 - 2008)*, ed. J. Gatt-Rutter and G. Papalia (Italian Australian Institute, 2009), 89–104. Among the most recent contributions, see Giulia Po, *Scrivere la diversità: autobiografia e politica in Clara Sereni* (Firenze: Franco Cesati Editore, 2012); Ernesto Livorni, 'Clara Sereni's *Casalinghitudine*: Recipes for Political History', in *Representing Italy Through Food*, ed. Peter Naccarato, Zachary Nowak and Elgin K. Eckert (London: Bloomsbury Publishing), 77–93; Elisa Gambaro, *Diventare autrice. Aleramo, Morante, de Céspedes, Ginzburg, Zangrandi, Sereni* (Milan: Edizioni Unicopli, 2018).

6 Paola Gaglianone and Giorgio Luti (eds), *Conversazione con Clara Sereni: Donne, Scrittura e Politica* (Rome: Omicron, 1996), 5.

7 Sereni, *Keeping House*, 47. 'Quel pranzo fu la prima rivelazione: sui rapporti con mio padre, per le cose terribili che mi diceva; ed anche sui suoi rapporti con il mondo esterno, per l'agio con il quale si muoveva nel ristorante d'alta classe, per l'alterigia che mostrò nella scelta del vino (a casa non se ne beveva), per la naturalezza con cui pagò il conto'. *Casalinghitudine*, 39–40.

8 David Del Principe, 'Consuming Women and Animals in Clara Sereni's *Casalinghitudine*', *Italica* 76, no. 2 (1999): 211.

9 Iaia Caputo and Laura Lepri (eds), *Conversazioni di fine secolo* (Milan: La Tartaruga Edizioni, 1995), 173.

10 Sereni, *Casalinghitudine*, 69.

11 Sereni, *Keeping House*, 69. 'Mi piace pensare che gli involtini di cavolo – credo di tradizione slava – discendano da lei, ma non è affatto detto che sia così. Come incerte sono tutte le cose che mi sono giunte della sua vita'. Sereni, *Casalinghitudine*, 67.

12 Adalgisa Giorgio, *Writing Mothers and Daughters: Renegotiating the Mother in Western European Narratives by Women* (New York and Oxford: Berghahn Books), 122.

13 Sereni, *Keeping House*, 40; 'Per Kippur zia Ermelinda, che non cucinava quasi mai, si preparava una cena eccezionale. Dovevano esserci varie leccornie, ma il fascino maggiore era esercitato dalle olive: nere, molto grosse [. . . .] Seduta a capotavola nel suo abito più elegante, zia Ermelinda si circondava allora di piatti, piattini, bicchieri e posate in gran numero: la nostra cena normale si illuminava un po' della sua cerimonia, e qualche oliva per me c'era sempre'. Sereni, *Casalinghitudine*, 30–1.

14 Sereni, *Keeping House*, 28. 'La regola aurea, in cucina, era molto semplice: "quel che viene in tavola si mangia." [. . . .] Per fortuna il cibo si limitava generalmente a essere monotono e senza voli di fantasia; neanche la cucina kosher trovava grande spazio fra i suoi piatti, improntati sopratutto a criteri nutritivi e di grande economicità

[. . . .] Nonna Alfonsa era in grado di riciclare tutto: gli avanzi di bollito nelle polpette, i pezzetti di baccalà nelle frittelle.' Sereni, *Casalinghitudine*, 16–17.

15 Sereni, *Keeping House*, 28; 'Quando ho cominciato a farli in casa mia, i crostini, per un certo tempo ho usato il pane fresco: bisogna pur sprecare qualcosa, per recidere un cordone ombelicale', Sereni, *Casalinghitudine*, 17.

16 'Mi aveva visto battere a macchina e ciclostilare, mi aveva portato qualche panino quando proprio non potevo smettere e non ne potevo più: avevo paura di non riuscire a scrollarmi di dosso il ruolo di "angelo del ciclostile"'. Clara Sereni, *Via Ripetta 155* (Florence: Giunti, 2015), 105.

17 'Ci svegliammo presto [. . . .] Mi affrettai a preparare bevande calde, temendo le recriminazioni che a buon diritto mi sarebbero piombate sulla testa'. Sereni, *Via Ripetta 155*, 47.

18 '[Stefano] avrebbe potuto utilizzare il tavolo del tinello, forse non lo faceva perché temeva il vapore della pastaciutta che continuavo a preparare per tanti, l'unto delle pentole per le quali inventavo ricette a poco prezzo, frittate in mille modi per non arrendermi all'abitudine o un sauté di poche poche cozze su tante tante fette di pane abbrustolito'. Sereni, *Via Ripetta 155*, 69.

19 The original Italian locution is 'angelo del ciclostile'.

20 Claude Lévi-Strauss is one of the fathers of the structuralist movement. In his 1964 book, *The Raw and the Cooked*, Lévi-Strauss explores nature/culture relations on a culinary level. Among the categories to be explored, he distinguishes between the raw and the cooked, the fresh and the rotten, the moist and the parched. Moreover, he analyses the way in which myth describes and explains the evolution of cooking techniques and rules, and the transformation of cooking into a cultural process.

21 Rosi Braidotti, *Nomadic Subjects: Embodiment and Sexual Difference in Contemporary Feminist Theory* (New York, Columbia University Press, 1994), 180.

22 As Giovanna Miceli Jeffries explains in the introduction of *Keeping House*: 'The original Italian title, *Casalinghitudine*, which the author created by combining *casalinga* (homemaker or housewife) with the sum of *abitudine*, *solitudine*, *negritudine* (habit, solitude, negritude), is now found as a neologism in the Italian dictionary of new words.'

23 'E siccome ero innamorata, e tutta presa dalla costruzione della coppia e di quel che le stava intorno, tante cose che accadevano poco più in là non le vedevo: per esempio il femminismo, che pure cambiò anche me ma non me ne accorsi. Sempre con quell'idea presuntuosa di essere già "nuova"'. Sereni, *Via Ripetta 155*, 164.

24 Biasin, *The Flavors of Modernity: Food and the Novel*, 27.

25 Sereni, *Keeping House*, 81. 'A casa di Aldo e Maria il menu era fisso, pastasciutta scotta e ascetiche frittate insapori: il massimo di economicità, il minimo tempo in cucina, servire il popolo era adeguarsi ai suoi standards più bassi e incolti, una norma che il gruppo non osava porre in discussione'. Sereni, *Casalinghitudine*, 83.

26 Mirna Cicioni, '"Better losers than lost": Self, Other and Irony in Clara Sereni's Autobiographical Macrotext', in *Across Genres, Generations and Borders, Italian Women Writing Lives*, ed. Susanna Scarparo and Rita Wilson (Newark: University of Delaware Press 2004), 88.
27 Ibid.
28 Mirna Cicioni and John Gatt-Rutter (eds), 'Il cibo come linguaggio nella narrativa di Clara Sereni', *Quaderni dell'Istituto Italiano di Cultura di Melbourne. Numero speciale per Simonetta Magnani* (2009): 93.
29 'riscalda l'anima'. Clara Sereni, *Passami il sale* (Milan: Rizzoli, 2002), 47.
30 Cicioni and Gatt-Rutter (eds),'Il cibo come linguaggio nella narrativa di Clara Sereni', 93.
31 Sereni, *Passami il sale*, 19.
32 Barthes wrote about food in *Mythologies* (New York: Hill and Wang, 1972); *Empire of Signs* (New York: Hill and Wang, 1983); 'Toward a Psychosociology of Contemporary Food Consumption', originally 'Vers une psycho-sociologie de l'alimentation moderne', *Annales: Économies, Sociétés, Civilisations* 5 (1961): 977–86.
33 Menozzi, 'Food and Subjectivity in Clara Sereni's Casalinghitudine', 221.
34 Gambaro, *Diventare autrice*, 252.
35 Stephen Kolsky, 'Clara Sereni's *Casalinghitudine*: The Politics of Writing. Structure and Intertextuality', *Italian Quarterly* XXXIV (1997): 49.
36 Francesca Calamita, *Linguaggi dell'esperienza femminile. Disturbi alimentari, donne e scrittura dall'Unità al miracolo economico* (Padua: Il Poligrafo, 2015), 21.
37 Gaglianone and Luti (eds), *Conversazione con Clara Sereni: Donne, Scrittura e Politica*, 5.
38 Caputo and Lepri (eds), *Conversazioni di fine secolo*, 173.

Chapter 13

1 An earlier and significantly shorter version of my analysis of Gianna Schelotto's 'La ragazza che mangiava la luna' has been deposited in the e-repository of the School of Advanced Study, University of London. From December 2013 to July 2014, I was Visiting Fellow at the Centre for the Study of Contemporary Women's Writing where I worked on a postdoctoral research project on eating disorders by contemporary female novelists. See http://sas-space.sas.ac.uk/5643 (accessed 8 November 2019).
2 It is challenging to link *Volevo essere una farfalla* to a specific literary genre. The book is an autobiographical novel that references intertextually previous writings by Marzano. This is not one of the many diaries by former anorexics where readers can find advice on how to recover quickly; rather, the book portrays a controversial

experience where Marzano's philosophical knowledge of the body, women's social role in Italy and her personal path to recovery come together. The author herself clarifies this point by stating that in her novel there are no recipes for recovering from eating disorders. Marzano, *Volevo essere una farfalla: come l'anoressia mi ha insegnato a vivere* (Milan: Mondadori, 2011), 90. I reviewed *Volevo essere una farfalla* in 2012. See Francesca Calamita, 'Book review of *Volevo essere una farfalla: come l'anoressia mi ha insegnato a vivere* by Michela Marzano', *La Libellula – Rivista di Italianistica* 4, no. 1 (2012): 143–4.

3 Except otherwise stated, all translations are mine; the original Italian quotes appear in footnotes. 'Mi ero convinta che se fossi riuscita a diventare leggera come una farfalla, tutto sarebbe andato a posto.' Marzano, *Volevo essere una farfalla*, 45.

4 Alessandra Arachi, *Briciole, storia di un'anoressia* (Milan: Feltrinelli, 2002); *Non più briciole* (Milan: Feltrinelli, 2015); Nadia Fusini, *La bocca più di tutto mi piaceva* (Milan: Mondadori, 2004); Margherita De Bac, *Per fortuna c'erano i pinoli* (Rome: Newton, 2014).

5 Gianna Schelotto, *Una fame da morire* (Milan: Mondadori, 1992).

6 American Psychiatric Association, 'Feeding and Eating Disorders', in *Diagnostic and Statistical Manual of Mental Disorders* (DSM-5) (Arlington: American Psychiatric Association, 2013), 329–54 (339).

7 APA, DSM-5, 345.

8 I am borrowing this expression from Lilian R. Furst and Peter W. Graham's *Disorderly Eaters: Texts in Self-Empowerment* (University Park: The Pennsylvania State University Press, 1992).

9 I am not suggesting that the ultra-thin bodies proposed by media do not influence women's relationship with their own body and food. Undoubtedly, contemporary culture and the constant objectification of women on television and other media influence women's psyche and their attitude towards the notion of perfect beauty and dreamed shape, as several authors, such as Natasha Walter and Naomi Wolf, have demonstrated. In this discussion however, I have chosen to focus on the family environment and the socio-cultural issues that the protagonists of contemporary women writers face and how their relationship with food reflects those issues. See Naomi Wolf, *The Beauty Myth: How Images of Beauty Are Used against Women* (New York: W. Morrow, 1991); Natasha Walter, *Living Dolls: The Return of Sexism* (London: Virago, 2010).

10 'L'anoressia è un sintomo di una parola che non riesce ad esprimersi altrimenti'. Marzano, *Volevo essere una farfalla*, 27.

11 Susie Orbach, *Fat Is a Feminist Issue: The Anti-Diet Guide to Permanent Weight Loss* (New York: Paddington Press, 1978); *Hunger Strike: The Anorectic's Struggle as a Metaphor for Our Age* (London: Penguin, 1993); Kim Chernin, *The Hungry Self: Women, Eating and Identity* (London; Virago, 1986); Marilyn Lawrence, *The*

Anorexic Experience (London: Women's Press, 1984); Morag MacSween, *Anorexic Bodies: A Feminist and Sociological Perspective on Anorexia Nervosa* (London: Routledge, 1993).

12 Mara Selvini Palazzoli, an Italian psychiatrist, wrote *L'anoressia mentale* in 1963, one chapter of which considered the rapid increase of anorexia among young women in the 1950s and the early 1960s. The 1970s–80s feminist perspectives on eating disorders were anticipated by her pioneering study: 'Today, in fact, women are expected to be beautiful, smart and well-groomed and to devote a great deal of time to their personal appearance even while in business or the professions. They must have a career and yet be romantic, tender and sweet, and in the marriage play the part of the ideal wife cum mistress and cum mother who puts away her hard-earned diploma to wash nappies and perform other menial chores.' ('Oggi, in sostanza, si chiede alla donna di essere bella, elegante e ben tenuta, di dedicare molto tempo alle cure della persona; ma ciò non le deve impedire di competere intellettualmente con gli uomini e con le altre donne, di far carriera, ed anche di innamorarsi romanticamente di un uomo, di essere tenera e dolce con lui, di sposarlo, e di rappresentare il tipo ideale di moglie-amante e di madre oblativa, pronta a rinunciare ai diplomi faticosamente conseguiti per occuparsi di pannicelli e faccende domestiche'). See, Mara Selvini Palazzoli, *L'anoressia mentale* (Milan: Feltrinelli, 1963), 75–9. Mara Selvini Palazzoli, *Self-starvation: From Individual to Family Therapy in the Treatment of Anorexia Nervosa*, trans. Arnold Pomerans (New York: J. Aronson, 1985), 35.

13 Lawrence, *The Anorexic Experience*, 13.

14 Susan Bordo, *Unbearable Weight: Feminism, Western Culture, and the Body* (Berkeley and Los Angeles: University of California Press, 2003), xix.

15 Ibid., xix–xxv.

16 '[Mio padre] immagina che l'anoressia sia come un raffreddore che si prende per strada se non ci si copre bene. Ma quando finirà questa [. . .] battaglia?' Marzano, *Volevo essere una farfalla*, 21 and 29.

17 Orbach, *Hunger Strike*, 82–3.

18 *Una fame da morire* is made up of two short-stories: 'La ragazza che mangiava la luna' and 'La mamma in un boccone' (Mum's in one bite). In the foreword, Gianna Schelotto states that these narratives come from her personal experience as a woman, with particular reference to her adolescence and her relationship with her mother, as well as her practice as a psychotherapist: 'facts that really happened to someone somewhere' (fatti accaduti realmente a qualcuno, in qualche luogo).

19 'Hai mangiato del cioccolato! [. . .] Dov'era? Dove l'hai trovato?' Schelotto, 'La ragazza che mangiava la luna', in *Una fame da morire*, 15.

20 'Livia è un nome bellissimo, leggero, leggero. Si pronuncia in un soffio, per questo l'ho scelto per la ragazza magra che è nascosta in me.' Ibid., 16.

21 MacSween, *Anorexic Bodies*, 107.

22 On women and eating disorders in Western history, see Joan Jacobs Brumberg, *Fasting Girls: The History of Anorexia Nervosa* (Cambridge, MA: Harvard University Press, 1988).

23 Maree Burns, 'Eating Like an Ox: Femininity and Dualistic Constructions of Bulimia and Anorexia', *Feminism & Psychology* 14, no. 1 (2004): 269–95 (289).

24 '[n]on esistono *le* anoressiche e *le* bulimiche. Esistono solo tante persone che utilizzano il cibo per dire qualcosa.' Marzano, *Volevo essere una farfalla*, 59.

25 'Non farlo papà [. . .] son certa che prima o poi la mangerei.' Schelotto, 'La ragazza che mangiava la luna', 27.

26 '[M]i protegge da tutto o quasi. Dimagrendo dovrei entrare in un mondo nuovo che i miei organi e i miei sensi non riconoscerebbero.' Schelotto, Ibid., 34.

27 Orbach, *Fat is a Feminist Issue*, 45–6.

28 'malate diabolicamente intelligenti' Schelotto, 'La mamma in un boccone', 155.

29 'l'orgoglio dell'istituto', Arachi, *Briciole*, 17.

30 'ad ogni pagina, ad ogni riga, mi comparivano montagne di budini e torte al cioccolato.' Ibid., 17.

31 'Ormai lo sapevo: quelle visite sarebbero diventate quattro sedute a settimana per almeno due, tre se non addirittura, quattro o cinque anni . . . E mi ero convinta che la psicanalisi non avrebbe potuto fare niente per me. Rivolevo Massimiliano. Volevo essere bella come Sofia Loren. Intelligente come Maria Curie [. . .] Cosa poteva darmi di tutto questo quell'inutile lettino anatomico del dottor Costantino Bricaro?' Ibid., 93.

32 Sheila McLeod, *The Art of Starvation: A Story of Anorexia and Survival* (London: Virago, 1981), ix.

33 Orbach, *Fat Is a Feminist Issue*, 45–6.

34 'Brutta cicciona!' Schelotto, 'La ragazza che mangiava la luna', 30.

35 In the studies of sexual deviance edited by Richard Laws and William T. O'Donohue in *Sexual Deviance*, sexual sadism is described as the desire to humiliate others physically and verbally in order to gain sexual pleasure. Giorgio humiliates Sara with his constant requests in order to feed his own needs. While there is no physical sadism, the psychological pain he inflicts on his victim is evident. Forcing someone to feed herself is a form of abuse; the perpetrator knows his emotional power on his victim, and he uses it to his own advantage. Even if sexual sadism is often related to murder, *Sexual Deviance* argues that many other abnormal attitudes towards sexuality belong to this category. In particular, see Pamela M. Yates, Stephen J. Hacker and Drew A. Kingston, 'Sexual Sadism: Psychopathology and Theory', in *Sexual Deviance: Theory, Assessment and Treatment*, ed. Richard Laws and William T. O'Donohue (New York: Guildford Press, 2008), 213–30.

36 Orbach, *Hunger Strike*, 82.

37 Throughout their anorexic or bulimic experience, disorderly eaters restrict significantly not only their food intake but also the number of dishes that they eat, allowing themselves to eat everything they wish only if they can eliminate it by vomiting, purging or exercising excessively.

38 'Ma non è me che chiama! Io sono Livia!' Schelotto, 'La ragazza che mangiava la luna', 97.

39 'è così che hai smesso' Ibid., 88.

40 'Quel giorno ero decisa: con due dita in gola si vomitava, lo dicevano tutti i manuali di pronto soccorso.' Arachi, *Briciole*, 11.

41 'Svanire piano piano dentro i vestiti mi avrebbe allontanata dalla realtà. Ogni giorno sempre di più.' Ibid, 13.

42 Leslie Heywood, 'When Descartes Met the Fitness Babe: Academic Cartesianism and the Late Twentieth-Century Cult of Body', in Susan Bordo, *Feminist Interpretations of René Descartes* (University Park: Pennsylvania State University Press, 1999), 261–79.

43 Heywood, 'When Descartes Met the Fitness Babe', 274.

44 Grazia Menechella, 'La rappresentazione dell'anoressia nel discorso medico e nei testi di Alessandra Arachi, Nadia Fusini e Sandra Petrignani', *Italica* 78, no. 3 (2001): 387–409 (393).

45 Menechella, 'La rappresentazione dell'anoressia', 393.

46 On Elena's love affairs and her development of eating disorders, see 'On the Verge of Emotional Hunger: Anorexia, Bulimia and Interpersonal Relationships in Contemporary Italian Women's Writing', in *Starvation, Food Obsession and Identity: Eating Disorders in Contemporary Women's Writing*, ed. Petra Bagley, Francesca Calamita and Kathryn Robson ('Studies in Contemporary Women's Writing', Oxford: Peter Lang, 2017), 67–89.

47 *Bulimanografie* is an umbrella term I coined to refer to all narratives where eating disorders take centre stage. This expression was first used in the Italian context; however, it could be applied also to other worldwide literatures. See Calamita, 'On the Verge of Emotional Hunger', 67–89.

Chapter 14

1 Silvia Ballestra, *Amiche mie* (Milan: Mondadori, 2014).

2 For a discussion of political engagement in Ballestra's fiction, see Claudia Bernardi, '*Impegno* in the Work of Silvia Ballestra: A Space of Political Engagement Between Realism and Postmodernism', *Studi d'Italianistica nell'Africa Australe/Italian Studies in Southern Africa* 24, no. 1 (2011): 151–76.

3 See Carol Helstosky, *Garlic and Oil: Food and Politics in Italy* (Oxford: Berg, 2004); John Dickie, *Delizia! The Epic History of the Italians and Their Food* (London: Sceptre, 2007); Federico Neresini and Valentina Rettore (eds), *Cibo, cultura, identità* (Rome: Carocci, 2008); Massimo Montanari, *L'identità italiana in cucina* (Rome – Bari: Laterza, 2010), also published in English as *Italian Identity in the Kitchen, or Food and the Nation* (New York: Columbia University Press, 2013); Matthew Hibber, 'National Tastes: Italy and Food Culture', in *Food, Drink, and Connoiseur Culture*, ed. Jeremy Strong (Lincoln: University of Nebraska Press, 2011), 81–104; Roberta Sassatelli (ed.), *Italians and Food* (London: Palgrave Macmillan, 2019).

4 See the two special issues of the journal *MicroMega* dedicated specifically to food and political engagement, with an introduction by the founder of the Slow Food movement, Carlo Petrini, *I quaderni di MicroMega: Il cibo e l'impegno*, supplement to *MicroMega* 4 (2004), and *I quaderni di MicroMega: Il cibo e l'impegno/2*, supplement to *MicroMega* 5 (2004); Roberta Sassatelli and Federica Davolio, 'Consumption, Pleasure and Politics: Slow Food and the Politico-Aesthetic Problematization of Food', *Journal of Consumer Culture* 10, no. 2 (2010): 202–32; Cristina Grasseni, 'Food Activism in Italy as an Anthropology of Direct Democracy', *Anthropological Journal of European Culture* 23, no. 1 (2014): 77–98.

5 'Carole Counihan, 'Gendering Food', in *The Oxford Handbook of Food History*, ed. Jeffrey M. Pilcher (Oxford: Oxford University Press, 2018), DOI: 10.1093/oxfordhb/9780199729937.0130006.

6 Maria Giuseppina Muzzarelli and Lucia Re (eds), *Il cibo e le donne nella cultura e nella storia. Prospettive interdisciplinari* (Bologna: CLUEB, 2005). See also Maria Giuseppina Muzzarelli and Fiorenza Tarozzi, *Donne e cibo: una relazione nella storia* (Milan: Mondadori, 2003).

7 Francesca Calamita, *Linguaggi dell'esperienza femminile. Disturbi alimentari, donne e scrittura dall'unità al miracolo economico* (Padua: Il Poligrafo, 2015).

8 'Milano da bere', translatable both as 'Milan to drink' and 'drinkable Milan', is the catchphrase of an advertising campaign created in 1985 for the alcoholic drink Amaro Ramazzotti. It came to symbolize the consumeristic, hedonistic culture of 1980s Milan, portrayed by the media as the financial, fashion and advertising capital of Italy and defined by its vibrant cafe culture. For critics of that culture, that expression captured the superficiality, individualism and political disengagement of those years with their long-lasting effect. See Paolo Morando, *'80. L'inizio della barbarie* (Milan: Laterza, 2016).

9 'I supermercati non lo so, i cibi di sicuro, e non da oggi! (Le madeleine, le pappe al pomodoro, i piattini di Montalbano, le indagini-denuncia-thriller di tanti scrittori [. . .]). Dal cibo passa ogni discorso, il cibo è una cosa di cui le persone parlano molto [. . . .] Qui in particolare si parla di cibo "pubblico" [. . .] dunque un cibo in qualche modo "amministrato, politicizzato, partecipato" oltre che somministrato ai cittadini più piccoli e sensibili alla qualità [. . . .] Mi interessava anche misurare

la distanza tra il cibo "sognato" della televisione [. . .] e quello reale del quotidiano (mense, aperitivi, surgelati di casa) con conseguente riposizionamento delle donne rispetto a preparazione e conoscenza.' (My translation. All translations from Italian in this chapter are mine). Chiara Valerio, 'Quattro amiche al bar. Mogli e madri si raccontano un mondo. Il nuovo romanzo di Silvia Ballestra', *L'Unità*, 18 March 2014: 17. Available online on Silvia Ballestra's website: http://silviaballestra.it/sez/stampa/ (accessed 1 December 2019).

10 While the year of the novel's action is never mentioned explicitly in the text, there are several references to the ongoing fallout from the global financial crisis of 2008 and to the earthquake that devastated the Marche and Abruzzo regions in 2009. The controversy about the 'hairy lasagna' at the centre of the narrative echoes directly the real scandal of the poor-quality meals served in schools that enraged public opinion in Milan in the winter-spring of 2009–2010. Therefore, it can reasonably be argued that the action of the novel is set between November 2009 and May 2010.

11 Silvia Ballestra, *Compleanno dell'iguana* (Ancona: Transeuropa; Milan: Mondadori, 1991); *La guerra degli Antò* (Ancona: Transeuropa; Milan: Mondadori, 1992); *Gli orsi* (Milan: Feltrinelli, 1994).

12 Silvio Berlusconi, the controversial real estate and media magnate, founded the political party Forza Italia in 1994 and, through various alliances with other centre-right and right-wing parties, he served as the prime minister of four Italian governments in 1994–5, 2001–5, 2005–6 and 2008–11. His political career was and still is marred by controversies, allegations of corruptions, legal challenges and personal scandals. For a brief profile of Berlusconi, *berlusconismo* and the 'personalization' of politics under his rule, see Mark Donovan and Mark Gilbert, 'Silvio Berlusconi and Romano Prodi', in *The Oxford Handbook of Italian Politics*, ed. Erik Jones and Gianfranco Pasquino (Oxford: Oxford University Press, 2015), DOI: 10.1093/oxfordhb/9780199669745.013.30.

13 Silvia Ballestra, *Joyce L. Una vita contro: diciannove conversazioni incise su nastro* (Milan: Baldini & Castoldi, 1996).

14 *La giovinezza della signorina N.N. Una storia d'amore* (Milan: Baldini & Castoldi, 1998); *Nina* (Milan: Rizzoli, 2001); *Il compagno di mezzanotte* (Milan: Rizzoli, 2002).

15 *Tutto su mia nonna* (Turin: Einaudi, 2005). See in particular chapter 31, which delves into the matrilinear culinary traditions, eating habits, general attitudes to food and the language used to speak of it in the narrator's family.

16 *La seconda Dora* (Milan: Rizzoli, 2006).

17 *I giorni della Rotonda* (Milan: Rizzoli, 2009).

18 *Contro le donne nei secoli dei secoli* (Milan: Il Saggiatore, 2006).

19 *Piove sul nostro amore. Una storia di donne, medici, aborti, predicatori e apprendisti stregoni* (Milan: Feltrinelli, 2008).

20 *Christine e la città delle dame*, with art by Rita Petruccioli (Rome and Bari: Laterza, 2015).

21 Ballestra, *Amiche mie,* p. 273. See also Davide Rampello and Marco Amato, *Storie di cibo, racconti di vita* (Food Stories, Life Stories, Milan: Skira, 2012). The theme of Expo 2015, held in Milan from 1 May to 31 October 2015, was 'Feeding the Plane, Energy for Life', with a focus on food sustainability across the globe. The ethics of globalized food production appear also at the margin of Ballestra's most recent novel, *La buona stagione* (The Good Season, Milan: Bompiani, 2019), where the female protagonists feel deeply conflicted about having to sell their land to a multinational company specialized in producing and distributing out-of-season fruit across the world.

22 'per effetti di avvicinamento e distanziamento a seconda delle cose che vanno raccontate'. Valerio, 'Quattro amiche al bar', 14.

23 'percorso [. . .] a spirale, si parte dal pubblico e si arriva al privato'. Severino Colombo, 'Silvia Ballestra e le lasagne pelose', *Corriere della sera,* 14 April 2014. Available online on Silvia Ballestra's website: http://silviaballestra.it/sez/stampa/ (accessed 1 December 2019).

24 Ballestra, *Amiche mie*, 7.

25 Tangentopoli, translated as 'Kickback City' or 'Bribesville', is the moniker adopted by Italian media to refer to the corruption system engrained in the Italian political world both at local and national level that was uncovered in 1992 by the wide-ranging *Mani pulite* (Clean Hands) investigation. The fallout was devastating for the traditional political classes that had administered Italy since the end of the Second World War, ending many prominent careers and resulting in the dissolution of political parties, thus opening the way to new, not necessarily less corrupt, political forces, including Berlusconi's Forza Italia. As Sofia points out in the novel, the investigation was triggered by a case of bribery involving a cleaning company and a member of Milan's city council. For a succinct summary of the history and legacy of Tangentopoli, see Martin Rhodes, 'Tangentopoli – More than 20 Years On', in *The Oxford Handbook of Italian Politics*, ed. Erik Jones and Gianfranco Pasquino (Oxford: Oxford University Press, 2015), DOI: 10.1093/oxfordhb/9780199669745.013.24.

26 Despite the growing research on the subject, orthorexia nervosa is not currently recognized as an eating disorder by the *Diagnostics and Statistics Manual of Mental Disorders (DSM-5).* For a review on the literature about orthorexia, see Thomas M. Dunne and Steven Bratman, 'On Orthorexia Nervosa: A Review of Literature and Proposed Diagnostics Criteria', *Eating Behaviors* 21 (2016): 11–17.

27 'Che ne sapevano? Cosa ne sapevano loro di quando mi era cominciata la preoccupazione! Lo sapeva il padre? No, non era mica stato lui a doversi occupare di come nutrire quei due piccoletti sin dal loro primo apparire.

Nutrirli, allattarli, svezzarli e allevarli.

[....]

I bambini, dopo un po', non se ne sarebbero più ricordati. I padri raramente si occupavano di questa parte di incombenze. E quindi lo sapevano le mamme e lo sapevano le nonne, lo sapevano le tate o lo sapevano le maestre.

Lo sapevano le donne, insomma'. Ibid., 39–43.

28 Counihan, 'Gendering Food'.

29 'il più classico dei cibi di conforto italiani, il piatto del ricordo.' Ballestra, *Amiche mie*, 32.

30 'Era stato importante per lei ricevere quel cibo cucinato, some un segno di vicinanza e aiuto fattivo a superare quei momenti di sbando totale e distacco dalle incombenze minute della quotidianità. Mangiare, tenersi su'. Ibid., 237–8.

31 Ibid., 168.

32 Manuela Galetto, et al. identify 'precarity in the workplace' and the 'sustained attacks on women's right to autonomous control of their bodies and sexuality' as the two most significant issues that affected women during the second and third Berlusconi governments (2001–6). Manuela Galetto, et al., 'Feminist Activism and Practice: Asserting Autonomy and Resisting Precarity', in *Resisting the Tide: Culture of Opposition under Berlusconi (2001-06)*, ed. Daniele Albertazzi, Clodagh Brook, Charlotte Ross and Nina Rothenberg (London: Bloomsbury, 2011), 190–203 (192).

33 'Un tempo cucinava e quando cucinava lui, allora tutti dovevano dire "buonissimo!", sempre. E che bravo questo 'uomo che cucina! Capito, come? Che favore che faceva? Che concessione? Del fatto che adesso cucino io, sempre, a pranzo e cena, invece frega un cavolo a nessuno'. Ibid., 151.

34 Counihan, 'Gendering Food'.

35 'come un uccellino'. Ballestra, *Amiche mie*, 246.

36 'almeno usa un piatto, non mangiare così alla brutta direttamente dalle vaschette di plastica e dalla scatoletta, dài, cerca di mantenere un po' di forma, se vuoi li lavo io dopo ma ti prego almeno i piatti, la tovaglia un po' di pane fresco'. Ibid., 253.

37 'magari gli sbatto lì delle focacce, due formaggi su un piatto, e certe volte non gli faccio trovare il pane che è il suo terrore atavico'. Ibid., 152.

38 'Carla disse a tutti loro che, pensando di sprovincializzarsi, stavano facendo i ragionamenti più provinciali del mondo.' Ibid., 132.

39 'una forma degenerata di pasto'. Ibid., 23.

40 'Chiuse le fabbriche, in rovina le aziende, poco attraenti le università, tutto quello che aveva saputo produrre la città, ultimamente, erano stati dei bar. Dei localini. Dei beveroni, per dimenticare.' Ibid., 23.

41 Galetto, et al., 'Feminist Activism and Practice', 198.

Bibliography

Introduction

Bagley, Petra, Francesca Calamita and Kathryn Robson, eds. *Starvation, Food Obsession and Identity: Eating Disorders in Post-1968 Women's Writing*. Oxford: Peter Lang, 2017.

Calamita, Francesca. *Linguaggi dell'esperienza femminile: disturbi alimentari, donne e scrittura dall'Unità al Miracolo Economico*. Padua: Il Poligrafo, 2015.

Chernin, Kim. *The Hungry Self: Women, Eating and Identity*. London: Virago, 1986.

Colella, Anna. *Figura di vespa e leggerezza di farfalla. Le donne e il cibo nell'Italia borghese di fine Ottocento*. Florence: Giunti, 2003.

Colombi, Marchesa. *Un matrimonio in provincia*. Milan: Galli, 1885.

Lawrence, Marilyn. *The Anorexic Experience*. London: Women's Press, 1984.

MacSween, Morag. *Anorexic Bodies: A Feminist and Sociological Perspective on Anorexia Nervosa*. London: Routledge, 1993.

Morandini, Giuliana. *La voce che è in lei. Antologia della narrativa femminile italiana tra '800 e '900*. Milan: Bompiani 1980.

Muzzarelli, Maria Giuseppina and Fiorenza Tarozzi. *Donne e cibo: una relazione nella storia*. Milan: Mondadori, 2003.

Muzzarelli, Maria Giuseppina and Lucia Re, eds. *Il cibo e le donne nella cultura e nella storia. Prospettive interdisciplinari*. Bologna: CLUEB, 2005.

Orbach, Susie. *Fat Is a Feminist Issue: The Anti-Diet Guide to Permanent Weight Loss*. New York: Paddington Press, 1978.

Orbach, Susie. *Hunger Strike: The Anorectic's Struggle as a Metaphor for Our Age*. London: Penguin, 1993.

Chapter 1

Armenise, Gabriella. *Amore, eros, educazione in Paolo Mantegazza*. Lecce: Pensa, 2005.

Artusi, Pellegrino. *La scienza in cucina e l'arte di mangiar bene* introduzione di Piero Camporesi. Torino: Einaudi, 2007.

Ashley, Hollows, Steve Jones and Ben Taylor. *Food and Cultural Studies*. London and New York: Rouledge, 2004.

Bergman, Jerry. 'The History of the Teaching of Female Inferiority in Darwinism'. *CEN Technical Journal* 14(U1) (2000): 117–26.

Bordo, Susan. *Unbearable Weight: Feminism, Western Culture, and the Body*. Berkeley and Los Angeles: University of California Press, 2003.

Brumberg, Joan. *Fasting Girls: The History of Anorexia Nervosa*. Cambridge: Vintage Books Press, 2000.

Calamita, Francesca. *Linguaggi dell'esperienza femminile. Disturbi alimentari, donne e scrittura dall'Unità al miracolo economico*. Padova: Il Poligrafo, 2015.

Costantino, Ludovica. *La ricerca di un'immagine. L'anoressia mentale*. Napoli: Liguori, 2004.

D'Epiro, Peter and Mary Desmond. *Sprezzatura: 50 Ways Italian Genius Shaped the World*, 201–9. New York: Anchor Books, 2001.

Fourier, Charles. *The Passions of the Human Soul and Their Influence on Society and Civilization*. Translated by Hugh Doherty. New York: A. M. Kelley, 1968.

Gigante, Denise. *Gusto: Essential Writings in Nineteenth-Century Gastronomy*. New York and London: Routledge, 2005.

Knepper, Paul and Per Jorgen Ystehede. *The Cesare Lombroso Handbook*, 51. New York: Routledge, 2013.

Lombroso, Cesare. *Il delitto poltico e le rivoluzioni*. Fratelli Bocca Editori, 1890.

Lombroso, Cesare. *La donna delinquente: La prostituta e la donna normale*. Fratelli Bocca Editori, 1903.

Mantegazza, Paolo. *La mia mamma*. G. Barbera, 1866.

Mantegazza, Paolo. *Elementi di Igiene*. Gaetano Brigola Editore, 1871.

Mantegazza, Paolo. *Fisiologia del piacere*. Gaetano Brigola e Co., 1879.

Mantegazza, Paolo. *Commemorazione di Carlo Darwin*. Coi Tipi Dell'Arte della Stampa, 1882.

Mantegazza, Paolo. *Fisonomia e mimica*. Fratelli Dumolard, 1883.

Mantegazza, Paolo. *Fisiologia della donna*. Fratelli Treves, 1893.

Mantegazza, Paolo. *La bibbia della speranza*. Editrice Razionale, 1909.

Mantegazza, Paolo. *Igiene d'epicuro*. Società Editrice Partenopea, 1910.

Mantegazza, Paolo. *Igiene della cucina. Igiene della casa*. Casa Editrice Madella, 1912.

Mitchell, Katharine. 'La Marchesa Colombi, Neera, Matilde Serao: Forging a Female Solidarity in Late Nineteenth-Century Journals for Women'. *Italian Studies*. Taylor and Francis, 18 July 2013. https://www.tandfonline.com/doi/abs/10.1179/007516308X270137

Moorey, James. *Living with Anorexia and Bulimia*. Manchester: Manchester University Press, 1991.

Puccini, Sandra. 'I viaggi di Poalo Mantegazza: Tra divulagazione, letteratura e antropologia'. In *Paolo Mantegazza e l'Evoluzionismo in Italia*, edited by Chiarelli and Pasini, 53–78. Firenze: Firenze University Press, 2010.

Rajberti, Giovanni. *L'arte di convitare* a cura di Giovanni Maffei. Salerno Editrice, 2001.

Re, Lucia. 'Passion and Sexual Difference: The Risorgimento and the Gendering of Writing in Nineteenth-Century Italian Culture'. In *Making and Remaking Italy*, edited by Albert Russell Ascoli and Krystyna von Henneberg, 155–200. Oxford: Berg, 2001.

Ricci, Maria Teresa. 'Grace and Sprezzatura in the Works of Baldassare Castiglione'. *Bibliothèque d'humanisme et renaissance; travaux et documents* 65, Issue 2 (1 January 2003): 233–48.

Schino, June di and Furio Luccichenti. *Il cuoco segreto dei papi: Bartolomeo Scappi.* Rome: Grangemi editore, 2011.

Tanini, Francesco. *La donna secondo il giudizio dei dotti e dei proverbi di tutti i popoli.* Fratelli Tanini, 1886.

Turnaturi, Gabriella. *Signore e signori d'Italia. Una storia delle buone maniere.* Milan: Feltrinelli, 2011.

Chapter 2

Bittman, Mark. 'Remembering Marcella'. *New York Times*, 6 November 2013.

Boni, Ada. *Il talismano della felicità.* Rome: Colombo, 1929.

Boni, Ada. *The Talisman Italian Cookbook.* Translated by Matilda La Rosa. Introduced by Mario A. Pei. New York: Crown, 1950.

Capatti, Alberto and Massimo Montanari. *Italian Cuisine: A Cultural History.* Translated by Aine O'Healy. New York: Columbia University Press, 2003.

Claiborne, Craig. 'There Was a Time She Couldn't Cook'. *New York Times*, 15 October 1970.

Daley, Bill. 'The Legacy of Marcella Hazan'. *Chicago Tribune*, 12 September 2014.

Di Schino, June and Fabio Luccichenti. *Il cuoco segreto dei papi: Bartolomeo Scappi e la confraternita dei cuochi.* Rome: Gangemi, 2007.

Grieco, Allen. 'The Social Politics of Pre-Linnaean Botanical Classification'. *I Tatti Studies: Essays in the Renaissance* 4 (1991): 131–49.

Grieco, Allen. 'From the Cookbook to the Table: A Florentine Table and Italian Recipes of the Fourteenth and Fifteenth Centuries'. In *Du manuscrit à la table: essais sur la cuisine au moyen âge et répertoire des manuscrits médiévaux contenant des recettes culinaries*, edited by Carole Lambert, 29–38. Montreal: Université de Montréal, 1992.

Grieco, Allen. 'From Roosters to Cocks: Italian Renaissance Fowl and Sexuality'. In *Erotic Cultures of Renaissance Italy*, edited by Sara F. Matthews-Grieco, 110–22. Surrey: Ashgate, 2010.

Harris, Marvin. *Good to Eat: Riddles of Food and Culture.* Long Grove: Waveland Press, 1998.

Hazan, Marcella. *The Classic Italian Cookbook.* New York: Harper's Magazine Press, 1973.

Hazan, Marcella. *More Classic Italian Cooking.* New York: Knopf, 1978.

Hazan, Marcella. *Marcella Cucina.* New York: HarperCollins, 1997.

Hazan, Marcella. *Amarcord: Marcella Remembers*. New York: Penguin, 2008.

Hazan, Marcella. *Food and Knowledge in Renaissance Italy: Bartolomeo Scappi's Paper Kitchens*. New York: Routledge, 2017.

Lakoff, Robin. *Language and Woman's Place: Text and Commentaries*. Edited by Mary Bucholtz. Oxford: Oxford University Press, 2004.

Marchetti, Domenica. '3 Years Gone, Marcella Hazan Speaks to us Still through New Book "Ingredienti"'. *Chicago Tribune*, 22 July 2016.

Martellotti, Anna. *I ricettari di Federico II: Dal 'Meriodionale' al 'Liber de coquina'*. Florence: Olschki, 2005.

Meldini, Piero. 'A tavola e in cucina'. In *La famiglia italiana dall'ottocento a oggi*, edited by Piero Bairati and Lucetta Scaraffia, 417–63. Rome: Laterza, 1998.

Messisbugo, Cristoforo. *Banchetti, compositioni di viuande et apparecchio generale*. Ferrara: Giouanni de Buglhat et Antonio Hucher compagni, 1549.

Notaker, Henry. *A History of Cookbooks: From Kitchen to Page Over Seven Centuries*. Berkeley: University of California Press, 2017.

O'Healy, Aine. *La cucina italiana: storia di una cultura*. Rome: Laterza, 2005.

Scully, Terence. *The* Opera *of Bartolomeo Scappi: L'arte et prudenza di un maestro cuoco*. Toronto: University of Toronto Press, 2011.

Seligman, Craig. 'Warped, Battered, Torn and Stained'. *Salon*, 27 December 1999.

Seligman, Craig. 'Classic Italian'. *New York Times*, 3 October 2008.

Serventi, Silvano and Françoise Sabban. *Pasta: The Story of a Universal Food*. New York: Columbia University Press, 2002.

Simon, Scott. 'Marcella Hazan: Italian Cooking with a Master'. *NPR*, 8 January 2005.

Sipress, Davis. 'Marcella Hazan Changed My Life'. *New Yorker*, 30 September 2013.

Steed, Michael and Claudia Woloshin, directed by 'Italian'. *The Mind of a Chef*, PBS, 23 November 2003.

Wheaton, Barbara Ketcham. 'Cookbooks as Resources for Social History'. In *Food in Time and Place: The AHA Companion to Food History*, edited by Paul Freedman, Joyce E. Chaplin and Ken Albala, 276–300. Berkeley: University of California Press, 2014.

Chapter 3

Agnello Hornby, Simonetta. *La Mennulara*. Milan: Giangiacomo Feltrinelli Editori, 2002.

Agnello Hornby, Simonetta. *Un filo d'olio*. Palermo: Sellerio, 2011.

Agnello Hornby, Simonetta. *Il pranzo di Mosè*. Florence and Milan: Giunti, 2014.

Ahmed, Sara. 'Killing Joy: Feminism and the History of Happiness'. *Signs* 35, no. 3 (2010): 571–94.

Allison, Anne. 'Japanese Mothers and *Obentōs*: The Lunch-Box as Ideological State Apparatus'. In *Food and Culture: A Reader*, edited by Carole Counihan and Penny Van Esterick, 3rd edn, 154–72. New York and Oxford: Routledge, 2013.

Blackwood, Robert J. and Stefania Tufi. *The Linguistic Landscape of the Mediterranean: French and Italian Coastal Cities*. London: Palgrave Macmillan, 2015.

Burns, Jennifer. *Migrant Imaginaries: Figures in Italian Migration Literature*. Oxford: Peter Lang, 2013.

Chiaricati, Federico. 'Economia e cultura dei consumi alimentari degli anni Ottanta'. *Storia e Futuro* 27 (2011). Online: http://storiaefuturo.eu/economia-e-cultura-dei-consumialimentari-degli-anni-ottanta-le-fonti/ (accessed 22 February 2019).

DeSalvo, Louise. *Vertigo: A Memoir*. New York: Dutton, 1996.

DeSalvo, Louise. *Crazy in the Kitchen: Food, Feuds and Forgiveness in an Italian American Family*. New York: Bloomsbury, 2004.

di Leonardo, Micaela. 'The Female World of Cards and Holidays: Women, Families, and the Work of Kinship'. *Signs* 12, no. 3 (1987): 440–53.

Duruz, Jean. 'Home Cooking, Nostalgia, and the Purchase of Tradition'. *Traditional Dwellings and Settlements Review* 12, no. 2 (2001): 21–32.

Ecker, Gisela. '*Zuppa Inglese* and *Eating up Italy*'. In *Performing National Identity*, edited by Manfred Pfister and Ralf Hertel, 307–22. Amsterdam and New York: Rodopi, 2008.

Giunta, Edvige. 'Memoir as Cross-Cultural Practice in Italian American Studies'. *Assay: A Journal of Nonfiction Studies* 5, no. 1 (2018). Online: https://www.assayjournal.com/uploads/2/8/2/4/28246027/__5.1_giunta.pdf (accessed 22 February 2019).

Giunta, Edvige and Louise DeSalvo. *The Milk of Almonds: Italian American Women Writers on Food and Culture*. New York: The Feminist Press at CUNY, 2003.

Huyssen, Andreas. *Present Pasts: Urban Palimpsests and the Politics of Memory*. Stanford: Stanford University Press, 2003.

Hom, Stefania Malia. 'Italy without Borders: Simulacra, Tourism, Suburbia and the New Grand Tour'. *Italian Studies* 65, no. 3 (2010): 367–97.

'Il pranzo di Mosè'. *RealTime*, 11 September 2014–13 December 2014. http://www.realtimetv.it/programmi/il-pranzo-di-mose/ (accessed 22 February 2019).

Lovell, Terry. 'Thinking Feminism with and against Bourdieu'. In *Reading Bourdieu on Society and Culture*, edited by Bridget Fowler, 27–48. Oxford: Blackwell Publishers, 2000.

Morley, David. *Home Territories: Media, Mobility and Identity*. Oxford and New York: Routledge, 2000.

Skeggs, Beverley. *Formations of Class and Gender: Becoming Respectable*. London: SAGE Publications, 1997.

Sprio, Margherita. *Migrant Memories: Cultural History, Cinema and the Italian Post-War Diaspora in Britain*. Bern: Peter Lang, 2013.

Woolf, Virginia. *Mrs. Dalloway*. London: Hogarth Press, 1925.

Zandy, Janet. *Calling Home: Working Class Women's Writings*. New Brunswick: Rutgers University Press, 1990.

Chapter 4

Arslan, Antonia and Gabriella Romani. 'Scenes from Nineteenth-Century Italy: Delightful Stories on Those Long, Long Winter Evenings'. In *Writing to Delight: Italian Short Stories by Nineteenth-Century Women Writers*, edited by Antonia Arslan and Gabriella Romani, 3–18. Toronto: University of Toronto Press, 2006.

Artusi, Pellegrino. *La scienza in cucina e l'arte di mangiar bene*. Turin: Einaudi, 1970.

Banti, Anna. *Matilde Serao*. Torino: UTET, 1965.

Bruni, Francesco. 'Nota introduttiva'. In *Il romanzo della fanciulla. La virtù di Checchina*, edited by Francesco Bruni, I–XXXVI. Naples: Liguori, 1985.

Calamita, Francesca. Wellington 2013 – 'Tastefulness: Fashion, Food, Lust and Domesticity in Matilde Serao's *La virtù di Checchina* (1884)'. *Altrelettere* (2015): 1–20. DOI: 10.5903/al_uzh-28

Colella, Anna. Figura di *vespa e leggerezza di farfalla. Le donne e il cibo nell'Italia borghese di fine Ottocento*. Florence: Giunti, 2003.

Collodi, Carlo. *The Adventures of Pinocchio. Le avventure di Pinocchio*. Translated by Nicolas Perella. Berkeley and Los Angeles: University of California Press, 1991.

Colombi, Marchesa. *Un matrimonio in provincia*. Milano: Galli, 1885.

Colombi, Marchesa. *La gente per bene. Galateo*. Novara: Interlinea, 2000.

D'Annunzio, Gabriele. 'Il piacere'. In *Prose di romanzi by Gabriele D'Annunzio*, edited by Annamaria Andreoli and Niva Lorenzini, vol. I, 3–358. Milan: Mondadori, 1988–1989.

De Marchi, Emilio. *Demetrio Pianelli*. Milan: Mursia, 1985.

Flaubert, Gustave. *Madame Bovary: Provincial Manners*. Oxford: Oxford University Press, 2004.

Ghirelli, Antonio. *Donna Matilde*. Venice: Marsilio, 1995.

Gistucci, Martin. *L'ouvre Romanesque de Matilde Serao*. Grenoble: PUG, 1973.

Mitchell, Katharine. *Italian Women Writers: Gender and Everyday Life in Fiction and Journalism, 1870–1910*. Toronto: University of Toronto Press, 2014.

Neera. *Teresa*. Milan: Galli, 1886.

Neera. *L'indomani*. Milano: Galli, 1889.

Orlando, Francesco. *Gli oggetti desueti nelle immagini della letteratura. Rovine, reliquie, rarità, robaccia, luoghi inabitati e tesori nascosti*. Torino: Einaudi, 2015.

Palazzeschi, Aldo. 'La passeggiata'. In *Tutte le poesie*, edited by Adele Dei, 295–8. Milan: Mondadori, 2002.

Pirandello, Luigi. *Il fu Mattia Pascal*. Milann: Mondadori, 1988.

Serao, Matilde. *Fantasia*. Turin: Casanova, 1883.

Serao, Matilde. *Il ventre di Napoli*. Milan: Treves, 1884.

Serao, Matilde. *La virtù di Checchina*. Catania: Giannotta Editore, 1884.

Serao, Matilde. *La virtù di Checchina*. Edited by Natalia Ginzburg. Milan: Emme Edizioni, 1974.

Serao, Matilde. *La conquista di Roma*. Edited by Wanda De Nunzio Schilardi. Rome: Bulzoni, 1997.

Serao, Matilde. *La virtù di Checchina*. Lecce: Piero Manni, 2000.

Svevo, Italo. *Una vita*. Ilano: Rizzoli, 2001.

Verga, Giovanni. *I Malavoglia*. Turin: Einaudi, 1995.

Chapter 5

Abarca, Meredith. *Voices in the Kitchen: Views of Food and the World from Working-Class Mexican and Mexican American Women*. College Station: Texas A&M University Press, 2006.

Baccini, Ida. *La mia vita. Ricordi autobiografici*. Rome: Società Editrice Dante Alighieri, 1904.

Benedetti, Laura. *The Tigress in the Snow: Motherhood in Twentieth Century Italy*. Toronto: Toronto University Press, 2007.

Brady, Emily. 'Smells, Tastes, and Everyday Aesthetics'. In *The Philosophy of Food*, edited by David M. Kaplan, 69–86. Berkeley: University of California Press, 2012.

Chodorow, Nancy. *The Reproduction of Mothering*. Berkeley: University of California Press, 1999.

De Rogatis, Tiziana. *Parole chiave*. Rome: Edizioni e/o, 2018.

Ferrante, Elena. *L'amore molesto*. Rome: Edizioni e/o, 1999.

Ferrante, Elena. *I giorni dell'abbandono*. Rome: Edizioni e/o, 2002.

Ferrante, Elena. *La figlia oscura*. Rome: Edizioni e/o, 2006.

Goddard, Victoria A. *Gender, Family, and Work in Naples*. Oxford: Berg, 1996.

Irigaray, Luce. *Thinking the Difference*. New York: Routledge, 1989.

Kroha, Lucienne. 'The Novel 1870–1920'. In *A History of Women's Writing in Italy*, edited by Letizia Panizza and Sharon Wood, 164–76. Cambridge: Cambridge University Press, 2000.

Martin-Gistucci, Marie-Gracieuse. *L'Oeuvre Romanesque de Matilde Serao*. Grenoble: Grenoble University Press, 1973.

Pappalardo, Armando. 'Matilde Serao, la più grande scrittrice del secolo, la fondatrice e direttrice del "Giorno", si è spenta ieri'. *Il Giorno*, 17 July 1927. Available online: http://www.identitainsorgenti.com/il-documento-90-anni-fa-ci-lasciava-matilde-serao-cosi-la-ricordavano-i-suoi-giornalisti-sul-giorno/ (accessed 19 October 2019).

Sambuco, Patrizia. *Corporeal Bonds: The Daughter-Mother Relationship in Twentieth Century Italian Women's Writing*. Toronto: Toronto University Press, 2012.

Serao, Matilde. *Piccole anime*. 1883. Naples: Libreria Economica, 1907.

Serao, Matilde. 'Terno secco.' 1888. In *All'erta Sentinella!*, 117–64. Milan: Baldini & Castoldi, 1914.

Serao, Matilde. *Il ventre di Napoli*. 1884. Naples: Torre editrice, 1992.

Whitaker, Elizabeth Dixon. *Measuring Mamma's Milk: Fascism and the Medicalization of Maternity in Italy*. Ann Arbor: University of Michigan Press, 2000.
Wilson, Perry, ed. *Gender, Family, and Sexuality: The Private Sphere in Italy 1860–1945*. London: Palgrave Macmillan, 2004.

Chapter 6

Almerico, Gina. 'Food and Identity: Food Studies, Cultural, and Personal Identity'. *Journal of International Business and Cultural Studies* 8 (June 2014): 1–7.
Anderson, Susan. *The Journey from Abandonment to Healing: Turn the End of a Relationship into the Beginning of a New Life*. New York: Berkley, 2000.
Avakian, Arlene. *Through the Kitchen Window: Women Writers Explore the Intimate Meanings of Food and Cooking*. Boston: Beacon Press, 1998.
Avakian, Arlene and Barbara Haber. 'Feminist Food Studies: A Brief History'. *Feminist Studies* 40, no. 2 (2014): 1–26.
Balina, Marina and Evgeny Dobrenko. *Petrified Utopia: Happiness Soviet Style*. London: Anthem Press, 2011.
Belasco, Warren. *Food: The Key Concepts*. Oxford: Berg, 2008.
Boni, Ada. *Il Talismano della felicità*. Roma: Colombo, 1984.
Castaldi, Marosia. *La fame delle donne*. San Cesario di Lecce: Manni, 2012.
Ceretta, Luisella. *Le donne e la cucina nel ventennio*. Sant'Ambrogio: Susalibri, 2008.
Charles, Nickie and Marion Kerr. *Women, Food and Families*. Manchester: Manchester University Press, 1990.
Counihan, Carole. 'Female Identity, Food and Power in Contemporary Florence'. *Anthropological Quarterly* 61 (1988): 51–62.
Counihan, Carole. *Anthropology of Food and Body*. New York: Routledge, 1999.
Desavahayam, Teresa. 'Power and Pleasure around the Stove: The Construction of Gendered Identity in Middle-Class South Indian Hindu Households in Urban Malaysia'. *Women's Studies International Forum* 28, no. 1 (2005): 1–20.
Ferrante, Elena. *I giorni dell'abbandono*. Roma: Edizioni e/o, 2002.
Gilmore, David. 'Men and Women in Southern Spain: "Domestic Power" Revisited'. *American Anthropology* 92 (1990): 953–70.
Giorgio, Adalgisa. '"Allegorie" di Napoli. Marosia Castaldi e Giuseppe Montesano tra tradizione e innovazione'. *Nuova Corvina* 19, no. 6 (2007): 121–39.
Giorgio, Adalgisa. 'Writing Versions of Home: Marosia Castaldi's *Per quante vite* and the Poetics of the Visible'. *Journal of Romance Studies* 10, no. 2 (2010): 77–96.
Hamburg, Myrte, Catrin Finkenauer and Carlo Schuengel. 'Food for Love: The Role of Food Offering in Empathic Emotion'. *Frontiers in Psychology* 5 (31 January 2014): 1–19.
Koc, Mustafa and Jennifer Welsh. 'Food, Identity, and the Immigrant Experience'. *Canadian Diversity* 1, no. 1 (2002): 46–8.

Lockford, Lesa. *Performing Femininity. Rewriting Gender Identity*. Walnut Creek: AltaMira Press, 2004.

McIntosh, Wm. Alex and Mary Zen. 'Women as Gatekeepers of Food Consumption: A Sociological Critique'. In *Food and Gender: Identity and Power*, edited by Carole Counihan and Steven L. Kaplan. 125–44. Amsterdam: Harwood Academic Publishers, 1998.

Moro, Elisabetta. 'Sette donne su dieci ancora a casa nel Sud'. *Il Mattino*, 8 marzo 2019.

Muzzarelli, Maria Giuseppina. *Nelle mani delle donne. Nutrire, guarire, avvelenare dal Medioevo ad oggi*. Roma: Ed. Laterza, 2013.

Schlessinger, Laura. *The Proper Care and Feeding of Husbands*. New York: Harper, 2006.

Sereni, Clara. *Casalinghitudine*. Milano: Giunti editore, 2015.

Soule, Gardner. 'The New Kitchen Built to Fit Your Wife'. *Popular Science* 163, no. 3 (September 1953): 172–3.

Speciale Ritratti. Intervista con Giuseppina Torregrossa (seconda parte), 7 December 2009. https://www.youtube.com/watch?v=Vjlex6iWoh0 (retrieved 11 December 2017).

Tavella, Paolo. '8 marzo, cresce il numero delle donne, al vertice, ma il Sud resta indietro'. *La Presse*, 8 March 2019. https://www.lapresse.it/politica/8_marzo_cresce_il_numero_delle_donne_al_vertice_ma_il_sud_resta_indietro-1218333/news/2019-03-08/ (retrieved 4 October 2019).

Torregrossa, Giuseppina. *Manna e miele, ferro e fuoco*. Milano: Mondadori, 2011.

Torregrossa, Giuseppina. *Panza e prisenza*. Milano: Oscar Mondadori, 2013.

Torregrossa, Giuseppina. *L'assaggiatrice*. Soveria Mannelli (CZ): Rubbettino, 2014.

Chapter 7

A tu per tu, directed by Sergio Corbucci. Adige Films, 1984.

Acapulco, prima spiaggia... a sinistra, directed by Sergio Martino. Cinematografica Alex, 1983.

Anzaldua, Glória. *Borderlands/La Frontera*. San Francisco: Aunt Lute Books, 1999.

Bakhtin, Mikhail. *Problems of Dostoevsky's Poetics*. Minneapolis: University of Minnesota Press, 1984.

Banfield, Edward Christie. *The Moral Basis of a Backward Society*. Glencoe: Free Press, 1958.

Bomber, directed by Michele Lupo. Elio Scardamaglia, 1982.

Calamita, Francesca. 'Voracious Dolls and Competent Chefs: Negotiating Femininities and Masculinities in Italian Food Advertisement of the 1990s–2010s'. *Gender/Sexuality/Italy* 1 (2014): 1–13.

Cheney, Ann M. 'Emotional Distress and Disordered Eating Practices among Southern Italian Women'. *Qualitative health research* 22, no. 9 (2012): 1247–59.

Cinzia Leone imita Marisa Laurito, *Avanzi*, 11/18 March 1991. https://bit.ly/2XHhbsN

Di Raimondo, Alessia. 'Fatima Trotta, l'intrattenimento innato di una donna Made in Sud'. *Il giornale digitale*, 2016, 29 February 2016. https://bit.ly/2F91inE

Dickie, John. 'The South as Other: From Liberal Italy to the Lega Nord'. *The Italianist*, no. 14 [Special Issue - Culture and society in southern Italy: past and present] (1994): 124–40.

Dussel, Enrique D. 'Europe, Modernity, and Eurocentrism'. *Nepantla: Views from South* 1, no. 3 (2000): 465–78.

Feldman, Allen. 'Violence and Vision: The Prosthetics and Aesthetics of Terror'. *States of Violence* 10, no. 1 (2006): 425–68.

FF.SS. – Cioè: ...che mi hai portato a fare sopra a Posillipo se non mi vuoi più bene?, directed by Renzo Arbore. Eidoscope Productions, 1983.

Giorgioni, Livio. 'Pane, amore e fantasia: il cibo nel cinema italiano dal dopoguerra ad oggi'. In *La grande abbuffata: percorsi cinematografici fra trame e ricette*, edited by Livio Giorgioni, Federico Pontiggia and Marco Ronconi, 11–34. Cantalupa: Effatà Editrice, 2002.

Gribaudi, Gabriella. 'Images of the South: The Mezzogiorno as seen by Insiders and Outsider'. In *The New History of the Italian South: The Mezzogiorno Revisited*, edited by Robert Lumley and Jonathan Morris, 83–113. Exeter: University of Exeter Press, 1997.

Il tango della gelosia, directed by Steno. Ypsilon Cinematografica, 2015.

Messina, Marcello. 'Matteo Garrone's Gomorra: A Politically Incorrect Use of Neapolitan Identities and Queer Masculinities?'. *Gender/Sexuality/Italy* 2 (2015): 179–87.

Messina, Marcello. 'Gendered Metaphors of Territorial Subordination, Theologies of Independence and Images of a Liberated Future: Sodaro & Di Bella's Làssami as a Sicilian Decolonial Allegory'. *Muiraquitã* 5, no. 2 (2017): 91–143.

Messina, Marcello and Teresa Di Somma. 'Unified Italy, Southern Women and Sexual Violence: Situating the Sexual Assault TV "Prank" against Emma Marrone within the Dynamics of Contemporary Italy as a Scopic Regime'. *Tropos* 6, no. 1 (2017): 1–18.

Mi faccia causa, directed by Steno. Fulvio Lucisano, 1984.

Niceforo, Alfredo. *L'Italia barbara contemporanea: Studi e appunti*. Milan and Palermo: R. Sandron, 1898.

Oxa, Anna. 'Imitazione di Marisa Laurito'. *Fantastico 1988*, 1988. https://youtu.be/uMclRRQoTDs

Palombo, Lara. 'The Drawing of the Sovereign Line'. In *Transmediterranean: Diasporas, Histories, Geopolitical Spaces*, edited by Joseph Pugliese, 39–58. Brussels: Peter Lang, 2010.

Palomba, Salvatore and Eduardo Alfieri. *Il babà è una cosa seria*. Fonit Cetra, 1989.

Pelúcio, Larissa. 'Traduções e torções ou o que se quer dizer quando dizemos queer no Brasil?' *Revista Periódicus* 1, no. 1 (2014): 68–91.

Perera, Suvendrini. 'Dead Exposures: Trophy Bodies and Violent Visibilities of the Nonhuman'. *Borderlands-e-Journal* 13, no. 1 (2014): 1–26.
Pugliese, Joseph. 'Assimilation, Unspeakable Traces and the Ontologies of Nation'. In *Asian and Pacific Inscriptions: Identities, Ethnicities, Nationalities*, edited by Suvendrini Perera, 229–54. Victoria: Meridian, 1995.
Pugliese, Joseph. 'Whiteness and the Blackening of Italy: La guerra cafona, extracommunitari and Provisional Street Justice'. *PORTAL Journal of Multidisciplinary International Studies* 5, no. 2 (2008): 1–35.
Putnam, Robert D. *Making Democracy Work: Civic Traditions in Modern Italy*. Princeton: Princeton University Press, 1993.
Ruggiero, Giovanni Maria and Marcello Prandin. 'Tradition, Transition, and Social Cognition in Italy: Are they Correlated with Eating Disorders?'. In *Eating Disorders in the Mediterranean Area: An Exploration in Transcultural Psychology*, edited by Giovanni Maria Ruggiero, 127–39. New York: Nova Biomedical Books, 2003.
Sketch di Miss'Illude. *Made in Sud*, 4 April 2016. https://youtu.be/_tj2xLHV6D0
Sketch di Miss'Illude e Peppe Step. *Made in Sud*, 12 April 2016. https://youtu.be/-l5mX-QNCT0
Sketch di Peppe Step, Miss'Illude and Nonno Moderno. *Made in Sud*, 30 May 2016. https://youtu.be/Z1Jm3oUU0HQ
Slim Fast. *Spot con Marisa Laurito*, n.d. https://youtu.be/pasChLWuMh4

Chapter 8

Buckley, Réka. 'Marriage, Motherhood, and the Italian Film Stars of the 1950s'. In *Women in Italy, 1945–1960: An Interdisciplinary Study*, edited by P. Morris, 35–49. New York: Palgrave Macmillan, 2006.
De Grazia, Victoria. *Irresistible Empire: America's Advance Through Twentieth-Century Europe*, Cambridge, MA: Harvard University Press, 2005.
De Santi, Gualtiero and Manuel De Sica. *Ieri oggi domani di Vittorio De Sica: Testimonianze. interventi, sceneggiatura*. Rome: Associazione Amici di Vittorio De Sica, 2002.
Gatta, Alessandro. *Sophia Loren*. Roma: Gremese, 2014.
Gundle, Stephan. 'Sophia Loren: Italian Icon'. *Historical Journal of Film, Radio, and Television* 15, no. 3 (1995): 367–85.
Helstosky, Carol. *Pizza: A Global History*. London: Reaktion Books, 2008.
Hotchner, Aaron Edward. *Sophia: Living and Loving*. New York: William Morrow and Company, Inc., 1974.
Ieri, oggi, domani [Film], directed by Vittorio De Sica. Italy: Carlo Ponti, 1964.
Loren, Sophia. *In cucina con amore*. Milano: Rizzoli, 1971.
Loren, Sophia. *Women & Beauty*. New York: William Morrow and Company, 1984.

Loren, Sophia. *Yesterday, Today, Tomorrow: My Life*. New York: Atria Books, 2014.

L'oro di Napoli [Film], directed by Vittorio De Sica. Italy: Ponti-De Laurentiis, 1954.

May, Elaine Tyler. *Homeward Bound: American Families in the Cold War Era*. New York: Basic Book, 2008.

Pensotti, Anita. *Le italiane*. Milano: Simonelli, 1999.

Reich, Jacqueline. *Beyond the Latin Lover: Marcello Mastroianni, Masculinity, and Italian Cinema*. Bloomington: Indiana University Press, 2004.

Snyder, Stephan. 'Hiding in the Light: De Sica's Work in the 1960s'. In *Vittorio De Sica: Contemporary Perspectives*, edited by H. Curle and S. Snyder, 226–41. Toronto: University of Toronto Press, 2000.

Tambor, Molly. 'Mothers, Workers, Citizens: Teresa Noce and the Parliamentary Politics of Motherhood'. In *La mamma: Interrogating a National Stereotype*, edited by P. Morris and P. Willson, 51–76. New York: Palgrave Macmillan, 2018.

Umberto D. [Film], directed by Vittorio De Sica. Italy: Rizzoli, 1952.

West, Rebecca. '"What" as Ideal and "Who" as Real: Portraits of Wives and Mothers in Italian Postwar Domestic Manuals, Fiction, and Film'. In *Women in Italy, 1945–1960: An Interdisciplinary Study*, edited by P. Morris, 21–34. New York: Palgrave Macmillan, 2006.

Chapter 9

Alaimo, Stacy. *Bodily Natures: Science, Environment and the Material Self*. Bloomington: Indiana University Press, 2010.

Barthes, Roland. 'Toward a Psychosociology of Contemporary Food Consumption'. In *Food and Culture: A Reader*, edited by Carole Counihan and Penny Van Esterik, 22–4. New York: Routledge, 2008.

Biasin, Gian-Paolo. *The Flavors of Modernity: Food and The Novel*. Princeton: Princeton University Press, 1993.

Braidotti, Rosi. *Nomadic Subjects: Embodiment and Sexual Difference in Contemporary Feminist Theory*. New York: Columbia University Press, 1994.

Calamita, Francesca. *Linguaggi dell'esperienza femminile. Disturbi alimentari, donne e scrittura dall'Unità al miracolo economico*. Padua: Il Poligrafo, 2015.

Calamita, Francesca. Wellington 2013 – 'Tastefulness: Fashion, Food, Lust and Domesticity in Matilde Serao's *La virtù di Checchina* (1884)'. *Altrelettere* (2015): 1–20. DOI: 10.5903/al_uzh-28

De Lauretis, Teresa. 'Eccentric Subjects: Feminist Theory and Historical Consciousness'. *Feminist Studies* 16, no. 1 (1990): 115–50.

Farnetti, Monica. *Il centro della cattedrale. I ricordi d'infanzia nella scrittura femminile. Dolores Prato, Fabrizia Ramondino, Anna Maria Ortese, Cristina Campo, Ginevra Bompiani*. Mantua: Tre Lune, 2002.

Giorgio, Adalgisa. 'Moving Across Boundaries: Identity and Difference in the Work of Fabrizia Ramondino'. *The Italianist* 18 (1988): 170–86.

Giorgio, Adalgisa, ed. 'Non sto qui a Napoli sicura di casa'. *Identità, spazio e testualità in Fabrizia Ramondino*. Perugia: Marlocchi Editore, 2013.

Greene, Paula. 'Writing Home to her Mother: Fabrizia Ramondino's *Althénopis*'. In *Across Genres, Generations and Borders: Italian Women Writing Lives*, edited by Susanna Scarparo and Rita Wilson, 117–39. Newark: Newark University Press, 2004.

Gribaudi, Gabriella. *Guerra totale. Tra bombe alleate e violenze naziste. Napoli e il fronte meridionale 1940–44*. Turin: Bollati Boringhieri, 2005.

Hauck-Lawson, Annie. 'When Food Is the Voice: A Case Study of a Polish-American Woman'. *Journal for the Study of Food and Society* 2, no. 1 (1998): 21–8.

Hauck-Lawson, Annie and Jonathan Deutsch, eds. *Gastropolis: Food and New York City*. New York: Columbia University Press, 2009.

Kaplan, M. David, ed. *The Philosophy of Food*. Berkeley and Los Angeles: University of California Press, 2012.

Lucamante, Stefania. '*Teatro di guerra*. Of History and the Fathers'. In *Under Arturo's Star: The Cultural Legacies of Elsa Morante*, edited by Stefania Lucamante and Sharon Wood, 221–56. West Lafayette: Purdue University Press, 2006.

Luzzatto Fegiz, Pierpaolo. 'Alimentazioni e prezzi in tempo di guerra: 1942–43'. *Annali triestini* 18, no. 2a (1948): 139–344.

Mazzoni, Cristina. 'Cucina, donne e santità: dalla pratica alla scrittura'. In *Il cibo e le donne nella cultura e nella storia. Prospettive interdisciplinari*, 67–81. Bologna: CLUEB, 2006.

Montanari, Massimo. *Food Is Culture*. New York: Columbia University Press, 2006.

Moyer-Nocchi, Karima. *Chewing the Fat: An Oral History of Italian Foodways from Fascism to Dolce Vita*. Perrysburg: Medea, 2015.

Muzzarelli, Giuseppina and Lucia Re, eds. *Il cibo e le donne nella cultura e nella storia. Prospettive interdisciplinari*. Bologna: CLUEB, 2005.

Orbach, Susie. *Hunger Strike: Starving Amidst Plenty. 1985*. New York: Other Press, 2011.

Pollan, Micheal. *In Defense of Food: An Eater's Manifesto*. New York: Penguin, 2008.

Ramondino, Fabrizia. *Althénopis*. Turin: Einaudi, 1981.

Ramondino, Fabrizia. *Storie di Patio*. Turin: Einaudi, 1983.

Ramondino, Fabrizia. *Althénopis*. Translated by Michael Sullivan. Manchester: Carcanet, 1988.

Riley, Gillian. *The Oxford Companion to Italian Food*. Oxford: Oxford University Press, 2007.

Sepe, Franco. *Fabrizia Ramondino – rimemorazione e viaggio*. Naples: Liguori, 2011.

Wilson, Rita. 'Personal Histories: Fabrizia Ramondino'. In *Speculative Identities: Contemporary Italian Women's Narrative*, edited by Rita Wilson, 83–98. Leeds: Northern University Press, 2000.

Chapter 10

Angelini, Francesca. 'Food and Identity in Laila Wadia and Igiaba Scego'. *Anuario de Literatura Comparada* 3 (2013): 249–57.

Barilli, Renato. 'Relazione 1'. In *Gruppo 63. Il romanzo sperimentale*, edited by Nanni Balestrini, 11–26. Milan: Feltrinelli, 1966.

Brioni, Simone. *The Somali Within: Language, Race and Belonging in Minor Italian Literature*. London: Routledge, 2017.

Brogi, Daniela. 'Smettiamo di chiamarla «letteratura della migrazione?'. *Nazione Indiana*, 23 March 2011. Available online: https://www.nazioneindiana.com/2011/03/23/smettiamo-di-chiamarla-%C2%ABletteratura-della-migrazione%C2%BB/ (accessed 17 July 2018).

Calamita, Francesca. 'Storytelling and Female Eating Habits at the Turn of the Twentieth Century: Italo Calvino's *Zio Lupo* and Neera's *Uno Scandalo*'. *AUMLA* (Special Issue Refereed Proceedings of the 2011 AULLA Conference: Storytelling in Literature, Language and Culture), (2012): 67–75.

Calamita, Francesca. 'Natalia Ginzburg e la rappresentazione dell'esperienza femminile'. In *Linguaggi dell'esperienza femminile: disturbi alimentari, donne e scrittura dall'Unità al Miracolo Economico*. Padua: Il Poligrafo, 2015. Available online: http://www.nuoviargomenti.net/la-narrativa-postbellica-di-natalia-ginzburg-e-la-rappresentazione-dellesperienza-femminile (accessed 17 July 2018).

Calamita, Francesca. 'On the Verge of Emotional Hunger: Anorexia, Bulimia and Interpersonal Relationships in Contemporary Italian Women's Writing'. In *Starvation, Food Obsession and Identity: Eating Disorders in Contemporary Women's Writing. Studies in Contemporary Women's Writing*, edited by Petra Bagley, Francesca Calamita and Kathryn Robson, 67–89. Bern: Peter Lang, 2017.

Calamita, Francesca. 'Resistance through Starvation: Refusal of Food, Empowerment and Eating Disorders in Natalia Ginzburg's Short Story *La madre* (1948)'. In *Women in the Public Sphere in Modern and Contemporary Italy*, edited by Marina Spunta, Simona Storchi and Maria Morelli, 41–52. Leicester: Troubador, 2017

Camilotti, Silvia. 'Saperi e sapori d'altrove: le scrittrici (si) raccontano'. *Questioni di Cibo, supplemento a Scienze e Ricerche* 2, no. 7 (2015): 84–7.

Chohra, Nassera. *Volevo diventare bianca*. Rome: e/o, 1993.

Comberiati, Daniele. *La quarta sponda. Scrittrici in viaggio dall'Africa coloniale all'Italia di oggi*. Rome: caravan edizioni, 2009.

Comberiati, Daniele. *Scrivere nella lingua dell'altro*. Bern: Peter Lang, 2010.

Dangarembga, Tsitsi. *Nervous Conditions*. 1988. Reprinted. London: Seal Press, 2004.

Derrida, Jacques. *Monolingualism of the Other or, The Prosthesis of Origin* (*Le Monolinguisme de l'autre*. Paris: editions Galilée, 1996). Translated by Patrick Mensah. Stanford: Stanford University Press, 1998.

Erichsen Skalle, Camilla. 'Nostalgia and Hybrid Identity in Italian Migrant Literature: The Case of Igiaba Scego'. *Bergen Language and Linguistics Studies*, no. 7 (2017):

73–86. Available online: http://dx.doi.org/10.15845/bells.v7i0 (accessed 27 November 2018).

Horn, Vera. 'Assaporare la tradizione. Cibo, identità e senso di appartenenza nella letteratura migrante'. *Revista de Italianistìca* 19–20 (2010): 156–75.

Janeczek, Helena. 'What went Wrong?'. *Minima&Moralia*, 2014. Available online: http://www.minimaetmoralia.it/wp/what-went-wrong/ (accessed 20 July 2018).

Lakhous, Amara. *Scontro di civiltà per un ascensore a Piazza Vittorio*. Rome: e/o, 2006.

Lakhous, Amara. *Clash of Civilization over an Elevator in Piazza Vittorio*. Translated by Ann Goldstein. New York: Europa Editions, 2013.

Paci, Franca Romana. 'Cibo e narrativa africana'. *Africa e Mediterraneo. Cultura e Società* 8, no. 12 (2014): 5–13.

Parati, Graziella. *Mediterranean Crossroads: Migration Literature in Italy*. Madison: Fairleigh Dickinson University Press, 1999.

Parati, Graziella. *Migration Italy: The Art of Talking Back in A Destination Culture*. Toronto: University of Toronto Press, 2005.

Parati, Graziella and Mary Orton. *Multicultural Literature in Contemporary Italy*. Madison: Fairleigh Dickinson University Press, 2007.

Pezzarossa, Fulvio. 'Cibi dei migranti'. In *Banchetti letterari. Cibi, pietanze e ricette nella letteratura italiana da Dante a Camilleri*, edited by Gian Mario Anselmi, 101–7 and 377–8. Rome: Carocci, 2011.

Pezzarossa, Fulvio and Ilaria Rossini, eds. *O: Vent'anni di scritture della migrazione*. Bologna: Clueb, 2011.

Proto Pisani, Angela. 'Igiaba Scego, scrittrice post coloniale in Italia'. *Italies* 14 (2010): 427–49. Available online: http://italies.revues.org (accessed 7 July 2018).

Sceats, Sarah. *Food, Consumption and the Body in Contemporary Women's Fiction*. Cambridge: Cambridge University Press, 2002.

Scego, Igiaba. *Rhoda*. Rome: Sinnos, 2004.

Scego, Igiaba. 'Dismatria'. In *Pecore nere*, edited by Emanuele Cohen and Flavia Capitani, 5–21. Rome/Bari: e/o, 2005.

Scego, Igiaba. 'Salsicce'. In *Pecore nere*, edited by Emanuele Cohen and Flavia Capitani, 23–36. Rome-Bari: e/o, 2005.

Scego, Igiaba. 'Sausages'. Translated by Giovanna Bellesia and Vittoria Offredi Poletto, *Metamorphoses* 13, no. 2 (2005): 214–25. Available online: http://www.warscapes.com/retrospectives/food/sausages (accessed 7 July 2018).

Scego, Igiaba. *Oltre Babilonia*. Rome: Donzelli, 2008.

Scego, Igiaba. *La mia casa è dove sono*. Turin: Loescher, 2010.

Scego, Igiaba. 'Exmatriates'. In *Rome Tales*, edited by Helen Constantine, translated by Hugh Shankland, 232–54. New York: Oxford University Press, 2011.

Scego, Igiaba. *Beyond Babylon*. Translated by Aaron Robertson. San Francisco: Two Lines Press, 2019.

Spivak, Gayatri. *The Post-Colonial Critic: Interviews, Strategies, Dialogues*. New York and London: Routledge, 1990.

Spivak, Gayatri. *A Critique of Postcolonial Reason*. Boston: Harvard University Press, 1999.

Chapter 11

Atwood, Margaret. *The Edible Woman*. Toronto: McClelland & Stewart, 1969.

Atwood, Margaret. *The Handmaid's Tale*. Toronto: McClelland & Stewart, 1985.

Ballaro, Beverly. 'Making the Lesbian Body: Writing and Desire in Dacia Maraini's *Lettere a Marina*'. In *Gendered Contexts*, edited by Laura Benedetti, Julia L. Hairston and Silvia M. Ross, 177–87. New York: Peter Lang, 1996.

Bono, Paola and Sandra Kemp. *Italian Feminist Thought: A Reader*. Cambridge, MA: Blackwell, 1991.

Chernin, Kim. *The Hungry Self: Women, Eating and Identity*. New York: Times Books, 1985.

Cixous, Hélène. 'Extreme Fidelity'. In *The Hélène Cixous Reader*, edited by Susan Sellers, 129–38. New York and London: Routledge, 1994.

Davidson, Arnold E. and Cathy N. Davidson, eds. *The Art of Margaret Atwood: Essays in Criticism*. Toronto: Anansi, 1981.

Diaconescu-Blumenfeld, Rodica and Ada Testaferri, eds. *The Pleasure of Writing: Critical Essays on Dacia Maraini*. West Lafayette: Purdue University Press, 2000.

Fanning, Ursula. 'Generation through Generation: Maternal and Paternal Paradigms in Sibilla Aleramo and Dacia Maraini'. In *Women's Writing in* Western *Europe: Gender, Generation and Legacy*, edited by Adalgisa Giorgio and Julia Waters, 248–62, Cambridge: Cambridge Scholars Publishing, 2007.

Friedan, Betty. *The Feminine Mystique*. New York: W. W. Norton & Company, 2012.

Gabriele, Tommasina. *Dacia Maraini's Narratives of Survival: (Re)Constructed*. Madison: Fairleigh Dickinson University Press, 2016.

Gaglione, Paola, ed. *Conversazione con Dacia Maraini: Il piacere di scrivere*. Rome: Omicron, 1995.

Haber, Barbara. 'Follow the Food'. In *Through the Kitchen Window: Women Writers Explore the Intimate Meanings of Food and Culture*, edited by Arlene Voski Avakia, 67–74. Boston: Beacon, 1977.

Halberstam, Jack. *Female Masculinity*. London: Duke University Press, 1998.

Kristeva, Julia. *Powers of Horror: An Essay on Abjection*. Translated by Leon S. Roudiez. New York: Columbia University Press, 1982.

Lombardi, Giancarlo. *Rooms with a View: Feminist Diary Fiction, 1952–1999*. Madison: Fairleigh Dickinson University Press, 2002.

Maraini, Dacia. *Memorie di una ladra*. Milan: Bompiani, 1972.

Maraini, Dacia. *Donna in guerra*. Milan: Rizzoli (Edizione BUR Scrittori Contemporanei), [1975] 2008.

Maraini, Dacia. 'On *Of Woman Born*'. Translated by Mary Jane Ciccarello. *Signs* 4, no. 4 (1979): 687–94.

Maraini, Dacia. *Storia di Piera*. Milan: Rizzoli (Edizione BUR Scrittori Contemporanei), [1980] 2006.

Maraini, Dacia. *Lettere a Marina*. Milan: Rizzoli (Edizione BUR Scrittori Contemporanei), [1981] 2008.
Maraini, Dacia. *Letters to Marina*. Translated by Dick Kitto and Elspeth Spottiswood. London: Camden Press, 1981.
Maraini, Dacia. *Woman at War*. Translated by Mara Benetti and Elspeth Spottiswood. New York: Italica Press, 1981.
Maraini, Dacia. *Il treno per Helsinki*. Milan: Rizzoli (Edizione BUR Biblioteca Universale), [1984] 2000.
Maraini, Dacia. *La bionda, la bruna e l'asino*. Milan: Rizzoli, 1987.
Maraini, Dacia. *I digiuni di Santa Catarina*, in *Fare teatro 1966-2000*. Milan: Rizzoli, [1995] 2000.
Maraini, Dacia. *La nave per Kobe: diari giapponesi di mia madre*. Milan: Rizzoli, 2001.
Maraini, Dacia. *Chiara di Assisi. Elogio della disobbedienza*. Milan: Rizzoli, 2014.
Muzzarelli, Maria Giuseppina and Lucia Re. 'Introduzione'. In *Il cibo e le donne nella cultura e nella storia. Prospettive interdisciplinari*, edited by Maria Giuseppina Muzzarelli and Lucia Re, 7–27. Bologna: CLUEB, 2005.
Pallotta, Augustus. 'Dacia Maraini: From Alienation to Feminism'. *World Literature Today* 58, no. 3 (1984): 359–62.
Picchietti, Virginia A. *Relational Spaces: Daughterhood, Motherhood, and Sisterhood in Dacia Maraini's Fiction and Films*. Cranbury: Associated University Press, 2002.
Rich, Adrienne. *Of Woman Born: Motherhood as Experience and Institution*. New York: W. W. Norton & Company, 1976.
Rich, Adrienne. 'Compulsory Heterosexuality and Lesbian Existence'. *Signs* 5 (1980): 631–60.
Sambuco, Patrizia. 'Immaginario alimentare e femminismo in Dacia Maraini'. In *Femminismo e femminismi nella letteratura italiana dall'Ottocento al XXI secolo*, edited by Sandra Parmegiani and Michela Prevedello, 177–19. Florence: Società Editrice Fiorentina, 2019.
Sumeli Weinberg, M. Grazia. *Invito alla lettura di Dacia Maraini*. Pretoria: University of South Africa Press, 1993.
'Tre Domande a Dacia Mariani'. *Il Resto del Carlino*, 18 November 1975. Available online: http://www.daciamaraini.it/romanzi/testi_critici/donnainguerra.htm (accessed 24 November 2017).

Chapter 12

Accademia degli Scrausi, Valeria della Valle, ed. *Parola di scrittore. La lingua della narrativa italiana dagli anni Settanta a oggi*, 61–84. Rome: Minimum Fax, 1997.
Biasin, Gian-Paolo. *The Flavors of Modernity: Food and the Novel*. Princeton: Princeton University Press, 1993.

Braidotti, Rosi. 'Becoming Woman: Or Sexual Difference Revisited'. *Theory, Culture & Society* 20, no. 3 (1993): 43–64.

Braidotti, Rosi. 'Embodiment, Sexual Difference, and the Nomadic Subject'. *Hypatia* 8, no. 1 (1993): 1–13.

Calamita, Francesca. *Linguaggi dell'esperienza femminile. Disturbi alimentari, donne e scrittura dall'Unità al miracolo economico*. Padua: Il Poligrafo, 2015.

Caputo, I. and Laura Lepri, eds. *Conversazioni di fine secolo*, 159–73. Milan: La Tartaruga Edizioni, 1995.

Carotenuto, Carla. *CIdentità femminile e conflittualità nella relazione madre-figlia. Sondaggi nella letteratura italiana contemporanea: Duranti, Sanvitale, Sereni*. Pesaro: Metauro, 2012.

Cicioni, Mirna. '"Better Losers than Lost": Self, Other and Irony in Clara Sereni's Autobiographical Macrotext'. In *Across Genres, Generations and Borders, Italian Women Writing Lives*, edited by Susanna Scarparo and Rita Wilson, 86–99. Newark: University of Delaware Press, 2004.

Cicioni, Mirna and John Gatt-Rutter, eds. 'Il cibo come linguaggio nella narrativa di Clara Sereni'. In *Quaderni dell'Istituto Italiano di Cultura (2003 - 2008)*, edited by Gatt-Rutter and G. Papalia , 89–104. Italian Australian Institute, 2009.

Del Principe, David. 'Consuming Women and Animals in Clara Sereni's *Casalinghitudine*'. *Italica* 76, no. 2 (1999): 205–19.

Gaglianone, Paola and Giotgio Luti, eds. *Conversazione con Clara Sereni: Donne, Scrittura e Politica*. Rome: Omicron, 1996.

Giorgio, Adalgisa, ed. *Writing Mothers and Daughters: Renegotiating the Mother in Western European Narratives by Women*. New York and Oxford: Berghahn Books, 2002.

Kolsky, Stephen. 'Clara Sereni's *Casalinghitudine*: The Politics of Writing. Structure and Intertextuality'. *Italian Quarterly* XXXIV (1997): 47–58.

Livorni, Ernesto. 'Clara Sereni's *Casalinghitudine*: Recipes for Political History'. In *Representing Italy Through Food*, edited by Peter Naccarato, Zachary Nowak and Eligin K. Eckert, 77–93. London: Bloomsbury Publishing, 2017.

Menozzi, Giuliana. 'Food and Subjectivity in Clara Sereni's *Casalinghitudine*'. *Italica* 71, no. 2 (1994): 217–27.

Sereni, Clara. *Sigma Epsilon*. Venice: Marsilio, 1974.

Sereni, Clara. *Casalinghitudine*. Turin: Einaudi, 1987.

Sereni, Clara. *Il gioco dei regni*. Florence: Giunti, 1993.

Sereni, Clara. *Da un grigio all'altro*, dialogo con Clara Sereni. Rome: Di Renzo Editore, 1998.

Sereni, Clara. *Passami il sale*. Milan: Rizzoli, 2002.

Sereni, Clara. *Keeping House: A Novel in Recipes*. Translated by Giovanna Miceli Jeffries and Susan Briziarelli. New York: State University of New York Press, 2015.

Sereni, Clara. *Via Ripetta 155*. Florence: Giunti, 2015.

Chapter 13

American Psychiatric Association. 'Feeding and Eating Disorders'. In *Diagnostic and Statistical Manual of Mental Disorders* (DSM-5), 329–54. Arlington: American Psychiatric Association, 2013.

Arachi, Alessandra. *Briciole, Storia di un'anoressia*. Milan: Feltrinelli, 2002.

Bell, Rudolph M. *Holy Anorexia*. Chicago: University of Chicago Press, 1995.

Bordo, Susan. *Unbearable Weight: Feminism, Western Culture, and the Body*. Berkeley and Los Angeles: University of California Press, 2003.

Bruch, Hilde. *The Golden Cage: The Enigma of Anorexia Nervosa*. Cambridge, MA: Harvard University Press, 1978.

Brumberg, Joan Jacobs. *Fasting Girls: The History of Anorexia Nervosa*. Cambridge, MA: Harvard University Press, 1988.

Burns, Maree. 'Eating Like an Ox: Femininity and Dualistic Constructions of Bulimia and Anorexia'. *Feminism & Psychology* 14, no. 1 (2004): 269–95.

Bynum, Caroline Walker. *Holy Feast and Holy Fast: The Religious Significance of Food to Medieval Women*. Berkeley and Los Angeles: University of California Press, 1987.

Calamita, Francesca. 'Filling the Void: Bulimarexic Characters in Contemporary Italian Women's Writing'. *Conference or Workshop Item, SAS-repository*. (2014) http://sas-space.sas.ac.uk/5643

Calamita, Francesca. 'Book review of Michela Marzano's *Volevo essere una farfalla. Come l'anoressia mi ha insegnato a vivere*'. *La Libellula—Rivista di Italianistica* 4, no. 1 (2012): 143–4.

Calamita, Francesca. *Linguaggi dell'esperienza femminile. Disturbi alimentari donne e scrittura dall'Unità al miracolo economico*. Padua: Il Poligrafo, 2015.

Calamita, Francesca. 'On the Verge of Emotional Hunger: Anorexia, Bulimia and Interpersonal Relationships in Contemporary Italian Women's Writing'. In *Starvation, Food Obsession and Identity: Eating Disorders in Contemporary Women's Writing*, edited by Petra Bagley, Francesca Calamita and Kathryn Robson ('Studies in Contemporary Women's Writing'), 67–89. Oxford: Peter Lang, 2017.

Chernin, Kim. *The Obsession: Reflections on the Tyranny of Slenderness*. New York: Harper & Row, 1981.

Chernin, Kim. *The Hungry Self: Women, Eating and Identity*. London: Virago, 1986.

Faccio, Elena. *Il disturbo alimentare: Modelli, ricerche e terapie*. Rome: Carocci, 2001.

Furst, Lilian R. and Peter W. Graham. *Disorderly Eaters: Texts in Self-Empowerment*. University Park: Pennsylvania State University Press, 1992.

Gordon, A. Richard. *Anorexia and Bulimia: Anatomy of a Social Epidemic*. Oxford and Cambridge, MA: Blackwell, 1990.

Heywood, Leslie. 'When Descartes Met the Fitness Babe: Academic Cartesianism and the Late Twentieth-Century Cult of Body'. In *Feminist Interpretations of René Descartes*, edited by Susan Bordo, 261–79. University Park: The Pennsylvania State University Press, 1999.

Krugovoy, Silver Anna. *Victorian Literature and the Anorexic Body*. Cambridge: Cambridge University Press, 2002.

Lawrence, Marilyn. *The Anorexic Experience*. London: Women's Press, 1984.

MacSween, Morag. *Anorexic Bodies: A Feminist and Sociological Perspective on Anorexia Nervosa*. London: Routledge, 1993.

Marzano, Michela. *La filosofia del corpo*. Genoa: Il Melangolo, 2010.

Marzano, Michela. *Sii bella e stai zitta: Perché l'Italia di oggi offende le donne*. Milan: Mondadori, 2010.

Marzano, Michela. *Volevo essere una farfalla: Come l'anoressia mi ha insegnato a vivere*. Milan: Mondadori, 2011.

McEachern, Patricia. *Deprivation and Power: The Emergence of Anorexia Nervosa in Nineteenth-Century French Literature*. Westport: Greenwood Press, 1998.

McLeod, Sheila. *The Art of Starvation: A Story of Anorexia and Survival*. London: Virago, 1981.

Menechella, Grazia. 'La rappresentazione dell'anoressia nel discorso medico e nei testi di Alessandra Arachi, Nadia Fusini e Sandra Petrignani'. *Italica* 78, no. 3 (2001): 387–409.

Orbach, Susie. *Fat Is a Feminist Issue: The Anti-Diet Guide to Permanent Weight Loss*. New York: Paddington Press, 1978.

Orbach, Susie. *Fat Is a Feminist Issue II: A Program to Conquer Compulsive Eating*. New York: Berkley Books, 1982.

Orbach, Susie. *Hunger Strike: The Anorectic's Struggle as a Metaphor for Our Age*. London: Penguin, 1993.

Palazzoli, Selvini Mara. *L'anoressia mentale*. Milan: Feltrinelli, 1963.

Palazzoli, Selvini Mara. *Self-starvation: From Individual to Family Therapy in the Treatment of Anorexia Nervosa*. Translated by Arnold Pomerans. New York: J. Aronson, 1985.

Raimbault, Ginette and Caroline Eliacheff. *Le indomabili, figure dell'anoressia: Simone Weil, l'Imperatrice Sissi, Caterina da Siena, Antigone*. Milan: Leonardo Editore, 1989.

Schelotto, Gianna. *Una fame da morire: Bulimia e anoressia, due storie vere*. Milan: Mondadori, 1994.

Stagi, Luisa. *La società bulimica: Le trasformazioni simboliche del corpo tra edonismo ed autocontrollo*. Milan: Franco Angeli, 2002.

Walter, Natasha. *Living Dolls: The Return of Sexism*. London: Virago, 2010.

Wolf, Naomi. *The Beauty Myth: How Images of Beauty Are used against Women*. London: Vintage Books, 1991.

Yates M. Pamela, Stephen J. Hucker and Drew A. Kingston. 'Sexual Sadism: Psychopathology and Theory'. In *Sexual Deviance: Theory, Assessment and Treatment*, edited by Richard Laws and William T. O'Donohue, 213–30. New York: Guildford Press, 2008.

Zanardo, Lorella. *Il corpo delle donne*. Milan: Feltrinelli, 2010.

Video

'L'intervista a Michela Marzano di Daria Bignardi (Interview with Michela Marzano by Daria Bignardi)' in the TV programme 'Le invasioni barbariche'. 2 March 2012. http://www.la7.it/le-invasioni-barbariche/video/lintervista-a-michela-marzano-03-03-2012-95962

Chapter 14

Ballestra, Silvia. *Compleanno dell'iguana*. Ancona: Transeuropa and Milan: Mondadori, 1991.

Ballestra, Silvia. *La guerra degli Antò*. Ancona: Transeuropa and Milan: Mondadori, 1992.

Ballestra, Silvia. *Gli orsi*. Milan: Feltrinelli, 1994.

Ballestra, Silvia. *Joyce L. Una vita contro: diciannove conversazioni incise su nastro*. Milan: Baldini & Castoldi, 1996.

Ballestra, Silvia. *La giovinezza della signorina N.N. Una storia d'amore*. Milan: Baldini & Castoldi, 1998.

Ballestra, Silvia. *Nina*. Milan: Rizzoli, 2001.

Ballestra, Silvia. *Il compagno di mezzanotte*. Milan: Rizzoli, 2002.

Ballestra, Silvia. *Tutto su mia nonna*. Turin: Einaudi, 2005.

Ballestra, Silvia. *La seconda Dora*. Milan: Rizzoli, 2006.

Ballestra, Silvia. *I giorni della Rotonda*. Milan: Rizzoli, 2009.

Ballestra, Silvia. *Amiche mie*. Milan: Mondadori, 2014.

Ballestra, Silvia. *Christine e la città delle dame*. Art by Rita Petruccioli. Rome and Bari: Laterza, 2015.

Ballestra, Silvia. *La buona stagione*. Milan: Bompiani, 2019.

Bernardi, Claudia. '*Impegno* in the Work of Silvia Ballestra: A Space of Political Engagement between Realism and Postmodernism'. *Studi d'Italianistica nell'Africa Australe/Italian Studies in Southern Africa* 24, no. 1 (2011): 151–76.

Calamita, Francesca. *Linguaggi dell'esperienza femminile. Disturbi alimentari, donne e scrittura dall'unità al miracolo economico*. Padua: Il Poligrafo, 2015.

Colombo, Severino. 'Silvia Ballestra e le lasagne pelose'. *Corriere della sera*, 14 April 2014. Available online: http://silviaballestra.it/sez/stampa/ (accessed 1 December 2019).

Counihan, Carole. 'Gendering Food'. In *The Oxford Handbook of Food History*, edited by Jeffrey M. Pilcher. Oxford: Oxford University Press, 2018. DOI: 10.1093/oxfordhb/9780199729937.0130006

Dickie, John. *Delizia! The Epic History of the Italians and Their Food*. London: Sceptre, 2007.

Donovan, Mark and Mark Gilbert. 'Silvio Berlusconi and Romano Prodi'. In *The Oxford Handbook of Italian Politics*, edited by Erik Jones and Gianfranco Pasquino. Oxford: Oxford University Press, 2015. DOI: 10.1093/oxfordhb/9780199669745.013.30

Dunne, Thomas and Steven Bratman. 'On Orthorexia Nervosa: A Review of Literature and Proposed Diagnostics Criteria'. *Eating Behaviors* 21 (2016): 11–17.

Galetto, Manuela, Chiara Lasala, Sveva Magaraggia, Chiara Martucci, Elisabetta Onori and Charlotte Ross. 'Feminist Activism and Practice: Asserting Autonomy and Resisting Precarity'. In *Resisting the Tide: Culture of Opposition under Berlusconi (2001–06)*, edited by Daniele Albertazzi, Clodagh Brook, Charlotte Ross and Nina Rothenberg, 190–203. London: Bloomsbury, 2011.

Grasseni, Cristina. 'Food Activism in Italy as an Anthropology of Direct Democracy'. *Anthropological Journal of European Culture* 23, no. 1 (2014): 77–98.

Helstosky, Carol. *Garlic and Oil: Food and Politics in Italy*. Oxford: Berg, 2004.

Hibber, Matthew. 'National Tastes: Italy and Food Culture'. In *Food, Drink, and Connoiseur Culture*, edited by Jeremy Strong, 81–104. Lincoln: University of Nebraska Press, 2011.4

I quaderni di MicroMega: Il cibo e l'impegno. MicroMega 4 (2004).

I quaderni di MicroMega: Il cibo e l'impegno/2. MicroMega 5 (2004).

Marazzi, Alina. *Vogliamo anche le rose* [Film]. Italy and Switzerland: Mikado Films, 2007.

Montanari, Massimo. *L'identità italiana in cucina*. Rome and Bari: Laterza, 2010.

Montanari, Massimo. *Italian Identity in the Kitchen, or Food and the Nation*. New York: Columbia University Press, 2013.

Morando, Paolo. *'80. L'inizio della barbarie*. Milan: Laterza, 2016.

Muzzarelli, Maria Giuseppina and Fiorenza Tarozzi. *Donne e cibo: una relazione nella storia*. Milan: Mondadori, 2003.

Muzzarelli, Maria Giuseppina and Lucia Re, eds. *Il cibo e le donne nella cultura e nella storia. Prospettive interdisciplinari*. Bologna: CLUEB, 2005.

Neresini, Federico and Valentina Rettore, eds. *Cibo, cultura, identità*. Rome: Carocci, 2008.

Rampello, Davide and Marco Amato, eds. *Storie di cibo, racconti di vita*. Milan: Skira, 2012.

Rhodes, Martin. 'Tangentopoli – More than 20 Years On'. In *The Oxford Handbook of Italian Politics*, edited by Erik Jones and Gianfranco Pasquino. Oxford: Oxford University Press, 2015. DOI: 10.1093/oxfordhb/9780199669745.013.24

Sassatelli, Roberta, ed. *Italians and Food*. London: Palgrave Macmillan, 2019.

Sassatelli, Roberta and Federica Davolio. 'Consumption, Pleasure and Politics: Slow Food and the Politico-Aesthetic Problematization of Food'. *Journal of Consumer Culture* 10, no. 2 (2010): 202–32.

Valerio, Chiara. 'Quattro amiche al bar. Mogli e madri si raccontano un mondo. Il nuovo romanzo di Silvia Ballestra'. *L'Unità*, 18 March 2014, 17. Available online: http://silviaballestra.it/sez/stampa/ (accessed 1 December 2019).

Index

www.ingramcontent.com/pod-product-compliance
Lightning Source LLC
Chambersburg PA
CBHW060251100726
47907CB00003B/839